The Holocaust Across Borders

Lexington Studies in Jewish Literature

Series Editor: Victoria Aarons, Trinity University

Jewish literature is an evolving field drawing upon a rich intersection of contexts: cultural, historical, religious, linguistic, interpretive, and political. As an essentially interdisciplinary field of study, Jewish literature transcends geographical and temporal boundaries, taking us back to ancient texts as it moves into new and evolving directions and patterns. This series welcomes original scholarship that explores a wide range of diverse perspectives, approaches, and methodologies that advance our understanding and appreciation of Jewish literature. The series will cover all geographical areas and all periods and movements in the field of Jewish literature, including such diverse areas as American Jewish literature; modern and ancient Hebrew literature; Jewish immigrant writing; Holocaust literary representation; Jewish writing around the globe; movements and theoretical approaches, such as cultural studies, psychoanalysis, feminism, gender studies, etc.; and Jewish cinema. We invite scholarly contributions that cover a range of genres: memoirs; fiction, including novels, graphic narratives, and short stories; poetry; and film. We welcome original monographs and edited volumes as well as English-language translations of manuscripts originally written in other languages.

Titles in the Series
The Holocaust Across Borders: Trauma, Atrocity, and Representation in Literature and Culture, edited by Hilene S. Flanzbaum
The Stolen Narrative of the Bulgarian Jews and the Holocaust, by Jacky Comforty with Martha Aladjem Bloomfield
May God Avenge Their Blood: A Holocaust Memoir Triptych, by Rachmil Bryks
Translated Memories: Transgenerational Perspectives on the Holocaust, edited by Ursula Reuter & Bettina Hofmann
Keepers of Memory: The Holocaust and Transgenerational Identity, by Jennifer Rich
The Animal in the Synagogue: Franz Kafka's Jewishness, by Dan Miron
I Was a Doctor in Auschwitz, by Gisella Perl
The Midrashic Impulse and the Contemporary Literary Response to Trauma, by Monica Osborne

The Holocaust Across Borders

Trauma, Atrocity, and Representation in Literature and Culture

Hilene S. Flanzbaum

LEXINGTON BOOKS
Lanham • Boulder • New York • London

Published by Lexington Books
An imprint of The Rowman & Littlefield Publishing Group, Inc.
4501 Forbes Boulevard, Suite 200, Lanham, Maryland 20706
www.rowman.com

6 Tinworth Street, London SE11 5AL, United Kingdom

Copyright © 2021 The Rowman & Littlefield Publishing Group, Inc.

All rights reserved. No part of this book may be reproduced in any form or by any electronic or mechanical means, including information storage and retrieval systems, without written permission from the publisher, except by a reviewer who may quote passages in a review.

British Library Cataloguing in Publication Information Available

Library of Congress Cataloging-in-Publication Data

Names: Flanzbaum, Hilene, editor.
Title: The Holocaust across borders : trauma, atrocity, and representation in literature and culture / edited by Hilene S. Flanzbaum.
Description: Lanham : Lexington Books, [2021] | Series: Lexington studies in Jewish literature | Includes bibliographical references and index. | Summary: "In this book, scholars with expertise in various national literatures and cultures explore how the Holocaust has been represented in novels, memoirs, film, television, and architecture. This book provides a unique vantage point for the scholar and student to compare how national context impacts representations of the Holocaust"—Provided by publisher.
Identifiers: LCCN 2021014913 (print) | LCCN 2021014914 (ebook) |
 ISBN 9781793612052 (cloth) | ISBN 9781793612069 (ebook)
 ISBN 9781793612076 (pbk)
Subjects: LCSH: Holocaust, Jewish (1939-1945), in literature.
Classification: LCC PN56.H55 H644 2021 (print) | LCC PN56.H55 (ebook) |
 DDC 808.8/0358405318—dc23
LC record available at https://lccn.loc.gov/2021014913
LC ebook record available at https://lccn.loc.gov/2021014914

Contents

The Holocaust Across Borders: An Introduction   1
Hilene Flanzbaum

1   Selling the Holocaust in Twenty-First-Century France   15
    Hilene Flanzbaum

2   Life Is Beautiful, or Not: The Myth of the Good Italian   33
    Shira Klein

3   Not My Holocaust: *MAUS* and Memory in the Polish Classroom   53
    Holli Levitsky

4   Germans, Migration, and Holocaust Memory in Contemporary Literature   71
    Agnes C. Mueller

5   The Burden of the Third Generation in Germany: Nora Krug's *Belonging: A German Reckons with History and Home*   89
    Victoria Aarons

6   An Impossible Homecoming: Ruth Klüger's Austria   113
    Sarah Painitz

7   Fractures and Refractions in Argentina: Prosthetic Memory and Edgardo Cozarinsky's *Lejos de dónde*   133
    Amy Kaminsky

8   Anglicization and the Holocaust in Judith Kerr and Eva Tucker's Fictions   157
    Joshua Lander

9	Collective Disengagement: Canada's National Holocaust Monument *Lizy Mostowski*	179
10	Forgetting and Remembering: The Holocaust in Contemporary Australian Fiction *Ira Nadel*	201
11	"We Are the New Children": Shoah and Israeli Childhood in Nava Semel's *And the Rat Laughed* *Ranen Omer-Sherman*	217
12	Representing the Holocaust and Jewishness in Contemporary Television: The Cases of *The Man in the High Castle, Hunters,* and *Juda* *Marat Grinberg*	239

Index	271
About the Contributors	287

The Holocaust Across Borders

An Introduction

Hilene Flanzbaum

THE CASE OF *THE READER*

In 2009, I attended a conference with the compelling title "The Holocaust, Art and Taboo," at the University of Hamburg in Germany.[1] The organizer, Susanne Rohr, had been inspired to her topic after reading Melvin Bukiet's *After*,[2] a novel which tells the story of three Holocaust survivors who, after the war, engage in a series of illegal and immoral profiteering—the most grievous of which is "liberating" 18 tons of golden ingots that have been made from the fillings of dead Jews. For Rohr, Bukiet breaks a taboo when she portrays the survivors as criminals. In Germany, as well as in the United States, Holocaust survivors had become heroes, symbols of courage, strength, and even saintliness. In the United States, Bukiet's work had drawn some favorable reviews; in Germany, however, it qualified as a major breach of Holocaust etiquette.[3]

Invited to the conference as an expert on Americanization, I met fellow presenters from Northern Europe, Canada, and the United States who spoke about literature, film, and visual art. Scholars spoke about artifacts which had, at one time or another, been viewed, in their countries, as provocative, offensive, or even blasphemous. The curator of the Jewish museum in New York City, for instance, recalled the uproar resulting from an artwork they had displayed in 2002: a construction of Auschwitz made out of LEGOs.[4] Upon hearing about this exhibit, no one paused to express outrage or endorsement. As scholars of Holocaust representation, we knew the contours of this debate too well and had not come this distance to rehearse them. Rather, we were there to compare the differences, across borders, of what constitutes transgression.

It wasn't, however, until I overheard a discussion among a group of Germans scholars that I realized how personal such distinctions would become. Agnes Mueller[5] said—not as the point of her remarks but simply offered as a passing comment on which she assumed consensus—on her way to a larger point which I cannot remember—that Bernhard Schlink's *The Reader*[6] was a reprehensible text. With derision, she chided those who taught it, implying that they were at best, misguided and at worst, suborning denial. There I stood: A seasoned and, I liked to think, enlightened professor of Holocaust literature—who had taught this novel at least *a half a dozen times*. What was I missing? What was wrong with teaching *The Reader*? And how had I—respected scholar of Holocaust literature, indeed, an invited speaker to the conference—committed such a violation? There comes in every career, if one is paying attention, a moment of reckoning. That was mine.

For those not familiar with the criticism that surrounds this text, its clamorous reception is worth noting. Only twenty-five years in print, *The Reader* has attracted scads of scholarly attention, while at the same time, it struck gold in popular culture—not a common confluence of events. First published in Germany in 1995 and in the United States the following year, Schlink's book sold millions of copies and has the singular distinction of being the first book translated from German ever to reach the bestseller list in the United States. In Germany, *The Reader* was called the literary event of the decade. In that country, the reasons for its popularity are contentious and complicated (and also beyond my expertise).[7] In the United States, however, its destiny becomes inevitable when Oprah chooses it for her famous list.

While it is possible to admire many of Oprah's choices over the years, this particular road to popular acclaim often provokes academics to frenzy, replaying the predictable *pas de deux* where arbiters of high culture feel honor bound to cast aspersions on what general audiences admire. In the case of *The Reader*, Cynthia Ozick's review, though stronger in rhetoric, typifies the usual charges of the opposition. Her article published in the notably conservative *Commentary* exclaimed, "that it was the most vile novel she had ever read," and her reasons amount to the usual complaint that "fiction can lie" and that the book is not "realistic enough."[8]

But if this were the only reason critics shunned it, I reasoned, I was in the clear. The demand for realism, in Holocaust representation, was no longer compulsory. As venerable and important a critic as Ozick has been, her stipulation, which may have been necessary when she began her career in the 1970s, was now obsolete. Not only were audiences thoroughly familiar with what happened, in the last quarter-century, scholars had become appropriately suspicious of modes of realism: documentaries, memory, and even testimony itself.[9] Imagining the Holocaust in fictional genres did not—had not—encouraged denial, despite critics' worst fears.[10] Rather, Americans had been so inundated by graphic representations—of the Holocaust and everything else—that in the twenty-first century, artists needed to move beyond images that now seemed too familiar: The piles of hair or shoes, the skeletal bodies, and stacks of bones that had so shocked viewers seventy years ago had in fact become ordinary, as unfortunate as that is. While scholars always stand ready to counter denial, they no longer unilaterally scoff at fictional representations of the Holocaust in texts, film, graphic novels, or even social media. Instead, they devote themselves to careful and nuanced readings of these artifacts.

The Reader did draw sophisticated study. Much of the debate centers on whether or not the text rationalizes or somehow excuses the actions of the main character, Hannah, an illiterate former Nazi prison guard, who is involved in leaving 300 Jewish women locked in a church as it burns to the ground. During her trial, the other indicted prison guards use Hannah as a scapegoat, accusing her of writing the order which authorized the action. Hannah could not have done this, because she is illiterate. Ashamed to confess this to the court, she receives a harsher sentence than those who were "more responsible." The novel raises complicated questions of law and ethics, among them: If the reader outside the text, or the judge and jury inside of the text, understand why Hannah has done what she has, does this mean we forgive her? And if we forgive her, does that mean we believe she should not be punished? Are there extenuating circumstances which excuse criminal behavior? Is Schlink portraying Hannah as "a good German"?[11]

The debate over Hannah's actions and Schlink's exoneration or condemnation of her has been widely and energetically waged; I cannot settle it here.[12] I do notice, however, that the most negative reactions come from Germany. Although there have been harsh reviews from American scholars (as Ozick's piece aptly demonstrates), they compose a smaller sample of the pile. My reading of the interpretive crisis aligns with that of writer and critic, Eva Hoffman, a second- generation naturalized American citizen. While admitting that Schlink does not go far enough "into the destructive side of the human soul," Hoffman praises *The Reader* for "saying some honest things about delicate and difficult matters." Praising the book and simultaneously fleshing out issues of moral complexity, Hoffman writes:

> How are we to understand someone such as Hanna—an ordinary person capable of desire and yearning, who turns her hand to monstrous work for a time? By what criteria is she to be appraised, and what would constitute true justice for her? What is demanded of us in retribution or compassion?[13]

I need go no further than the first question—how are we to understand Hanna, an ordinary person capable of desire and yearning who turns to monstrous work for a time?—to advocate for the continued teaching of *The Reader* in American classrooms.

This penetrating question must be confronted. Hanna is an ordinary person—or in other words, just like you and me. For my well-intentioned and largely unsophisticated students to understand that the performance of what they consider evil does not always immediately appear as itself, or that is not as clearly delineated as they might wish thought requires them to take a huge conceptual leap. As Americans, they can easily vilify and dehumanize Nazis—a group—cast them as the enemy so far from them; they might as well have been another species: they are little surprised by Steven's Spielberg's characterization of the monstrous Amon Göth in *Schindler's List*, they have been seeing Nazis depicted in popular culture since they were born.[14]

Moreover, my students have grown accustomed to the one-dimensional villains they see in superhero movies and need prodding to acknowledge moral complexity.[15] Teaching *The Reader*, I work very hard to make Hanna's actions human, not because I wish to defend the Nazis (as some critics imagine I must be doing) but because my students gain a great deal if they can accept that human beings perform evil with what they *believe to be perfectly good reasons*, or perhaps what they convince themselves are good reasons—out of convenience, or greed, or, as in Hannah's case, shame. This does not excuse as much as humanize her; for we gain nothing when we think of her as "a monster." Whether we like to admit it or not, the Nazis were—at least in the literal sense—human beings. Hitler and his inner circle may have been sociopathic or psychopathic, yet many lower-rung war criminals had flaws which would not put them in institutions or prisons if they lived next door to us today. Sadly, they were just people—ambitious or thoughtless, or afraid to challenge authority rather than confront it, who, in some cases, turned their backs on nagging questions of moral conscience because paying attention to them meant to be severely inconvenienced, impoverished, or even imprisoned.

Many of my colleagues, here and abroad, condemn the pivotal moment in the text when Hannah turns to the judge and asks "what would you have done?" because it elicits too much sympathy for the character—as if to say that Schlink's worst sin is in creating a situation where a criminal gets to ask this question. But it is more than a valid question; for my students, it is the most important one. They know—*they know*—that they have been far from exemplary in their own behaviors—taken shortcuts, cyberbullied, used products that were made in sweatshops. If they understand enough of themselves to realize, "I could have done the same thing" I create a transformative teaching moment. That realization does not excuse Hanna's actions as much as it condemns the reader, both inside the text (Michael, the narrator) and outside the text (you and me)—condemns us because Hannah's weaknesses have led her to do something monstrous. Be advised—so might yours or mine. Her fatal flaw is illiteracy; yours is ambition; mine is laziness. It seems almost too obvious to state—but nonetheless must be: A text like *The Reader*, or any other (about the Holocaust or not) for that matter, cannot be read in Germany—where righteous citizens have viewed themselves as perpetrators of the most barbarous crimes, heirs of guilt and shame—as it does in the United States where readers have viewed themselves as liberators, and have been shaped by a national ethos of blamelessness and, in the case of the Holocaust, a collective memory of heroism.

In Germany, professional readers fret that *The Reader* lets off its citizenry too easily; critics worry that general readers so enjoy this novel because it offers them exculpation—that Schlink makes Hannah's illiteracy a "justification" for her actions, and therefore makes it possible to excuse her and all ignorant Germans. I can appreciate this argument in that context. Nor is the necessity of censuring one's own people specific to Germany—but this particular criticism is. In other words, the great energy put into either constructing or debunking the myth of "The Good German" has none of the same momentum in the United States as it does in Germany. In the United States, we have had no trouble accepting the truly evil nature of Nazis: we have held them to be—in every avenue of popular culture—the most villainous of all villains for over fifty years.

TURNING POINT

My longer essay on *The Reader* that is cited at the beginning of this essay, and the seeds of this volume, took root at the moment that I overheard that comment. Indeed, such can be the unexpected benefits of international meetings.[16] That juncture—when I was compelled to examine the relative use of Holocaust literature across national boundaries—became a turning point in my scholarly career. As I understood with some force that my German colleague's view of what was taboo—in *The Reader* or elsewhere—could not realistically apply to my students in Indiana,[17] I was compelled to consider why that conclusion felt like both a revelation and a breach of Holocaust etiquette. Why did acknowledging that novels about this topic could generate different readings feel like perfidy when for the past forty years, literary critics had taken for granted the historical and national contingencies of literary evaluation? Although new historicism may have its detractors, it had been almost half a century since it had first galvanized a great number of literary scholars; cultural critique was well-established—even if not universally practiced. Why had Holocaust Studies been largely exempted from poststructuralism and its many offshoots?[18]

Once configured in those terms, an explanation emerges: the fear of giving aid and comfort to deniers, or those that would trivialize the immensity of the Holocaust, has often prevented scholars from engaging in contemporary strategies of reading. Many believed that the project of memory would be threatened by any destabilization of meaning. Contingencies of value, as Herrnstein-Smith labeled it over thirty years ago, stalwarts feared, took us down the path toward moral relativism that in the case of the Holocaust was not only misguided—it was evil.[19] How many detractors of postmodern theory had ended their invectives by invoking Holocaust denial as the likely destination of deconstruction?[20]

This was the profane territory that Rohr feared she had stepped into while reading *After*. Of course Bukiet's novel did not make *her* question the veracity of survivors' stories; rather, she must have feared what others might think. The reasoning might go something like this: "I know, of course, that survivors are only human—not saints—but if someone more ignorant that I read it, they could think that if the son of a Holocaust survivor portrays survivors like this, he must be right. Survivors must be really bad people—cheaters and liars, not the heroes they are usually portrayed as. How can we trust any of their stories?" Even if sophisticated and well-intentioned readers do not comb artworks for evidence that supports Holocaust denial, some imagine anti-Semitic readers, always ready to pounce, to point and accuse.

Efforts to preserve the "uniqueness" argument also pertain here. Invested in a global consensus that what happened to the Jews of Europe was far worse than any other genocide in history, Holocaust scholars of earlier generations argued that comparing the Holocaust to atrocities that occurred in other places and time trivialized it—and again opened the door to denial. Such entrenched debates are too difficult to unpack here, though, I believe that time has settled the issue in practice—if not theory. In the twenty-first century, it has become apparent to educators and scholars—that central to the preservation of Holocaust memory is the emphasis on similarities between it and more recent global catastrophes. In doing so, they keep the Holocaust relevant for this generation and for those in the future.

In the past two decades, scholarly trends have sought to find among diverse entities those issues that transcend national boundaries or ethnic categorizations. Trauma studies, in particular, has been a windfall for scholars of the Holocaust who have seen their subject remain integral to current conversations. For while middle-school teachers have known for decades that the literature of the Holocaust can serve as fuel for broad-based discussions of human cruelty and political savagery, only of late, when the uniqueness debate has faded from favor, have such approaches been granted legitimacy among Holocaust scholars.[21]

While this project does not compare the genocide of the Jews to others more recent ones, the essays herein compare different literary responses to the

Holocaust and thus contribute to the ongoing project of Holocaust memory, which is neither static nor monochromatic. From country to country, the writers herein weigh the relative importance and multiple meanings of the event as they analyze the various strategies of representation. And they do so confident in the knowledge that all of its readers accept wholly and without reservation that Hitler and his henchmen were responsible for the murder of six million European Jews.

SOME PERSONAL HISTORY AND THE ESSAYS

My first scholarly work on the Holocaust was published in the latest 1990s and dealt with how American writers represented the Holocaust.[22] In the decade when I began this work, the United States Holocaust Museum and Memorial opened; *Schindler's List* won the Academy Award for best picture, and Steven Spielberg endowed a multitude of Visual Testimony libraries at universities across the country. Between 1995 and 2000, three of the five documentaries awarded Oscars were about the Holocaust and another was about the founding of the state of Israel.[23] "One Survivor Remembers," the story of a survivor that married her liberator, won an award for best short film. The Holocaust was so pervasive in the American consciousness that it would be quite naive of me to assume that the subject just came to me out of the blue. Surely, it did not.

Both my professional and personal life would change as a result of the Holocaust fever that rose around me. As an Americanist scholar and a Jew, I wanted to make sense of what this surge in popularity signified—even though I had been trained as a scholar of poetry and had been hired to teach in that field. During that same time, I moved to Indianapolis and shortly thereafter gave birth to two daughters—two enormous life changes. For the first time, I lived in a city that did not have a significant Jewish population. I had grown up in New York, and then lived in Boston, Washington DC, and Philadelphia and was thus unprepared for the scarcity of Jewish life and Jewish people. As I thought about how my daughters would grow up and observed the renewal of Holocaust memory all around me, my scholarly focus changed direction and I began to question my own cultural identity.

I was a third-generation American—born half a century after my grandparents immigrated to the United States from Eastern Europe—along with three million other Jews. But the situation of my father's mother differed from my other grandparents who escaped pogrom: my paternal grandmother fled Poland to an arranged, unhappy and short-lived marriage in America—while her mother, eight siblings, a niece, and a nephew bought their way into France—where they believed they would be safe. Five of the eleven who emigrated to France perished there. I had never thought of my grandmother as a Holocaust survivor; she had not survived by hiding, or running, or enduring a concentration camp. She had been safe in Brooklyn. Yet now, as I looked again at her life, I remembered the whispering, the conversations behind closed doors. I saw the vestiges of terror, loss, and guilt. For the first time, I had a vision of my father's childhood and adolescence as partially shaped by the cataclysm that had not even touched his native soil.

My personal journey and my professional life continued to feed each other. In 1996, I began to teach a Literature of the Holocaust course, the first my home university had ever offered. The syllabus was not unique: *Night*, *MAUS*, *The Painted Bird*, *Survival at Auschwitz*. Yet I soon discovered that in order to teach these books properly, I had to know enough to answer my students' questions.

So Primo Levi was a resistance fighter? What was the Resistance? Did other nations have them? Were they successful? Why didn't all nations have a Resistance, and so on.

As a new student of European history, I learned the comparative circumstances of each nation during World War II, for the first time understanding that individual national circumstances had affected how successful Hitler had been implementing the final solution. That the murder of Jewish-Europe had proceeded at different speeds and with different levels of tolerance from the non-Jewish citizens surprised and fascinated me. This realization threw light into the dark corners of my own history. Six of my grandmother's family survived the Nazi occupation of France and five had not. How had that happened? How does it occur that those in the same family, living in the same apartment, were divided: half of them escaping, half of them captured. It mystified me. I would come to realize that the version of the Holocaust I had always known was the Holocaust *in Poland*—a massive, thorough and unrelenting persecution that took every Jew with no exceptions, broke down walls, dug up underground bunkers, and relied on the anti-Semites to inform against their neighbors.

Further, when I read the appendices to Irene Nemirovsky's novel, *Suite Française*, I had learned that the novelist and her husband had been captured and killed in Auschwitz, while her mother and children survived. That peculiarity, added to what I had wondered about my own family, launched the scholarly and personal journey that I am still on today, including my vision for this book. And while this is not a history book, these chapters examine literature, film, television, and architecture taken together, they inform us of the national frameworks that shape the representation of the Holocaust.

My contribution to this collection examines the success of two twenty-first-century French novels, *Suite Française* and *Sarah's Key*, in order to argue that their popular reception is linked to France's acceptance of their own collaboration in the murder of its Jews—after decades of uneven and negligible acknowledgment. In the twenty-first century, the issue of individual national culpability emerges as a central concern. In chapters by both Holli Levitsky, about her Polish students' reaction to Art Spiegelman's MAUS, and in Shira Klein's contribution, about how and why the myth of "the Good Italian" continues to prevail in the popular culture of Italy, despite historical evidence to the contrary, the reader is led to consider the tendency of nations to deny or bury their own criminal behavior.

In Germany, where acknowledging culpability has at times been a national project, two contributors discuss contemporary works written by third-generation writers. In Nora Krug's *Belonging: A German Reckons with History and Home*, Victoria Aarons discusses Krug's inheritance as a grandchild of those who might have been Nazis. The difficulty in negotiating the porous distinctions among the categories of perpetrator, collaborator, and bystander mark this as a distinctly German artifact. Agnes Mueller, on the other hand, takes up the work of third-generation German-Jewish writers and explains how this minority group employs different strategies to topple majority discourses. The displacement of the Jewish subject disturbs other German language literature as well. In a study of the career of Austrian novelist Ruth Klüger, contributor Sarah Painitz observes that in order to survive, the novelist must reconcile her disparate selves and accept a life marked by exile, homelessness, and constant journeying.

From nations that were not conquered by Germany, and whose Jewish population was left untouched, representation of the Holocaust acquires another layer of complexity. In a discussion of two British novelists, Joshua Lander finds that Anglo-Jewish novelists Judith Kerr and Eva Tucker struggle to express their ethnic ties in the face of British anti-Semitism and a pressure to Anglicize. And yet, he simultaneously finds that new attention to colonial atrocities committed by that nation has brought new energy to Holocaust writing. Such paradoxes also appear in artifacts from Great Britain's former provinces. Lizy Mostowski, writing about the National Holocaust Memorial in Canada, finds that ambivalence and erasure are written into the design and content of the building itself. In his study of Australian literature, Ira Nadel describes an ambivalent mode of expression wherein popular writers like Heather Morris use documentary evidence of the Holocaust, and then distort it in order to conform to the national tendency toward evasion of political and social conflict.

In the single contribution about South America, a continent left ostensibly untouched by World War II, Amy Kaminsky writes about Argentinian writer

Edgardo Cozarinsky's novel *Lejos de dónde (Far from Where)*. Finding that Cozarinsky's novel elaborates upon diasporas, refractions, repetitions, and contradictions that are at the center of Holocaust memory in Argentina, Kaminsky sheds light on the unique situation of the nation that gave refuge to both survivors and perpetrators of the genocide.

The collection concludes with essays on Israel and the United States, nations in which Holocaust memory has been sacrosanct for over half a century. Ranen Omer-Sherman studies several novels that appeared in the thirty-year career of novelist, playwright, poet, and screenwriter Nava Semel. Semel published the first Israeli second-generation novel and her attention to intergenerational family trauma and the lasting scar of the Holocaust, Omer-Sherman suggests, is only in the twenty-first century getting its due. In the final essay, Marat Grinberg discusses whether shadows and images of the Holocaust in American and Israeli science-fiction television programming can still remain vital on both a historical and aesthetic level. In the United States, where the Holocaust is widely taught, represented, and used as both tool and metaphor by which to measure other atrocities, this culminating question is most pressing. And yet, surely this would not be the case in Australia, where the representation of the Holocaust is just now becoming widespread; nor in Italy, where the popular audience does not recognize their nation's complicity. Undoubtedly, comparisons such as these, as well as the discussion of previously unfamiliar materials to American readers, direct the reader to the importance and singularity of this collection.

NOTES

1. The first part of this essay is partially adapted from my earlier essay, "Reading the Holocaust: Right Here, Right Now" Hilene Flanzbaum. "Reading the Holocaust: Right Here, Right Now," *Holocaust Studies* 17, no. 1 (2011), 63–84, DOI: *10.1080/17504902.2011.11087274*

2. Bukiet, Melvin. *After.* London: Picador, 1997.

3. It might be equally accurate to say that the novel drew only a meager share of attention in the US, not even drawing a review in the *New York Times*.

4. Polish artist Zbigniew Libera (b. 1959) created the controversial LEGO concentration camp 'toy' in 1996. The kit was made to resemble an actual LEGO kit as it would be sold in stores, complete with packaging that depicts how the fully-constructed kit should look. Libera used actual LEGO blocks and figurines but made his own modifications. In the fully-assembled model, the Jews are presented as skeletons, while the Nazi guards are dressed in black uniforms. Among other things, the model depicts large electrified fences surrounding drab, grey dormitory facilities and crematoriums, as well as torture beds. LEGO Group provided Libera with the blocks and its permission to use its products in the display; however, Libera drew the company's ire

when he indicated on the models packaging that his work was 'sponsored' by LEGO. The company began a lawsuit against Libera but eventually withdrew the suit. The model was exhibited as part of an exhibit at the Jewish Museum in New York called 'Mirroring Evil: Nazi Imagery/Recent Art'. The exhibit ran from 17 March to 20 June 2002.

5. Agnes Mueller has written an essay for this collection.

6. Schlink, Bernhard. *The Reader*. New York: Vintage, 1997.

7. For a positive German reception of the novel see Swales, 'Sex, Shame and Guilt', and Roth, 'Reading and Misreading *The Reader*'. For a more critical approach see Metz, '"Truth is Woman"'; Prager, 'The Good German as Narrator'; and Alison, 'The Third Victim in Bernhard Schlink's *Der Vorleser*'.

8. Cynthia Ozick, "The Rights of History and the Rights of Imagination," *Commentary*, March 1999, 22.

9. There is much to say here. Current work on trauma has contributed to our understanding that even direct testimony does not constitute objective truth. I would also point out that the great documentary, *Shoah*, by Claude Lanzmann—perhaps one of the strictest adherents to realism—is no longer understood as "objective" truth. For a discussion of this, and related topics, see PMLA.

10. Some would argue that Holocaust denial is increasing. I would not dispute it—but would point out that it is not doing so among among well-intentioned, rational and fair-minded individuals anywhere—and that we err when we shape our reactions in fear of what anti-Semites might say or do.

11. The myth of the Good German holds that "though the Germans, as a whole, were bad, my uncle, or my father, actually helped the Jews." Holli Levitsky and Shira Klein in their essays herein discuss national variations of the Good German myth, in Poland and Italy respectively.

12. These questions have captivated legal scholars. In 2004, the academic journal *Law and Literature* devoted an entire issue to *The Reader* in which it contemplates the legal and ethical implications of the issues presented.

13. Eva Hoffman, "The Uses of Illiteracy," *New Republic*, March 23, 1998, 36.

14. *Austin Powers*, directed by Jay Roach (1999–2002; Burbank, CA: New Line Cinema, 2006),

15. I am thinking especially of the Marvel superhero movies, particularly *Guardians of the Galaxy* series, which has been the highest grossing franchise of the last two decades.

16. I write this during the Covid-19 crisis, when international travel has come to a halt, and where US citizens have been even prohibited from entering Canada.

17. For a more particular and thorough discussion of teaching my experience teaching literature of the Holocaust in midwestern America, I direct you again to "Right Here, Right Now."

18. "As everyone knows, literary study in the past few years has undergone a sudden, almost universal turn away from theory in the sense of an orientation toward language as such and has made a corresponding turn toward history, culture, society, politics, institutions, class and gender conditions, the social context, the material base in the sense of institutionalisation, conditions of production, technology, distribution,

and consumption of 'cultural products,' among other products. This trend is so obvious everywhere as hardly to need description." Miller, "Presidential Address 1986," 283.

19. Smith, Barbara Herrnstein. "Contingencies of Value." *Critical Inquiry* 10, no. 1 (September 1983): 1–35.

20. In 1987, I was a beginning graduate student at the University of Pennsylvania and traveled to the Center for Cultural Analysis at Rutgers University to hear Jacques Derrida speak. At the end of Derrida's lecture, what looked like another grad student stood up and asked, "But what about Apartheid?" to which Derrida replied, "Apartheid is wrong. Next question."

21. See Rothberg, Michael. "From Gaza to Warsaw: Mapping Multidirectional Memory." *Criticism* 53, no. 4 (2011): 523–48. Among other things, Rothberg argues that the Holocaust should be considered alongside other representations of oppressions and genocides because such intersections yield more penetrating readings of such artifacts.

22. Flanzbaum, Hilene. *The Americanization of the Holocaust.* Baltimore: Baltimore: JHU Press, 1999.

23. In order, Academy Award-winning documentaries were: 1995, *Anne Frank Remembered* for which Miep Gies accepted the award; 1997, *The Long Way Home*, edited by Morgan Freeman, tells the story of survivors, who after liberation have nowhere to go; 1999, *One Day in September* is not quite on point, but is about the murder of the Israeli Olympians in Munich 2000: *Into the Arms of Strangers: Tales of the Kindertransport*. During this same period, 1998, *Life is Beautiful* won the Academy Award for best foreign film.

REFERENCES

Alison, Jane, 'The Third Victim in Bernhard Schlink's *Der Vorleser*'. *The Germanic Review* 81, no. 2 (2006): 163–77.

Barnouw, Dagmar, 'True Stories: Oprah, Elie Wiesel, and the Holocaust'. *History News Network*, 18 March 2006.

Brinkley, Robert, and Youra, Steven, 'Tracing Shoah'. *PMLA*, Volume 111, no. 1 (Special Topic: The Status of Evidence (Jan., 1996)): 108–127.

Flanzbaum, Hilene. *The Americanization of the Holocaust.* Baltimore: Johns Hopkins University Press, 1999.

Flanzbaum, Hilene. '"But Wasn't It Terrific?": A Defense of Liking *Life is Beautiful*'. *The Yale Journal of Criticism* 14, no. 1 (2001): 273–86.

Flanzbaum, Hilene. 'Reading the Holocaust: Right Here, Right Now'. *Holocaust Studies* 17, no. 1 (2011): 63–84.

Hoffman, Eva. 'The Uses of Illiteracy'. *The New Republic* (23 March 1998): 36.

Metz, Joseph, '"Truth is Woman": Post-Holocaust Narrative, Postmodernism, and the Gender of Fascism in Bernhard Schlink's "Der Vorleser"'. *The German Quarterly* 77, no. 3 (2004): 300–23.

Miller, J. Hillis, 'Presidential Address 1986. The Triumph of Theory, the Resistance to Reading, and the Question of the Material Base'. *PMLA* 102, no. 3 (1987): 281–91.

Ozick, Cynthia, 'The Rights of History and the Rights of Imagination'. *Commentary* (March 1999): 22.
Prager, Brad, 'The Good German as Narrator: On W.G. Sebald and the Risks of Holocaust Writing'. *New German Critique* 96 (Fall 2005): 75–102.
Roth, Jeffrey I., 'Reading and Misreading *The Reader*'. *Law & Literature* 16, no. 2 (2004): 163–76.
Rothberg, Michael, *Multidirectional Memory*. Stanford, CA: Stanford University Press, 2009.
Smith, Barbara Herrnstein. 'Contingencies of Value'. *Critical Inquiry* 10, no. 1 (September 1983): 1–35.
Swales, Martin, 'Sex, Shame and Guilt: Reflections on Bernhard Schlink's *Der Vorleser* (The Reader) and J. M. Coetzee's *Disgrace*'. *Journal of European Studies* 33 (2003): 7–22.

Chapter 1

Selling the Holocaust in Twenty-First-Century France

Hilene Flanzbaum

In 2018, the Polish Institute of National Remembrance (IPN) passed a law that "Whoever accuses, publicly and against the facts, the Polish nation, or the Polish state, of being responsible or complicit in the Nazi crimes committed by the Third German Reich . . . shall be subject to a fine or a penalty of imprisonment of up to three years."[1] This edict marked a notable moment in the history of Holocaust memory, constituting a turnaround in what some viewed as progress toward individual countries accepting responsibility for their participation in the murder of their Jews.

In 1996, *Hitler's Willing Executioners*[2] Daniel Goldhagen advanced the supposition that Nazis so successfully murdered Jews because the anti-Semitic Germans were glad to oblige. While Goldhagen's work has been subject to challenge, the major thrust of his argument has remained intact: the efficiency of the final solution, to a large degree, depended upon whether or not individual citizens had chosen to cooperate with the Nazis, and that choice was to a large extent determined by how much antisemitism was a fact of national life. Legendary, for instance, is the case of Denmark, where the king ordered all Danish citizens to wear the yellow star, creating enough confusion for him to facilitate the safe passage of all Danish Jews into Sweden. While this story is not factual, it does correctly characterize the extraordinary efforts on the part of the Danish government to protect its Jewish citizens. The result was that only 120 of 7,500 Jews met their deaths, or roughly 1.6 percent.[3] Stories from Poland are the stuff of nightmare rather than legend: in both nonfiction and imagination, readers have found details of collaboration, of neighbor turning on neighbor, of Jews murdered when they returned after the war, of Polish indifference toward the peculiar stench of chimney smoke. To what extent these images provide a wholly truthful picture is left to debate; however, Poland's bad rap bears out in the numbers: over 90 percent of their population of three million Jews met their deaths.[4] And still, it is illegal for Poles to examine their own complicity in the extermination of the Jews. Blaming the Germans for their racial policies, or not even acknowledging the genocidal aspect of World War II (i.e., that the Jews were singled out for extermination) is an all too common stance that scholars liken to outright denial. In 2017, American President Trump made a similar maneuver when on Holocaust Remembrance Day: he omitted any mention of the Jews.[5] Lawrence Grossman, the director of publications for the American Jewish Community, responded by saying

> President Trump's statement marking International Holocaust Remembrance Day without mentioning Jews was stunning, as was the White House refusal to retract and clarify. . . . In doing so he joined a number of other world leaders who have already made such denial a pattern. This year's statement from the White House . . . is just the latest iteration of Holocaust "memory" that "forgets" the identity of the actual victims.[6]

White House chief of staff at the time, Reince Priebus, shrugged these criticisms off, stating: "I don't regret the words. I mean, everyone's suffering in the Holocaust."[7] Careless, inaccurate, and insensitive, Priebus's words demonstrate just how much can go wrong as the memory of the Holocaust is figured and refigured. Among these issues at stake, how nations weigh their own culpability in the execution of their Jewish citizens—as Jews (and not as Poles, or Hungarians, or Greeks)—takes on long-ranging significance. From a global perspective, it seems urgent that nations be able to hold themselves accountable for crimes against humanity. And yet, even with an event as egregious as the Holocaust, the record of accountability is uneven and inaccurate.

Of the almost twenty nations where Jews were endangered, *because they were Jews,* the case of France stands out. Because the political situation of that nation was unique and complicated—involving an occupied Zone; a government-in-exile; the unoccupied "free-France," the Vichy government, and a strong Resistance movement—France emerged as a site of continuing fascination and contested reality. Irregular laws and boundaries created opportunities, and a fertile field for imagination. As early as 1942, just two years after the Germans overran France, a movie like *Casablanca,* demonstrated how personal agency could make the difference between good and evil, life, and death.[8] In the film, sly Captain Renault figures as the ideal Frenchman who manages to convince the Nazis he is cooperating with them, when he is actually helping the hero, Rick, a Resistance fighter. Based on a true story, and brought to life by Jewish-American screenwriters, the film not once mentions the Jews; on the other hand, it emphasizes personal courage and independent thought as tools to fight the Nazis. The ambiguous political boundaries of the war in France, the interstices between collaboration and resistance, the continual *pas-de-deux* between German and French officials, and the potential for individuals to be heroic, or villainous, or somewhere-in-between renders "what happened" in France, especially subject to interpretation. Not surprisingly then, representations of the French as heroic crowded popular literature and film for half a century.

Until the early 1990s, few French collaborators appeared in literature or film. Judging by the artistic output in the first ten years after the war, one might have concluded that the preponderance of French men and women fought in the Resistance.[9] Films like *Tonight We Raid Calais* (1943), *Paris After Dark* (1943), *Paris Underground* (1945), *The Battle of Rails* (1946), and *Odette* (1950) created the impression that every French man and woman acted with conscience and courage; of course, the historical record proves otherwise. Yet even these exaggerated portrayals of universal heroism seldom included helping the Jewish population or even an acknowledgment that there was a Jewish population, endangered or not.

An early benchmark in French representations of the Holocaust, *Night and Fog*, also does not mention Jews. Among the earliest visual records of the atrocities committed, this short documentary was financed by the *Comité d'histoire de la Deuxième Guerre mondiale*, (Committee on the History of World War II) and the *Réseau du souvenir* (Network of Memory),[10] directed by the young Alan Resnais and written by Jean Cayrol, poet, Resistance fighter, and deportee to Mauthausen. Today, the film still shocks for its graphic images: the clearing of bodies, giant cranes with claws emptying bones into mass graves, the skeletal frames of the living. Thus, the film was deemed not suitable—nor was it ever intended for—a popular audience. Its short documentary format mandated special viewings rather than theatrical release. Since 1956, when it was first screened at the Cannes Film Festival, however, the film had been widely shown to generations of pupils and students.[11] "*Nuit et Brouillard* was mostly shown in France in schools, film clubs, universities, societies and commemorations";[12] over time; however, the film was seen by millions of school children across the Western Hemisphere, thus making it a cornerstone of Holocaust education.[13]

Before the film was released even to these select audiences, however, government censors demanded that certain pieces of footage be eliminated. Resnais's original version showed French police brutalizing Jewish prisoners and offering no resistance to Nazi orders.[14] In *Night and Fog*, then, the graphic depiction of the atrocities covered new ground but otherwise the same myth prevailed: only the Germans were responsible, and the victims were all the Allies. Thirteen years later, when *The Sorrow and The Pity* premiered, little had changed. Through personal interviews, the filmmakers documented the collaboration of French officials with the Nazis for unconscionable reasons, including lust for power, cowardice, and antisemitism. Although 600,000 people saw the film in theaters and were strongly affected, the French government refused to televise *The Sorrow and the Pity*, explaining that "certain myths are necessary for a people's well-being and tranquillity."[15]

Still, scholars view *The Sorrow and the Pity* as a milestone toward representing the long and tortured road toward the French acknowledgment of their own complicity.[16] One might make a similar case about *Au Revoir les Enfants* (1987) which although not as explicit about collaboration reached a much larger audience and may have prompted a much larger *crise de foi*. Three-and-a-half million French bought tickets to what critics called Louis Malle's masterpiece, a semi-autobiographical story of a young Catholic boy, Julien, who inadvertently betrays his Jewish friend who is being hidden by the priests in his boarding school.[17] Merely a glance by Julien in the Jewish friend's direction dooms the latter to capture and death. Julien, the viewer is led to believe, has spent his lifetime regretting that single instant and weighing his own complicity. Also in the film, Malle gives us a view of the honorable French—priests who risked their lives to save Jewish children, as well as a discontented and lower-class worker who informs against the priests. Viewers are then left to consider where they fit in the spectrum of good and evil: the young protagonist's unwitting denunciation of his friend generates an emotional and intellectual crisis. By not indicting all of the French, and by presenting a dramatic situation where collaboration can be viewed as unintentional, Malle presents a conducive apparatus by which one can examine their own conscience, which may partially explain the popularity of the film. It had taken the larger French audience forty-two years to get to this crisis.

Such reversals are never sudden, nor are they reversals at all. Change is gradual. It is impossible to mark the exact moment when the French national mythos definitively alters. The protests at the commemoration for the fiftieth anniversary of the incident at Vel D'Hiv in 1992, for instance, may have seemed like a sudden change in public sentiment, when actually attitudes had been slowly altering all along.

Fifty-two years after the Nazis occupied France, but only five years after *Au Revoir, Les Enfants* premiered in French cinemas, protesters demanded that then-president Francois Mitterand acknowledge the nation's complicity in the murder of its Jews. That occasion, the fiftieth anniversary of what is known as the incident at Vel D'Hiv, was as likely a time as any for such a movement. The first round-up of women and children and the conditions that these 13,000 people suffered—dehydration, starvation, for almost a week while French officers watched, awaiting further orders from the Germans—is the most graphic illustration of French complicity in the murder of the Jews.[18] Mitterand, however, denied the public's request, some believed due to his personal history in the Vichy government.[19] The death of Mitterand, and the succession of Jacques Chirac to the presidency, began a new era in French politics.

Chirac had been in office only a few months before he made the now-famous public statement that the "French people 'handed those who were under its protection over to their executioners.'"[20] This is widely viewed as the beginning of France's official and public reckoning with their responsibility for the murder of their Jewish population. A landmark in French history, this admission changed France in profound ways, and was responsible for a sea change in literary representations of the Holocaust. In the eleven years between Chirac's dramatic reversal and the opening of a vastly improved and expanded Memorial and Museum de la Shoah in the fourth arrondissement,[21] several groundbreaking books appeared. Widely embraced by the public, these stories fully acknowledged the assumption of French responsibility—and indeed, their success partly depended on this acknowledgment. The commercial success of the novels *Suite Francaise* (2004) and *Sarah's Key* (2006) can be understood as culminating chapters in the torturous tale of a nation grappling with, and then accepting responsibility for, its crimes against humanity—a feat for which the French should be applauded, and which, arguably, few other nations have achieved.[22]

The enthusiastic public reception to these artistic indictments demonstrates the extent to which the national mythos has altered; the literary marketplace, quite sensibly, responds to changing appetites. Perhaps the strongest evidence for this comes in the discovery of previously "lost" or "repressed" stories. Written by Jewish women in mortal danger, books like *Le Journal d'Hélène Berr* and *Suite Francaise* would never have emerged from their hiding places prior to 2000.[23] In 2010, another forgotten memoir, *A Bookshop in Berlin* recounts the life of Françoise Frenkel and her flight to safety—from Germany through France to Switzerland. Originally published in 1945, it promptly sank into obscurity until it was rediscovered in a jumble sale in Nice in 2010. Republished in 2015, the current edition includes a preface by Patrick Modiano, Nobel Prize-winning author and survivor, and will no doubt attract its share of attention.[24] That these books appear, or reappear, in contemporary France, must draw our attention.

The case of *Suite Francaise* fascinates for several reasons: first, it demonstrates the difference between French attitudes "then" (in 1943, when it was written) and "now" (the early twenty-first century when it was published). And second: while the book contains fiction, it is not only fiction. A good deal of it cannot correctly be labeled a novel, and therefore it manages to capitalize on the blurred distinction between truth and imagination. *Suite Francaise* may be best considered a collection, containing two novellas by Nemirovksy, but also an assortment of other documents: notes for an unwritten third novella by Nemirovsky, historical appendices, a long preface (or epilogue depending upon the edition), which recounts Nemirovky's fate as a "stateless Jew" in occupied France. This, along with appendix one (Nemirovsky's notes for the rest of the planned series and her editorial comments) and appendix two (her husband's correspondence with various French officials to ask for Irene's release), complement the novellas, supplying a jarring counterpoint to the fictional content that was never completed. Between the same covers where the fictional narratives appear, one sees documentation of Nemirovsky's capture and arrest, her husband's futile appeals to people in high places to secure a release, her frantic search to find caretakers for her children, and finally her execution.[25]

Surprisingly, critics have not viewed the book as a multi-generic document, rather they have focused only on its fictional components. They have praised the novellas, and only glanced at the historical documents. The critic for the *New York Times* mentions that Nemirovsky "wrote the exquisitely shaped and balanced fiction of *Suite Francaise* almost contemporaneously with the events that inspired them,"[26] and calls that feat remarkable. Focusing mostly on the invented story, the critic is amazed that Nemirovsky can write so well in the face of mortal danger. Fair enough; however, such praise neither accounts for the power nor the popularity of the book as a whole. Without the appendices, *Suite Francaise* would have gone the way of Nemirovsky's earlier books: popular in their time, but forgotten within a few years. As Nathan Zuckerman observes in *The Ghost Writer*, the potency of Anne Frank's story would rapidly fade if the world discovered she had not died in Bergen-Belson.[27]

Moreover, without the appendices, the book could not be correctly considered inside the genre of "Holocaust Literature" as we now call it. The story, however intricate or subtle, follows only French characters living under the German occupation: in the first novella, *Storm*, the reader sees the German defeat of France and the behavior of those that must flee Paris; in the second, *Dolce*, the author closely observes a town in the French countryside where the inhabitants find themselves in ambiguous and ambivalent relations with their captors. A best-selling author, Nemirovksy knew what makes popular fiction: the novellas are chock full of the virtuous and the not-so-virtuous, the needy and the not-so-needy, the cowardice of some French soldiers and the courage of others. It is well-written and readable, but hardly remarkable. Not once does it refer to the fate of the Jews—her own fate—an omission that in the twenty-first century feels noteworthy, but in the 1940s made a great deal of sense, an argument we will follow shortly.

This sixty-year period—*history*—between *Suite's* creation and its reception is responsible for the success of the book. When Nemirovsky senses she does not have much time, she gives two completed sections and notes for section three (in a suitcase) to her older daughter, Denise, who along with her sister spends the remaining war years hiding from the Nazis, first in a Catholic orphanage (the girls had taken communion before the war) and then in various cellars of Bordeaux. Half-a-century passes before Denise finds the courage to look inside the suitcase her mother had given her. She recalls that she thought the pages to be autobiographical, retelling the events of her wartime ordeal—events that she could not bear to live through again. Only in 1992, when she is forty-six, does she look closely enough to see that the pages inside the suitcase are fiction. Ostensibly, the manuscript has little to do with what her family suffered. The year that Denise finds the courage to look at the contents of the suitcase, of course, corresponds to the wider French awakening and may well reflect Denise's position within a cultural zeitgeist that has turned to face the past. With relief and curiosity, Denise begins the difficult process of deciphering this inheritance—the ink has smeared, the pages are brittle, and her mother's handwriting is cramped and blurry.

Two years after Denise found and deciphered the manuscript, she sent it to the publisher, Éditions Denoël, who already had a relationship with her sister.[28] Almost immediately, it became a bestseller in France and was soon translated into English and thirty-one other languages. Undoubtedly, Nemirovsky's two daughters and even their publishers had the noblest of intentions when publishing it, but we should not overlook how market forces played a central role in providing readers access to Nemirovsky's work. Denise's newfound determination and the editor's enthusiasm are not coincidental. They are undoubtedly influenced by the larger cultural attitudes about French culpability and the publisher's belief that she had a hot commodity on her hands.

Students of literary history should ask themselves how such fortunes turn around, why manuscripts reappear and ignite. Such information is crucial to the commercial market, of course, but also reveals a narrative about cultural change and vexing questions of taste. For half-a-century, *what happened to the Jews in France* had been filed under the heading of *what happened to all French people during the German occupation*; thus, few would have embraced Nemirovsky's full story. Because French attitudes toward accepting culpability had evolved, attaching Nemirovsky's fiction to her history and biography has become more than likely. And quite paradoxically, then, *Suite Francaise* became a book—about the murder of the Jews— despite the author's complete omission of the topic (a subject we will get to shortly). In its ordering of sections, the French edition of the book preempts the possibility of misapprehending the potency of *Suite Francaise*. Positioning the facts before the fiction immediately establishes the book as a product of the Holocaust and illustrates how contemporary markets are responding to the marked increase in public interest, as well as putting the events in the novellas into a much more dire context.

For readers in Nemirovsky's time, and a half-century beyond, World War II was not about the murder of the Jews. It was a much more personal tragedy: the loss of nationhood, honor, autonomy, and freedom. The distasteful word, "collaboration," had not been used in connection to the Jewish problem; rather, it indicated giving aid and succor to the Germans. As Nemirovsky's novellas properly demonstrate, the fate of the Jews was barely on anyone's mind. Anecdotally, I can report that when I teach this book in my Literature of the Holocaust class, my students are confused about why I have asked them to read it. There is no recognizable "Holocaust" in this book. It is a relief, a brief respite in an agonizing reading list: no death, no torture, no brutal scenes of execution, no politically incorrect antisemitism. Reading the appendices only partially illuminates them. Even when they learn the horrible fate of the writer, they cannot attach it to the novellas, "Storm" or "Dolce." One could make the case that Nemirovsky's searing indictment of her French characters—for instance, the Catholic priest who cannot bear to be in contact with human beings because they are too messy—indicts her countrymen, and by extension, may extend to their callous treatment of the Jews.[29] But such an explanation is subtle medicine for a generation that has been reared on *Schindler's List* and *Night*. For generations X and Y, in the United States, at least, World War II is almost synonymous with discussing the Holocaust— they know more about concentration camps than they do about the bombing of Pearl Harbor. It is unusual to find a college-age student who has not seen *Inglourious Basterds* or read *The Boy in the Striped Pajamas*, while the one or two lessons they might have had about the bombing Pearl Harbor in high school history class does not often leave a similar impression.

As I have been suggesting, Nemirovsky's decision not to mention the Jews has historical verisimilitude but has still been controversial. Nemirovsky may have been Jewish by Hitler's rules, but she and her husband, Michel, had converted to Catholicism in 1939.[30] These decisions have led several critics to accuse Nemirovsky of being a self-hating Jew. Writing for the *New Republic*, Ruth Franklin argued, for instance, that Nemirovsky's blindness to Jewish issues, her conversion and a portrayal of an unsympathetic Jewish character in an earlier novel provided reason enough to never read anything she wrote.[31] Such criticisms surprise in their ahistoricism and obscure the importance of the book. One should compare her professional decisions to those of other writers under threat, or in captivity. An apt comparison might be to Phillis Wheatley whose poems appear to praise her white masters.[32] In the 1960s, some critics condemned her for toadying; Franklin is similarly ahistorical when she argues that *Suite* is best forgotten. Fortunately, more informed readings of Wheatley's work prevailed—now we realize that Wheatley's work would never have been printed had she criticized her white masters, or their peculiar institution, and benefit from critical attention devoted to finding the double-consciousness of the speaker. We could read *Suite* with similar intentions, for Nemirovsky's sharp criticism of the French bourgeoisie might well be understood as having been aimed at that population's refusal to risk their security for the sake of the Jews or any other endangered party.

Understanding other similarities between these two writers provides a clearer understanding of the twentieth-century writer. Wheatley's ability to get her poetry into public view depended on pleasing those with the power to publish and that desire stems from more than just the desire to be read, or even to make money. In her case, publication lifted her from abject poverty and a lifetime of grueling work. In retrospect, literary historians have understood how shrewdly Wheatley managed her career, given the material circumstances of her life. Similarly, the possibility of criticizing the Nazis in print—in Nazi-occupied France—is as impossible as it sounds. In France, of course, there was an underground press which published sporadically and reached a select few. Those that resisted too loudly were arrested.[33]

In order to save her own life, Nemirovsky needed to make a splash and to stay clear of dangerous political alliances. Her first novel, *David Golder*, brought her a degree of fame and fortune that had given her access to the first tier of French society—a status she could not, as a foreign-born Jew, otherwise maintain in 1940. In 1929, this status felt as if it were her due, necessary to this well-born and wealthy Ukrainian. The main character, Golder is Jewish, unattractively so—a fact that has fed accusations of Nemirovky's anti-Semitism or fostered the notion that the writer was "a self-hating Jew."[34] Critic Susan Suleiman has done a convincing job of debunking these claims, arguing among other things that Nemirovksy wrote from the "inside of a Jewish community" and might well be compared to Philip Roth who felt that he was writing from a safe perch from which to portray Jews, with all their human idiosyncrasies intact.[35] Yet in light of what the next decade brought, Nemirovksy's unflattering portrayal of Jews has taken on more troubling dimensions than Roth's—but of course, as Suleiman argues, Nemirovksy could not have predicted Hitler's final solution. Yet in *Suite*, Nemirovsky does not portray Jewish characters at all, sparing them her usual critical scrutiny. Instead, she saves that for the French, portraying them as, at best, passive and at worst cowardly, selfish, and vain—at the same time, her omission of the Jewish question makes her more like her countryman, and less likely to attract notice. Paraphrasing Sartre, Nemirovsky must have hoped that she "could enjoy all the rights of a French citizen, as long as she wasn't so Jewish."

In Nazi-occupied France, status did more than satisfy vanity. Distinguishing oneself from the mass of foreign-born Jews who had looked to France for refuge was a matter of life and death. Those who had status, or money, or friends in high places had a much higher survival rate than those without resources or connections. In cases of prominent Jews—that the Nazis judged to have international significance, and whose murders might draw too much attention—emigration was encouraged. Thomas Mann had been escorted out of Germany; as is well-known, Freud had been politely—and then not so politely—asked to leave Austria. In *Two Lives: Gertrude and Alice*, Janet Malcolm does a thorough job of explaining how Gertrude Stein and Alice B. Toklas moved around the French countryside with the help of some powerful friends in government and only slight inconvenience.[36]

Nemirovksy must have understood that she was not of Freud's or Stein's echelon; still she had come from a background of wealth and privilege and her first novel had made her name recognizable. Irene's husband Michel tried to trade on that. Besides being "a novelist of very great talent," Michel wrote to the authorities, my "younger brother Paul was a personal friend of the Grand-Duke Dmitri" and Irene's father, he tells them, "was often received by the Grand Duke Alexander." He made additional pleas based on their anti-Communist and anti-Jewish credentials: "she does not speak of the Jews with any affection in her works," he offers, as ammunition for her release from detention.[37] His pleas, of course, did no good. Both Irene and Michel met their end in Auschwitz in 1942. Sixty-two years after her death, then, Irene's wish to write a novel that lifted her from obscurity was finally granted.

Indeed, part of the miracle of *Suite Francaise* is that it has managed to capture the attention of two audiences—that do not often meet at the bookstore—the first: professional readers, literary critics, and professors and the second, a more general reading audience that is typically female, and between the ages of 25 and 75.[38]

What the latter group reads, of course, is a much more accurate barometer of what the French people think about their wartime behavior than what professors and professional historians think, or know.

For that reason, I will briefly discuss the popular novel, *Sarah's Key*, which, published only a year after *Suite* is an even larger blockbuster and a much more explicit condemnation of the French. While *Suite* has attracted critical attention, *Sarah's Key* is a book that most academics would be happy to ignore—yet as a marker of cultural change, it is definitive. In it, two stories unravel side-by-side: in the first, a transplanted American, Julia, now working for a French magazine. is given the assignment of writing an anniversary piece for the 60th anniversary of the massacre at Vel D'Hiv—an event about which she previously knew very little; the second takes place in 1943 when the eponymous Sarah and her family are captured and taken to that notorious velodrome. Her family will perish at Auschwitz but Sarah escapes to tell the sorrowful tale. The day of her family's arrest, Sarah hides her younger brother in a wardrobe and locks him in, planning to retrieve him later. His body is left to an unknown but presumably horrific fate. The two narratives merge when Julia learns that her husband—with whom she is growing increasingly alienated, because he is a narcissist and a philanderer—grew up in that very apartment, unaware of what had transpired there, nor does he know anything about the historical event. In fact, no one Julia meets in France knows about it. Thus, Julia tells the story several times and each time she does, her listeners are astonished, but accepting—except the bad husband. De Rosnay creates this angry, depressed, and soon-to-be-revealed adulterous husband to represent all of his unrepentant and right-leaning French. Furious at his wife, the husband accuses Julia of enjoying "yet another chance to show your compatriots how devious we Frogs were, collaborating with the Nazis and sending those poor innocent families to their death. What are you going to do? Rub our noses in it? Nobody cares."[39]

But of course the reader knows the opposite to be true: everyone cares. By 2006, the villainous husband is the outlier. Only he doesn't want to confront the past—thereby symbolizing those French citizens who refuse to take stock of their own culpability. As is often the case in popular novels, the good are rewarded and the bad are punished: the family that lived in the apartment where Sarah's family once lived is swamped by guilt and regret. At the end of the novel, the husband who refuses to condemn the blindness of his parents' generation is loveless and embittered, while the persevering heroine is rewarded with family, a clear conscience, and a renewed sense of identity. Not to worry, readers, Julia will have a new love interest before the book ends.

One is not likely to see *Sarah's Key* on a syllabus for a Literature of the Holocaust course. The hackneyed writing, the vague scene rendering, and the happy ending (the reviled component of so much Holocaust representation) would make it more at home in the paperback rack of a drugstore. Yet the book's great success must be noted. Even the "best" of bestsellers seldom breaks convention: instead they confirm what the reader already believes—or at least suspected or feared. Only rarely do bestsellers or hit movies neither challenge popular notions of good and evil nor ask their audiences to question values or beliefs. Rather, they deliver clear meanings and mete out deserved rewards and punishments, and in most cases, reaffirm what readers already believe. Neither *Sarah's Key* nor *Suite Francaise* could have gathered such an audience—or in the case of the former, even been pulled out of the suitcase, if the zeitgeist had not been right.

The making of Holocaust memory in France has been bitterly fought over for the last seventy years; its trajectory does not advance in a straight line, but circles and curves and collapses unto itself. Any generalization one might make about what the French believe today or even what they did in 2006 is subject to challenge and eternal revision. And yet, having said this, one must still applaud the French for being able to face, at least in one generation, what so many other Europeans cannot.

Thirteen days before France's first round of voting for its 2017 presidential election, far-right candidate Marine Le Pen denied Vichy's presence in France, announcing on French television: "I don't think France is responsible for Vel d'Hiv," an action that sparked fury among French citizens and politicians alike.[40] Jean-Maire Le Pen, Marine's father, was an outspoken Holocaust minimizer who founded the National Front party, which Marine led from 2012 until her presidential campaign in 2017. Like his daughter, he downplayed the severity of the Holocaust, stating that gas chambers were merely a "detail" of World War II. Jean-Marie was punished for his statements in 1987 when he was charged 1.2 million Francs under the Gaysott Act, which makes it an offense to deny or question crimes against humanity, such as the Holocaust.[41] Le Pen's presidential loss and besmirched reputation were the consequence of her own statements.[42] At least for now then, France provides a lesson for all of us.

NOTES

1. Adam Easton, "Poland Holocaust Law: Government U-turn on Jail Threat," *BBC*, June 27, 2018, https://www.bbc.com/news/world-europe-44627129.

2. Daniel Goldhagen, *Hitler's Willing Executioners* (New York: Knopf, 1996).

3. "Jewish Population of Denmark," United States Holocaust Memorial Museum, Washington, DC, accessed May 6, 2020, https://encyclopedia.ushmm.org/content/en/article/denmark.

4. Adam Easton, "Jewish Life Slowly Returns to Poland," *BBC*, April 20, 2012, https://www.bbc.com/news/world-radio-and-tv-17741185.

5. Trump's exact words: "It is with a heavy heart and somber mind that we remember and honor the victims, survivors, heroes of the Holocaust. It is impossible to fully fathom the depravity and horror inflicted on innocent people by Nazi terror. . . . I pledge to do everything in my power throughout my Presidency, and my life, to ensure that the forces of evil never again defeat the powers of good." "Statement by the President on International Holocaust Remembrance Day," Statments and Releases, White House, issued January 27, 2017, https://www.whitehouse.gov/briefings-statements/statement-president-international-holocaust-remembrance-day/.

6. Lawrence Grossman, "Holocaust Memory Without Jews," *American Jewish Community*, January 31, 2017, https://www.ajc.org/news/holocaust-memory-without-jews.

7. Jonah Engel Bromwich, "Reince Priebus Defends Holocaust Statement that Failed to Mention Jews," *New York Times*, January 29, 2017, https://www.nytimes.com/2017/01/29/us/politics/reince-preibus-holocaust-remembrance-day.html.

8. *Casablanca*, directed by Michael Curtiz (1942; Burbank: Warner Bros, 1991), DVD.

9. Movies about the French Resistance have been too numerous to get completely listed here. *Tonight We Raid Calais*, directed by John Brahm (1943; Los Angeles, CA : 20th Century Fox, 2007), DVD; *Paris After Dark*, directed by Léonide Moguy (1943; Los Angeles, CA: 20th Century Fox, 2013), DVD; *Paris Underground*, directed by Gregory Ratoff (1945; Beverly Hills, CA: United Artists, 2005), DVD; *Bataille Du Rail* (The Battle of Rails), directed by René Clément (1946; Paris, France: Union Française de Production Cinématographique, 2006), DVD; *Odette*, directed by Herbert Wilcox (1950; London, England: British Lion Films, 2019), DVD.

10. Donald Reid, "Teaching *Night and Fog*: Putting a Documentary Film in History," *Teaching History: A Journal of Methods* 33, no. 2 (Fall 2008): 3.

11. Jean-Marc Dreyfus, "Censorship and Approval: The Reception of *Nuit et Brouillard* in France," in *Uncovering the Holocaust The International Reception of Night and Fog*, ed. Ewout van der Knaap (London: Wallflower Press, 2006), 35.

12. Ibid., 36.

13. As part of school curricula, Night and Fog has been shown in French, German, American, and British classrooms. Dreyfus, "Reception of *Nuit et Brouillard*," 35, 61, 116, 162.

14. Richard Raskin, *Night and Fog by Alain Resnais: On the making, Reception and Functions of a Major Documentary Film* (Aarhus: Aarhus University Press, 1987), 30.

15. Julian Jackson, *France: The Dark Years, 1940–1944* (Oxford: Oxford University Press, 2003), 613.

16. Jackson, *France: Dark Years*, 613.

17. One reviewer wrote that it was "so flawless and overwhelming is this film that it is tempting to call it Louis Malle's masterpiece, but this would be to overlook not only "Lacombe, Lucien" but also "Atlantic City." It's enough to say that "Au Revoir Les Enfants" . . . which is France's entry in the Oscar race for best foreign-language film, is one of the best films of this or any other year. Leonard Klady, "Box Office Champs, Chumps," *Los Angeles Times*, January 8, 1989, https://www.latimes.com/archives/la-xpm-1989-01-08-ca-258-story.html

18. "The Vélodrome d'Hiver (Vél d'Hiv") Roundup," United States Holocaust Memorial Museum, Washington, DC, assessed May 6, 2020, https://encyclopedia.ushmm.org/content/en/article/the-velodrome-dhiver-vel-dhiv-roundup.

19. Romain Brunet, "France's Role in Deporting Jews: The Changing Political Views Over 70 Years," *French 24*, April 11, 2017, https://www.france24.com/en/20170411-france-role-deporting-jews-political-stances-through-70-years.

20. On Chirac -- what he said, and more: "These dark hours forever sully our history and slander our past and our traditions. Yes, French people, the French State, assisted the occupier in its criminal madness. . . . France, the motherland of the Enlightenment and Human Rights, land of welcome and of asylum, France, on that

day, committed the unredeemable. Breaking her word, she delivered her protégés to their executioners. . . . France owes the victims an everlasting debt." Liam Hoare, "How the Late French President Jacques Chirac Started France's Reckoning with the Holocaust," *Jewish Telegraphic Agency*, September 26, 2019, https://www.jta.org/2019/09/26/opinion/how-the-late-french-president-jacques-chirac-started-frances-reckoning-with-the-holocaust.

21. Included in these improvements are the French records where Jews were taken from, and where they ended up. Much more visibly, perhaps, a visitor can see the wall of remembrance – ten feet obsidian blocks of black slabs on which the name of every French-Jewish victim is etched. "The Spaces of the Museum-Memorial," Memorial de la Shoah, accessed May 14, 2020, http://www.memorialdelashoah.org/en/the-memorial/the-spaces-of-the-museum-memorial/the-wall-of-names.html.

22. Certainly, this is a controversial and enormous topic about which scholars, depending upon their political and national affiliations, reach different conclusions. To begin research on this topic, one might look at "Collaboration and Complicity during the Holocaust," United States Holocaust Memorial Museum, accessed May 26, 2020, https://www.ushmm.org/information/press/press-releases/collaboration-and-complicity-during-the-holocaust; Orlando Crowcroft, "The History of the Holocaust is Being Re-written and Historians are Fighting Back," *Euronews*, January 27, 2020, https://www.euronews.com/2020/01/27/the-history-of-the-holocaust-is-being-re-written-and-historians-are-fighting-back.

23. *Le Journal d'Hélène Berr (The Journal of Hélène Berr)* was published in 2008. Studying Russian and English at Sorbonne University (though not allowed to pass her final exams due to anti-Semitic policies), Berr began making journal entries in April 1942 about Paris, her love life, friends, experiences at Sorbonne University as well as her time spent volunteering at holding camps, watching over children whose parents had been deported, which were complemented by Shaksphere and Keats quotes. The last entry is in February of 1944, shortly before Berr and her family were deported to Drancy internment camp, then transferred to Auschwitz and then Bergen-Belsen. Berr died at Bergen-Belsen concentration camp, five days before liberation. Jason Burke, "France Finds its Own Anne Frank as Young Jewish Woman's War Diary Hits the Shelves," *The Guardian*, June 6, 2008, https://www.theguardian.com/world/2008/jan/06/biography.secondworldwar; Hélène Berr, *The Journal of Hélène Berr,* trans. David Bellos (New York: Weinstein Books, 2008).

24. Patrick Modiano, "Patrick Modiano on the Bookshop Owner Who Escaped the Nazis," *Lit Hub*, January 27, 2020, https://lithub.com/patrick-modiano-on-the-bookshop-owner-who-escaped-the-nazis/.

25. The details of Nemirovsky's life, capture and execution (at least what is known about it) is discovered in the third appendix to the novel in English – but this third appendix appeared as the Preface to the book in the original French version, which means that immediately upon opening, French readers knew what they were getting into.

26. Paul Gray, "As France Burned," *New York Times*, April 9, 2006, https://www.nytimes.com/2006/04/09/books/review/09gray.html.

27. Philip Roth, *The Ghost Writer* (New York: Farrar, Straus and Giroux, 1979), 145.

28. Cynthia Zarin, "A Strange but Beautiful Book about a Mother who Disappeared," *New Yorker*, May 15, 2017,https://www.newyorker.com/books/page-turner/a-strange-and-beautiful-book-about-a-mother-who-disappeared. DeNoel had already published Nemirovsky's biography, a few years earlier.

29. In fact, Nemirovsky''s judgment of the French might be more harsh than fair - an understandable bias given her predicament. While the behavior of the French is despicable at times, it would be unfair to say that no one helped the Jews. But we should remember that at this time, Nemirovksy is frantically searching for someone to take her daughters in – after her own mother who is living in safety, refuses.

30. Irene Nemirovsky, *Suite Francaise* (New York: Random House, 2006), 425.

31. Ruth Franklin, "Scandale Française," *New Republic*, January 30, 2008, https://newrepublic.com/article/61151/scandale-francaise.

32. Addison Gayle Jr. stated "Some soft-headed whites and blacks have been led to believe that her poetry deserves to be considered as something more than a historical relic and everyone's been trying to make excuses...[Wheatley] wrote...'as a Negro reacting not as a Negro' . . . black writers have traveled the road of Phillis Wheatley. They have negated or falsified their racial experiences in an attempt to transform the pragmatics of their everyday lives into abstract formulas and theorems." Amiri Baraka wrote: "The mediocrity of what has been called 'Negro Literature' is one of the most loosely held secrets of American culture. From Ph[i]llis Wheatley to Charles Chesnutt to the present generation of American Negro, the only recognizable accretion of tradition readily attributable to the black producer of a formal literature in this country, with a few notable exceptions, has been of an almost agonizing mediocrity." Addison Gayle Jr., *The Black Aesthetic* (New York: Anchor Books, 1972), 71, 384; Amiri Baraka, *Home: Social Essays* (New York: Akashic Books, 2009), 105.

33. Jackson, *France: Dark Years*, 406.

34. Franklin, "Scandale."

35. Robert Zaretsky, "No Easy Answers: Susan Rubin Suleiman on 'The Nemirovsky Question,'" *Los Angeles Review of Books*, November 24, 2016, https://lareviewofbooks.org/article/no-easy-answers-susan-rubin-suleiman-on-the-nemirovsky-question/; Susan Rubin Suleiman, "Irène Némirovsky and the "Jewish Question" in Interwar France," *Yale French Studies* 2012, no. 121 (2012): 23.

36. Janet Malcolm, *Two Lives: Gertrude and Alice* (New Haven: Yale University Press, 2007).

37. Nemirovsky, *Suite Francaise*, 404.

38. Amy Watson, "Share of Adults Who Have Read a Book in Any Format in the Last 12 Months in the United States in 2019, by Age Group," *Statista*, October 9, 2019, https://www.statista.com/statistics/249787/book-reading-population-in-the-us-by-age/. Jamie Ballard, "Women Report Reading More Books than Men Do," *YouGov*, August 14, 2018, https://today.yougov.com/topics/lifestyle/articles-reports/2018/08/14/reading-books-men-women.

39. Tatiana de Rosnay, *Sarah's Key* (New York: St. Martin's Press, 2007), 51.

40. Associated Press, "Marine Le Pen criticized for denying French role in WWII roundup of Jews," *Los Angeles Times*, April 10, 2017, https://www.latimes.com/world/la-fg-le-pen-wwii-roundup-denial-20170410-story.html; Margaux Deygas and James Masters, "Marine Le Pen sparks outrage over Holocaust comments," *CNN*, April 10, 2017, https://edition.cnn.com/2017/04/10/europe/france-marine-le-pen-holocaust/.

41. Anonymous, "Jean-Marie Le Pen referred to justice for his remarks on the Occupation," *La Monde*, July 13, 2006, https://web.archive.org/web/20060720121511/http://www.lemonde.fr/web/article/0,1-0@2-3224,36-794895@51-776560,0.html.

42. Victor Mallet, "Resurgent Marine Le Pen Revels in Macron's Woes," *Financial Times*, January 30, 2020, https://www.ft.com/content/6d8b9c7a-412c-11ea-a047-eae9bd51ceba.

REFERENCES

Anonymous. "Jean-Marie Le Pen Referred to Justice for his Remarks on the Occupation." *La Monde*, July 13, 2006. https://web.archive.org/web/20060720121511/http://www.lemonde.fr/web/article/0,1-0@2-3224,36-794895@51-776560,0.html.

Associated Press. "Marine Le Pen Criticized for Denying French Role in WWII Roundup of Jews." *Los Angeles Times*, April 10, 2017. https://www.latimes.com/world/la-fg-le-pen-wwii-roundup-denial-20170410-story.html.

Ballard, Jamie. "Women Report Reading More Books than Men Do." *YouGov*, August 14, 2018. https://today.yougov.com/topics/lifestyle/articles-reports/2018/08/14/reading-books-men-women.

Baraka, Amiri. *Home: Social Essays*. New York: Akashic Books, 2009.

Berr, Hélène. *The Journal of Hélène Berr*. Translated by David Bellos. New York: Weinstein Books, 2008.

Brahm, John, dir. *Tonight We Raid Calais*. 1943; Los Angeles, CA: 20th Century Fox, 2007. DVD.

Bromwich, Jonah Engel. "Reince Priebus Defends Holocaust Statement that Failed to Mention Jews." *New York Times*, January 29, 2017. https://www.nytimes.com/2017/01/29/us/politics/reince-preibus-holocaust-remembrance-day.html.

Brunet, Romain. "France's Role in Deporting Jews: The Changing Political Views Over 70 Years." *French 24*, April 11, 2017. https://www.france24.com/en/20170411-france-role-deporting-jews-political-stances-through-70-years.

Burke, Jason. "France Finds Its Own Anne Frank as Young Jewish Woman's War Diary Hits the Shelves." *The Guardian*, June 6, 2008. https://www.theguardian.com/world/2008/jan/06/biography.secondworldwar.

Clément, René, dir. *Bataille Du Rail*. 1946; Paris, France: Union Française de Production Cinématographique, 2006. DVD.

Crowcroft, Orlando. "The History of the Holocaust is Being Re-written and Historians are Fighting Back." *Euronews*, January 27, 2020. https://www.euronews

.com/2020/01/27/the-history-of-the-holocaust-is-being-re-written-and-historians-are-fighting-back.
Curtiz, Michael, dir. *Casablanca*. 1942; Burbank, CA: Warner Bros, 1991. DVD.
de Rosnay, Tatiana. *Sarah's Key*. New York: St. Martin's Press, 2007.
Deygas, Margaux, and James Masters. "Marine Le Pen Sparks Outrage Over Holocaust Comments." *CNN*, April 10, 2017. https://edition.cnn.com/2017/04/10/europe/france-marine-le-pen-holocaust/.
Dreyfus, Jean-Marc. "Censorship and Approval: The Reception of *Nuit et Brouillard* in France." In *Uncovering the Holocaust The International Reception of Night and Fog*, edited by Ewout van der Knaap, 35–46. London: Wallflower Press, 2006.
Easton, Adam. "Jewish Life Slowly Returns to Poland." *BBC*, April 20, 2012. https://www.bbc.com/news/world-radio-and-tv-17741185.
Easton, Adam. "Poland Holocaust Law: Government U-turn on Jail Threat." *BBC*, June 27, 2018. https://www.bbc.com/news/world-europe-44627129.
Franklin, Ruth. "Scandale Française." *New Republic*, January 30, 2008. https://newrepublic.com/article/61151/scandale-francaise.
Gayle Jr., Addison. *The Black Aesthetic*. New York: Anchor Books, 1972.
Goldhagen, Daniel. *Hitler's Willing Executioners*. New York: Knopf, 1996.
Gray, Paul. "As France Burned." *New York Times*, April 9, 2006. https://www.nytimes.com/2006/04/09/books/review/09gray.html.
Grossman, Lawrence. "Holocaust Memory Without Jews." *American Jewish Community*, January 31, 2017. https://www.ajc.org/news/holocaust-memory-without-jews.
Hoare, Liam. "How the Late French President Jacques Chirac Started France's Reckoning with the Holocaust." *Jewish Telegraphic Agency*, September 26, 2019. https://www.jta.org/2019/09/26/opinion/how-the-late-french-president-jacques-chirac-started-frances-reckoning-with-the-holocaust.
Jackson, Julian. *France: The Dark Years, 1940–1944*. Oxford: Oxford University Press, 2003.
Klady, Leonard. "Box Office Champs, Chumps." *Los Angeles Times*, January 8, 1989. https://www.latimes.com/archives/la-xpm-1989-01-08-ca-258-story.html
Malcolm, Janet. *Two Lives: Gertrude and Alice*. New Haven: Yale University Press, 2007.
Mallet, Victor. "Resurgent Marine Le Pen Revels in Macron's Woes." *Financial Times*, January 30, 2020. https://www.ft.com/content/6d8b9c7a-412c-11ea-a047-eae9bd51ceba.
Memorial de la Shoah. "The Spaces of the Museum-Memorial." Accessed May 14, 2020. http://www.memorialdelashoah.org/en/the-memorial/the-spaces-of-the-museum-memorial/the-wall-of-names.html.
Modiano, Patrick. "Patrick Modiano on the Bookshop Owner Who Escaped the Nazis." *Lit Hub*, January 27, 2020. https://lithub.com/patrick-modiano-on-the-bookshop-owner-who-escaped-the-nazis/.
Moguy, Léonide, dir. *Paris After Dark*. 1943; Los Angeles, CA: 20th Century Fox, 2013. DVD.
Nemirovsky, Irene. *Suite Francaise*. New York: Random House, 2006.

Raskin, Richard. *Night and Fog by Alain Resnais: On the Making, Reception and Functions of a Major Documentary Film*. Aarhus: Aarhus University Press, 1987.

Ratoff, Gregory, dir. *Paris Underground*. 1945; Beverly Hills, CA: United Artists, 2005. DVD.

Reid, Donald. "Teaching Night and Fog: Putting a Documentary Film in History." *Teaching History: A Journal of Methods* 33, no. 2 (Fall 2008): 59–74.

Roth, Philip. *The Ghost Writer*. New York: Farrar, Straus and Giroux, 1979.

Suleiman, Susan Rubin. "Irène Némirovsky and the "Jewish Question" in Interwar France." *Yale French Studies* 2012, no. 121 (2012): 8–33.

United States Holocaust Memorial Museum. "The Vélodrome d'Hiver (Vél d'Hiv") Roundup." Assessed May 6, 2020. https://encyclopedia.ushmm.org/content/en/article/the-velodrome-dhiver-vel-dhiv-roundup.

United States Holocaust Memorial Museum. "Collaboration and Complicity during the Holocaust." Accessed May 26, 2020. https://www.ushmm.org/information/press/press-releases/collaboration-and-complicity-during-the-holocaust.

United States Holocaust Memorial Museum. "Jewish Population of Denmark." Accessed May 6, 2020. https://encyclopedia.ushmm.org/content/en/article/denmark.

Watson, Amy. "Share of Adults Who Have Read a Book in Any Format in the Last 12 Months in the United States in 2019, by Age Group." *Statista*, October 9, 2019. https://www.statista.com/statistics/249787/book-reading-population-in-the-us-by-age/.

White House. "Statement by the President on International Holocaust Remembrance Day." Issued January 27, 2017. https://www.whitehouse.gov/briefings-statements/statement-president-international-holocaust-remembrance-day/.

Wilcox, Herbert, dir. *Odette*. 1950; London, England: British Lion Films, 2019. DVD.

Zaretsky, Robert. "No Easy Answers: Susan Rubin Suleiman on 'The Nemirovsky Question.'" *Los Angeles Review of Books*, November 24, 2016. https://lareviewofbooks.org/article/no-easy-answers-susan-rubin-suleiman-on-the-nemirovsky-question/.

Zarin, Cynthia. "A Strange But Beautiful Book about a Mother who Disappeared." *New Yorker*, May 15, 2017. https://www.newyorker.com/books/page-turner/a-strange-and-beautiful-book-about-a-mother-who-disappeared.

Chapter 2

Life Is Beautiful, or Not
The Myth of the Good Italian
Shira Klein

The year is 1939. The place is a sleepy town somewhere in Italy. A jovial Jewish waiter, Guido, enjoys a rare moment of rest during a busy evening party, when another waiter comes running toward him.

"Guido, I've looked everywhere for you!" he says, breathless.
"What is it?" asks Guido, still cheerful.
"Your uncle," pants the man. "Something's happened. Come outside, quickly!"

Guido rushes out and sees his uncle Eliseo and his uncle's horse, both in a state of agitation. The horse has been painted green, its stomach has on it the words "DANGER: JEWISH HORSE." Guido gives it a glance, then turns to comfort Eliseo. "Come, uncle, don't be upset," he says merrily. Eliseo voices some vague and brief words of warning; soon they all return to the party.

This scene takes place in *Life is Beautiful* (*La Vita è Bella*), the 1997 Italian blockbuster film about the Holocaust[1] that perfectly displays the myth of Italian benevolence toward Jews. Though Italians did far worse to Jews than vandalize their horses, the film scarcely shows the effects of Italian anti-Semitism. This scene, as others in the film, portrays Italian crimes toward Jews as minimal—there's nothing so very terrible about painting a horse, after all.

Life is Beautiful illustrates a popular misconception about Italy's role in the Holocaust. The film features *the good Italian* and the warped view that Italy treated Jews kindly in the late 1930s and during World War II. Historians have proven this claim to be grossly exaggerated, arguing that Italians persecuted Jews vigorously. Yet popular representations of the past—films, novels, museum exhibits, and websites—continue to give credence to the notion that Italians were overwhelmingly good to Jews. Although France and Germany cultivated similar self-acquitting myths in the decades immediately after the war, they eventually moved on to accept the more difficult truths about the past. Italy, however, has not moved on; the narrative of the good Italian is still very much alive. *Life is Beautiful*, the most famous Italian production about the Holocaust to date, both reflects and bolsters this warped view of the past. This essay surveys, first, what actually happened to Jews between 1938 and 1945 in the Italian peninsula, summarizing the broad scholarly consensus that Italy pursued a brutal and relentless persecution of its Jews. The essay then lays out the myth of Italian benevolence and its origins, using *Life is Beautiful* as an example of how the past has been misremembered.

WHAT REALLY HAPPENED TO JEWS IN ITALY

On the eve of Italy's attack on Jews in 1938, the Italian peninsula comprised some 45,000 Jews (a tenth of a percent of the total population), the majority of whom were well integrated into the fabric of Italian society.[2] In July 1938, the government published a manifest declaring, "Jews don't belong to the Italian race."[3] Laws passed in September and November defined Jews biologically, expelled all Jewish children and teachers from school, and targeted Jewish livelihoods.[4] The regime forbade Jews from owning real estate or large businesses, fired Jews working for the government and the industries it sponsored, and expelled them from the Fascist Party and the military.[5] In 1939, the government attacked Jewish jobs in the private sector, including doctors, pharmacists, lawyers, accountants, and architects.[6] In June 1940, upon Italy's entrance into war, the government interned 6,383 (out of 9,000) foreign Jews in concentration camps. A further 400 Italian Jews were arrested as well.[7] In 1942, the regime sent almost 2,000 Jews to forced labor, usually involving difficult menial tasks such as lugging lumber and loading trucks.[8] Italy passed all its anti-Jewish laws, scholars have shown, with little if any pressure from Germany.[9]

Italy's racial laws and regulations turned Jews into social outcasts. One decree banned marriages between Jews and "Aryans," another forbade Jews from changing their surnames to "Aryan"-sounding names, publishing advertisements or death notices, or going to vacation resorts.[10] Propaganda produced by the regime showed Jews as the ultimate enemy, as suggested by radio programs like "Judaism Wanted This War," "Judaism Against Civilization," and "Bolshevik Judaism is the Mortal Enemy of Europe."[11]

Most ordinary Italians either accepted or supported these anti-Semitic measures. The racial campaign certainly did not dampen admiration for Mussolini or Fascism, who remained popular until late 1942.[12] Indeed, Italians slowly but steadily turned against their Jewish neighbors, acquaintances, and coworkers. Physical violence erupted often and spontaneously, as non-Jewish Italians sacked synagogues, beat up rabbis, and smashed Jewish shops. Shopkeepers and café owners, with no prodding from the law, took to hanging large placards on their facades, saying "Jews Not Welcome," "This Store is Aryan," and "No Dogs or Jews."[13] Non-Jewish Italians throughout the peninsula denounced Jews for evading the racial measures. One study found hundreds of denunciations sent to Italian police, most often anonymous and unsolicited.[14]

Even as Italy persecuted Jews in the peninsula, the Fascist regime protected some Jews outside its borders, a fact Italians would later emphasize. Between June 1940 and September 1943, when Germany deported Jews from Italian-occupied Greece, Yugoslavia, and southern France to killing centers, Italians secured exemptions for thousands under their control. On the other hand, Italian authorities in Yugoslavia routinely turned away Jewish refugees at the Italian-Croatian border, knowing that they would face death camps if caught by the Germans, and rape, torture, starvation, and murder, if the Croatian Ustaša movement found them.[15]

From 1943 to 1945, when German soldiers began deporting Jews from the peninsula, Italians played a key role in the roundups. The tragic events of those years began with a seemingly promising development in the war, the landing of the Allies in Sicily in July 1943. The king and several Fascist officials, seeing that the tide was changing in favor of the Allies, decided to switch sides. They ousted Mussolini, and on September 8, broadcast to the world that they had signed an armistice with the Allies. That very same day, in response, Germany poured its troops into Italy. The country now split in two, north and south. The Allies occupied the south, liberating Jews as the front line inched upward.[16] In the north, where most Jews lived, the Germans ruled jointly with Mussolini, who was reinstated at the helm of a reborn Fascist regime, the RSI (Italian Social Republic).

Until December 1943, the Germans deported Jews on their own.[17] But on the last day of November 1943, the Italian authorities in the north decided they, too, wanted a hand in rounding up Jews. "All Jews," the RSI government ordered in a directive known as Police Order Number 5, "whatever their nationality . . . shall be sent to special concentration camps. All their property, mobile and real estate, shall be immediately confiscated."[18] A neat division of labor began; Italian policemen searched for, arrested, and imprisoned Jews, while German soldiers loaded the prisoners on convoys to Auschwitz. Put another way, Italians delivered Jews to the Nazis for deportation. This police order was an entirely Italian initiative—the Italians retained full control over the police—with no German prodding.[19] In fact, the Germans only heard about the order several days after it came out. Italian police vied with German soldiers for the right to round up Jews, so as to confiscate Jewish property at the time of arrest.[20] After every arrest, Italian authorities took everything owned by Jews, from villas to cars, from grand pianos to socks. Objects worth billions of lire ended up in the homes of Fascist Party officials or policemen.[21]

Italian Police Order Number 5 sealed the fate of the Jews in Italy. From December 1943 until the end of the war, Italian policemen rounded up all the Jews they could find, women and men, young and old. While German soldiers continued to arrest Jews as well, their Italian colleagues were far more efficient. They knew the language and its dialects, the back allies where Jews might escape. They received tips from informers and had census records replete with addresses. The statistics are telling: almost half of all deported Jews that we know of were arrested by Italian policemen working on their own or in collaboration with Germans.[22]

Some non-Jewish Italians did save Jews from arrest and death—a fact that Italians would highlight in the postwar years. About 30,000 Jews in Italy, foreign and Italian, survived the war, a high survival rate compared to tallies in eastern European countries. Many survivors received some degree of assistance from non-Jewish Italians, in the form of fake papers, shelter, or food.[23] But the relatively high rate of survival in Italy, compared to eastern European countries, stemmed from other crucial factors as well. The peninsula's proximity to neutral Switzerland enabled 6,000 Jews to escape into safety across the Alps, a non-existent option in any of the eastern European states. Additionally, Jews in Italy could often receive help without disclosing they were Jewish, because they blended in with millions of other displaced people, including army deserters in hiding. Finally, the deportations from Italy only began in September 1943, almost two years after they had started in eastern Europe, meaning that Jews in Italy had to spend far less time escaping death.

While some non-Jewish Italians helped Jews survive, others turned them in, a point that Italians would later gloss over. Scholarship shows that without the relentlessness collaboration of Italians, the extermination of Italian Jews would not have reached the scale it did.[24] As before 1943, Italians continued to denounce Jews to the authorities, but with far more fatal consequences than before. Out of 428 testimonies carried out by the University of Southern California Shoah Foundation Institute with Italian-speaking survivors, a quarter of the interviewees mentioned a betrayal. That proportion would have increased if those who perished in Auschwitz could have given testimony, because denounced Jews were arrested at a greater rate. In Rome alone, postwar trials against collaborators show that over 200 Jewish victims were either denounced or arrested by Italians, and one scholar estimated that denunciations in the capital numbered in the "hundreds and hundreds."[25] Informing on Jews was profitable, for the Germans offered a prize of 5,000 lire for every Jewish person delivered to them—more than six months' worth of a factory worker's wages.[26] Criminals made a lucrative business of capturing Jews. Bands of violent thugs, like the Koch Gang in Rome, La Muti in Milan, and Carità in Tuscany, blackmailed Jews in return for supposed protection. After the Jewish captives had given all they had, the gang turned them over to the Germans and claimed the prize.[27]

Despite these examples, it is important to note that the majority of Italians neither helped nor betrayed Jews; they ignored them. Among these was the Pope; as is now commonly accepted, the Vatican did little to help the Jews—and would not even apologize for its inaction until 1998.

In the face of this historical record, one can only wonder how the myth of good Italian prevailed, and survives, into the twenty-first century.

THE MYTH OF THE GOOD ITALIAN

Immediately after the war, Italians crafted a narrative that de-emphasized their involvement in the persecution of the Jews and highlighted the actions of the Germans. According to Italians, their country had very little to do with the suffering of the Jews; to the contrary, they had done everything they could to help Jews. Italy was the oddity, the Axis country that had saved Jews. In some versions of this story, Germany bore the responsibility for all that the Jews had suffered, and Italy was its helpless captive. In other versions, Mussolini and a handful of his henchmen stood to blame, but the rank and file of Italians heroically defended Jews. Either way, the Italian people featured as innocents. Historians describe these narratives as a myth—the myth of the *brava gente*, "good people."

Italians' self-acquitting narrative began as soon as the war had ended. In 1945, authorities portrayed their country's war record in a positive light, hoping to shape the Allied-authored peace treaty (signed in 1947). A punitive treaty, Italians feared, would lead to painful territorial losses for Italy and crippling war reparations.[28] If Italians could retell the past to cast themselves in a favorable light, they might secure a better deal. Politicians, diplomats, and cultural figures worked hard to present a positive image of Italy, insisting that Italians had treated Jews fairly.[29] On the one hand, postwar diplomats highlighted the cases in which Italian authorities had saved Jews—particularly in southern France and the Balkans; on the other hand, they de-emphasized Fascist policy toward Jews at home, skimming over the years 1938–1943, when Italy had persecuted Jews entirely on its own, and omitting any mention of Police Order Number 5. For instance, in September 1945, when a Belgian journalist asked for information on the fate of Jews in Italy, Italian government officials decided to "underline that the Italian initiatives in the race matter . . . [were] merely a formality." They insisted that "the administrative authorities who were supposed to implement the laws [had] actually competed with one another to sabotage them."[30] In this way, Italian officials wove a story that was very different from what had actually transpired.

The narrative of the "Good Italian" also gained currency, because few Fascists were punished after the war, forging the impression that few had committed any crimes. Although in 1945 thousands of imprisoned Fascists awaited trial for their actions against partisans, Allied prisoners of war, and Jews, most of them walked free. Italians could not agree on how to define and place blame, and in July 1946, the Ministry of Justice declared a blanket amnesty.

Yet another cause for the positive image of Italians lay in Italy's internal politics. The groups highlighting Fascist cruelty tended to be the communists and socialists, who had formed the bulk of the partisans fighting in the Resistance. These groups became increasingly marginalized in the postwar years. In April 1948, a center-right coalition came to power, prosecuting former partisans and thereby silencing those who called attention to the wrongdoings of the Fascist regime. Britain and America supported these developments, because they wanted the peninsula on their side in the Cold War.[31] Further, as in Germany and France, calling out Fascists for crimes they had committed toward Jews, partisans, or POWs, would have posed bureaucratic challenges. As one senior British army officer put it, "If we get rid of everyone who collaborated in the Fascist administration, we are left with practically no one of any use for carrying on."[32]

The narrative about Italy's commendable conduct spread internationally. *The New York Times* ran an article in June 1945 that declared "anti-Semitism never made much headway with the great masses of Italians." Another article claimed that "anti-Semitism was something imposed on the Italians from without." A third piece carried the sensational headline, "Mussolini Regime Fought Berlin Anti-Semitism," and asserted that there was "no popular support for the racial laws," thanks to Italy's "friendliness" and "humane" attitude.[33]

In the decades that followed, the myth of the good Italian resurfaced periodically, both in Italy and abroad. Cinema and literature preserved the gilded narrative. A smattering of Holocaust-related films in the 1940s and 1950s all ignored or misrepresented events that had taken place in the peninsula. The film *L'Ebreo Errante* (*The Wandering Jew*, 1948) did not even take place in Italy. It was set in Frankfurt, Jerusalem, and Paris. A second film, Il *Monastero di Santa Chiara* (*The Monastery of Santa Chiara*), belittled the Italians' part in the persecution by focusing the plot on an absurd romantic affair between a Jewish singer and an SS officer. The screenplay of a third film, *Febbre di Vivere* (*Eager to Live*, 1953), told a far more realistic story about a non-Jewish Italian, Massimo, who betrays his Jewish friend to the

Nazis. But the filmmakers judged it too controversial and removed the Jewish tale from the screenplay.[34]

From the 1960s onward, the Holocaust became the theme of celebrity-starring films and best-selling books, but the message remained the same: Italians had played no role in the persecution of Jews. Hannah Arendt's famous report of the trial of Nazi criminal Adolf Eichmann, *Eichmann in Jerusalem* (1963), again reinforced the story of Italian benevolence. "The great majority of Italian Jews were exempted" from the racial laws, Arendt claimed— wrongly—in her brief section on Italy. "Even convinced Italian anti-Semites seemed unable to take the thing seriously," she stated, echoing the same tropes that had been circulating since the end of the war. She praised "Italian humanity," and posited—again, wrongly—that "all anti-Jewish measures were decidedly unpopular." Arendt made no mention of Italy's homegrown race laws or their acceptance by the population, Italy's police order from November 30, 1943, to arrest Jews or the widespread phenomenon of ordinary Italians informing on Jews in hiding.[35] Her book may have greatly contributed to the proliferation of the myths—it was published in seventeen languages and printed in twenty-two editions in Italy alone. Almost as popular was the film *Kapò* (1960), which is set entirely outside of Italy, and therefore deflected attention from what happened in the peninsula. Slightly more daring was the film *The Garden of the Finzi-Continis* (1970; based on a novel by Jewish author Giorgio Bassani), it showed Fascist authorities arresting Jews and therefore acknowledged their role in the manhunt of 1943–1945. But this film was an exception in cinematic representations of the Holocaust in Italy.[36]

We should note that Italy was not alone in attempting to whitewash their crimes. Other countries in western Europe, particularly France and Germany, did the same. Yet the Italian myth has held out far longer. In the postwar years, the French cultivated what came to be called the "Vichy Syndrome," the claim that the Vichy government's racist policies were entirely a German imposition and that most of the French had chosen anti-German Resistance, not collaboration. Germans, too, crafted a self-acquitting memory, fueled by Cold War politics. East Germans described the war as a battle of capitalist Fascism against communist anti-Fascism, and in doing so downplayed the involvement of non-Jewish Germans in harming Jews. West Germans, in turn, focused on their own plight at the hand of the Soviets, and also denied the role of the German masses in persecuting the Jews. These rosy narratives, however, began to crack in the 1960s and 1970s. In France, the release of Marcel Ophüls's documentary *The Sorrow and the Pity* triggered a shift in public opinion by featuring interviews with French citizens who had been indifferent to discrimination against Jews. The student uprisings of 1968, De Gaulle's death in 1970, and the publication in 1972 of Robert Paxton's book *Vichy France* all prompted the French to revisit their past and begin to acknowledge French responsibility for Jewish suffering. In Germany, the Eichmann trial in 1961, the counter-culture in the 1960s, and the 1978 American *Holocaust* miniseries (wildly popular in Germany) had a similar effect. They led Germans to admit that ordinary people, not just Hitler or the SS, had played a role in the persecution of Jews.[37]

In Italy, however, no such revision has taken place, except among scholars. In the late 1980s, historians began to poke holes in the gilded narrative of the good Italian. Yet the scholarship has had little effect on the public. Even after historians showed the extent of Italian brutality, non-scholarly representations of Italy's past continued—and still continue—to portray Italians as non-racist do-gooders who helped Jews. Italy had no equivalent to France's *The Sorrow and the Pity*, no documentary hoping to challenge public opinion. In fact, in 1986, Italian television broadcast *The Courage and the Pity*, a clear play on Ophüls's title. This documentary bore the exact opposite message of *The Sorrow and the Pity*, as it reconfirmed German culpability and Italian benevolence by stressing that "Italians behaved better than everyone else in Europe."[38]

The single most famous and popular film about the Holocaust in Italy is Roberto Benigni's 1997 film *Life is Beautiful*. The film's two-part plot begins in 1939 with Guido Orefice, a funny and kind Jewish man in the sleepy town of Arezzo, who gets work as a waiter in a hotel restaurant. While walking through town, he meets Dora, a lovely Christian teacher, who falls in love with him and breaks off her engagement to another man. The couple marry, Guido opens the book store he's always wanted, and he and Dora have a son, Giosué. Then tragedy strikes: Guido and Giosué get picked up and deported to a concentration camp. Dora rushes to the station and demands to get on the train with her husband and son. The second part of the film is set in the camp, apparently Auschwitz. Dora is put in one section, while Guido and Giosué are in an adjacent one. To spare his son from the horrors of the camp and keep him safe, Guido pretends everything is a game—the barracks, the forced labor, the hunger. He succeeds in protecting his son, but not himself; at the end of the film, Dora and little Giosué reunite, while Guido is shot to death by camp guards.

Public reception to the film was stupendous. It won the most prestigious prizes possible in several countries—seven nominations and three awards in the Oscars, three nominations and one win in the BAFTA Awards in Britain, and nine David di Donatello Awards in Italy. It received the prestigious Grand Prix at the Cannes Film Festival, several Golden Globe awards, as well as accolades in Germany, Spain, Poland, Czech Republic, Greece, Norway, Australia, Japan, Russia, and Canada.[39] With a worldwide box office revenue of $230 million, *Life is Beautiful* also set a record of more than 16 million viewers when released on Italian television in October 2001.[40] *Life is Beautiful*'s popularity quickly surpassed the *Garden of the Finzi Continis* (1970), which is largely unknown to younger audiences today. In the months and years that followed its appearance, it received positive reviews across the world. In Italy, the newspaper giant *La Repubblica* called it a "story of the tender, the sweet, the humane," marveling at its capability to move its audiences. "There is love and memory, grace and tenderness, forgiveness and recklessness, lost feelings that caress the heart," wrote the reviewer.[41] Israeli newspaper *Globes* agreed, praising the film for humanizing survivors: "*Life is Beautiful* . . . is a movie about people, humans, and not symbols, as Holocaust victims are sometimes understood."[42] Reviews in the *Los Angeles Times* described the film as "a poignant drama" of "overarching sincerity," and called its director, Benigni, a "ray of light."[43] One American reviewer praised its "delicate balance between sweetness and sorrow," while another appreciated that Benigni "took a great risk" and managed to "make moving statements on the evils of dictatorships."[44]

Judging by the metrics of the digital age, the public remains passionate about the film. *Life is Beautiful* appears in every online list of "most popular Holocaust films," and on IMDB it enjoys over half a million user ratings, an extremely high number for a Holocaust movie, topped only by *Schindler's List* and *The Pianist*. IMDB users have given it a high vote—8.6 out of 10 —and posted over a thousand reviews. One review, entitled "The Best Movie I've Seen for a Long Time," declared, "it provided me with something that everyone . . . needs—hope." Another reviewer wrote, "No piece has ever before combined laughter and tears of sadness in me before and that is the miracle of the movie." According to a third, "Please see it for yourself. Have a box of tissues handy. Best film ever seen!!!"[45]

While popular audiences loved the film, most academics and professional critics argued that it grossly misrepresented history, especially Nazi camps. If the camp in the film is supposed to be the Auschwitz concentration camp complex—the number tattoo on Guido's arm suggests as much, as Auschwitz was the only camp to tattoo prisoners—then the mild conditions shown in the film are disturbingly warped. In the fictional camp, wrote Ilona Klein, "no one seems to be dying. No human waste is detected . . . no filth is noticeable . . . [and] there are no rotting corpses." The film's concentration camp, wrote Kobi Niv, is "too nice, too amusing a place, too devoid of death." Instead of seeing "the brutality, the starvation, the beatings, the humiliation, the endless standing to attention day and night, or the daily executions," he states, "we are actually shown a softened, sugar-coated, and outright false version of the truth."[46] While children who survived actual concentration camps went from healthy to emaciated in a matter of days, the hunger in Benigni's film is barely visible—young Giosué's face stays nice and round until the very end.[47] David Denby condemned the film for claiming that love was enough to save a Jewish child from the Nazis. "Is playing make-believe inside a death camp possible? Does it make any sense, even as a fable? . . . Surely [Benigni] knows that a young child entering Auschwitz would be immediately put to death, and that at every camp people were beaten and humiliated at random. He shows us nothing like that."[48] In one scene in the film, Guido manages to manipulate a guard to broadcast Offenbach into the camp's loudspeakers; in another, he purposely mis-translates orders from German to Italian to a barracks full of prisoners. In the real Auschwitz (indeed, in any other Nazi concentration camp), such stark breaches of discipline would have resulted in swift executions.

What critics rarely speak about, however, is the first part of the film, set in the peninsula. *Life is Beautiful* portrays a distorted picture of Jewish life in late 1930s Italy, thereby perpetuating the myth of the good Italian. Practically every minute set in Italy downplays the brutality of Fascist anti-Jewish policy and highlights, instead, the evil of Nazi Germany. Take the very first scene, set in 1939. Two cheery friends, soon to be revealed as Jewish, whiz down a beautiful countryside road to the sound of merry music, spouting poetry. They haven't a care in the world. In reality, the year 1939 was anything but cheerful for Jews. The racial laws had been in place for months, destroying the livelihoods of thousands and casting them out as social pariahs.

When Italian anti-Semitism does make an appearance in the film, it is so mild as to be laughable. The scene with the painted horse, set in 1939, ends with Uncle Eliseo warning Guido, "They'll start with you too," as though there are no anti-Jewish policies in place by then; they have yet to start. Until that happens, graffiti on a horse appears to be the height of Italian brutality. As Guido responds, laughingly, "What could possibly happen to me? The worst they can do is undress me, paint me yellow, and write, '. . . Jewish waiter.'" It is true that Guido ends up being murdered by the Germans, and it is indisputable that Italian Jews did indeed die mostly at the hands of the Germans; but by inserting this dialogue, the film signals to viewers that nothing very serious was happening to Jews in 1939 Italy, when in fact, the racial laws had dealt a tremendous blow to Italian Jews, robbing them of both income and dignity. Similar attempts to minimize Italy's race measures recur in other scenes. Guido arrives at the school where Dora works, posing as a government official, and discovers he is expected to speak about race. This episode barely acknowledges anti-Semitism—one of the characters mentions a "race manifesto" but viewers have no idea what that means—and certainly gives no inkling of the race laws' monumental effect on Italian schools. Audiences have no idea that at the time the scene is set, not a single Jewish student was allowed in school.

The film places Jews in historically impossible situations. It shows Guido and Dora as a married couple in 1943, so that the wedding must have taken place sometime between their meeting in 1939 and their deportation in 1943. Yet this could not have happened, because a law from November 1938 expressly forbade the marriage of a Jew to a non-Jew. "The marriage of an Italian citizen of the Aryan race with a person belonging to another race is prohibited," said one clause, while another threatened a fine of up to 5,000 lire to anyone officiating at such a marriage.[49] Another unlikelihood is Dora and Guido's evident wealth in 1943, when in fact the racial laws had by then pauperized Jews. Dora, though apparently disowned by her affluent mother, still wears beautiful suits, the family lives in an elegant apartment, and on Giosué's birthday, they prepare a lavish feast. Compare this to the birthday of a real Jewish boy, Nedo Fiano, living through that time. Nedo grew up in Florence, an hour's drive from the fictional Giosué, and he too celebrated his birthday after the passage of the racial laws. Since his father was fired from the post office where he had worked for twenty years, and his mother lost the license to her boarding home, the family plunged into poverty. Unlike Giosué, Nedo's birthday celebration consisted of a plate with two small pastries and a note: "This year I can't give more than this. Happy birthday, Papà."[50]

Multiple times throughout the film, the director finds ways to compare Fascist and Nazi anti-Semitism, always showing that Italian anti-Semitism both stemmed from German racism—and paled in comparison to it. Even if anti-Jewish sentiment existed in Italy, suggests the film, it came from Germany. In the horse scene, the warning "DANGER," appears in German, "ACHTUNG." In reality, anti-Jewish slurs were unlikely to have been in German in 1939. After all, there were no German troops there yet; Italian anti-Semitism evolved independently until September 1943. Yet viewers get the message that the Italian language simply lacked the vocabulary needed for anti-Jewish language, and therefore had to borrow from its evil counterpart, Germany.

In another scene comparing diabolical Germany to benign Italy, the head-mistress at Dora's school wishes that Italian children were as good at math as their German counterparts. By giving an example of a German mathematical problem, she reveals the Nazis' gruesome approach to the mentally and physically challenged. "A lunatic costs the state four marks a day," says the headmistress, evidently quoting a German textbook. "A cripple, four and a half marks. An epileptic, three and a half marks . . . how much would the state save if these individuals were eliminated?" While the script portrays the Italian headmistress in an unflattering light—she marvels at German children's capacity to do the math, not bothered in the slightest about the prospect of eliminating humans—Germany is the real culprit. The Nazis are smarter than Italians could hope to be, and more importantly, they are more evil than Italians—German children can calculate human death in a heartbeat, while Italian children stumble and fail. In the final scene that occurs in Italy, the officials rounding up the Jews are German soldiers (identifiable by their helmets), not Italian policemen, though we know that they participated in the manhunt. There is not a single hint in the film of Police Order Number 5; viewers have no inkling that Italian policemen played as central a role as Germans in the hunt for Jews.

Another recent film preserving the myth of the good Italian is *Unfair Competition* (*Concorrenza Sleale*, 2001).[51] Although less well-known and successful than *Life is Beautiful*, it too won a David Di Donatello award as well as several other prizes, and it boasted a superstar set, with director Ettore Scola and actor Gérard Depardieu. *Unfair Competition* acknowledges the racial laws to a far greater extent than Benigni's film does—the entire film is set in 1938, long before the Germans arrived—but it also tells an unlikely tale that casts non-Jewish Italians in a positive light. A Christian tailor, Umberto Melchiori, and a Jewish haberdasher, Leone DellaRocca, are vicious competitors, until the racial laws so disgust Umberto that he befriends Leone. In reality, non-Jewish business competitors welcomed the racial laws more than anyone else. Attorneys betrayed attorneys, doctors betrayed doctors, and so on.[52] Yet in *Unfair Competition*, the racial laws trigger compassion among bitter competitors.

The film portrays Fascist anti-Semitism as meek and incompetent. The police inspector that confiscates Jewish property shows reluctance, pleading, "I didn't make these laws . . . we're just pawns who need to follow orders." When the inspector sees how upset Leone's father is at having to surrender his radio, he is even willing to bend the law for him, offering, "Come listen to the radio here, the custodian will keep it [for you]." Another officer, a blundering idiot with a tear in his pants, can't clean his own gun without accidentally shooting himself in the leg. In reality, Fascist officials implemented the racial laws with unsparing efficiency, but according to the film, there were no competent anti-Semites in Italy.

As in *Life is Beautiful*, hints abound in *Unfair Competition* that Germany is the cause of Italy's racist turn. Just before the laws begin to make Jewish life miserable, the camera shows a Swastika hanging nearby a picture of the Duce, as though to suggest that the Nazis caused the impending ugliness. In another scene, one of the Jewish characters declares about the racial laws, "It was obvious that this is how Hitler's visit in April [1938] would end." Similarly, Umberto's anti-Fascist brother remarks disgustedly, "We're pandering to the Germans!" In reality, Germany far from forced Italy into passing its race laws; Italians concocted the racial campaign entirely on their own, echoing policies they had implemented against blacks in East Africa.

In *Unfair Competition*, as in *Life is Beautiful*, Italian anti-Semitism features as a pale imitation of German racism, with Italians portrayed as too kind, but also too lazy, to do anything truly brutal—"the contrast between the evil German and the good Italian."[53] The comparison between the two countries is voiced by a German Jewish refugee who has opened a watch shop in Italy. "How fortunate you are to be Romans. If your sun were to shine in our countries, perhaps there wouldn't be such brutality." "Italians don't respect any law," he continues, voicing an oft-repeated stereotype of "the backward Italian" riddled with inefficiency and incompetence.[54] It goes to follow that they wouldn't respect the racial laws, leading the refugee to declare, "I'm happy to live here in Italy." The refugee reiterates this claim later in the movie: "Everyone knows that in Italy they make laws, but nobody respects them." While he does not fare well—we later learn he has been sent to an Italian concentration camp, as indeed most foreign Jews in Italy were—his favorable opinion of Italy never wanes.

The viewer and critic are now left to ponder: are movies like *Life is Beautiful* and *Unfair Competition*, which depict misleading versions of the past, unworthy of screening? Film critic David Denby certainly suggested as much when he wrote that *Life is Beautiful*'s false portrayal of the camps made it "a benign form of Holocaust denial."[55] Yet as Hilene Flanzbaum has pointed out, the demand for realism may be an unfair one to begin with.[56] *Life is Beautiful*'s rave reviews stem precisely from its creative license, from its ability to pluck at our heartstrings, from the fact that it is *not* a documentary blow-by-blow account of everything that happened to Italian Jews from 1939 to 1943.[57]

Still, films like *Life is Beautiful* do preserve some persistent untruths. In the context of Italy, the problem lies in how widespread these manipulations of the past have become, not just in Italy but abroad too. Consider the titles of these recent books and films, revealing just how popular the myth of the good Italian still is among non-scholarly audiences: *The Righteous Enemy* [referring to Italians in World War II] (1994); *Bad Times, Good People* [again, referring to Italians] (1999); *It Happened in Italy: How the People of Italy Defied the Horrors of the Holocaust* (2009); *Road to Valor: A True Story of WWII Italy* (2012); and *My Italian Secret: The Forgotten Heroes* (2014).[58] All of these continue to highlight the heroism of Italians when it came to Jews and minimize the uglier facts, such as the common phenomenon of Italians informing on their Jewish neighbors and acquaintances. Even an institution as reputable as the United States Holocaust Memorial Museum echoes the oft-repeated claims about Italy's innocence. Its online encyclopedia essay on Italy, the first hit on a Google search of the words "Italy" and "Holocaust," informs readers (as of the time of my writing this in 2020) that the 1938 racial laws resulted from "pressure from Nazi

Germany" and that Italian authorities "did not always aggressively enforce the legislation," when in fact scholars have proven otherwise. The article correctly remarks on the "unwillingness of many non-Jewish Italians . . . to participate in or facilitate the roundups" but fails to mention the other side of the coin, such as the fact that Italian authorities participated in half of all the roundups.[59]

The selective memory of what Italians did to Jews is part of a larger amnesia about Italy's role in the war. Italians have promoted the myth of the good Italian in other ways as well. Most Italians, goes the claim, abhorred Fascism, backed the Resistance, and worked to topple Mussolini. In fact, historians have shown that from 1943 to 1945, of a population of roughly 20,000,000 under joint Nazi-Fascist control, at most 250,000 (1.25 percent) joined the Resistance, and even that was only toward the end of the war, when it was clear the Allies were winning. For most of the occupation, the Resistance numbered about 100,000. A similar number, 100,000–200,000, fought for on the side of the Fascists and Nazis against the Resistance, in what amounted to a bloody civil war. The overwhelming majority of Italians in the north took no organized action whatsoever.[60] Similarly, there is a widespread assumption that Italians led a benign colonization of Africa from the 1910s to the 1940s.[61] That, too, strays far from the truth; research has revealed that Italian rule in the colonies claimed tens of thousands of lives. Italy used poison gas on Africans, even though it was banned by the international community, and subjected Africans to mass population transfers, forced marches, detention in concentration camps, as well as rape.[62]

In the same vein, many think that Italians were gentle occupiers of the Balkans between 1940 and 1943. The Hollywood movie *Captain Corelli's Mandolin* (2001) is a prime example, contrasting peaceful Italians with demonic Germans on the occupied Greek island of Cefalonia. The Italian officer, played by the dashing Nicholas Cage, is more interested in courting a local beauty (Penelope Cruz) than in waging war, while the bloodthirsty Germans commit endless atrocities. The film is not wrong, per se; the Germans in Cefalonia did indeed massacre thousands in September 1943.[63] But Italians in Greece and the Balkans also committed atrocities. Historians have shown that they carried out massacres, raped women, shot hostages and partisans who had surrendered, and burned down villages. Italian troops deported 110,000 men, women, and children from Croatia, Slovenia, and Montenegro, to concentration camps, some of which were in such dire condition that prisoners died within weeks of arrival.[64] No Hollywood film shows this side of Italian history.

Whether we like it or not, films play a monumental role in shaping what people know—or think they know—about history. What Italians know of their past is crucial, particularly with tens of thousands of refugees arriving to the peninsula every year and triggering debates about the limits of Italian tolerance. Watching a film like *Life is Beautiful* will make Italians feel good about their country, even as that same country turns ever more intolerant toward present-day refugees. In reality, there isn't much to feel good about; films like *Life is Beautiful* repeat the entrenched, false narrative that Italian persecution of Jews was mild, existed only because of Germany, and involved none of the rank and file of Italians. Perhaps one day, viewers watching *Life is Beautiful* will have access to a tool like Amazon's X-Ray feature, enabling them to see (in real time) what is wrong in the film. In truth, Italy persecuted its Jews independently and ruthlessly for five long years, between 1938 and 1943. It had its own racial laws, its own racial propaganda, and its own government mechanisms to exclude the Jews from Italian society. Life in Italy, for Jews, was far from beautiful.

NOTES

1. *La Vita è Bella*, directed by Roberto Benigni (1997; Italy: Cecchi Gori Group Tiger Cinematografica).
2. Roberto Bachi, "La Demografia dell'Ebraismo Italiano," *Rassegna Mensile di Israel* 12, no. 7/9 (1938): 263.
3. "Manifesto degli Scienziati Razzisti," *Giornale d'Italia*, July 14, 1938.
4. Royal Decree Law, September 23, 1938, n. 1630. See also Annalisa Capristo, "The Beginnings of Racial Persecution," in *Jews in Italy under Fascist and Nazi Rule, 1922–1945*, ed. Joshua D. Zimmerman (New York: Cambridge, 2005), 82–83.
5. Royal Decree Law, November 17, 1938, n. 1728, Articles 10, 13.
6. Royal Decree Law, June 29, 1939, n. 1054, Articles 2, 4, 21.
7. Michele Sarfatti, *The Jews in Mussolini's Italy: From Equality to Persecution* (Madison: University of Wisconsin Press, 2006), 141–142, 146–147. Mario Toscano, "L'Internamento degli Ebrei Italiani," in *I Campi di Concentramento in Italia*, ed. Costantino Di Sante (Milano: F. Angeli, 2001), 102, 107–108.
8. Sarfatti, *The Jews*, 148–149. Daniela Adorni, "Modi e Luoghi della Persecuzione," in *L'Ebreo in Oggetto*, ed. Fabio Levi (Torino: S. Zamorani, 1991), 62.
9. For explanations of Italy's anti-Jewish turn, see Ilaria Pavan, "An Unexpected Betrayal?" *Holocaust Studies* 15, no. 1–2 (2009): 136–137. Ugo Caffaz, *L'Antisemitismo Italiano sotto il Fascismo* (Firenze: Nuova Italia, 1974), 16. Enzo Collotti, *Il Fascismo e gli Ebrei* (Roma: Laterza, 2003), 58. Mauro Raspanti, "I Razzismi del Fascismo," in *La Menzogna della Razza*, ed. David Bidussa (Casalecchio: Grafis, 1994), 86. Franklin Adler, "Why Mussolini Turned on the Jews," *Patterns of Prejudice* 39, no. 3 (2005). Nicola Labanca, "Il Razzismo Istituzionale Coloniale," in *Storia della Shoah in Italia*, vol. 1, ed. Marcello Flores (Torino: UTET, 2010).

10. Royal Decree Law, July 13, 1939, n. 1055. Sarfatti, *The Jews*, 139–140, 151–152, 156–157. David Bidussa, *La Menzogna della Razza: Documenti e Immagini del Razzismo e dell'Antisemitismo Fascista* (Casalecchio di Reno: Grafis, 1994), 211.

11. The first three are radio transmissions from October 1941, cited in *Menzogna della Razza*, 211. The fourth is an article in the pamphlet *Il Problema Ebraico*, Year 2, Number 5, May 1943, p. 5.

12. On the trajectory of Italian public opinion, see Philip Morgan, *The Fall of Mussolini* (New York: Oxford, 2007), 43–44; Marco Fincardi, "Italian Society under Anglo-American Bombs," *Historical Journal* 52, no. 4 (2009): 1025.

13. Sarfatti, *The Jews*, 158–159, 357n342. Mimmo Franzinelli, *Delatori: Spie e Confidenti Anonimi* (Milano: Mondadori, 2001), 145. Maura Hametz, "The Ambivalence of Italian Antisemitism," *Holocaust and Genocide Studies* 16, no. 3 (2002): 391–392.

14. Franzinelli, *Delatori*, 136.

15. Davide Rodogno, "Italiani Brava Gente? Fascist Italy's Policy toward the Jews in the Balkans," *European History Quarterly* 35, no. 2 (2005): 222–28.

16. For an overview of the war's development in Italy, see Morgan, *The Fall*, Chapters 1–6.

17. Liliana Picciotto, "The Shoah in Italy," in Zimmerman, *Jews in Italy*, 211, 222n15.

18. Ministry of Interior to Heads of Provinces, November 30, 1943, quoted in Liliana Picciotto, "Statistical Tables on the Holocaust in Italy," *Yad Vashem Studies* 33 (2005): 317–218.

19. Ibid., 319.

20. Picciotto, "Shoah in Italy," 215.

21. Simon Levis Sullam, *The Italian Executioners* (Princeton: Princeton, 2018), Ch. 4.

22. Picciotto, "Statistical Tables," 343.

23. For examples of Italians helping Jews survive, see Shira Klein, *Italy's Jews from Emancipation to Fascism* (NY: Cambridge University Press, 2018), 119, 121–124.

24. Sullam, *Italian Executioners*, Ch. 5–8.

25. Ibid., 125–130.

26. Frauke Wildvang, "The Enemy Next Door: Italian Collaboration in Deporting Jews during the German Occupation of Rome," *Modern Italy* 12, no. 2 (2007): 191. Michele Sarfatti, "Raffaele Jona ed il Soccorso agli Ebrei del Piemonte durante la Repubblica Sociale Italiana," in *Dalle Leggi Razziali alla Deportazione. Ebrei tra Antisemitismo e Solidarietà*, ed. Alberto Lovatto (Borgosesia: Istituto per la storia della Resistenza, 1992), 65.

27. Wildvang, "Enemy Next Door," 195–197.

28. Ilaria Poggiolini, "Translating Memories of War and Co-Belligerency into Politics," in *Memory and Power in Post-War Europe*, ed. Jan-Werner Müller (New York: Cambridge, 2002), 224. Focardi et al., "War Crimes," 335.

29. Guri Schwarz, "On Myth Making and Nation Building," *Yad Vashem Studies* 36, no. 1 (2008): 116. Oscar Österberg, "Taming Ambiguities: The Representation

of the Holocaust in Post-War Italy," in *The Holocaust on Post-War Battlefields*, ed. Klas-Göran Karlsson and Ulf Zander (Malmo: Sekel, 2006).

30. Circular sent by Ministry of Interior to prefects, September 21, 1945, quoted in Schwarz, "On Myth Making," 121–122.

31. Focardi et al., "War Crimes," 343. Poggiolini, "Translating Memories," 230–231.

32. Quoted in Isobel Williams, *Allies and Italians under Occupation* (Basingstoke: Palgrave, 2013), 127.

33. Virginia Lee Warren, "Jews' Future Seen Better in Europe," *New York Times*, June 18, 1945, 8. Milton Bracker, "Italians Apologetic," *New York Times*, August 26, 1945, 34. Delbert Clark, "Fascist Rescues of Jews Revealed," *New York Times*, May 22, 1946, 6.

34. Emiliano Perra, *Conflicts of Memory* (New York: Peter Lang, 2010), 29, 31–34, 40.

35. Hannah Arendt, *Eichmann in Jerusalem* (New York: Viking Press, 1963), 160–161.

36. *Kapò*, directed by Gillo Pontecorvo (1960; Italy: Cineriz). *Il Giardino dei Finzi Contini*, directed by Vittorio De Sica (1970; Italy: Documento Film).

37. On France, see Joan Wolf, *Harnessing the Holocaust* (Stanford: Stanford, 2004), 6, 13, 19, 21, 62, 66. Wiedmer, *Claims of Memory* (Ithaca: Cornell, 1999), Ch. 2. On Germany, see Jeffrey Herf, *Divided Memory* (Cambridge: Harvard, 1997), 38–39, 80–84. Roderick Stackelberg et al., eds., *The Nazi Germany Sourcebook* (London: Routledge, 2002), 394–407. Robert Moeller, "Germans as Victims?" *History & Memory* 17, no. 1/2 (2005): 151–182.

38. *Il Coraggio e la Pietà*, directed by Nicola Caracciolo (1986; Italy: RAI Channel 2).

39. Awards list of *Life is Beautiful*, IMDB, accessed July 23 2019, https://www.imdb.com/title/tt0118799/awards?ref_=tt_awd

40. Screened on channel RAI 1, 7–17–2013 RAI television guide, "La Vita è Bella," www.ufficiostampa.rai.it/mb_index.aspx?file=mb_98053.html (accessed April 2015).

41. Vittorio Zucconi, "E negli USA è già cult," *La Repubblica*, February 10, 1999.

42. Nir Kipnis, "Hachayim Yafim," *Globes*, April 28, 2003.

43. Boudreaux, Richard. "Champagne Flows in Benigni's Village," *Los Angeles Times*, March 23, 1999. Turan, Kenneth. "Movie Review; the Improbable Success of Life is Beautiful," *Los Angeles Times*, October 23, 1998.

44. Glenn Whipp, "Life is Beautiful Balances Dad's Sweetness, Nazi Terror," *Daily News*, October 23, 1998. Brian McIntyre, "Humor & Hope Survive the Holocaust," *The Salt Lake Tribune*, November 06, 1998.

45. Reviews of *Life is Beautiful*, IMDB, accessed July 23 2019, https://www.imdb.com/title/tt0118799/reviews?ref_=tt_ov_rt

46. Kobi Niv, *Life is Beautiful but Not for Jews* (Lanham: Scarecrow Press, 2003), xvi–xvii.

47. Ilona Klein, "Life is Beautiful, or Is It? Asked Jakob the Liar," *Rocky Mountain Review* 64, no. 1 (Spring 2010): 22.

48. David Denby, "In the Eye of the Beholder: Another Look at Roberto Benigni's Holocaust Fantasy," *The New Yorker*, March 15, 1999, 98.
49. Royal Decree Law, November 17, 1938, n. 1728, Articles 1–7.
50. Nedo Fiano, *A 5405: Il Coraggio di Vivere* (Saronno: Monti, 2004), 41.
51. *Concorrenza Sleale*, directed by Ettore Scola (2001; Italy: Medusa Film)
52. See for example anonymous note to police, Milan, May 1939, cited in Franzinelli, *Delatori*, 153. For more such cases, see Chapter 6 and 7 of Franzinelli's book, and Klein, *Italy's Jews*, 106–107.
53. Filippo Focardi, "Italy's Amnesia over War Guilt," *Mediterranean Quarterly* 25, no. 4 (2014): 21.
54. John Agnew, "Time into Space: The Myth of 'Backward' Italy," *Time & Society* 5, no. 1 (1996): 38.
55. Denby, "In the Eye of the Beholder," 99.
56. "Life is Uncomfortable? Spielberg Guarded in Opinion of Benigni's Holocaust Story," *Daily News*, Mar 17, 1999.
57. Flanzbaum, "'But Wasn't It Terrific?'" 283–284.
58. Walter Wolff, *Bad Times, Good People: A Holocaust Survivor Recounts His Life in Italy during World War II* (Long Beach: Whittier, 1999). Elizabeth Bettina, *It Happened in Italy: Untold Stories of How the People of Italy Defied the Horrors of the Holocaust* (Nashville: Thomas Nelson, 2009). Aili McConnon et al., *Road to Valor: A True Story of WWII Italy, the Nazis, and the Cyclist Who Inspired a Nation* (New York: Crown, 2012). *My Italian Secret: The Forgotten Heroes*, directed by Oren Jacoby (2014; United States: Storyville Films).
59. "Italy," United States Holocaust Memorial Museum website, https://encyclopedia.ushmm.org/content/en/article/italy, accessed 20 July 2020.
60. Claudio Pavone, *Una Guerra Civile* (Torino: Bollati Boringhieri, 1991), Chapter 5. See also Paolo Pezzino, "The Italian Resistance between History and Memory," *Journal of Modern Italian Studies* 10, no. 4 (2005): 396.
61. On the assumption of Italian goodness in Africa, see Angelo Del Boca, "The Myths, Suppressions, Denials, and Defaults of Italian Colonialism," in *A Place in the Sun: Africa in Italian Colonial Culture from Post-Unification to the Present*, ed. Patrizia Palumbo (Berkeley: University of California Press, 2003). Luigi Cajani, "The Image of Italian Colonialism in Italian History Textbooks for Secondary Schools," *Journal of Educational Media, Memory, and Society* 5, no. 1 (2013): 76–83.
62. Ben-Ghiat et al., *Italian Colonialism*, 1. Angelo Del Boca, *I Gas di Mussolini* (Roma: Editori Riuniti, 1996). Giulia Barrera, "The Construction of Racial Hierarchies in Colonial Eritrea," in *A Place in the Sun: Africa in Italian Colonial Culture*, ed. Patrizia Palumbo (Berkeley: University of California, 2003).
63. Philip Morgan, *The Fall of Mussolini* (New York: Oxford, 2007), 111.
64. H. James Burgwyn, "General Roatta's War against the Partisans in Yugoslavia: 1942," *Journal of Modern Italian Studies* 9, no. 3 (2004): 319, 322–323. Lidia Santarelli, "Muted Violence: Italian War Crimes in Occupied Greece," ibid. 289–294. Focardi et al., "War Crimes." Focardi, "Italy's Amnesia," 8; Davide Rodogno, *Fascism's European Empire* (New York: Cambridge, 2006), Ch. 10.

BIBLIOGRAPHY

Adorni, Daniela. "Modi E Luoghi Della Persecuzione (1938–1943)." In *L'ebreo in Oggetto : L'applicazione Della Normativa Antiebraica a Torino, 1938–1943*, edited by Fabio Levi, 39–119 (Torino: S. Zamorani, 1991. Agnew, John. "Time into Space: The Myth of 'Backward' Italy in Modern Europe." *Time & Society* 5, no. 1 (1996): 27–45).

Arendt, Hannah. *Eichmann in Jerusalem: A Report on the Banality of Evil*. New York: Viking Press, 1963.

Bachi, Roberto. "La Demografia Dell'ebraismo Italiano Prima Della Emancipazione." *Rassegna Mensile di Israel* 12, no. 7/9 (1938): 256–320.

Bettina, Elizabeth. *It Happened in Italy: Untold Stories of How the People of Italy Defied the Horrors of the Holocaust*. Nashville: Thomas Nelson, 2009.

Burgwyn, H. James. "General Roatta's War against the Partisans in Yugoslavia: 1942." *Journal of Modern Italian Studies* 9, no. 3 (2004): 314–29.

Bidussa, D. *La Menzogna della Razza: Documenti e Immagini del Razzismo e dell'Antisemitismo Fascista* (Casalecchio di Reno: Grafis, 1994), 211.

Capristo, Annalisa. "The Beginnings of Racial Persecution: The Exclusion of Jews from Italian Academies." In *Jews in Italy under Fascist and Nazi Rule, 1922–1945*, edited by Joshua D. Zimmerman, 81–95. New York: Cambridge University Press, 2005.

Concorrenza Sleale, directed by Ettore Scola (2001; Italy: Medusa Film)

Fiano, Nedo. *A 5405: Il Coraggio Di Vivere*. Saronno: Monti, 2004.

Flanzbaum, Hilene. "'But Wasn't It Terrific?' A Defense of Liking Life is Beautiful." *The Yale Journal of Criticism* 14, no. 1 (2001): 273–86.

Focardi, Filippo. "Italy's Amnesia over War Guilt: The 'Evil Germans' Alibi." *Mediterranean Quarterly* 25, no. 4 (2014): 5–26.

Filippo Focardi et al., "The Question of Fascist Italy's War Crimes: The Construction of a Self-Acquitting Myth (1943–1948)," *Journal of Modern Italian Studies* 9, no. 3 (2004): 343

Franzinelli, Mimmo. *Delatori: Spie E Confidenti Anonimi: L'arma Segreta Del Regime Fascista*. Milano: Mondadori, 2001.

Hametz, Maura Elise. "The Ambivalence of Italian Antisemitism: Fascism, Nationalism, and Racism in Trieste." *Holocaust and Genocide Studies* 16, no. 3 (2002): 376–401.

Il Giardino dei Finzi Contini, directed by Vittorio De Sica (1970; Italy: Documento Film).

Kapò, directed by Gillo Pontecorvo (1960; Italy: Cineriz).

Klein, Ilona, "Life is Beautiful, or Is It? Asked Jakob the Liar." *Rocky Mountain Review* 64, no. 1 (2010), 17–31.

Klein, S. *Italy's Jews from Emancipation to Fascism* (NY: Cambridge University Press, 2018), 119, 121–124.

La Vita è Bella, directed by Roberto Benigni (1997; Italy: Cecchi Gori Group Tiger Cinematografica).

McConnon, Aili, and Andres McConnon. *Road to Valor: A True Story of WWII Italy, the Nazis, and the Cyclist Who Inspired a Nation.* New York: Crown, 2012.

Morgan, Philip. *The Fall of Mussolini: Italy, the Italians, and the Second World War.* Oxford: Oxford University Press, 2007.

My Italian Secret: The Forgotten Heroes, directed by Oren Jacoby (2014; United States: Storyville Films).

Niv, Kobi. *Life is Beautiful but Not for Jews.* Lanham, MD: Scarecrow Press, 2003.

Österberg, Oscar. "Taming Ambiguities: The Representation of the Holocaust in Post-War Italy." In *The Holocaust on Post-War Battlefields: Genocide as Historical Culture*, edited by Klas-Göran Karlsson and Ulf Zander. Malmo: Sekel, 2006.

Pavone, Claudio. *Una Guerra Civile : Saggio Storico Sulla Moralità Nella Resistenza.* Nuova Cultura. Torino: Bollati Boringhieri, 1991.

Perra, Emiliano. *Conflicts of Memory: The Reception of Holocaust Films and TV Programmes in Italy, 1945 to the Present.* New York: Peter Lang, 2010.

Picciotto, Liliana. "The Shoah in Italy: Its History and Characteristics." In *Jews in Italy under Fascist and Nazi Rule, 1922–1945*, edited by Joshua Zimmerman, 209–23. Cambridge: Cambridge University Press, 2005 (Picciotto, Liliana, "Statistical Tables on the Holocaust in Italy." *Yad Vashem Studies* 33 (2005)).

Poggiolini, Ilaria. "Translating Memories of War and Co-Belligerency into Politics: The Italian Post-War Experience." In *Memory and Power in Post-War Europe: Studies in the Presence of the Past*, edited by Jan-Werner Müller, 223–43. Cambridge: Cambridge University Press, 2002.

Rodogno, Davide. "Italiani Brava Gente? Fascist Italy's Policy toward the Jews in the Balkans, April 1941–July 1943." *European History Quarterly* 35, no. 2 (2005): 213–40.

Santarelli, Lidia. "Muted Violence: Italian War Crimes in Occupied Greece." *Journal of Modern Italian Studies* 9, no. 3 (2004): 280–99.

Sarfatti, Michele. "Raffaele Jona Ed Il Soccorso Agli Ebrei Del Piemonte Durante La Repubblica Sociale Italiana." In *Dalle Leggi Razziali Alla Deportazione. Ebrei Tra Antisemitismo E Solidarietà*, edited by Alberto Lovatto, 55–73. Borgosesia: Istituto per la storia della Resistenza, 1992.

Sarfatti, Michele. *The Jews in Mussolini's Italy: From Equality to Persecution.* Madison: University of Wisconsin Press, 2006.

Schwarz, Guri. "On Myth Making and Nation Building: The Genesis of the 'Myth of the Good Italian'." *Yad Vashem Studies* 36, no. 1 (2008): 111–43.

Sullam, Simon Levis. *The Italian Executioners: The Genocide of the Jews of Italy.* Princeton, NJ: Princeton University Press, 2018.

Toscano, Mario. "L'internamento Degli Ebrei Italiani 1940–1943: Tra Contingenze Belliche E Politica Razziale." In *I Campi Di Concentramento in Italia. Dall'internamento Alla Deportazione (1940–1945)*, edited by Costantino Di Sante, 95–112. Milano: F. Angeli, 2001.

Wildvang, Frauke. "The Enemy Next Door: Italian Collaboration in Deporting Jews during the German Occupation of Rome." *Modern Italy* 12, no. 2 (2007): 189–204.

Williams, Isobel. *Allies and Italians under Occupation: Sicily and Southern Italy, 1943–45.* Basingstoke: Palgrave Macmillan, 2013.

Wolff, Walter. *Bad Times, Good People: A Holocaust Survivor Recounts His Life in Italy During World War Ii.* Long Beach, NY: Whittier, 1999.

Chapter 3

Not My Holocaust
MAUS *and Memory in the Polish Classroom*
Holli Levitsky

In Poland, in the several decades leading up to World War II, Jews and non-Jews lived as neighbors, interacted in markets and on the streets, and occasionally cooperated in business, and professional and social engagements. In major cities, such as Warsaw and Krakow, Jewish and non-Jewish Poles spoke each other's languages and for the most part, lived as much a Polish life as a Catholic or Jewish one. Although one's religious identity was public knowledge, religious difference was not always an issue. That did not mean that anti-Semitism did not have an impact on the lives of Polish Jews, but Jews were part of Poland, and Polish culture was, in part, Jewish.

Although these two communities were deeply connected, each carried different memories of their history. Jews had been living in Poland since at least the Middle Ages, where they enjoyed relative autonomy and tolerance and developed a rich social and cultural life. Throughout the nineteenth century, they made up between a quarter and half of the population in Poland's larger cities (in some smaller towns, they made as much as 90 percent) and fought alongside Polish fighters seeking independence during a series of uprisings.

After World War I, Poland became a democratic independent state with significant minority populations, including Ukrainians, Belorussians, Lithuanians, and ethnic Germans; Jews, however, made up the largest minority. As World War II approached and Polish nationalism surged, violence against Jews became more common. Yet, on the eve of World War II, three-and-a-half million Jews, or about 10 percent of the population, lived in Poland, giving it the highest percentage of Jews in any European country.[1]

Within the first two months of the Nazi occupation of Poland in September 1939, the German military killed 20,000 Jews, bombed tens of thousands of Jewish businesses, and destroyed hundreds of synagogues in 120 Jewish communities. Restrictions were placed on Jews almost immediately. Jews in every profession were targeted for removal, including Jewish physicians and lawyers, despite their having made up more than 50 percent of those professional classes. Hundreds of thousands of Polish refugees—Jews and non-Jews—fled to eastern Poland, hoping the Polish army would successfully defend the country against the German invaders. After Germany and the Soviet Union partitioned Poland, the Polish government fled the country and established a government-in-exile in London. Under the Soviets, hundreds of thousands of residents were arrested and deported by the secret police. It wasn't until the breach of the non-aggression Molotov-Ribbentrop Pact between the Soviet Union and Nazi Germany that eastern Poland came under German control and that the lives of Polish Jews and non-Jews dramatically diverged. While Polish citizens faced the prospect of a long exile, they were neither the subject of ever more restrictive laws (such as the enactment of the "Nuremburg Laws") nor the object of government-sanctioned terror.

The fate of Polish Jews in World War II has encouraged a narrative that overshadows the reality that, for centuries, Poland had allowed millions of Jewish residents to practice their religion openly. Before the outbreak of World War II, Poland held the second largest Jewish community in the world and served as a mecca for Jewish culture. Developing, sustaining, and growing such a thriving culture had to have included positive interactions outside the Jewish community. To cast the entire Polish nation as anti-Semitic misses the rich and varied history of the two groups. My own family history attests to this complicated history: How had my great-grandparents been successful merchants if they had not benefited from peaceable and positive relations with neighbors, townspeople, and local officials?

The important, but often overlooked, history between Poles and Polish Jews complicated my objective to teach intercultural competency and cultural diplomacy in a place where Jewish life had all but vanished as a result of genocide. I sought a text that could help process these complexities for uninformed Polish students, as well as providing a broad introduction to what Americans commonly refer to as Holocaust. With Art Spiegelman's graphic novel *Maus*,[2] I found a text that documented this complicated connection between Jewish and non-Jewish Poles; that acknowledges a world in which identities frequently shifted and where Jewish residents had over a period of two or three decades gone from agreeable neighbors and colleagues to dangerous undesirables.

In this essay, I'll discuss my own experience teaching *Maus* to Polish students at the University of Warsaw. I'll share some of my observations about (1) my personal background before I got to Poland (2) the nature of the differing narratives (3) the putative motivation for the Polish narrative, and (4) *Maus* as a way to grapple with a complex of competing—as well as cooperating—narrative threads.

In early September 2001, I arrived at the University of Warsaw as a Fulbright Distinguished Chair in American Literature. I had chosen Poland because of my family background (both maternal grandparents were born there). Before World War II, the major cities included many assimilated Jews who were, in terms of practice and mother tongue, far more Polish than Jewish. My grandfather's family expected him to become a rabbi and had sent him to a yeshiva in Warsaw. For whatever reason, including the lures of assimilation, he left school and went to work in sales at a large department store.

My grandfather's sister had self-published a family memoir,[3] describing their emigration at the turn of the twentieth century from the village of Modliborzyce to America. Even the market towns, or shtetls, like Modliborzyce, that have come to represent the lives of Jews in Eastern Europe were, to some extent, mixed communities of Jews and non-Jews, Poles, and other minorities. In her book, my aunt evoked a little town "made up of small buildings surrounding a square. The square was a marketplace every Thursday. If anybody got married the ceremony was in the square under the stars. The whole town—the Jewish part—went to the wedding"[4] She goes on to describe "the Jewish part": characters like Sarah Chuck, the town water carrier; Schmuel Baer, the town "dummy"; and her father, a "good-looking young man," who attracted the attention of "all sorts" of diverse women. She describes her mother, the daughter of a wealthy Jewish doctor in whose home many townspeople worked as servants; her numerous siblings (including my grandfather, who stayed in Warsaw for another decade), and the journey she takes from Polish shtetl to American life in 1912. She never discusses the "other" women who swooned over her father, her grandparents' non-Jewish servants, the customers for her father's shoes and her mother's fabric business. She documents their interactions only obliquely: "The busiest time was before Christmas. Everyone would make a lot of money because people would come from all over to buy and sell."[5] Together, in 1912, the Jews and non-Jews made up the "whole town." It wasn't as if the Polish non-Jews had vanished from history. But they weren't part of the Jewish narrative.

Growing up in Detroit, I knew plenty of kids and families from the neighboring city of Hamtramack, which at the time was a vibrant center of Polish-American life and culture. Polish surnames commonly appeared on school rosters and in the trade publications. My father's collegiality with Polish electricians included working for each other on their respective holy days and holidays. At the time, I didn't know much about the country or its history, but in Jewish communities in the 1960s and 1970s, I often heard condemnations of Polish anti-Semitism and their conduct in the Holocaust. This put an inflexible barrier between our communities. We could be neighbors, but we could not be friends, based on the seemingly immutable characteristic of Jew-hatred.

So-called "Polack jokes," based on negative stereotypes and meant to mock Poles, Polish culture or habits, had become part of the American lexicon, and in some ways could be seen as a kind of twisted revenge on the assumed anti-Semitism of the Polish people.[6] Despite these antagonisms of history, in an American metropolis, Polish and Jewish immigrants co-existed—without becoming friends.

When she came to America, my aunt must have wondered about the family she left behind. As Americans learned about the atrocities that had been committed against the Jews of Europe, it was impossible not to think about the Poles of her town. Did their neighbors assist her family? Had they been bystanders when her family was captured? Had they turned against the Jews they'd known forever?

As for modern Poland and its politics, I knew next to nothing, and no one I knew seemed to know much about it either. Among American Jews—native born and refugees from Europe—Poland was mostly seen as a Jewish cemetery. "Why would you want to go there?" my parents asked. Friends misheard us say "Portland," and when we began complaining about how hard living there might be, they reminded us how much we loved the Pacific Northwest. The strangest thing people said was to bring toilet paper since there would be none to buy in Poland. The image of Poles standing in endless queues for toilet paper and other necessities was a remnant of the Communist era, where such necessities were in short supply. Since that era ended with the fall of Communism and rise of democracy in 1989, it was clear that Americans knew little about life in contemporary Poland. As for Jews, were there any left?

What I did know was that moving to a country from which my Jewish grandfather barely escaped was fraught with history and memories that weren't even my own. Then, just days after arriving in Europe, while en route to Poland by car from Sweden, 9/11 occurred. My husband, daughter, son, and I wound our way through Germany to Warsaw in a fog. As we took the northern route through grim forests, full of anxiety about America, past and present blurred. In terms of Polish-Jewish history,[7] it was not out of line to think that Poles might align themselves not with American victims but with those who hated Americans and wanted them dead. I wondered: Would I be safe in Poland? How much of this fear had to do with what had happened there three-quarters of a century and how much was inspired by international tensions in 2001 remains unclear.

Once we arrived, my Polish colleagues, students, neighbors, shopkeepers, and even strangers offered sympathy and support. Eventually, I recognized that modern Poland had a deep respect for and interest in all things American, and most of my fear evaporated under their good will and curiosity. Teaching in one of the two American Studies Institutes attached to Warsaw University,

I had colleagues with specialties in African-American, Latin-American, and Native-American literatures. Within the two different American Studies associations in Poland, Polish scholars presented papers and published articles on the hyphenated ethnic-American at their annual conferences. Their courses on these topics were packed with students eager to learn about anything American. I witnessed it in my own classroom. During a heated discussion on "Southern American literature," the class insisted that Poland was a gothic landscape—and bore similarity to the American South. In the divided class system, amid lost aristocracy, and through their mutual attachment to the land, Faulkner, McCullers, Welty, and other Southern writers mined the same gothic history for the "tragic separateness" of its people. My Polish students began to teach me their own understanding of their history as much as I would teach them. In my students' identification with America's dark history, I found other lessons to learn about Poland and the Polish people.

As a visiting professor at Warsaw University's Pedagogical Institute, I offered their first course on "American Writers on the Holocaust." It filled quickly with Master's students in American literature, who, I learned, knew very little about Jews and the Holocaust. Nearly all locales in Poland housed Jewish citizens before World War II, yet I discovered that it was unlikely my students had ever met a Jewish person before they met me. Faced with the task of teaching Polish students about their own history, and events that took place on their land, I wondered why it had not been taught in schoolbooks or by their teachers, and had instead vanished into an untold history.

I discovered that they knew nothing about the Jewish history of their hometown or of Poland because they were not taught Polish-Jewish history. For decades, under Communism, Polish textbooks subsumed Polish-Jewish history into general Polish history. The stories of Jewish lives were not seen as distinct or separate. Furthermore, with time, Jews had vanished from current Polish memory. This made it hard for students to understand Poland's thriving Jewish population and quotidian interactions between Poles and Jews before the war. I told them about my own family residing in Poland for generations—and how as a young Polish man my grandfather worked as a salesman in a large department store in Warsaw that still stood—just down the street from our Institute. I reminded them that I was teaching them Polish-Jewish history as a descendent of the three million plus Jews who had formerly inhabited their villages, towns, and cities.

My Polish students did not know the extent of Jewish life lost because they did not know the extent of Jewish life in Poland—period. While I was prepared to teach the Holocaust, the Holocaust they were expecting me to teach was not my Holocaust. I approached my pedagogy through the American Holocaust narrative, where the primary victims were European Jews who were targeted by the Nazis for death by genocide. Within this view, Poles were seen as bystanders at best, perpetrators at worst. Fortunately, the literature classroom offers a safe space for such charged discussions, so that we could unpack our certainties and assumptions about Jews in Poland and open them up to each other for scrutiny. As I brought more verifiable facts to the discussion, I found that that students' own Holocaust education had burdened them with a vanished history that floated like a vapor over our work together. Poles (including my students) were educated through their teachers and textbooks and the national narrative to believe that they were the primary victims. They saw Jews at best as part of the greater Polish catastrophe, at worst as the cause of the catastrophe. To many Poles, *Maus* could not have value as a family Holocaust story because it wasn't the story the Poles knew.

As a Fulbright Distinguished Chair, I was charged with improving *intercultural relations, cultural diplomacy, and intercultural competence* between the people of the United States and Poland. Thus, my teaching had to balance two conflicting narratives, while diplomatically constructing a productive way to move students toward a deeper, intercultural understanding of the catastrophe. To provide a stage for conflicting narratives to engage, I had to find a way to see Polish-Jewish history, the Holocaust, and its aftermath through the eyes of my Polish students. In order to apply the lessons of the Holocaust to *where they are now*, I needed to see it through their eyes.

In "Reading the Holocaust: Right Here, Right Now,"[8] an essay that inspired my own thinking about Holocaust pedagogy, Hilene Flanzbaum considers the difference between teaching a novel like Bernhard Schlink's *The Reader*[9] in her Indiana classroom and a colleague that had been teaching the book in Germany. For Americans, praised as liberators and heroes, the book blurs the rigid lines of certainty between villainous and heroic behavior. The "villain" in Schlink's story is Hannah, a rather ordinary street car conductor who turns out to have been a voluntary (and illiterate) concentration camp guard. The story offers a kind of warning to Americans who may be surprised to learn that a villain can be "an ordinary person capable of desire and yearning, who turns her hand to monstrous work for a time,"[10] as Hannah did during the War. The book will not have the same implications for Germans, shamed as a perpetrator nation, for whom geography and history are everyday reminders Germans cannot avoid. Locating "different meanings in the Holocaust hardly feels surprising," Flanzbaum writes, but abstracting "different lessons from artwork feels groundbreaking."[11]

I felt similarly as I tried to teach *Maus* to Polish students. As an oral narrative that struggles to represent the spoken memories of a Holocaust survivor through a graphic format, it is especially effective at inviting emotional involvement and is "much more accessible to a general audience than many other accounts."[12] To the primarily non-Jewish students in my Los Angeles classroom, the book was a game-changer: visually gripping and full of expected comic book tropes and structures, the story was, for them, deeply nuanced, multi-layered, suspenseful. It spoke to new generations of students, weaned on victim culture, who were longing to read personal stories of hardship and redemption. It was a very *American* story: first-generation immigrants seeking the American dream and a better life for their children with the second generation trying to find their place in the family drama.

To Polish students, the book was both dangerous and alluring. Poles largely had rejected its value from the beginning (which I will go into shortly), and it took a decade for the book to be translated into Polish and published in Poland. The most groundbreaking, as well as controversial, element of *Maus* is Spiegelman's rendering of nationality. Each character of a particular nation is drawn as its own animal species, which both essentializes national characteristics and masks individuality. Spiegelman's choice of pigs to represent Poles associates them with crude, boorish behavior. But embodying Poles as pigs also unleashes layers of historical animosity between Jewish law and Polish culture. Dietary laws prohibiting Jews from eating pork must have seemed foolish if not offensive to Poles given their national love for all forms of pork products. Drawing Poles as pigs made sense as shorthand to convey the absolute difference between Jews and non-Jews.

It also tapped into long-held German anti-Polish sentiments. In October 1939, a directive from Nazi Germany's Propaganda Ministry stated:

> It must be made clear even to the German milkmaid that Polishness equals subhumanity. Poles, Jews and gypsies are on the same inferior level.... This should be brought home as a *leitmotiv*, and from time to time, in the form of existing concepts such as "Polish economy," "Polish ruin," and so on, until everyone in Germany sees every Pole, whether farm worker or intellectual, as vermin.[13]

Thinking through "Nazi" point of view, it also made sense that Poles would be pigs, but for a different reason. Poles (like pigs) were unredeemable by virtue of their low status, but they could provide hard labor before they too would be eliminated from the Reich.

At first, animal identities in *Maus* are stable and objective. When Jewish characters need to conceal their religion, they wear a pig mask; no other animals wear masks. Likewise, when Spiegelman as a character feels like an imposter in *Maus II*, he wears a mask to depict his anxiety of not being "Jewish enough." In one scene, a German prisoner is depicted both as a mouse for the Nazis and a cat for the other inmates: here identity is imposed from the outside, and a matter of perspective. The easy animal classifications become more confused and contentious throughout the book, suggesting that identity is never fully self-evident or even decipherable. Because Poland was the setting for most of *Maus,* and Polish was the language of his parents and his own mother tongue, the translation of *Maus* into Polish was of considerable importance to Spiegelman, yet as I mentioned earlier, the Polish translation encountered difficulties. As early as 1987, when Spiegelman planned a research visit to Poland, the Polish consulate official who approved his visa questioned him about the Poles' depiction as pigs and pointed out how serious an insult it was.[14]

As narrated by Vladek Spiegelman, a Pole and a Jew, to his American Jewish son, Art, *Maus* uses the conventions of the graphic novel—a complex interplay of text and illustrations—to construct a sequential narrative. The frames run parallel stories: the book opens with Vladek and Art talking in the present, but as Vladek recounts his memories of life before and during the war years, the frames follow that earlier story as well, documenting the big and small changes in the world—for Jews in particular.

Spiegelman slowly unpacks the changes and prohibitions against Jews, at times using an entire page (or several frames) to emphasize a dramatic shift in his landscape, such as the public visibility of the swastika. While the non-Jewish Poles basically ignore the looming red-and-black banners strewn across the cities, Jews acknowledge its threat and vocalize their fear of what may follow.[15] By presenting these visual and textual fields as complex layers of remembered history, Vladek Spiegelman's memories project Polish self-determination alongside Jewish lack of self-determination without necessarily bringing them into conflict. *Maus* sublimates the central conflict into a shared story, where competing narratives of non-Jewish Poles and Jewish Poles co-exist.

By the time my students were assigned the book, the national debates that had questioned the role and representation of Poles as pigs in the book was in embers. Once it was in the bookstores, it was purchased and read widely. However, some Polish readers and critics continued to question its value, even referring to it as a racist text, as this commentary on the book by a Polish writer makes clear:

> The pigs for the most part are not presented in a sympathetic way or as cute. They are portrayed as bad-tempered or frightened and unwilling to help. It is never explained why. It is suggested that Poles killed Jews. The kapos in the camp are brutal pigs. A priest (pig) prisoner consoles Vladek. The idea that there were prisoners other than Jews at Auschwitz makes an occasional appearance but is never fully explored. Earlier in the story there is a female pig who hides Vladek's family but money seems to be the motivation. Finally, vodka drinking pigs undertake to smuggle Vladek and Anja into Hungary but only betray them to the Germans.[16]

As this writer points out, the pigs aren't the problem, their behavior is. If the pigs were portrayed as sympathetic or cute, and the characters acted "piggishly," it would not be so bad because they'd still be "sympathetic" and "cute," which may well be how Poles—and pigs—see themselves.

My students eagerly entered these public debates. During our lively class discussions, we analyzed characters and interrogated the Holocaust stories being told. I was sympathetic to student concerns about the depiction of Poles as bad pigs, and they in turn became more intrigued by their nation's Jewish-Polish history. As their Holocaust "misinformation" emerged, a powerful tension grew between what they had learned in school and what I was telling them. When I gently corrected a student who said the Polish people never had prejudice against Jews as a people, that it was an economic problem since Jews owned the land, he got defensive. He insisted that King Kazimierz[17] had favored the Jews over other minorities and thus they had these advantages until this day. They disputed the number of Jews who were murdered during the Holocaust and continued the line of thinking that Poles suffered as much as the Jews. Their misinformation about Polish-Jewish history and Holocaust history gave me a door into their reality. Walking through that door allowed me to correct those errors.

Our discussions led directly to their final project, which was to interview a family member who was alive during World War II and to ask them what they remembered about Jews from before and during the War. From this interview they were to creatively "tell the story" of the relative, as Art tells his father's story through the graphic novel—allowing me to see the Holocaust through their eyes, providing an intimate lens through which to learn personal and cultural histories.

Their stories inclined toward the heroic and the tragic (in their own right), including grandparents fighting Nazis in the Warsaw Uprising or with the Home Army, and relatives sent away as slave laborers; almost every student shared that someone in their family had saved or helped a Jew or Jewish family, though no one could actually cite the name of a "saved Jew."

But once the interviews began, students made surprising discoveries that burst asunder many of the platitudes they shared in class. I'll share two examples. In "Interview With My Father," "Anna" interviewed her father, who loved history and frequently quizzed her on facts and dates from Polish history. While he "doesn't know any Jews," he tells "Anna" what he heard from her grandfather, a shoemaker. "They were cunning as foxes . . . and joined their forces to make Polish sellers bankrupt. . . . They took us for enemies and in consequence we considered them as such. . . . What really makes me angry is that they always called themselves Polish Jews . . . They separated themselves from the society . . . your grandfather strongly disliked them. He often told Jewish jokes and he laughed at them." Her father continues to deny remembering any Jews but adds that "Jews were always villains," and their very presence caused a stir that "often led to war."

Unfortunately, she neither reflects on the deeper historical ramifications suggested by her grandfather's hateful words nor does she call out her father's anti-Semitic views.

In "Fragments of My Grandfather's War," "Pawel" interviewed his grandfather, a carpenter who fought in the Home Army. He relates the respect received by Polish officers in the POW camps, how the Poles received so many packages from international organizations that the Germans bought bread from them, and how they were encouraged to sing Polish songs, including their national anthem. Rumors of Jewish ancestry had long been circulating in the family, and "Pawel" is disappointed that he can't get his grandfather to verify the "innuendo" that his grandmother was Jewish ("by descent"). He has sound suspicions, writing that "her physical type was rather distinctive. But both of my grandparents denied." He describes the source of "this denial, or . . . repression" as emerging from an incident in a forced labor camp in Ravensbruck where his grandmother had a relatively easy post. A coworker who wanted her job reported her to the commander as a Jew. "Pawel" concludes that "she managed to clear herself. Obviously, if she did not, she probably would have been executed right on the spot or at best deported to a death camp. This, as well as the post-war persecution of Jews, would probably be more than enough to conceal her 'racial' identity for the whole life."

As I considered their family stories, one thing became clear: my students did not know much about Jews, and what they did know was full of misinformation. They were convinced Judaism was a racial category, that it was immutable, and that, at times, it was better to hide it if you could. If their beloved parents and grandparents could hold anti-Semitic views, maybe they were right. When the 2018 Polish legislation passed that would essentially criminalize any mention of Polish complicity in the Holocaust, the heated global controversy underscored, for me, how differently Jewish and non-Jewish Poles perceive their entire history.

While I found this deficiency unsettling, it was not surprising because, at least in 2001, Polish secondary school textbooks did not mention Jews specifically in relation to World War II. Their focus was primarily on the German war against the Poles, and for purposes of counting victims, Jews were included within the Polish casualty count.[18] Over the years, reports from the Jewish Historical Institute examining the inclusion of Jewish history in Polish textbooks confirmed that popularly used textbooks provided little or no context to Jewish life. Although Jews had lived in the country for over 1,000 years, contemporary textbooks didn't make clear why they disappeared suddenly from the Polish landscape. Furthermore, the Holocaust was discussed as an act against Poles; Jews were seen as passive in their destruction and even though they had active resistance cells of their own, only Poles were reported as resistance fighters.

In short, Polish national pride dictated the way history was told. The standards for secondary history curricula highlighted Polish heroism—much like American textbooks focused on American heroism as a major factor in winning World War II. Challenging the national narrative with such thorny ethical issues as Polish bystanders and collaborators—Polish neighbors who turned Jews in to the Nazis, and others who turned a blind eye—would have meant teaching students about Polish complicity with crimes against Jews. This reckoning with the past could not be easily integrated into a history curriculum that privileged Poles' victimhood and heroism. Many Polish people helped Jews—courageously—and Poles were certainly victims of the Nazis. But seventy years after the Polish Communist government declared that all Poles were victims of the Nazis—as one body—students' stories reveal the extent to which there is still just one narrative. For all these reasons and more, the teaching of *Maus* to Polish students presented a challenge.

As I mentioned earlier, Polish publishers and commentators refused to deal with the book for fear of public protests and boycotts. Poles love Poland and stand prepared to defend her honor. While this behavior could be seen as "piggish," the Poles felt the portrayal made them a homogenous mass of Polish swine, their country a pigsty. In order to publish *Maus* in Polish, Piotra Bikont, a journalist for *Gazeta Wyborcza*, had to set up his own publishing house. Demonstrators protested publication and burned the book in front of *Gazeta*'s offices. Bikont's response was to show his own acceptance as a "Polish pig," so he donned a pig mask and waved to the protesters from the office windows. The book's translation into Polish was delayed for a decade due to the ferocity of public resistance.[19]

Several coinciding elements contributed to such forceful public resistance to the graphic novel, suggests Polish Holocaust scholar Tomek Lysak.[20] First, given the narrow focus of Holocaust education in Poland, Poles generally see themselves as deeply victimized by this past. Not in and of themselves targeted for immediate death, they were used for slave labor and marked for eventual extinction by the Nazis. Hostilities by other nations toward Polish people pre-dated the Holocaust, but it reached a particular peak during World War II, when Poles became the subject of ethnic cleansing on an unprecedented scale. To the Poles, *Maus* omitted their victimhood.

A second element was the publication of Jan Gross's book *Neighbors*,[21] also in 2001, which examined the pogrom against the Jews of Jedwabne perpetrated by their Polish neighbors in 1941. *Had* every family saved a Jew? Not according to Jan Gross, whose research disputed that statement unequivocally by showing that, in fact, in a barn in the village of Jedwabne, Poles killed their Jewish neighbors. The publication of the book belied the image Poles have of themselves as heroes and victims and led to more public debates that called into question deeply rooted beliefs of Polish nationalism and pride. It also re-opened public discussion of the Polish sense of guilt surrounding the Holocaust, a debate which dealt with the dark past of Polish collective memory.

A third element was the attitude toward Polish comic culture. Children's comics had developed over the last century, but in general comics continued to be seen by cultural critics as "mindless entertainment."[22] In *Words Without Borders,* one Polish popular culture critic writes that today, "Much of the media still does not recognize the existence of this art form, and many critics still practice the old cultural prejudice, seeing comics as something inferior, not understanding their language, aesthetics, special qualities, their difference from literature or film."[23] The many comics for children, and the few series for adults, have mostly been stories that laughed at unpopular politicians or public figures, scandals and other national shortcomings, and general human stupidity. There was no tradition of comics or graphic novels that provided a serious platform to tell a story of suffering and loss, such as *Maus* succeeds in doing.

The year 2001 was just over a decade after Communism fell in Poland. In terms of memory culture, the Communist regime privileged Poles as victims of the Nazis. The lack of specificity of Jewish victims and Jewish victimhood was made apparent as post-Communist memory culture tried to atone for the buried past of Polish Jews and Polish-Jewish life. Still, even after Communism was replaced by a form of democracy, the debates over who were the greater victims continued. Spiegelman's graphic novel—first published in English in 1991, then in Polish in 2001—as well as Gross's book, presented the best textual opportunity to work through the thorny questions posed by these contradictions.

Spiegelman's brilliant layering of Polish and American history, Holocaust memoir, and family biography creates a bridge between American Holocaust culture and Polish history and culture. As seen through a Polish perspective, some of the text's frames present normal relations between Poles and Jews: seated together on trains, the nurse and loyal governess attending Art's mother, a dancehall with Jewish and Polish couples dancing side by side. When Vladek, the Jewish-Polish protagonist, is drafted into the Polish Army Reserves, Polish and Jewish soldiers march alongside. In one frame, a Polish officer sneaks over to help Vladek in the battlefield improve his shooting position. These scenes of Poles and Jews living parallel lives confirmed the self-image of Poles as helpful, friendly people who lived side by side with their peaceful neighbors. Such depictions of "normalized" relations between Poles and Jews reinforced the Polish national narrative of master victim, and the notion that all was good for everyone until it wasn't.

Another illustration of a Polish perspective, though more complicated, shows an increasingly larger (and seemingly more optimistic) series of frames that convey a spontaneous interaction between Vladek and a Polish woman named Motonowa. She had once hidden Vladek and his wife Anya, so Vladek feels somewhat safe around her. When she spots him, Motonowa cries, "Oh God! Oh God! Mr Spiegelman. You're alive! I'm so glad to see you! . . . Praise Mary. You're safe! I couldn't sleep, I felt so guilty about chasing you and your wife out."[24] It should be understood that the risk she takes in hiding them offered a far greater threat—certain death—than the loss of money meant to Vladek—although the exchange of money or other valuables were motivators for hiding Jews.

Motonowa wears her pig face openly, with no need to mask her identity. Vladek, on the other hand, has donned a pig mask over his mouse face (Motonowa recognizes him nonetheless). At that point in the story, Vladek is concerned but not yet existentially terrified about being in a world where he is hated for his Jewish identity. His fortitude and forward-looking attitude have kept him from recognizing the doom he is facing, but the need for a mask makes that clear to us.

She invites them to hide with her again. Although they are relatively safe in her house, they must remain in the cellar without food and water at times for days when her husband returns from the war. When Anya expresses her fear of the cellar's rats, Motonowa cheerfully replies that "you're better off with the rats than with the Gestapo . . . at least the rats won't kill you." But the couple, without masks, are drawn almost completely in shadow. The darkness suggests their helplessness and lack of agency, and their fear of immanent erasure. They must rely on the assistance of Poles, but they don't trust them.

Yet when Anya and Vladek are allowed into her house from the cellar, Spiegelman uses the last frame of the scene in Motonowa's house to convey their gratitude. Anya is shown bathing in a soapy tub, in a warmly lit room, Vladek standing nearby. She says, "It's good to be 'home,' eh Vladek?" and he replies, "It's a lot nicer than that cellar." They are grateful to be protected, but at the bottom of the same frame, Vladek expresses his ongoing concern about their safety under the Poles, "It was too many ways somebody could find us out."[25]

Discussing this scene in class, my students identified with Motonowa, seeing her behavior as a sign of continued Polish goodwill toward Jewish neighbors. One student verbalized what I sensed was a common sentiment: "In *Maus*, the fact that no Jews would have survived without help from Poles is never brought out." I made them aware that when the laws changed under occupation and being Jewish becomes criminalized—and by this new definition could be neither law-abiding nor citizens of the state—Polish citizens could keep their Polish identity and still live through the war. They could walk on the streets, shop in the stores, eat at restaurants, live in their own homes. They could reach out and help their neighbors, or not. Jews had no such choices. By laws, directives, and resolutions, Jews were required to gather and be removed when called. For Jews, the machinery of a final solution was in place. Life was uncertain for Poles and certainly difficult. But they were not presented with the same final terms as the Jews. This is where the perspective—and the narratives—diverge.

A darker and more insidious story emerges a few pages later when Vladek leaves the hiding place to arrange to be smuggled to Hungary. On the way, he has to pass a group of children playing. Although he is wearing his pig mask, the children see through the pretense. They have the certainty of their own identity as Polish children, thus they can easily identify his rootlessness. Immediately they see he is a Jew and run home to their mothers, screaming, "Help! Mommy! A Jew!!" Describing the scene from his memory, Vladek tells Art: "The mothers always told so: Be careful! A Jew will catch you to a bag and eat you . . . so they taught to their children."[26] Such frames call to mind the aphorism I heard from relatives, that "Poles imbibe anti-Semitism with their mothers' milk." In Vladek's memory, such incidents convey his understanding that he lived in a divided world, that his identity as a Pole was dependent on *how others viewed him*. His mask was a flimsy reminder that one's identity was not fixed (especially ethnic identities). Identity could be in the eye of the beholder.

Productively working through *Maus* and memory in the Polish classroom brought me closer to an understanding of the nature of the conflicting Holocaust narratives of Polish non-Jews and Jews. In *Multidirectional Memory*, Michael Rothberg conceives a space where such conflicting narratives confront one another, potentially—though not necessarily—creating sympathy between groups, suggesting that "memory works *productively* through negotiation, cross-referencing, and borrowing; the result of memory conflict is not less memory, but more—even of subordinated memory traditions."[27] But is it possible to work through these conflicting historical memories of the Holocaust without endorsing historically inaccurate narratives? Though the Polish students did not experience Polish victimhood firsthand, the traumatic memories of their grandparents and the older generations were transmitted as family lore. The literature classroom opened up a space where the "tragic separateness of experience"[28] could be identified, creating a common goal to understand the other's experience. The work produced more memory in everyone, succeeding in moving us forward.

My class learned that Jews were one of several minorities that had lived in Poland for centuries, and they had engaged each other in regular, even daily neighborly, social, commercial, and other kinds of interactions before World War II. We concluded that during the Holocaust, many of these Poles acted heroically toward their Jewish neighbors. Indeed, citizens of Poland have the world's highest count of non-Jewish individuals who risked their lives to save Jews, recognized in an honorific by Yad Vashem in Israel as Righteous Among the Nations. It is estimated that thousands of Poles concealed and aided thousands of their Polish-Jewish neighbors. Many of these initiatives were carried out by individuals, but there also existed organized networks of Polish resistance which were dedicated to aiding Jews.

Unfortunately, during the decades of Communist rule, Poland had one national Holocaust narrative. Despite its many Jewish citizens, each with a unique story, and despite the Polish perpetrators and bystanders who were neither helpful nor heroic, there was no priority on critical introspection. This tragic separateness left little room for nuance. Using *Maus* to teach Polish students the history of Jews in Poland was an opportunity to use creative literature as a practice "much closer to the truth by showing various attitudes, from sacrifice and compassion to indifference and betrayal."[29] The experience opened my mind, and my heart, to the personal stories of individual Poles, just as my stories opened their minds to questions they had not known to ask. That does not exempt moral failure, nor does it place blame on future generations: it asks that as teachers we strive to become cultural diplomats, seeking out partners within our shared texts to create interculturally competent citizens of the world.

NOTES

1. https://www.jewishvirtuallibrary.org/poland-virtual-jewish-history-tour
2. Art Spiegelman, *Maus: A Survivor's Tale* (New York: Pantheon Books, 1986).
3. Rachel Farber, *Horseradish: Jewish Roots* (Philadelphia: Self-published, 1981).
4. Ibid., 2.
5. Ibid., 4.
6. For example, using the light bulb joke to insinuate low intelligence in Polish people, as in the following: "How many Poles does it take to change a light bulb? Three—one to hold the bulb and two to turn the ladder."
7. Michael C. Steinlauf, *Bondage to the Dead* (New York: Syracuse University Press, 1997).
8. Hilene Flanzbaum, "Reading the Holocaust: Right Here, Right Now," *Holocaust Studies* 17, no. 1 (Spring 2011): 63–84.
9. Bernhard Schlink and Carol Brown Janeway, *The Reader* (New York: Pantheon Books, 1997).
10. Flanzbaum, "Reading the Holocaust," 78.
11. Ibid., 66.
12. Staub, "The Shoah Goes On," 33.
13. Bernt Wegner, *From Peace to War: Germany, Soviet Russia, and the World, 1939–1941* (New York: Berghahn Books 1997).

14. Lawrence Weschler, "Pig Perplex," *Lingua Franca* 11, no. 5 (July–August 2001) http://linguafranca.mirror.theinfo.org/print/0107/field_notes.html.
15. Spiegelman, *Maus,* 32–35
16. Peter Obst, "Maus by Art Spiegelman." http://www.polishcultureacpc.org.
17. Herman Rosenthal, "CASIMER III THE GREAT" (Polish spelling 'Kazi mierz') http://www.JewishEncylopedia.com
18. See for example: Lida Zessin-Jurek, "Hide and Seek with History-Holocaust Teaching at Polish Schools, Cultures of History Forum," http://cultures-of-history.uni-jena.de; and
    Burton Bollag, "In the Shadow of Auschwitz: Teaching the Holocaust in Poland," https://www.aft.org/sites/default/files/periodicals/bollag_spring1999.
19. Neal Conan, "'MetaMaus': The Story behind Spiegelman's Classic," NPR (October 5, 2011).
20. Łysak, Tomasz. "Contemporary Debates on the Holocaust in Poland: The Reception of Art Spiegelman's 'Graphic Novel'Maus." (2009): 469–479.
21. Jan Tomasz Gross, *Neighbors: The Destruction of the Jewish Community in Jedwabne, Poland* (New York: Penguin Books, 2002).
22. Annie Corrigan, "Michael Uslan: The Value of Comic Books." https://indianapublicmedia.org/arts/comic-books.php
23. https://www.wordswithoutborders.org/article/animal-farm-or-a-short-and-somewhat-political-history-of-comics-in-poland
24. Spiegelman, *Maus*, 146.
25. Ibid., 148.
26. Ibid., 149.
27. Michael Rothberg, "'We Were Talking Jewish'": Art Spiegelman's *Maus* as 'Holocaust' Production," *Contemporary Literature* 35, no. 4 (Winter, 1994), pp. 661–687.
28. Monica Adamczyk-Garbowska, "A New Generation of Voices in Polish Literature," *Prooftexts* 9, no. 3 (1989) 273–287.
29. Ibid., 282.

REFERENCES

Adamczyk-Garbowska, Monica, "A New Generation of Voices in Polish Literature," *Prooftexts* 9, no. 3 (1989): 273–287.
Bollag, Burton, "In the Shadow of Auschwitz: Teaching the Holocaust in Poland," https://www.aft.org/sites/default/files/periodicals/bollag_spring1999.
Conan, Neal, "'MetaMaus': The Story Behind Spiegelman's Classic," NPR (October 5, 2011).
Corrigan, Annie, "Michael Uslan: The Value of Comic books," https://indianapublicmedia.org/arts/comic-books.php
Farber, Rachel, *Horseradish: Jewish Roots* (Philadelphia: Self-published, 1981).

Flanzbaum, Hilene "Reading the Holocaust: Right Here, Right Now," *Holocaust Studies* 17, no. 1 (Spring 2011): 63–84.
Gross, Jan Tomasz, *Neighbors : The Destruction of the Jewish Community in Jedwabne, Poland* (New York: Penguin Books, 2002).
Jewish Virtual Library, jewishvirtuallibrary.org/poland-virtual-jewish-history-tour
Lysak, Tomasz, "Contemporary Debates on the Holocaust in Poland: The Reception of Art Spiegelman's 'graphic novel' '*Maus*,'" *Polin* 21 (2009): 469–479.
Obst, Peter, "Maus by Art Spiegelman," http://www.polishcultureacpc.org.
Rosenthal, Herman "CASIMER III THE GREAT," http://www.JewishEncyclopedia.com
Rothberg, Michael, "We Were Talking Jewish": Art Spiegelman's *Maus* as 'Holocaust' Production," *Contemporary Literature* XXXV, no. 4 (1994): 661–687.
Schlink, Bernhard, *The Reader,* trans. Carol Brown Janeway (New York: Pantheon Books, 1997).
Spiegelman, Art, k*Maus: A Survivor's Tale* (New York: Pantheon Books, 1986).
Staub, Michael, "The Shoah Goes On and On: Remembrance and Representation in Art Spiegelman's Maus," *MELUS* 20, no. 3, History and Memory (Autumn, 1995): 33.
Steinlauf, Michael C., *Bondage to the Dead* (New York: Syracuse University Press, 1997).
Wegner, Bernt, *From Peace to War: Germany, Soviet Russia, and the World, 1939–1941* (New York: Berghahn Books 1997).
Weschler, Lawrence, "Pig Perplex," *Lingua Franca* 11, no. 5 (July–August 2001).
Words without Borders, "Animal Farm or a Short and Somewhat Political History of Comics in Poland, https://www.wordswithoutborders.org/article/animal-farm-or-a-short-and-somewhat-political-history-of-comics-in-poland
Zessin-Jurek, Leda, "Hide and Seek with History-Holocaust Teaching at Polish Schools, Cultures of History Forum," http://cultures-of-history.uni-jena.de

Chapter 4

Germans, Migration, and Holocaust Memory in Contemporary Literature

Agnes C. Mueller

With Holocaust memory moving into greater temporal distance, questions of the commemoration and representation of the Shoah gain renewed urgency. This is especially true in a German context. And while the silence, Holocaust guilt, and repression of earlier postwar decades resulted in somewhat unexpected anti-Semitic acting out in literature—if we think of works by Günter Grass or Bernhard Schlink—as well as elusive involvement with the German past—W. G. Sebald comes to mind[1]—more recent writings from Germany engage Holocaust memory overtly and productively. Narrative fiction by German Jews writing in German demonstrates how different strategies of literary expression (irony, conscious, and self-conscious play with modes of fiction and authenticity, humor) are used creatively to engage and subvert any "normalizing" majority discourses. Analyses of texts by Mirna Funk, Olga Grjasnowa, and Dimitrij Kapitelman show how and why Jews in Germany today, while still taking the Shoah as a crucial point of orientation, are no longer dominated by its past discourses. In some recent texts, Israel has become a point of orientation for the Germans' reconsideration of Holocaust memory. The trajectory where Israel has become an important reference point, in some of the fiction, alludes to larger patterns of migration and war memory. Accordingly, my chapter explores the different ways in which several of these younger writers, born in the early 1980s, have created original and moving ways of expressing their newly emancipated place in the German–Jewish nexus. Untangling some of the conceptual iterations of Holocaust memory sheds light on how and why Israel has become an important point of reference for German Jewish Holocaust discourse, how this connects with migratory discourses, and how this is especially relevant for recent German Jewish fiction. Questions of memory and migration, as they pertain to national, cultural, and religious identities also bring up the knotty question of "cosmopolitanism."

"Cosmopolitan memory" emerges from the "historical link between the memories of the Holocaust and the emergence of a moral consensus about human rights."[2] This is how the term is described by Nathan Sznaider and Daniel Levy in *The Holocaust and Memory in the Global Age*, of 2006. "Cosmopolitanism" here seems to be associated with an explicitly positive way of conceptualizing, or remembering, the specificity of a place or a history. Our ambiguity toward contemporary Holocaust memory might then be wrapped up in this imagination of a "cosmopolitan" memory culture, in that it suggests Jewish particularity as well as the universalizing and normalizing attempts of German memorial culture. Of course, in 2006, "global" or "cosmopolitan" meant different things than it did in 2020, especially as we are trying to cope with a "global" pandemic. And perhaps those terms mean different things entirely for the memory of the Holocaust. Nevertheless, the very term "cosmopolitan memory" does suggest a universal, transnational, and transcultural dimension to memory, and one that might, at first consideration, eclipse the specificity of Jewish memory. But, for Sznaider, Jewish memory is simply an "instantiation" of memory, and hence not at odds with a larger, or "cosmopolitan," dimension.[3] There is, in other words, no hierarchy implied between different memory discourses. Therefore, we may be able to connect "cosmopolitan memory" easily with Michael Rothberg's concept of a "multidirectional memory," a way of remembering the Holocaust that connects it to other discourses of trauma throughout history.[4] For Rothberg, still, the Holocaust is the "original memory." But Jewish memory, and Jewish cosmopolitanism, is still always also a particular memory, and, compared with other memories, perhaps a privileged form of genocide, and trauma and cosmopolitan memories. An example from a 2007 text helps to illustrate this point:

> When Hamas threatened suicide attacks again a few days ago, it caused more worry in Germany than here [in Israel]. My friends wrote emails with the subject line "Are you still alive?"[5]

Thus observes the first-person Russian German Jewish narrator and protagonist named Anja in Lena Gorelik's novel *Hochzeit in Jerusalem* (*Wedding in Jerusalem*, 2007). That Israel's precarious situation might cause more worry in Germany than in Israel itself underlies the narrative. German critics reviewed Gorelik's text favorably, yet it received little attention outside of Germany, probably due to its rather conventional poetic style and the fact that the author was unknown. The plot covers the love story between Anja, and her German and Jewish friend Julian whom she has invited to the wedding of her family in Jerusalem. Julian wants to explore his newly discovered Jewish roots, and Anja wants to help him. The simply constructed story establishes a *locus amoenus* where Anja, the novel's first-person narrator, falls in love with Julian, who had been courting her since their first encounter via an online dating site for Jewish singles. This particular—perhaps unexpected—setting, where Israel is portrayed as an imagined location of healing appears as a place of nearly unambiguous positivity, where the encounters between Julian (who has only recently found out that his father was Jewish) and Anja's Jewish family enrich both protagonists. Curiously, Julian is able to fully realize his love for Anja only after a brief infatuation with an ultra-orthodox Jewish woman whom he meets at the wedding in Jerusalem (hence the title of the novel). It seems that Anja and Julian, who are both depicted as exceedingly well-integrated into German mainstream culture, are only able to explore their love when they are away from Germany, in Israel, a setting that is personified in the figure of Julian's Orthodox love interest.

Such an apparently uncritical and affirmative stance toward Israel might be surprising were it not reflected in several additional contemporary German Jewish texts, mostly by younger Jewish writers who were born after 1970. Born in 1981, Lena Gorelik, exemplifies this generation. The ethnically diverse background of this author is typical especially for this generation of German Jews. Benjamin Stein's *Die Leinwand* (2010), Olga Grjasnowa's *Der Russe ist einer der Birken liebt* (2014), Adriana Altaras's *Doitscha!* (2015), and Oliver Polak's *Der jüdische Patient* (2014) exhibit similar features. Works by these younger German and Jewish writers frequently imagine Israel as a place of desire, serving as a site in which to address traumas of the past. Individual and collective Holocaust memories, as well as other instances of ethnic persecution and genocide are topics of the plots, such as in Grjasnowa's 2014 novel.[6] Israel, in all these texts, is embedded into the narrative as a specific place of reconciliation.

Given the difficult and multiple unsatisfactory history of German Jewish relations and the persistence of anti-Semitic speech in every day contemporary German discourse,[7] how do we evaluate the positive stance that these contemporary texts take toward Israel? How does the Jewish experience of Diaspora, that affected previous generations of Jews, relate to this newfound optimism? In some narratives, the contemporary reality of an Israeli–Palestinian conflict is imagined as a foil that can turn previous trauma into productive or at least reflective experiences, and thus help the German Jewish subject heal, as perhaps most poignantly visible in Gorelik's text. Yet, considering the terror and violence that structure daily life in Israel, this seems paradoxical at the very least. Why and how exactly do culturally and ethnically diverse young German Jewish writers imagine Israel as a place for healing? How does this positive image of Israel bear on collective memories of the Shoah, both in Germany and beyond? How do the diverse, often migratory, fictional accounts of places of terror and mourning connect with the idea of healing and a *locus amoenus*? And, finally, how do these newer texts relate to notions of "cosmopolitan" or "multidirectional" memory?

Olga Grjasnowa's *Gott ist nicht schüchtern* (2017) does not, on the face of it, have anything to do with Jews, or with the Holocaust, and not even with memory of the event. It is a book about the Syrian refugee crisis. Readers are taken on a journey to witness the shocking and violent disruptions of the lives of young actress Amal and of the newly minted medical doctor Hammoudi. The critically acclaimed novel has been praised for its authenticity in describing wartime experiences, but also criticized for its depictions of violence that are deemed voyeuristic. In a recently published interview, Grjasnowa herself describes *Gott ist nicht schüchtern* as a "Jewish book." Taking into consideration the fact that authors' statements about their works are never to be taken at face value, what, if anything, makes this novel a "Jewish book"? This is a central question entangled with many of the issues that I will address below.

Conversely, Dimitrij Kapitelman situates his *Das Lächeln meines unsichtbaren Vaters* (*The Smile of My Invisible Father*; 2016) in Israel. His protagonist's story of a search for Jewish identity as the son of a Jewish father and a non-Jewish Ukrainian mother is the centerpiece of what some critics call a "new genre": the "father-observation." In Kapitelman's autobiographical novel, references to Judaism and to Jewish identity abound, yet Holocaust memory or German Jewish identity are not part of the narrative. We might think that the father in Kapitelman's text, as a Jew of the second generation after the Holocaust, is still an important witness to the memory of the Holocaust trauma, but this particular experience is seemingly absent, while Jewish clichés and stereotypes form the core of the narrative.

I seek to explore the tension between the two different kinds of absences in contemporary German Jewish writing. In one case, we are dealing with the absence of the Jewish experience in a war trauma narrative, and in the other, we see the absence of Holocaust reference in a Jewish experience. Both are absences complicated by specific migration narratives that invoke two very different survivor stories. Yet in both cases, Holocaust memory and the Jewish experience nevertheless function as the primary frames for the narratives.

Let us first consider the assertion of *Gott ist nicht schüchtern* (recently translated into English as *City of Jasmine,* 2019) as a "Jewish book." During the Arab Spring and the later battles around Aleppo of 2014, Amal and Hammoudi, protagonists in Grjasnowa's novel, are both refugees on their way to Berlin. Neither one of the protagonists is Jewish. Both Hammoudi and Amal are well-off, upper middle class, educated, and before the outbreak of the Syrian revolution are leading promising lives that resemble those of many Western, educated, and ambitious twentysomethings. Hammoudi dedicates his training as a surgeon to humanitarian aid after the outbreak of the war. When Amal finally flees Syria on a boat; in his devastated country, even the possibility for flight is a privilege. "It's the middle class who is able to escape—poor people remain behind in refugee camps. Those are the people who at one time had hoped for more from life than just to arrive in a safe country. They had ambitions and a future."[8] Amal's Russian-Syrian family had disintegrated even before the Arab Spring, and Hammoudi connects only to his love interest Claire who is safely settled in Paris, and whom he will never see again. Both protagonists are—at one point, had been—hopeful that the revolution can improve life for many, and thus the process of their flight and migration can be read as evidence of their disillusionment.

Such disillusionment recalls other migratory and traumatic war histories—the largest, of course, the memory of the Holocaust. As Holocaust memory continues to recede, a global or cosmopolitan Holocaust memory emerges that has become a "measure for humanist and universal identifications."[9] It might therefore not be a moral imposition to suggest that different historical atrocities can now cross-reference, build on, and enable each other as Rothberg suggests. In addition, we might consider that major forms and rituals of Holocaust remembrance with their iconic images, structuring narratives, and moral imperatives are now used for the remembrance of other stories of exclusion, expulsion, or genocide—whether we like it or not. Rather than competing for limited space and attention to traumatic historical events, the assertion of a multidirectional memory therefore *allows for* linking different acts of violence. The danger is of course that the specificity of an individual instance of violence and trauma is either denied or in some way minimized when we engage such a comparative perspective. The comparative shades over into the competitive all too easily. I'd like to briefly consider how this might or might not be the case in Grjasnowa's novel.[10] If we take seriously the question of the ability of literary works to move us, then authorial intention or identity are only an extension of the text itself, but not its center.

Amal and Hammoudi arrive in Berlin as refugees, as outsiders, and they also arrive as individuals who have witnessed and experienced atrocities that the residents of their host country, for the most part, did not experience, They are therefore foreigners twice over: once, because of their ethnicity, nationality, and religion, and again because of their experiences of war and violence in a specific political context. This present situation manifests itself in their struggles as they arrive in Berlin. Hammoudi death in an attack on a refugee camp is gut-wrenching considering what he had gone through to even get to Berlin. There is the added recognition that Amal survives and even becomes successful, in part because she built a nuclear family with Yussouf and their adopted daughter Amina. The plot could be considered overwrought of dramatic and gut-wrenching elements.

Yet, Grjasnowa's novel is not kitsch. The ways in which empathetic engagement work here and involve the reader in violence and trauma; while not an overt Holocaust story, nonetheless echoes our expectations of Holocaust memory. The means by which the novel achieves this kind of reader engagement is by employing an exceptionally bare language. The poetic style of this text is characterized by ellipses, by conversations that are not possible, by encounters that we wish could happen but do not. This narrative style, a bare and elliptical prose, emulates the experience of flight and expulsion. Just as individual words are isolated and sentences pared, so is the possibility for connection of the protagonists. The situation of the Syrian refugees thus applies to more than just their own experience when it comes to the ways in which readers perceive the narrative. Additionally, it engages our imagination and expectations relation to the parts that are missing. This, in turn, is a style (and content) that we are familiar with from the known trauma narratives of Holocaust memory. When Amal first becomes aware of the situation in Syria, he "knows exactly what could happen to her, but she doesn't know when and whether it will happen. This uncertainty lets her tremble. Too many people in her surroundings were incarcerated, tortured, or they just disappeared, which results in the same."[11] Therefore, Grjasnowa's novel is not so much a "Jewish book," in that it names or overtly specifies a "typically Jewish" experience of a Holocaust survivor. Yet her narrative style works by engaging absence in a way that alerts us to experiences of trauma, of loss, of violence. And those experiences are familiar to us from reading Holocaust trauma narratives (such as, for example, Primo Levi or Cynthia Ozick). With her unique and specific narrative style, the author invokes Holocaust trauma and memory and may even enhance contemporary readers' empathetic engagements—without being sentimental or reductive.

While the bare and elliptical style in *Gott ist nicht schüchtern* is the crucial and defining element that can narratively link the novel with Holocaust memory, the case is different in Kapitelman's *Das Lächeln meines unsichtbaren Vaters*. Here, we have a chatty, happy, overbearing narrative style and a characterization of the protagonists (the son and the father) as lively, carefree characters. If anything, this text comes across as an anti-Holocaust memoir. Dima, the son of the Jewish father Leonid and a largely absent mother who seems to not be Jewish is not considered Jewish according to the Halakha. Like many Russian Jewish immigrants, he feels Jewish only insofar that this marks him different from Germans, and also different from the Russians of his ancestry. Yet, the son-protagonist is hostile to any serious attempt to define or categorize identity, whether ethnic, religious, or otherwise. As much as the father–son trip to Israel is ostensibly about recovering

Judaism, a Judaism that had to be absent both in the Soviet system as well as in post-unification Germany, it is also about appreciating the idiosyncrasies of the father as a refugee:

> My father's life is marked by the self-evidence of being Jewish. At least that's how he presents himself. He relates all important life decisions to this. When he is doing well, he praises his luck of being Jewish. When he catches a cold, he complains about it. When he sees Dustin Hoffman being brilliant as Rain Man (one of Dad's favorite movies) he never forgets to note that Dustin Hoffman is also a Jew. With religious Judaism, on the other hand, he wants nothing to do. He does not follow traditions. He likes to eat pork with pork sauce. But his funeral is supposed to be at a Jewish cemetery. What exactly it means for my non-religious father to be Jewish that remained invisible to me until this day. The truth is: My father, Leonid Kapitelman, is invisible. And that is why I want to go to Israel with him. Because I have the idea that he will reveal himself in Israel. (My translation).[12]

Jewishness, as it is seen here—albeit just barely seen—is wrapped up entirely with external and stereotypical markers as they might be envisioned by a clueless German non-Jew: Jews don't eat pork (so he defiantly eats extra much); Jews identify with Jewish celebrities, and he complains a lot and is slightly neurotic, like Albert Brooks or Woody Allen. Marked as Jewish, he also rejects being Jewish. Of course, our narrator's father does not reveal himself in Israel— not to the son and not completely. At the end of the trip and of the book, we have only a vague idea of who Leonid is, and in terms of the father–son relationship itself, the excursion might as well have been a mere trip to Kaufland, the made-up name of a German department store, a recurring theme from the narrator's youth. That is to say, apart from a few humorous references, no meaningful encounter with Judaism or Jewish identity takes place and no transformative experiences. The invisibility of the father parallels the invisibility of Jewishness and Judaism. Thus, why is Israel such an important location? And what then, about Jewish identity, does the narrator hope to make visible?

It is important to note that Israel here functions, at least in the imagination of the narrator-son, as a place of desire and positive longing, as in the other texts I refer to in the introduction. Kapitelman's family had wanted to settle in Israel, but chose Germany, as "Wiedergutmachungsjuden,"[13] in the mid-1990s. Perhaps as a result, and due to the absence of a clear place of home and belonging, Israel has become a positive place of identification for the two protagonists. The imagination of Israel as a *locus amoenus* is the theme that is familiar from other German, German-Jewish, and German-Jewish-post Soviet texts. Yet, the explicit wish for some kind of transformation or revelation via travel to the location of Israel is especially pronounced in Kapitelman's narrative, and the overall humor of the equally explicit refusal of such a transformation makes his novel unique. Because, what remains invisible, but nevertheless forms a prevailing theme here, is not actually the father. Despite the enigmatic title of the novel, the father is not invisible. As the permanent subject of the narrator's gaze, he is quite visible. Also apparent are references to Judaism and Jewish life. Although it is viewed skeptically, religion becomes an important frame of reference (even though one that both protagonists reject). Even the Israeli–Palestinian conflict is visible, although not as a tragic or overbearing calamity. Yet, what does indeed remain invisible, and on the face of it has no bearing on the narrative, is the memory of the Holocaust. There are no references specifically engaging Holocaust remembrance. The haphazard comment about the "Wiedergutmachungsjuden" is the only clue that indicates that the Holocaust and German ways of dealing with the past has any bearing on the protagonists.

> We were welcome as make-good-again-jews. That was in 1994, that's since we've been here, but Papa never accepted Germany as his new home. I think it is because he's never been able to forgive the Germans for the Holocaust. He wouldn't put it like this. But when I say it out loud he also doesn't deny it. [. . .] Let's suppose I am wrong and my father has indeed forgiven the Holocaust—he certainly has not forgotten how people with a star could be made invisible.[14]

This text, emphasized in the title, thus metonymically switches the father with the memory of the Holocaust: it is not the father who is invisible, but, to a large extent, he functions as an explicit reference to Holocaust memory. This paragraph provides the only clear and direct reference to Holocaust memory, and of course it is in fact the inability of the father to forgive the Germans, preventing him from accepting Germany as a home, that so clearly constitutes his identity. Visible, instead, in the father's interactions is the legacy of flight, exile, and migration. Because it is due to Leonid's migratory experiences that the protagonists can have such an informed, clear, and untainted view of Israel, Judaism, and religion. The notion of a narrative as "father observation," as one German critic has termed the new genre of this novel (Jens Jessen in *Die Zeit*), is therefore also the observation of the previous generations' struggles with Holocaust memory and the German Jewish past. Indeed, much of the search for identity has to do with the narrator-son, as he seeks to make sense of his own migratory experience as it pertains to his status as a refugee entering the third grade of the local German elementary school:

> I don't know whether some of the third graders from back then are today in Meerane blocking buses with refugees and throwing stones at those needing

help. And I don't want to claim that they regularly buy cheap train tickets to travel to Dresden in order to support [right-wing] Pegida. That would not be fair. But I will not resort to the lie that I would find this surprising. From Dresden and elsewhere we can today feel the same kind of chill that I had felt back then in the class room in Meerane.[15]

This thought, the specificity of being discriminated as a migrant, of course, links Kapitelman's autobiographical narrative to Grjasnowa's new novel. Even though narrative style and diction differ, and the absences in both texts are different, they both evoke a migratory experience, and the memory of the Holocaust.

Less visible, but no less important in its very different recall of Holocaust memory and trauma in contemporary German literature is Katharina Höftmann's popular novel *Der Rabbi und das Böse* (2013), a sequel to the critically somewhat more acclaimed *Die letzte Sünde* (2012). Both crime novels center on the figure of Assaf Rosenthal, a Jewish and Israeli police detective charged with solving crimes in Tel Aviv and Jaffa. The interesting part of the conventional plot is that Höftmann's novels depict all kinds of national, religious, and cultural-ethnic identities: Arabs, Jews, Israeli, Lebanese, but not Germans—surprising given that the novel was written in German, by a German author, for a German audience. There are no references to the Holocaust, the German past, or German–Jewish relations. Israel is here seen as an exotic location that serves as a contemporary backdrop for ethnically motivated and somewhat religiously charged crimes. In spite of its popular appeal, the novel has not been translated into English and does not seem to have found much of an audience either within the German Jewish or the German mainstream. Nevertheless, Katharina Höftmann—born in 1982, the same year as Funk and Grjasnowa—is successful as a journalist and writes for Israeli news outlets while living in Tel Aviv, presumably with a view from the outside of Israeli politics. Her novels, easily categorized as popular literature, underscore the trend in German and non-Jewish literature in which Holocaust memory is neglected, or otherwise absent. The interesting twist here is that this happens even when the plot is set in Israel, and Jewish protagonists are front and center. This is different from Kapitelman's novel in which the German backdrop and German Jewish history are not referenced, and not even remotely evoked. This seems all the more surprising since Höftmann, who lives in Tel Aviv and grew up in East Germany, in the same generation as Kapitelman and Gjasnowa, was presumably confronted with German and German Jewish culture to the same extent as the immigrants, and might have included German Jewish issues in her novel. Yet, her migratory experience is different: as a native and non-Jewish German, she chooses Israel as her new home, apparently without ambivalence. While our assumption might be that the absence of German Jewish history and contexts depends upon the fact that Höftmann is not Jewish, we do not know this for sure—and the following example suggests that the author's religious or cultural identity is not the defining category.

The German Jewish writer Mirna Funk, born in 1981, is known mostly as a lifestyle journalist, and hence her author persona resembles Höftmann's. Yet, Funk's debut novel *Winternähe* (2015) was much more positively and widely reviewed, even winning a literary prize. It is a narrative closely bound to the protagonist's perspective, consistently related from a third-person perspective. It features the protagonist Lola's search for her father Simon who has been emotionally absent for most of her life; yet he is the Jewish parent who gives Lola her religious identity. Additionally, the story traces the fate of the GDR (German Democratic Republic), a theme that generally does not receive much attention in addressing the Holocaust past. Lola observes that in contemporary Berlin there is a "The-Holocaust-is-so-over side" and a "we-must-never-forget-what-happened side"—two opposing perspectives that are unresolvable in their seeming contradiction.[16] Lola identifies as unmistakably Jewish even though she knows that she can't be recognized by the Orthodox community, because her mother is not Jewish: "I grew up with a Jewish family, I experienced their sorrow, I absorbed their trauma, I have visited Israel every year since I was eleven years old, I can make aliyah and become an Israeli citizen, but I can't marry, and my children would be discriminated against and disadvantaged."[17]

The continuing and visible anti-Semitism in the midst of German society, which Lola feels acutely in Berlin, causes her to act out in destructive public gestures—rather than contributing to healing the conflict of her German Jewish identity. In the first scene of the novel, set in Berlin, Lola persecutes a couple for depicting her image with a photoshopped Hitler moustache on social media.

In Berlin, Lola meets, through Tinder, her great love Shlomo, an Israeli. When her life unravels, she decides to visit Shlomo in his hometown Tel Aviv, where her grandfather still lives. Lola arrives in Tel Aviv during the war of the summer 2014, occasioned by the kidnapping and then the murder of three Israeli teenagers by Hamas members. Both Shlomo and Lola are traumatized. When he served in the Israeli army, he had accidentally killed a Palestinian boy and as a result became a peace activist. Shlomo never tells Lola about the boy; she finds out from his friend by coincidence. Both traumas—personal in both cases, but, in Lola's case, evoked by the German Jewish history of anti-Semitism, and in Shlomo's case by the Israeli–Palestinian conflict—induce a particular kind of intimacy for the lovers. At the same time, Lola's inner conflicts leave her suspended in displacement. In Jerusalem, Lola observes on the occasion of viewing the exhibit of the glass booth in which Eichmann sat during his trial, that the Holocaust is neither explicable nor forgivable: "But what happened has happened. If it was terrible then one doesn't have to forgive. To forgive someone is as misguided as it is to forgive oneself" And: "Accept. Live with it. Not forget. Remember."[18] However, Lola can't follow this advice. The days with Shlomo are full of conflict and defined by the terrifying noise of the war. Instead of a *locus amoenus* Israel becomes a *locus terribilis*. When Lola's grandfather suddenly dies in the midst of the war, and Lola learns a secret about the grandmother's past, she travels to Thailand without saying good bye to Shlomo. Thailand is here coded as an exotic other, and also as an alternative to Israel. It almost seems as if Lola wants to live in a Diaspora, but one that frees her from both the German and the German Jewish and Israeli past.

When Lola accompanies Shlomo to the funeral of the Palestinian boy who Israelis killed in retaliation for the Hamas murder of the three young boys, she knows that it is not this particular boy who is on Shlomo's mind, but the boy whom he had accidentally killed. Curiously, the funeral takes place in Jerusalem, the place where both Shlomo and Lola visit as tourists (they disguise themselves as journalists to gain access to the funeral). Jerusalem functions as a dangerous place, whereas Tel Aviv works as a place of love and family. After the funeral, Lola's love for Shlomo is not diminished by her knowledge of his culpability.

With differently coded markers—in a shift from *locus amoenus* to *locus terribilis*—Israel is in Mirna Funk's text clearly signifies a place of terror and violence. As opposed to what happens in Gorelik's novel, the constant fear occasioned by the attacks and loud detonations of the missile defense system is the dominant emotion of Lola's experience in Tel Aviv. Lola associates those emotions with her German Jewish identity, specifically with the German anti-Semitism that resulted from Holocaust guilt,[19] and finally with Shlomo's trauma. What in Gorelik's text is articulated as humorous and trivial, namely that the Germans are more concerned with the war in Israel than the Israelis themselves, is in Funk's novel, the subject of serious consideration. As Funk explains, "For Lola everyone was a potential victim and a potential perpetrator. [. . .] Only those who were not conscious of those contradictions viewed themselves exclusively as victims even though they had turned into perpetrators a long time ago. Lola called this guilt anxiety."[20]

Holocaust memorial culture is thus moved to a non-German, exotically heightened location. Love and desire play an important role in this narrative: Lola's love for Shlomo initially draws her to Israel where she then reflects on her family history and identity. Lola's personal and individual engagement with what she calls "guilt anxiety" only starts in Israel, because of the physical experience of the terror of war. Israel as a place of desire as well as terror or trauma thus becomes, in Funk's period novel, a physical space for the experience of working through the past. The resulting terror, anxiety, and insecurity function as catalysts for confronting trauma, a confrontation that seems impossible in Germany. To write poetry after Auschwitz is thus perhaps no longer barbaric, but in Germany it may well have become increasingly difficult.[21]

The important question as to how art today can remember the Shoah and how this discourse of remembrance might remain relevant for future generations is therefore not only a question of "how" we engage in dealing with the past and memory. Instead, today we must also ask questions of "where" and "from where." What Rothberg and Snyder touch on in their interpretations of a new and changed minority discourse, but do not directly name, points straight to diachronic as well as synchronic questions of a changed locality. Who is speaking, and from which position? For whom? A view from the outside and a view of that which is seen differently allow for a new point of view. Place and migration are experiences that shaped generations differently but that have more recently become conflated with both current and transgenerational memories of war and expulsion. In several German and German Jewish fictional works, we see examples of projections of love and trauma, often via a specific yet imagined place that leads to actual and physical experiences of working through trauma. The imagination of the "other"—images of Jews, images of Israel, images of Germans, or images of Syrian refugees—become a part of the self. The new and changed conditions of the aesthetic in the discourse of Holocaust remembrance, as they are seemingly naively related in Gorelik's novel, indicate new markings in both form and content. Additionally, these texts engage in a complex staging of fiction—fiction and aesthetic difference reference itself. Such an emphasis on place and position in fiction gains its fullest expression in Funk's novel, precisely because it is NOT possible for the German and Jewish protagonist to name and call out the anti-Semitism that she finds herself confronted with in Germany. This is an experience that is recalled by Grjasnowa's Syrian protagonists as well as the narrator-son in Kapitelman. When interpreting this new form of remembrance, it is important to not gloss over textual differences where new media and hybrid forms (as they appear in many of the recent texts) are seen as synonymous with a new, "post-migrant" or "global" narrative. In the texts under discussion here, it is not true that remembrance is taking place at a random location or in a fictional context, since Israel and the Middle East are so clearly presented as the new location for an articulation of trauma.

Funk's novel can be read as the beginning of a new discourse on Holocaust remembrance, imagining Israel as both a place of exotic desire, and a site of productive engagement of horror and *personal* trauma. "Multidirectional memory" is here coalescing into specific, personal, local, and empirical markers of remembrance. The conflations that take place in the fictional texts—for example of Holocaust memory with the trauma of having killed a Palestinian boy—precisely do not relativize the horrors of the Shoah. Neither do they suggest that the memory of the Shoah and the adjacent discourse on anti-Semitism can be easily located in a globalized, post-migrant and multi-cultural society. Rather, the memory and working through—a reconciliation—of what had not been worked through by previous generations is invoked, and this time without attempting a universalizing, Europeanizing, or Orientalizing impulse of the well-rehearsed victim-perpetrator discourse.

The implications of a "cosmopolitan" memory discourse, a term that on the outset seems naïve and counterproductive due to its conflicting stance toward universal Enlightenment emancipation while glossing over local specificity, seems productive in this context. Kwame Anthony Appiah writes that this cosmopolitan memory discourse lies "beneath the facts of globalization."[22] As opposed to the narrower invocation of Israel as a global place of exotic desire and terrible destruction, German Jewish Holocaust remembrance enlists Israel's particularity to advance an emergent discourse that significantly expands on previous notions of empathy. Rather than engaging in a didactic stance—what Adorno tried to refute earlier—these literary texts confront the reader directly with the fictional and raw experiences of a new yet specific location. At stake here is not so much a "post-didactic" memorial culture, as formulated elsewhere, but rather a move to make traumatic memory emotionally and personally accessible. A memorial culture that is changed in this way still includes the strong German desire for a refutation of guilt of the German Nazi past. Yet, in these moments of narrated migratory experiences that translate into emergent cosmopolitan memory, Holocaust memory is now displaced to an attractive and terrible place, a precise place of trauma and desire, to make individual pain and individual guilt accessible. Accessible as these emotions are, too, in Grjasnowa's work. The disillusionment of a generation that sets out to live a positively coded and largely care-free cosmopolitan life—like Amal and Hammoudi—but whose trajectories are cruelly altered and turned into traumatic war and migratory experiences or who is confronted with racism and xenophobia in his supposed host country—the father in Kapitelman—echo the realization that past trauma, in the case of Holocaust memory, is never just past.

NOTES

1. Cf. Agnes C. Mueller, *The Inability to Love: Jews, Gender, and America in Recent German Literature*. Evanston, IL: Northwestern University Press, 2015. Published in German as *Die Unfähigkeit zu lieben. Juden und Antisemitismus in der Gegewartsliteratur*. Würzburg: Königshausen & Neumann, 2017.

2. Levy and Sznaider, *The Holocaust and Memory in a Global Age*. Philadelphia, PA: Temple UP, 2006, 20.

3. As pointed out by Stuart Taberner, "The Possibilities and Pitfalls of a Jewish Cosmopolitanism. Reading Natan Sznaider Through Russian-Jewish Writer Olga Grjasnowa's German-language Novel *Der Russe ist einer der Birken liebt* (*All Russians Love Birch Trees*). *European Review of History: Revue europeenne d'histoire*, 23, nos. 5–6 (2016): 912–930. Here 917.

4. Michael Rothberg, *Multidirectional Memory. Remembering the Holocaust in the Age of Decolonization*. Palo Alto: Stanford University Press, 2009.

5. All translations in this essay are my own. German original: "Als die Hamas vor ein paar Tagen wieder mit Selbstmordattentten drohte, löste das in Deutschland mehr Besorgnis aus als hier. Meine Freunde schrieben mir E-Mails in deren Betreffzeile stand: 'Lebst du noch?'" Gorelik, 163.

6. Rather than offering a "definition" of German Jewish literature, or German Jewish identity, I'd like to point to Dan Miron's astute observations, and think of "contiguity" as a descriptor for "Jewish literature." Dan Miron. *From Continuity to Contiguity: Toward a New Jewish Literary Thinking*. Palo Alto: Stanford UP, 2010. Further texts that fall into a similar paradigm but are not discussed here: Markus Flohr. *Wenn samstags immer Sonntag ist* (2011), and Katja Petrowskaja, *Vielleicht Esther* (2014).

7. For a full discussion of this phenomenon in recent German literature, see my book *The Inability to Love: Jews, Gender, and America in Recent German Literature*. Evanston, IL: Northwestern University Press, 2015. Published in German as *Die Unfähigkeit zu lieben*.

8. German original: "Es ist der Mittelstand der flieht, die Armen bleiben in den Flüchtlingslagern zurück. Es sind Menschen die sich mal mehr erhofft hatten vom leben, als nur in ein sicheres Land zu kommen. Die Ambitionen hatten und eine Zukunft." (Grjasnowa, *Der Russe ist einer*, 242).

9. Cf. Levy and Sznaider, *The Holocaust and Memory*, 21.

10. As a side note, the identity of the author as the granddaughter of a Holocaust survivor does not, in our consideration of the text and the ways in which we read this text, play a role, nor does her assertion that we are to read her novel as a "Jewish book."

11. German original: Amal weiss genau was ihr zustossen könnte, aber sie weiss nicht wann und ob es passieren wird. Diese Ungewissheit lässt sie erzittern. Zuviele Menschen in ihrer Umgebung wurden verhaftet, gefoltert, oder sind einfach verschwunden, was jedoch auf dasselbe hinausläuft." (Grjasnowa, *Der Russe ist einer*, 16).

12. German original: "Das Leben meines Vaters ist vom Selbstverständnis geprägt, ein Jude zu sein. So stellt er sich jedenfalls dar. Die entscheidenden Wendungen in seinem Leben führt er darauf zurück. Geht es ihm prächtig, lobt er sein Judenglück. Fängt er sich eine Erkältung ein, beklagt er es. Wenn er Dustin Hoffman als Rain Man (einer von Papas Lieblingsfilmen) brillieren sieht, vergisst er nie mit stolzem Grinsen anzumerken, dass Dustin Hoffman auch ein Jude sei. Mit dem religiösen Judentum hat er dagegen abgeschlossen. Traditionen befolgt er keine. Schweinefleisch isst

Papa am liebsten mit Schweinefleischsoße. Allerdings soll sein Begräbnis auf einem jüdischen Friedhof stattfinden. Was genau es also für meinen nichtreligiösen Vater bedeutet, Jude zu sein, das blieb für mich bis heute unsichtbar. Die Wahrheit ist: Mein Vater, Leonid Kapitelman, ist unsichtbar. Und deshalb möchte ich nach Israel mit ihm. Weil ich die Vorstellung habe, dass er sich in Israel offenbart." (Kapitelman, 7)

13. The term (literally, "make-good-again-Jews"), also "Kontingentflüchtlinge," refers to Jews that were welcomed into Germany in the early to mid-1990ies as part of a government program after German unification: Any Russian or Easter European "Jews" could immigrate into Germany, which led to an influx of non-German, Eastern European and Russian immigrants. Some of them were Jewish only by designation in their passports, leading to criticism of the program which was later disbanded.

14. German original: "Wir waren willkommene Wiedergutmachungsjuden. Das war 1994, seitdem sind wir hier, dennoch hat Papa Deutschland nie als neue Heimat akzeptiert. Ich glaube, weil er diesem Land den Holocaust nicht verziehen hat. Das sagt er so nicht. Aber wenn ich es ausspreche, verneint er es auch nicht. [. . .] Angenommen, ich irre mich und mein Vater hat Deutschland den Holocaust tatsächlich vergeben – vergessen, wie Menschen mit einem Stern unsichtbar gemacht wurden, hat er ganz gewiss nicht" (Kapitelman, 9).

15. German original: Ich weiß nicht, ob einige der Drittklässler von damals heute in Meerane Busse mit echten Flüchtlingen blockieren und mit Steinen nach Schutzsuchenden werfen. Und ich will auch nicht behaupten, dass sie sich regelmäßig Sachsentickets kaufen und mit der Bahn nach Dresden fahren, um Pegida zu unterstützen. Das wäre unfair. Aber ich werde mir nicht die Lüge abnötigen, dass ich das überraschend fände. Aus Dresden und anderswo weht dieselbe Kälte, die ich schon damals im Meeraner Klassenzimmer spürte (Kapitelmann, 11).

16. Mirna Funk, *Winternähe* (Frankfurt am Main: S. Fischer Verlag, 2015), 21.

17. German original: "Ich bin bei einer jüdischen Familie groß geworden, ich habe ihr Leid erfahren, ihr Trauma aufgenommen, ich habe Israel seit meinem elften Lebensjahr jedes Jahr besucht, ich darf Alija machen und israelische Staatsbürgerin werden, aber ich darf nicht heiraten, und meine Kinder würden diskriminiert und benachteiligt werden." Ibid., 259.

18. German original: "Aber das geschehene ist geschehen. Wenn es furchtbar war dann muss man es nicht verzeihen. Jemandem zu verzeihen ist genauso bescheuert, wie sich selbst zu verzeihen." Instead one is supposed to "Annehmen. Akzeptieren. Damit leben. Nicht vergessen. Sich erinnern." Ibid., 183.

19. Cf. Mueller, *The Inability to Love*, for a full consideration of secondary anti-Semitism in Germany, especially as it pertains to guilt induced anti-Semitism.

20. German orginal: "Für Lola war jeder Mensch ein potentielles Opfer und ein potentieller Täter. . . . Nur jene die sich dieser Widersprüche nicht bewusst waren, sahen sich selbst ausschliesslich als Opfer obwohl sie längst zu Tätern geworden waren. Lola nannte das Schuldangst." Funk, *Winternähe*, 85.

21. Theodor W. Adorno: "Jene Zwanziger Jahre [1962]," *Gesammelte Schriften*, 10, no. 2 (Frankfurt: Suhrkamp, 1977), 506, The discussion on the (mis)understanding of Adorno's quote is best explained here: https://persistentenlightenment.wordpress.com/2013/05/21/poetry-after-auschwitz-what-adorno-didnt-say/

Also, Samuel Weber's translation of the original quotation firms this up: "Cultural criticism finds itself today faced with the final state of the dialectic of culture and barbarism. To write poetry after Auschwitz is barbaric. And this corrodes even the knowledge of why it has become impossible to write poetry today. Absolute reification, which presupposed intellectual progress as one of its elements, is now preparing to absorb the mind entirely. Critical intelligence cannot be equal to this challenge as long as it confines itself to self-satisfied contemplation."

22. Kwame Anthony Appiah, *Cosmopolitanism. Ethics in a World of Strangers.* New York and London: W. W. Norton, 2006, xx.

BIBLIOGRAPHY

Adorno, Theodor W. "Kulturkritik und Gesellschaft." *Gesammelte Schriften* 10, no. 1: *Kulturkritikund Gesellschaft I, "Prismen. Ohne Leitbild."* Frankfurt am Main: Suhrkamp, 1977.
Appiah, Kwame Anthony. *Cosmopolitanism. Ethics in a World of Strangers.* New York/London: W. W. Norton, 2006.
Bernhard, Thomas. *Auslöschung. Ein Zerfall.* Frankfurt am Main: Suhrkamp, 1988.
Flohr, Markus. *Wo samstags immer Sonntag ist.* Munich: Kindler, 2011.
Foer, Jonathan Safran. *Here I Am.* New York: Farrar, Straus & Giroux, 2016.
Funk, Mirna. *Winternähe.* Frankfurt am Main: Fischer, 2015.
Gopnik, Adam. "Blood and Soil. A Historian Returns to the Holocaust." *The New Yorker*, September 21, 2015. http://www.newyorker.com/magazine/2015/09/21/blood-and-soil
Gorelik, Lena. *Hochzeit in Jerusalem.* Munich: SchirmerGraf, 2007.
Grjasnowa, Olga. *Der Russe ist einer der Birken liebt.* Munich: Hanser, 2012.
Grjasnowa, Olga. *Gott ist nicht schüchtern.* Berlin: Aufbau, 2017.
Hammerstein, Katrin and Julie Trappe. *Aufarbeitung der Diktatur – Diktat der Aufarbeitung Normierungsprozesse beim Umgang mit diktatorischer Vergangenheit.* Göttingen: Wallstein, 2009.
Höftmann, Katharina. *Der Rabbi und das Böse.* Berlin: Aufbau, 2013.
Horstkotte, Silke. "'Ich bin woran ich mich erinnere.' Benjamin Steins *Die Leinwand* und der Fall Wilkomirski." In *Der Nationalsozialismus und die Shoah in der deutschsprachigenGegenwartsliteratur.* Hg. Von Torben Fischer, Philipp Hammermeister, und Sven Kramer, 115–132. Amsterdamer Beiträge zur neueren Germanistik 84. Amsterdam, New York: Rodopi, 2014.
Kapitelmann, Dimitri. Das Lächeln meines unsichtbaren Vaters. Munich: Hanser, 2016.
LaCapra, Dominick. *Writing History, Writing Trauma.* Baltimore: Johns Hopkins University Press, 2001.
Levy, Daniel, and Natan Sznaider. *The Holocaust and Memory in a Global Age.* Philadelphia, PA: Temple University Press, 2006.
Margalit, Gilad. "Israel through the Eyes of the West German Press 1947–1967." *Jahrbuch für Antisemitismusforschung* 11 (2002): 235–248.

Miron, Dan. *From Continuity to Contiguity. Toward a New Jewish Literary Thinking.* Stanford: Stanford University Press, 2010.
Mueller, Agnes C. *The Inability to Love: Jews, Gender, and America in Recent German Literature.* Evanston, IL: Northwestern University Press, 2015.
Rothberg, Michael. *Multidirectional Memory. Remembering the Holocaust in the Age of Decolonization.* Stanford: Stanford University Press, 2009.
Seyhan, Azade. *Writing Outside the Nation.* Princeton, NJ: Princeton University Press, 2001.
Stein, Benjamin. Die Leinwand. Munich: Beck, 2010.
Taberner, Stuart. "The Possibilities and Pitfalls of a Jewish Cosmopolitanism. Reading NatanSznaider through Russian-Jewish Writer Olga Grjasnowa's German-language Novel *Der Russe ist einer der Birken liebt* (*All Russians Love Birch Trees*)." *European Review of History: Revue europeenne d'histoire* 23, nos. 5–6 (2016): 912–930.
Wilkomirski, Binyamin. *Fragments. Memories of a Wartime Childhood.* Translated from German by Carol Brown Janeway. Schocken Books 1996.

Chapter 5

The Burden of the Third Generation in Germany
Nora Krug's Belonging: A German Reckons with History and Home

Victoria Aarons

"Who am I in relation to my past," ask Dan Bar-On, Tal Ostrovsky, and Dafna Fromer, in their psychological studies of the lingering effects of the Holocaust on the third generation.[1] This is a complicated question for both the grandchildren of survivors and the descendants of Germans who were adults during the Nazi era and whose participation in the war, two generations later, remains the source of fraught deflection and uncertain speculation. For the grandchildren of those Germans who directly experienced National Socialism, in particular, the relational question opens itself up to uncertainties regarding the degree and extent of their relatives' involvement in the war: perpetrator, collaborator, bystander, resister. Such reckoning is, as Bar-On and others suggest, "a painful process because of the dialectical tension within memory and between memory and history."[2] Competing or absent memories, information lost or withheld, the denials and contortions of agency, and a re-envisioning or dismantling of history all destabilize one's perceived relation to the past. Such a process of identity-formation set within the circumferences of familial and cultural antecedents is thrown off balance by the position from which one views the past: one's responsibility to and for that history; one's perceived guilt and culpability; and one's inherited obligations to the past, and the ruptures and fault-lines in one's unavoidable legacy. As third-generation German scholar Oliver Fuchs posits, one's family history cannot be severed from place of origin and thus, for postwar generations, family histories are shaped by and "inextricably linked to national history and Germany's role during WWII."[3] In other words, one cannot separate oneself conceptually and affectively from place and from the identifying structures and complexion of the homeland, that is, the formative premises and the signifying structures upon which its foundation rests.

Questions regarding family histories, then, the position and involvement of individual family members and the possible—even likely—complicity in, or at the very least, indifference toward the events of the Holocaust as they unfolded, have implications for Germany's national character, the moral fiber of the homeland, as well as for those individuals involved and their descendants. Such a legacy is thus situated uneasily within twin narratives: family stories set against the larger encompassing and looming narrative of Germany's social, cultural, and political disposition leading up to, during, and after the war. The inheritance of the past, then, has dual and potentially dueling implications for postwar generations of Germans attempting to come to terms with their place in and a reckoning of that history. As Susanne Vees-Gulani suggests, "Revisiting the Nazi past and the Second World War in both the former East and West Germany has become an important basis for finding and defining a new national identity . . . as well as for establishing a personal identity. . . . Germans of all generations emphasize that the Nazi era is inseparable both from their family histories and from German society as a whole."[4] The unsettling question of ownership, of one's relation and obligation to the past and to place, *the* question of identity and accountability, is taken up by German-American writer Nora Krug in the 2018 third-generation graphic memoir, *Belonging: A German Reckons with History and Home*, the account of her apprehensive search for answers to questions regarding her relatives' involvement in German National Socialism, as well as the weight of her own place in that familial and cultural narrative. For, as Krug asks, "How do you know who you are, if you don't understand where you came from?"[5]

Generational attitudes and public discourses regarding Germany's identity and accountability to its genocidal past have changed as we move farther and farther in time from Germany's defeat, the end of the war, the liberation of the concentration camps, the numbers of victims tallied, and the extent and specificity of war crimes calculated. Ironically, as the temporal experience grows more distant, subsequent generations move closer to a reckoning of Germany's role in the war, encountering more directly the burden of Germany's obligation to remembrance and reparation. The German cultural and national narrative has shifted as subsequent generations respond to Germany's political and cultural ethos during and in the aftermath of the Holocaust and World War II. Such shifting generational responses both inform and are informed by public discourses about the war and the extent to which accountability for the actions and attitudes of the war generation is transferred intergenerationally. Such mutations in the ways in which World War II and the Holocaust are approached in public memory are complicated by the many fluctuating generational, cultural, and political influences brought to bear on collective cultural affect. Furthermore, the shift in public consciousness in Germany in the evolving generations since the war has changed the way memory and forms of remembrance are talked about. As Bernhard Giesen suggests:

> [The] shift to a public discourse about the Holocaust was closely associated with a change in the construction of memories. The first postwar generation still had immediate experiences and strong personal memories. . . . . They did not need an explicit discourse to revive and reconstruct the Nazi past. . . . Recalling the past was not their problem—it was always lingering, haunting their memories. These personal memories were missing in the new generation; they had to rely on an elaborate public discourse to cope with the Nazi past. Hence it was not only the conflict between generations but also a shift from personal memories, silenced or reconstructed . . . to the remembrance of the past by public discourse carried by those who did not take part and could not refer to personal memories.[6]

Despite the increasingly remote access to memories and direct testimonies of the war years, subsequent generations, as they proliferate from the point of traumatic origin, are haunted still by the specter of the war, the absent presence of that defining historical moment. Significantly, the shaping and transmission of memory is tied to collective, institutionalized expressions of guilt and accountability but also to the way in which memories were and continue to be confronted in domestic space, resulting in disruptions and disjunctions between institutional and personal memory.

Such a vacillation of public attitudes toward Germany's involvement in the National Socialist agenda exhibits patterns of retreat and retrieval. As Lars Rensmann explains, "In the immediate postwar period public consciousness had normalized its past as simply an unfortunate episode in the history of a proud nation."[7] The majority, as Jeffrey Herf suggests, "wished to avoid truths about the country's criminal past," and thus the burden of responsibility and an accounting of the heinousness of crimes committed were repressed, deflected, denied, and, effectively, silenced, at least in the short term.[8] In this way, the first generation, "the silent generation," came to define the immediate response to the war.[9] The initial un-speakability in the public consciousness of crimes committed by the Third Reich and "the silencing of the past after 1945," as Giesen suggests, eventually shifted to a "new narrative of the collective guilt of an entire generation [that] changed the notion of guilt," an evolving narrative that transcended generations and is now firmly cemented in Germany's institutional memory.[10] A narrative of collective guilt, the collective weight of Germany's complicity and moral obligations, has implications for a contemporary generation of Germans for whom, as Fuchs, speaking from his own third-generation position, argues, the effects of war "did not end its reign with those who were directly exposed to and involved with the Nazis."[11] For a contemporary generation twice removed from the immediacy of the war, the disposition and character of Germany's war years are tied up in their sense of identity and place, a precarious position given the legacy bequeathed to them and the generations of silence and resistance that preceded them. Here past, present, and future uneasily coalesce, the one a window through which to view the other. In response to this uneasy union, as Fuchs argues, "an awareness of our own sense of existence in relation to the past is essential for the development of a secure feeling of identity, belonging, and safety in the present," without which "a distinct sense of dislocation seems to exist . . . that perpetuates the disturbing relationship with that part of our history."[12] Such generational anxiety in response to the persistent and unresolved echoes of the past set against the instability of the contemporary moment in Germany, as well as prospects for the future, shapes Nora Krug's graphic memoir, as the author/illustrator attempts to comprehend her own haunted identity as a grandchild of those who participated in National Socialism.

The German title of Krug's graphic memoir is *Heimat*, the German word for home or homeland. Krug translates Heimat as *Belonging* in the English edition of the book, a significant turn of phrase signaling a possible shift in the syntactic function and extended meaning of the term. Early in the memoir Krug introduces the definition of Heimat from the German Brockhaus encyclopedia, defined, in part, as "the concept of an imaginarily developed, or actual landscape or location, with which a person . . . associates an immediate sense of familiarity . . . [an] experience imparted across generations, through family and other institutions, or through political ideologies . . . [T]he place . . . that largely shapes identity, character, mentality, and worldviews."[13] Heimat is an important concept for Krug, one that she grapples with throughout the memoir. While Heimat represents for her a kind of longing, a connection to the embrace of the familiar, it is also a charged and thus unstable construct largely because of its associations. The implications of the term for Krug are complicated by the political and ideological resonances and by its appropriation by National Socialist ideology and propaganda as a justification for xenophobia, expulsion, and extermination.

Significantly, then, Krug defines the term *Heimat* as *belonging* for the title of the English version of the memoir in order to extend its defining properties and establish her complex relation to her imagined and actual place of origin. Belonging implies both being of a certain time and place and a longing for, a return to, the stability and familiarity of that place and time. Belonging, thus straddles both past and present—belonging *to* as well as *reconstructing* place, a *return*—and establishes the foundational ground upon which identity is shaped. The origins of the prefix "be"—"about, around, on all sides"—suggest the all-encompassing aspect of *belonging*, that which surrounds one, containing, defining, inescapable. Throughout the memoir, Krug both seeks and rejects this notion of Heimat, ultimately redefining and thus reaffirming it as something that must be repudiated before it can be reconstructed and reimagined. As Krug belatedly comes to acknowledge, "Heimat can only be found again in memory, that it is something that only begins to exist once you've lost it."[14] Krug thus reconstructs the homeland as it emerges through images, photographs, reproductions of artifacts, and imprints, a montage of impressions that erect the blueprint of Germany's past. Her graphic narrative is, in large part, an attempt to reconcile her nagging sense of shame and longing, both evoked by the idea of homeland. She attempts to excise her sense of "German guilt," as she puts it, persistent feelings of guilt quieted neither by leaving Germany nor by marrying a Jewish man. It is against this figurative and literal landscape that Krug engages the implications and liabilities of homeland, both personally and collectively. Her memoir evokes the cultural and ideological shape of the past against an entrenched "coalition of silence," and her perceived moral inheritance of Germany's monstrous history and the indelible imprint of the Heimat on her own struggling identity.[15]

Belonging thus tells the story of Krug's attempt to piece together the fragments of her relatives' lives during the war in order to locate her own family narrative in the larger context of Germany's history under the Third Reich. Born in 1977 in Karlsruhe, a city in southwestern Germany, Krug knew little of her grandparents' histories. Her paternal grandparents died before she was born, and, while as a young child, she knew her maternal grandparents, their wartime past was not part of the family narrative. As she acknowledges, "My mother didn't talk about them much, and when she did, it was with the kind of weariness one feels when having to revisit a subject thought or talked about too many times before. In my mind, a family began with one's parents and ended with oneself," a kind of insularity that prevented trespass.[16] The past, for Krug, was enshrouded in a complicit intergenerational obfuscation. Only after her maternal grandparents' deaths can Krug piece together, though unevenly, the basic narrative of their lives. Reconstructing the past is, for Krug, an arduous process because of what is concealed in memory or elided from the family narrative. The gaps in the narrative invite questions regarding the extent of her grandfathers' involvement in Nazism, as well as that of the uncle she never knew, her father's older brother who was shot down over Italy, and for whom, disconcertingly, her father was named.

Krug's graphic memoir thus narrates her attempts to break through the silence and the "postwar family fantasy."[17] As Krug reveals in an interview, "*Belonging* is as much about my own family history in the Second World War as it is an attempt of looking for my own cultural identity—what it means to be a German growing up after the war."[18] The graphic memoir (both narrated and illustrated by Krug) is in many ways a post-memory narrative of return, an attempt, as she puts it, to find her way back, to transport herself back in time and place in order to gather the missing pieces of her family narrative and to reckon with her own unshakable sense of inherited guilt and accountability for the actions of her relatives but also for the country that formed her. As Krug acknowledges, "the atrocities my country committed during World War II cast a long shadow all throughout my entire childhood, and my years as a teenager were accompanied by a tremendous sense of inherited guilt. . . . By the time I learned about the Holocaust in school, around the age of 12 or 13, all my grandparents had died, and I had missed the chance to ask them directly about their lives within the Nazi regime."[19]

Despite the Holocaust education delivered in the school curricula when Krug was growing up in Germany—including wartime documents, photographs, films, and trips to concentration camps—there were decipherable gaps in her understanding of the events. For the young Krug, and, by implication, others of her generation, the Holocaust was a vague, if sinister, shadow concealed in remote history, an event that happened in the distant, unapproachable past. As Krug explains, "My generation had a rigorous war and Holocaust education . . . . It was good and very important, but we learned [broad] facts, not what went on in our home towns. Most Germans of my generation know fairly little about what happened in their own families."[20] Krug's knowledge of the period, like others of her generation—a generation distanced enough from the events but not so removed that they were unaware of the outline of the legacy passed down from their grandparents' generation—as she describes it, was mediated through, filtered through, an institutionalized set of requirements that subverted discussions of incidents relating to individual towns and communities. Her introduction to Nazism, to the Holocaust, in particular, was primarily academic, abstract platitudes about war, the stuff of school exercises.

Her generation, as she explains, was exposed to a formal education that offered facts and lessons about German history: the rise to power of the Third Reich; the catalog of battles waged; the dangers of Nazi propaganda; and the process of *Vergangenheitsbewältigung*, a "coming to terms" with one's political past—all, as she writes, "evidence of our collective guilt."[21] But, as Krug explains, what was fundamentally lacking in her generations' knowledge of that particular era was important information about their grandparents, the visage of their relatives within the abstractions and generalizations of war. As Krug puts it in an interview with *The Guardian*, "What I found problematic about the way in which we were taught at school about the Holocaust and the war was that it conveyed a very generalizing sense of guilt. You learned about the facts, but you weren't encouraged to research what happened in your own city, or your own family."[22] The abstractions of collective guilt seem to leave no space for the adequate expression of personal guilt, of individualized, extended, and inherited culpability and shame that "entangles" her and that leaves Krug with "a nagging sense of unease."[23] She seeks a personal connection: a face and a name, without which her own sense of identity was unstable, since, as she admits, "I am irrevocably intertwined with people and with places, with stories and with histories . . . the unescapability of who we are."[24] What Krug thus desires most, and that takes on in her memoir an urgency and immediacy of symptomatic requisite, is to reconstruct the family narrative: the missing pieces of her own felt history. "What does it take to reconstruct a fractured family?" she wonders; "Who would we be as a family if the war had never happened?"[25]

The caesura that existed, then, between the broad strokes of Germany's history that Krug learned in the public forum and what was gleaned in the domestic space of the family created a conspicuous absence, a complicit secrecy and silence that ran alongside her more formal education. Neither the Holocaust nor Germany's orchestration of events and involvement in the war were discussed directly in her home during her years growing up. Both her parents were born immediately after the war, in 1946, and their own family histories were only sketchily drawn. Their own knowledge of their parents' involvement was murky. Krug's paternal grandfather died when her father was a young boy, and her father's older brother who fought for the homeland died before her father's birth. Furthermore, Krug's father was estranged from his only other sibling, his older sister, from whom he might have gathered some information about the family's past. Because Krug's father "never knew much about his father, or his grandparents, or, in fact, anyone else in his family . . . [n]o shared family narrative was delivered from father to son to grandson, told over and over through generations."[26] This unknowing, as well as the burrowed sense of guilt and shame, was handed down intergenerationally. As Krug says of her childhood, "the war was present but unacknowledged," a kind of disruption in the unspooling of history, a time in which "something had once gone horribly wrong" but well "before my parents were born."[27] For the young child growing up in Germany two generations since the war, as Krug admits, the Jews "didn't exist outside of the Bible . . . like a long-extinct species."[28] In fact, as her father acknowledges, there was no collective memory of the prewar Jewish population of Külsheim, his home town in Germany. For Krug, the Holocaust was inaccessible, and yet carried with it a sense of continuing shame and guarded discomfort, dangerous and taboo, conscious and unconscious, and only warily spoken of, "something embarrassing to talk about, something that grown-ups discussed in whispers."[29] The secret and forbidden subject of Germany's involvement in the war, then, was compounded by the silence in her own family and by the "unhealed wounds," as she titles one of the chapters in her memoir, resulting from this past history.[30]

Thus Krug, in an attempt to "move beyond the abstract shame," returns to the origins of that time and place in order to "ask those questions that are really difficult to ask. . . . To return . . . go back to the beginning, follow the bread crumbs, and hope they'll lead the way home."[31] What she ultimately discovers, after delving through archives and government records, sorting through artifacts, testimonies, photographs, and family documents, and conducting interviews with those who were present at the time or had some knowledge of the events and people involved, is that both her maternal and paternal grandfathers were members of the Nazi Party and that her uncle, her father's older brother, died in 1944 at the age of 18 fighting for the Nazis. But even this unwelcome knowledge does not provide Krug with the information she really wants to know: the motivations for her young uncle's anti-Semitism and fervor for the homeland; the extent of her maternal grandfather's sympathies toward, knowledge of, and involvement in anti-Semitic measures; and thus—even more pronounced—the nature of her own legacy of "inherited sin . . . of having to bear the consequences of another generation's actions"[32] What she really wants to know, that is, are the answers that might exonerate her or that might pave the way to some sort of exculpation of her relatives' activities and thus her own expiation for the shame she carries with her, and the fear, though unarticulated, but finally exposed by her aunt's unwelcome question, "What would you do" under similar circumstances?[33]

But it is only from a temporal and geographical distance that Krug can begin to retrieve such knowledge and hope to come to terms with the past and its continuing impact on her own identity. Krug's memoir begins not in the country of her birth, but rather in New York City. It is only when Krug leaves the contours of the homeland that she can critically assess her place against the backdrop of Germany's burdened past. Significantly, it is only after relocating to America, establishing herself professionally, and marrying into a Jewish family that she is distant enough to confront the history she left behind. Having left Germany, Krug explains in an interview, makes her all the more aware of her German heritage:

> I never would have written this book if I hadn't left Germany. During my 17 years living abroad [first in the UK and then in the US], I felt more German than ever before. As a German living among non-Germans, I realized I would always be as much an individual as a representative of my country and therefore my country's history. I was often confronted with negative stereotypes towards German cultural identity, but I was also asked sincere questions about my family's past I didn't know how to answer. Over the years, I felt a growing urge to tackle my country's history in a new way. I realized that to overcome

the collective, abstract shame I had grown into as a German two generations after the war. . . . I needed to go back and ask questions about my family, my hometown, those questions I was too unreflective as a child and too afraid as a teenager to ask.[34]

Removal from the Heimat, paradoxically reifies, solidifies, and calls attention to Krug's German-ness, her ancestry and sense of difference, her otherness. Instead of seeing herself as a German in Germany, she views herself as a German outside of Germany. Her sense of guilt is made less abstract and more tangible a burden as she comes to see herself through the eyes of others.

Living abroad brings Krug face-to-face with reminders of Germany's horrendous past. It is only when she is away from Germany that she is confronted by a Holocaust survivor who, in a troubling way, moves to absolve her: "That was a long time ago," the woman offers, "I'm sure things have changed."[35] To make emphatic the way in which the past follows her, transcending time and space, Krug draws the topography of New York as a Holocaust cityscape where water towers atop buildings resemble guard turrets, rooftop foliage takes on the shape of crematoria flames emblazoned with Nazi insignia, and the clouds overhanging the fiery skyline are seared red. This is how she represents the world she inhabits. Krug confronts such reminders of Germany's of shameful history because of her deeply felt sense of inherited culpability embodied in being German; as she uncomfortably acknowledges, "history was in our blood . . . shame in our genes."[36] At the same time, there is a kind of relief in comeuppance that accompanies her self-critical posture. The willing embrace of collective guilt and shame may not exonerate her from her forbears' participation in Germany's monstrous past; however, it positions her to legitimately and authentically take it on. In doing so, she can censure and criminalize that history, thus making it marginally "easier to navigate [her] shame."[37]

Because of her sense of difference, and her connection to her Heimat, she sees the landscape through the filter of how others regard her homeland. In the United States, she feels surrounded by constant reminders of her German-ness by others who call her attention to it, so much so that, as she admits "after all these years, I still try to hide my accent": unwelcome stereotypes of Germans on American television; media depictions of Germany as the "homeland of Schadenfreude"; unsolicited warnings about German culture, "the land of the Huns and the Nazis"; assumptions of consanguinity when confronted by anti-Semitic insinuations; even the apologetic gestures of acquaintances who point to their own country's ignominious histories.[38] In other words, being out of the German context in which she was raised shifts the possibilities of a critical gaze. The "immediate sense of familiarity," or belonging, with which one associates the homeland, once out of the place of origin, is undermined by an uncanny, un-Heimat, sense of unfamiliarity, of difference, her attachment to the homeland destabilized by the reality of its history. As she says, "the longer I've lived away from Germany, the more elusive my idea of my identity becomes. My Heimat is an echo . . . an unrecognizable reverberation."[39] Repositioning herself spatially and in place provides an aperture through which she can see her homeland as it exists without her and as it is perceived through the gaze of others. The aperture through which she now views the homeland both distorts and compresses historical time, its portal telescopic, widening and magnifying, and, at the same time, myopic, collapsing and reducing her sight to a focal pinpoint. The focus converges on specific members of her own family, her relation to her family history, and her position in that extended narrative.

Place matters. That is, place—generational, geographical, temporal, and relational—influences and directs the critical gaze, framing the composition, as it is both interiorly and externally shaped, of the past. As Hilene Flanzbaum suggests, "where you are standing and *when* you are standing there makes all the difference."[40] In other words, place, the position from which one views the events of the past, "where you are standing," shapes not only one's perception of those events but also the perspective and interpretation of them. And it does so because positioning oneself in relation to the past becomes a means of locating and solidifying one's place in the world that one inhabits—the subjective, interior space, and the constraining and restraining structures of the external landscape. Place, in this context, suggests the position from which the gaze originates, but also the position from which, and the distance to which, it extends.

The parameters of place, for Krug, are crucial in two centrally defining ways: the original place of origin (the place to which she looks back) and the place from which she is writing. When place shifts for Krug, it positions her in a different relation to the original context, at once more expansive and more constricted. The spatial shift occasions the shift in temporality. Both the spatial and the temporal distance—"where you are standing and *when* you are standing there"—consort together for Krug to open the text of the past, to "recalibrate," as she says "what we believe to be our place in the world."[41] Krug's newly invented idea of her place in the world speaks to a generation twice removed, coming of age at a moment in history that will witness the end of direct eyewitnesses, of those who, as she says, "voted for Adolf Hitler. They chose him as their leader out of their own free will. To understand how this could happen, we need to understand their motives."[42] Krug writes, then, in a period of transition, a generation in the process of coming to terms with Germany's collective guilt, of repositioning and reassessing its relation to Germany's Nazi past and to the Holocaust. Thus, hers is an important generation to consider, one emerging at a critical moment in history. As Rensmann suggests,

> For understanding motivational structures and the processing of collective guilt in Germany, the most interesting generational cohort is the 'third generation' of West Germans (those born 1970 or after). Members of this generation are the first who grew up in a substantially democratized environment in which the Holocaust and national guilt had become relevant issues in the public sphere.[43]

The third generation, having reopened the conversation about the war, is in a position to approach the Holocaust and Germany's extended culpability with a kind of institutional sanction and authorization that was not as readily available to their parents who were much closer in proximity to the events but for whom the events of the recent past were both silent and silenced.

Writing against the silence of past generations, then, Krug's pursuit of her grandparents' and her uncle's participation in the war becomes a process of uncovering and peeling back the "infinite layers" of concealment and reticence, "each one exposing what was there before."[44] These tensions shape her return narrative, both in terms of text and image. Krug opens her graphic memoir with the metaphor of the unhealed wound, a wound covered, hidden, but one that leaves a scar nonetheless. The opening image in the book is a drawing of the German manufactured Hansaplast, a bandage that she associates with her childhood and her mother's nurturing care, "so reliable that it won't come off until your wound has fully healed . . . the most tenacious bandage on the planet, and it hurts when you tear it off to look at our scar."[45] While concealed, the scar remains. The wounds of the past, Krug implies, while determinedly sutured by time and evasion, nonetheless remain embodied on subsequent generations who have inherited that legacy.

The generational narrative as it extends beyond the war years is an important frame within which to explore the current position of the third generation and to understand the ambivalences and exigencies that give rise to Krug's attempt, as she explains it, to "understand the meaning of my history" and thus to know "where I belong. . . . Geographically. Historically. Genetically."[46] Krug and others of her generation have, as I've noted, grown up at a pivotal time in history, a time in which institutionalized acknowledgment of the collective guilt of the nation informs the public consciousness.[47] The current generational response to Germany's Nazi past is an outgrowth of the mutating responses to the Holocaust in Germany since the end of the war, a time that has increasingly invited collective and individual expression. Since 1945, postwar German culture has responded to the notion of *Vergangenheitsbewältigung*, a process of coping with or working through the past. While the generational narrative is, by necessity, reductive and overly simplified, it suggests important stages in the reckoning with the reality that has defined Germany arguably since 1930, with the rise of Nazism and the traumatic fallout and imprint on subsequent generations. The evolution involving first, second, and third-generational responses to the Holocaust, and its aftershocks situates the position of the current generation against the backdrop of the fluctuations and mounting tensions between distance and proximity.

While one wants to avoid making the kinds of sweeping generalizations that prevent sensitive readings of the complexities, contentions, and disparities in the generational attitudes and discourses in Germany about the Holocaust, the generational narrative, as it moves from the immediate aftermath of war to the early decades of the twenty-first century, reflects shifting patterns of direction from which Germany's past is viewed. Such shifts point to a move from evasion and denial to an incrementally more open acknowledgment of Germany's accountability. This changing attitude may, in fact, have something to do with temporal and affective distance, that is, one's dispositional and logistical relation to the events. After all, as Rensmann points out, the current generation in Germany is, "more distant from the past and their grandparents' potential personal involvement in the Nazi regime" and thus might be thought to have fewer personal claims to that history.[48] As such, the position from which the country's Nazi past is viewed and navigated by the grandchildren of those who were there, in that place and time, provides a less torturous route, if not less complicated, to censure, to an interrogation of the past, and, as Krug writes, to "dismantling history and our memory of it . . . to continue asking detailed and uncomfortable questions . . . to understand and stand up to the responsibility we have a carriers of our countries' pasts."[49]

It need not be said that this evolving attitude is not true for all Germans of Krug's generation. What does seem apparent in the literature and in various studies of third-generation Germans, however, is that, as Fuchs and others have argued, "Germany's WWII involvement remains to have a wounding effect on the grandchildren of the war generation."[50] These "young Germans," as Fuchs contends, continue to respond to the wounds of history by experiencing "a distinct disconnection within their identities . . . years after the end of the War."[51] As Krug acknowledges,

> I grew up feeling culturally disoriented because the war had such a major impact on our understanding of who we are. It's a feeling that hasn't gone away for Germans of my generation. Even though I was aware of this feeling growing up I didn't understand what I could do as an individual to address the feeling of paralysis and collective guilt, which I felt stood in the way of my taking responsibility and fully facing my country's past.[52]

Identity is inextricably linked to place and thus this "disconnection within their identities," as Fuchs puts it, would seem to be, in part, a response to the public/private dichotomy: the emergence of public discourses about Germany's complicity in the Holocaust set against the absence of disclosure regarding individual family involvement in the war.

This uneasy tension is especially problematic for those third-generation Germans like Krug, who, as she puts it, feel obligated to "take responsibility for our country's atrocious actions . . . who believe we need to continue to talk about our past and confront our country's atrocities," a generation who is torn between their own nostalgic memories of home and the realities of Germany's participation in genocide.[53] This is thus a confusing time to come to terms with the past because of the caesura between public remembrance and closeted family memories. As Vees-Gulani and Cohen-Pfister explain, "Since 1945, discussion . . . has transpired in a web of dichotomies: silence and speaking, guilt and responsibility, official discourses and family conversations, historical facts and individual memory."[54] Such tensions, contradictions, inconsistencies, and gaps in the narratives of culpability, participation, and responsibility complicate the transmission of memory but also subvert the very process of *Vergangenheitsbewältigung*, of coming to terms with the past that would seem to define the extended period since the end of the war. If as Ingrid Laurien points out, "[s]ince the end of the Second World War, Germans have been seeing the foundation of their identity in their shared historical responsibility for the atrocities of National Socialism and the Holocaust as well as for the Second World War," what, then, is the ethical measure of a generation's extended culpability?[55] How do generations locate their place in the legacy of the past, a legacy that threatens to sever one's identity from place of origin, "the war," as Krug says, "deeply buried in me"?[56]

By all accounts, the initial response in the direct aftermath of war by the first generation, that is, the generation that experienced the war and to one extent or another participated in it, was disturbingly labyrinthine, an amalgam of denial, of guilt, of fear of reprisal, and of shameful and thus repressed memories. Thus, there was no consistent national narrative of accountability in response to the war, to the harboring of anti-Semitism, and, in particular, to the Holocaust. There was, in the aftermath of the war, as Herf points out, a "marginalization of the Holocaust" in public discourse: "even within the framework of the Nuremberg war crimes' trials, the Jewish catastrophe did not occupy center stage in the Allied, and moreover, the German public memory of World War II."[57] Thus, there existed a wall of silence that was less a matter of forgetting than a mechanism of deflection and diversion of the tenor of the times and the atrocities committed. For the disposition of the times reflected something deeply embedded, ingrained in the character of the population, something "unsettling," as Krug poses, unspoken: anti-Semitic, xenophobic, malignant.[58] The disposition of character, as Krug fears, is not defined by political exigency. In other words, the Holocaust was a product, she suggests, of corrupt and barbarous character among the people of Germany, and thus may be suppressed upon defeat, but not necessarily eradicated. Krug, early on in the memoir, quotes from the 1945 US War Department training film delivered to the US troops: "It can happen again . . . . The German lust for conquest is not dead. Trust none of them."[59] Such a prelude to the narrative that follows establishes a haunting, prescient frame for the book's conclusion and its reference to the rise of neo-fascism and the new right in contemporary Germany.

The historical and political reality of the situation leading up to the Holocaust, as Gertrud Hardtmann argues, involved and depended on a population predisposed and susceptible to anti-Semitic Nazi propaganda and directives as early as 1933. Indeed, as Hardtmann contends, "Only a few Germans resisted. . . . What started in the neighborhood, in the housing area, in the village, and in the city ended in Auschwitz."[60] What was known but cloaked in silence "was not passed on openly in the family narration. . . . Even if National Socialism was described in the families, the Holocaust was not mentioned. Instead, stories of everyday life during the war were told. German children relying only on family narration for their knowledge of National Socialism would have had a fragmentary and deceiving, and thus false, picture."[61] The years in the wake of the war were defined by an absence of articulated agency, a defining "coalition of silence," as Giesen suggests, in which "very few spoke even of their responsibility as bystanders, collaborators, and party members with respect to the Holocaust."[62] This in itself was a failure of character. But if it was a "coalition of silence," it was also a "communicative silence," one passed on to subsequent generations, a framework and structure in which to contextualize, to deflect and circumvent the proximate realities of the Holocaust.[63]

Such a perceptible silence created, then, a gap in the narrative of accountability, as Giesen contends, an acknowledgment of

> the unspeakable or inconceivable horror, the dark abyss into which the German nation had been precipitating. There was no way of telling a story about how it could have happened. Nobody could bear to look at the victims. All those who had devoted years of their lives to a movement whose members had to consider themselves as collaborators in a mass murder could not repair their ruined moral identity even if they had been ready to confess their guilt.[64]

In other words, the war generation set the stage for the fraught relation between an identity politics of collective denial and individual identity formation that had to adopt a pose of denial while feeling a protuberance beneath it. The failure to confront the atrocities of the immediate past in the national discourse seems to mirror the silence within individual families, the one reinforcing and laying claim to the other. As Fuchs proposes, the war generation essentially buried the narrative: "thereby setting the stage for the legacies of silence that have been affecting subsequent generations of Germans ever since."[65] The mutually reinforcing coalition of silence generated in the wake of the war thus was transmitted to the second generation, the children of those who lived under the Nazi regime and who came of age in the midst of this ambivalence created by the presence of such a deeply entrenched absence.

The second generation, those born at the end of the war or in the years immediately following Germany's defeat, appears collectively to be divided in terms of their reaction to the silence that was beginning to give way to more public exposure. Based on psychological studies of generational responses, Fuchs and others found that "the second generation, born during or shortly after the war, were exposed to disturbing, erratic, and destructive behaviors on the part of their parents."[66] The reaction to such behaviors, even if—or especially if—cloaked in a veil of silence, as Fuchs contends, resulted in a complex set of symptoms and coping mechanisms among the children of the war generation. "Attempting to defend against" the psychological trauma caused by their parents' repressed or concealed memories, as Fuchs proposes, the second generation "learned to identify with the projections of their parents, thereby internalizing their guilt and shame . . . which prompted the creation of a mutually reinforced double wall of silence that made clear that Germany's role in the war, and families' narratives around the period, had to remain an unmentionable issue in post-War society, therefore perpetuating the conspiracy of silence."[67] In having "submitted to the silence between the generations," the second generation, to a significant extent, then, "continued their parents' legacy of denial," a position inevitably communicated to their own children.[68]

As Krug, a product of such silence, puts it, her parents' generation was raised in an "age of oblivion," one in which the crimes of war and the presence of the Holocaust were subverted, buried beneath Germany's attempts to emerge from its national disgrace and defeat and attendant vilification.[69] Thus, to be sure, for a host of reasons and complex motives, there was, as Hardtmann contends, a "long time of latency in Germany in the decades following the end of the war."[70] If, as Giesen suggests, "[a] tacitly assumed coalition of silence provided the first national identity after the war," then the second national identity might be characterized by a liminal period in which fissures were beginning to threaten the silent posture of the previous generation, but one nonetheless framed by concealed memories in both the public and personal spheres.[71] The second national identity thus seems to be in some essential way an identity deferred, on the threshold between suspension and reinvention.

The third-generational narrative of identity, then, one that has emerged from this transitional period of liminality and uncertainty is characterized by a more "open engagement with the national past—in contrast to the silence and denial that the first generation passed on to their children."[72] That is, the discourse of the third generation in Germany, as it emerges in the early decades of the twenty-first century, is more receptive to discussions and confrontations that were once concealed in subdued and muted memory. The national narrative, as it emerges in popular and literary discourse, seems more open to an acceptance of Germany's role in the atrocities perpetuated by Nazism and to a reckoning of individual legacies, as is suggested by the subtitle of Krug's graphic memoir. As Fuchs puts it, the grandchildren "who lived their adult lives during the days of National Socialism in Germany . . . grew up with an inherent notion that [they] have a special responsibility or duty regarding that particular chapter of national history," despite, as Fuchs admits, the difficulties in "conceptualiz[ing] what this obligation actually means or entails."[73] This is not to say, however, that the emerging attitude is generally accepted nor that it is without its detractors. According to a survey conducted by the Yougov Institute in January 2020, "1 in 5 Germans think the Holocaust gets too much attention."[74] The position from which Germany's continuing fault and requisite reparation is approached is thus seriously and precariously complicated.

Despite largely positive critical reviews of her memoir in Germany, as Krug admits, the response among the book's readers has been mixed: "I have received a lot of mail from German readers telling me the book has inspired them to do more research and confront their own families' history in a new way. But I have also received isolated messages from extreme right-wing Germans who accuse me of dragging Germany through the dirt and spreading anti-German propaganda."[75] As Krug further explains, "there is now a backlash from people who say they are fed up with having to feel guilty. There's a defensive attitude that can lead to the exact opposite. In my view, Germans still feel deeply insecure about all this. . . . I don't think we should no longer feel guilty. But there are paralyzing ways to feel guilt and there are constructive strategies for coping with guilt."[76] Writing and illustrating this book seems to be a way in which Krug attempts to cope with the weight of her abiding guilt and shame and the lingering responsibility she feels for her country's and her family's involvement in the crimes of National Socialism. Despite the supposition made by Doris Schroeder and Bob Brecher that "The grandchildren generation does not stand in any guilt-relation to the Holocaust, but rather in a responsibility-relation," for Krug guilt and responsibility are inextricably linked.[77] Thus, as Schroeder and Brecher propose, "while murder, torture and humiliation cannot be made good, respect can nevertheless be shown to those who suffered and died by acknowledging the deeds of their ancestors as those of their own society, and thus accepting obligations across generational borders."[78]

By and large, then, writing against the silence of previous generations, the third generation of Germans, the generation of the grandchildren of those who experienced National Socialism firsthand, have come of age at a pivotal time in history, one in which they have enough distance from the events of Germany's Nazi past and yet are still in reach of that difficult, if fractured, narrative through their grandparents' memories or by way of memories transferred and mediated by their parents. As William Safran suggests, "If there has been a growing admission of German responsibility for the Holocaust it is due in large measure to the fact that a generation that had nothing to do with the event came to constitute a majority of the German people; this generation could approach its country's history more honestly."[79] Despite external and institutional portals of public memory, a contemporary generation of Germans has emerged, as I've suggested, from an extended and deeply entrenched period of collective silence, and thus must make a conscious effort to reenter the past and to redirect the discourse on Germany's history of National Socialism toward more personalized and thereby accessible modes of reckoning. Krug's candid account of her own family's inexplicable past speaks to this trend in recent German literature. This is a generation that knows the shape of that history, the broad strokes of Germany's instigation and execution of the war against the Jews. What this generation does not know, because of the lack of direct proximity to the events and to the narratives of people involved, are the idiosyncratic, individualized chapters of family histories in the overall narrative of war. Thus, this is a generation that continues to be haunted by that history, by "the sense of underlying anxiety that results from the near constant need to defend against the threat of confrontation with a tainted family history."[80] Family histories are generally fraught places to enter for the grandchildren of victims of the Holocaust as well as those of perpetrators and bystanders.[81] But for the generation of the grandchildren of those who participated in the heinous project of National Socialism, their lineage is further complicated by feelings of shame, guilt, and the need for expiation, if only to free themselves from this haunting legacy. This generation, then, not entirely unlike the previous one, remains in something of a liminal position, one on the threshold of discovery but still contending with the silence that marked the generations since the war.

Family narratives, of course, are always part fantasy and part wish fulfillment. They speak to the desire for achievement and completion, as the family romance emerges as a vindication of identity. Family stories are shaped, fictionalized, and molded to justify an otherwise precarious sense of stability and moral legitimacy. Thus, Krug's return to the place of origin to uncover the truth of her grandparents' and uncle's wartime dispositions and activities is impeded by distorted, opaque, fragmented, and contradictory stories of the past, stories that recede even as she touches upon them. For example,

Krug's grandfather Willi Rock's 1946 letter of defense submitted to the public prosecutor affirming his "innocence" of wrongdoing, testimony that "proved that [he] was forced to enter the party in 1933 because of the conditions at the time, that [he] was in no way engaged in National Socialist activities and always vocalized [his] disregard for the party," is undermined by photographs that Krug uncovers of her grandfather in Nazi uniform, photographs that potentially tell a different story.[82] And even were she to determine with certainty that his conduct did not fall into any of the categories classified for the purposes of prosecution—Major Offender, Offender, Lesser Offender, Follower—she still cannot exonerate him. And even were she finally to determine his placement in the hierarchy of failures and atrocities as "an in-between man," "neither a resistance fighter nor a major offender," but rather, a "follower," such knowledge would be, as she confesses "hard to bear."[83] For her grandfather remains in memory as her mother and aunt need him to remain, to preserve not only his image but their own self-images and that of the family profile. Mustering together official archival documents, including her maternal grandfather's military file and paperwork verifying his membership in the Nazi Party and his self-proclaimed status as *Mitläufer*, or Follower, "a person lacking courage and moral stance," as well as personal family artifacts, such as photographs and personal testimonials, still fails to provide Krug with a stronghold on her grandfather's war history. The inherent abstraction of the definition blunts the potential force of moral accusation. Throughout her graphic memoir, Krug draws images of faces partially concealed, eyes occluded or covered as a way of making emphatic the locus of the buried self, unconscious impulses and instincts so hidden as to be impenetrable to the outside gaze. Motives are always in part hidden, concealed in the inexplicable and impenetrable defenses of the ego. There always will be nagging inconsistencies, inconsistences bred from the desire to maintain the family romance, the sense of stability and constancy that cannot be reinvented outside of the nostalgia of the equally fictional narrative of childhood security.

Thus, Krug finally will never know the subtleties, the motivations, the explanations, and rationalizations, the character of the man whom she only knew for a brief time as her grandfather, but who had an entire history behind him. The reasons for his participation in the war are foiled by the lengthening of time, by forgetfulness, by fear, and by her own desire, for it to have been otherwise. She would like to expiate the grandfather she knew and thus expiate herself, but finally, the justification for such relief is concealed in a memory not her own. One of the final images Krug draws of her grandfather is one in which his figure is vague, softly drawn, receding into the backdrop until, on the adjacent page, the image dissolves, lost to the white page, "the closest I will ever get," she acknowledges.[84] Her grandfather's cloaked past, contained and constricted in that time and place, remains hidden, beyond her reach and her reason. And, finally, Krug can only see herself against the backdrop of her family's clouded history. It is against this backdrop, a hazy, incomplete landscape that Krug, through her graphic memoir, will attempt to visualize, "to look where it seemed impossible to look before," to put a face on that increasingly remote history by illustrating the found voice of the past, as Krug's autobiographical narrator puts it, for, without the "story," there is "no history."[85]

"Wouldn't it be better," Krug wonders, "to leave the past behind?"[86] But turning from the past, the willful erasure of history, has implications for the worlds we continue to inhabit. Thus, *Belonging*, this graphic memoir of apprehension, conscience, and shame, written and illustrated by the grandchild of perpetrators of National Socialism, concludes with an uneasy warning for the future. The memoir comes to a close with the 2017 national election in Germany, one that "has given rise to a new right-wing party," an extreme right that "has claimed seats in parliament again, for the first time in more than half a century."[87] As Krug explains, writing the book occurred during a time of reactive political change, whose consequences paved the way for "a new extreme right-wing movement [that] emerged in Germany, a movement that . . . had long been underestimated . . . driven by fears of globalization and waves of migrants."[88] As Krug makes clear, the vestiges of the past continue to haunt generations of Germans, arousing complicated and ambivalent attitudes about identity and place in the unfolding national narrative. While the extent of engagement among the third generation is not easily measured, clearly the unfolding generational narrative redirects and readjusts ways of remembering the past and of "retelling the story in a new way."[89] Thus, the third generation is in the process of establishing a new chapter in Germany's narrative of identity, one that continues to ask difficult questions of identity and place. Psychoanalyst Helm Stierlin thus poses the following questions as fundamental to intergenerational dialogue in postwar Germany: "What are my sources, my roots? What made me into what I am? What formed my present identity? Into what conflicts—intrapsychic, interpersonal, and social—was I born?"[90] And while Krug ends her memoir with similarly unanswered questions, there is some relief for her in the recognition that she was not born in the time and place of her grandparents' generation, and thus responsible for the "unforgivable . . . suffering of millions," crimes that, finally, are not hers to atone.[91]

NOTES

1. Dan Bar-On, Tal Ostrovsky, and Dafna Fromer, "'Who am I in relation to my past, in relation to the other?' German and Israeli Students Confront the Holocaust and Each Other," in *International Handbook of Legacies of Multigenerational Trauma*, ed. Yael Danieli (New York: Plenum Press, 1998), 97.

2. Dan Bar-On, et al., "Who Am I in Relation to My Past," 97.

3. Oliver Fuchs, Lou-Marie Krüger, and Pumla Gobodo-Madikizela, "An Exploration of German Subjectivity Three Generations after the End of World War Two," *The Humanistic Psychologist* 41.2 (2013): 143, DOI: 10.1080/08873267.2012.694127.

4. Susanne Vees-Gulani, "Between Reevaluation and Repetition: Illa Hahn's *Unscharfe Bilder* and the Lasting Influence of Family Conflicts about the Nazi Past in Current Literature of the 1968 Generation," in *Generational Shifts in Contemporary German Culture*, eds., Laurel Cohen-Pfister and Susanne Vees-Gulani (Rochester, New York: Camden House, 2010), 56.

5. Nora Krug, *Belonging: A German Reckons with History and Home* (New York: Scribner, 2018), n.p.

6. Bernhard Giesen, "The Trauma of Perpetrators: The Holocaust and the Traumatic Reference of German National Identity," in *Cultural Trauma and Collective Identity*, ed. Jeffrey C. Alexander, Ron Eyerman, Bernhard Giesen, Neil J. Smelser, and Piotr Sztompka (Berkeley CA: University of California Press, 2004), 129–30.

7. Lars Rensmann, "Collective Guilt, National Identity, and Political Processes in Contemporary Germany," in *Collective Guilt: International Perspectives*, eds. Nyla R. Branscombe and Bertjan Doosje (Cambridge, England: Cambridge University Press, 2004), 180.

8. Jeffrey Herf, "The Holocaust and the Competition of Memories in Germany, 1945–1999," in *Remembering the Holocaust in Germany, 1945–2000: German Strategies and Jewish Responses*, ed. Dan Michman (New York: Peter Lang, 2002), 10–11.

9. Ingrid Laurien, "Germany: Facing the Nazi Past Today," *Literator* 30.3 (December 2009): 96.

10. Giesen, "The Trauma of Perpetrators," 130.
11. Fuchs et al., "An Exploration of German Subjectivity Three," 136.
12. Fuchs et al., "An Exploration of German Subjectivity Three," 136.
13. Krug, *Belonging*, n. pag.
14. Krug, *Belonging*, n. pag.
15. Giesen, "The Trauma of Perpetrators," 116.
16. Krug, *Belonging* n. pag.
17. Krug, *Belonging* n. pag.
18. "Nora Krug Asks Tough Questions about Her German Family's Wartime Past," CBC Radio (March 8, 2019), www.cbc.ca/radio/writersandcompany/nora-krug-asks-tough-questions-about-her-german-family-s-wartime-past-1.5048581.

19. Michael Sneff, "Graphic Novelist Nora Krug Accepts 2019 Lynd Ward Prize, Speaks at Penn State, *The Daily Collegian* (October 17, 2019), www.collegian.psu.ed/arts_and_entertainment/article_5cfd829a-f0e3-11e9-abf9-7b8ba33b9567.html.

20. Rachel Cooke, "A Graphic History of the rise of the Nazis," *The Guardian* (September 30, 2018), www.theguardian.com/books/2018/sep/30/graphic-history-of-the-rise-of-the-nazis.

21. Krug, *Belonging* n. pag.

22. Philip Oltermann, "Interview, Nora Krug: 'I would have thought, what's left to say about Germany's Nazi past?'" *The Guardian* (October 3, 2018): 6, https://www.the guardian.com/books/2018/oct/03/nora-krug-germany-nazi-past-heimat-memoir-author-illustrator.
23. Krug, *Belonging* n. pag.
24. Krug, *Belonging* n. pag.
25. Krug, *Belonging* n. pag.
26. Krug, *Belonging* n. pag.
27. Krug, *Belonging* n. pag.
28. Krug, *Belonging* n. pag.
29. Krug, *Belonging* n. pag.
30. Krug, *Belonging* n. pag.
31. Krug, *Belonging*, n. pag.
32. Krug, *Belonging*, n. pag.
33. Krug, *Belonging*, n. pag.
34. Apruzzese, "The Universal Memoir".
35. Krug, *Belonging*, n. pag.
36. Krug, *Belonging*, n. pag.
37. Krug, *Belonging*, n. pag.
38. Krug, *Belonging*, n. pag.
39. Krug, *Belonging*, n. pag.
40. Hilene Flanzbaum, "Reading the Holocaust: Right Here, Right Now," *Holocaust Studies: A Journal of Culture and History* 17.1 (Summer 2011): 66, DOI: 10.1080/17504902.2011.11087274.
41. Apruzzese, "The Universal Memoir".
42. Apruzzese, "The Universal Memoir".
43. Rensmann, "Collective Guilt, National Identity," 174.
44. Krug, *Belonging* n. pag.
45. Krug, *Belonging* n. pag.
46. Krug, *Belonging* n. pag.
47. Susanne Vees-Gulani and Laurel Cohen-Pfister, in the introduction to *Generational Shifts in Contemporary German Culture*, provide a useful, if loosely characterized, definition of those generations whose responses have evolved since the end of the war: "The first generation implies those who actually experienced, as adults, the Nazi era and subsequent transition to postwar German society; the second describes their children, born at the end of the war or shortly thereafter . . . while the third generation refers to the grandchildren of the first generation, who experienced unification mostly in their late teens and early twenties" (5–6).
48. Rensmann, "Collective Guilt, National Identity," 174.
49. Apruzzese, "The Universal Memoir".
50. Fuchs et al., "An Exploration of German Subjectivity Three," 135.
51. Fuchs et al., "An Exploration of German Subjectivity Three," 138.
52. Apruzzese, "The Universal Memoir".
53. Apruzzese, "The Universal Memoir".
54. Vees-Gulani and Cohen-Pfister, *Generational Shifts in Contemporary*, 5.

55. Laurien, "Germany," 94.
56. Cooke, "A Graphic History".
57. Herf, "The Holocaust and the Competition," 9.
58. Krug, *Belonging*, n. pag.
59. Krug, *Belonging*, n. pag.
60. Gertrud Hardtmann, "Children of Nazis: A Psychodynamic Perspective," in *International Handbook of Multigenerational Legacies of Trauma*, ed. Yael Danieli (New York: Plenum Press, 1998), 87.
61. Hardtmann, "Children of Nazis," 87–8.
62. Giesen, "The Trauma of Perpetrators," 117.
63. Giesen, "The Trauma of Perpetrators," 116.
64. Giesen, "The Trauma of Perpetrators," 116.
65. Fuchs et al., "An Exploration of German Subjectivity Three," 137.
66. Fuchs et al., "An Exploration of German Subjectivity Three," 137.
67. Fuchs et al., "An Exploration of German Subjectivity Three," 137.
68. Fuchs et al., "An Exploration of German Subjectivity Three," 138.
69. Krug, *Belonging*, n. pag.
70. Hardtmann, "Children of Nazis," 85.
71. Giesen, "The Trauma of Perpetrators," 116.
72. Fuchs et al., "An Exploration of German Subjectivity Three," 138.
73. Fuchs et al., "An Exploration of German Subjectivity Three," 134.
74. Toby Axelrod, "I in 5 Germans Think the Holocaust Gets Too Much Attention, Surveys Find," Jewish Telegraph Agency (January 26, 2020), www.jta.org/2020/01/26/global/ I-in-5-germans- think-the-holocaust-gets-too-much-attention-surveys-find.
75. Apruzzese, "The Universal Memoir".
76. Oltermann, "Interview, Nora Krug".
77. Doris Schroeder and Bob Brecher, "Transgenerational Obligations: Twenty-first Century Germany and the Holocaust, *Journal of Applied Philosophy*, 20.1 (2003): 52.
78. Schroeder and Brecher, 54–5.
79. William Safran, "Germans and Jews Since 1945: The Politics of Absolution, Amends, and Ambivalence," in *German Studies in the Post-Holocaust Age: the Politics of Memory, Identity, and Ethnicity*, ed. Adrian Del Caro and Janet Ward (Boulder, Colorado: University Press of Colorado, 2000), 50.
80. Fuchs et al., "An Exploration of German Subjectivity Three," 138.
81. See, for example, Victoria Aarons and Alan L. Berger, *Third-Generation Holocaust Representation: Trauma, History, and Memory* (Evanston, IL: Northwestern University Press, 2017) and Victoria Aarons, *Third-Generation Holocaust Narratives: Memory in Memoir and Fiction* (Lexington Books/Rowman & Littlefield, 2016).
82. Krug, *Belonging*, n. pag.
83. Krug, *Belonging*, n. pag.
84. Krug, *Belonging*, n. pag.
85. Krug, B*elonging*, n. pag.
86. Krug, *Belonging*, n. pag.

87. Krug, *Belonging*, n. pag.
88. Apruzzese, "The Universal Memoir".
89. Oltermann, "Interview, Nora Krug".
90. Helm Stierlin, "The Dialogue Between the Generations about the Nazi Era," in *The Collective Silence: German Identity and the Legacy of Shame*, trans. Cynthia Oudejans Harris and Gordon Wheeler, eds. Barbara Heimannsberg and Christoph J. Schmidt (San Francisco, CA: Jossey-Bass Pub., 1993), 143.
91. Krug, *Belonging*, n. pag.

REFERENCES

Aarons, Victoria. *Third-Generation Holocaust Narratives: Memory in Memoir and Fiction*. Lanham, MD: Lexington Books/Rowman & Littlefield, 2016.

Aarons, Victoria and Alan L. Berger. *Third-Generation Holocaust Representation: Trauma, History, and Memory*. Evanston, IL: Northwestern University Press, 2017.

Apruzzese, J. P. "The Universal Memoir: An Interview with Nora Krug. The NBCC Autobiography Award winner on Belonging: A German Reckons with History and Home" (May 5, 2019), http://www.publicseminar.org/2019/05/the-universal-memoir-an-interview-with-nora-krug/.

Axelrod, Toby. "I in 5 Germans Think the Holocaust Gets Too Much Attention, Surveys Find." Jewish Telegraph Agency (January 26, 2020). www.jta.org/2020/01/26/global/ I-in-5-germans-think-the-holocaust-gets-too-much-attention-surveys-find.

Bar-On, Dan, Tal Ostrovsky, and Dafna Fromer. "'Who Am I in Relation to My Past, in Relation to the Other?': German and Israeli Students Confront the Holocaust and Each Other." In, *International Handbook of Legacies of Multigenerational Trauma*, edited by Yael Danieli, 97–118. New York: Plenum Press, 1998.

Cooke, Rachel. "A Graphic History of the rise of the Nazis." *The Guardian*. September 30, 2018. www.theguardian.com/books/2018/sep/30/graphic-history-of-the -rise-of-the-nazis.

Flanzbaum, Hilene. "Reading the Holocaust: Right Here, Right Now." *Holocaust Studies: A Journal of Culture and History* 17.1 (Summer 2011): 63–84. DOI: 10.1080/17504902.2011.11087274.

Fuchs, Oliver, Lou-Marie Krüger, and Pumla Gobodo-Madikizela. "An Exploration of German Subjectivity Three Generations after the End of World War Two." *The Humanistic Psychologist* 41.2 (2013): 133–158. DOI: 10.1080/08873267.2012.694127.

Giesen, Bernhard. "The Trauma of Perpetrators: The Holocaust and the Traumatic Reference of German National Identity." In *Cultural Trauma and Collective Identity*, edited by Jeffrey C. Alexander, Ron Eyerman, Bernhard Giesen, Neil J. Smelser, and Piotr Sztompka, 112–154. Berkeley: CA, University of California Press, 2004.

Hardtmann, Gertrud. "Children of Nazis: A Psychodynamic Perspective." In *International Handbook of Multigenerational Legacies of Trauma*, edited by Yael Danieli, 85–95. New York: Plenum Press, 1998.

Herf, Jeffrey. "The Holocaust and the Competition of Memories in Germany, 1945–1999." *Remembering the Holocaust in Germany, 1945–2000: German Strategies and Jewish Responses*, edited by Dan Michman, 9–30. New York: Peter Lang, 2002.

Krug, Nora. *Belonging: A German Reckons with History and Home*. New York: Scribner, 2018.

Laurien, Ingrid. "Germany: Facing the Nazi Past Today." *Literator* 30.3 (December, 2009): 93–113.

"Nora Krug Asks Tough Questions about Her German Family's Wartime Past." CBC Radio. March 8, 2019. www.cbc.ca/radio/writersandcompany/nora-krug-asks-tough-questions-about-her-german-family-s-wartime-past-1.5048581.

Oltermann, Philip. "Interview, Nora Krug: 'I would have thought, what's left to say about Germany's Nazi past?'" *The Guardian* (October 3, 2018). https://www.theguardian.com/books/2018/oct/03/nora-krug-germany-nazi-past-heimat-memoir-author illustrator.

Rensmann, Lars. "Collective Guilt, National Identity, and Political Processes in Contemporary Germany." *Collective Guilt: International Perspectives*, edited by Nyla R. Branscombe and Bertjan Doosje, 169–190. Cambridge, England: Cambridge University Press, 2004.

Safran, William. "Germans and Jews Since 1945: The Politics of Absolution, Amends, and Ambivalence." *German Studies in the Post-Holocaust Age: The Politics of Memory, Identity, and Ethnicity*, edited by Adrian Del Caro and Janet Ward, 41–51. Boulder, Colorado: University Press of Colorado, 2000.

Schroeder, Doris and Bob Brecher. "Transgenerational Obligations: Twenty-first Century Germany and the Holocaust. *Journal of Applied Philosophy*, 20.1 (2003): 45–57.

Sneff, Michael. "Graphic Novelist Nora Krug Accepts 2019 Lynd Ward Prize, Speaks at Penn State. *The Daily Collegian*. October 17, 2019. www.collegian.psu.ed/arts_and_entertainment/article_5cfd829a-f0e3-11e9-abf9-7b8ba33b9567.html.

Stierlin, Helm. "The Dialogue Between the Generations about the Nazi Era." *The Collective Silence: German Identity and the Legacy of Shame*, translated by Cynthia Oudejans Harris and Gordon Wheeler, edited by Barbara Heimannsberg and Christoph J. Schmidt, 143–161. San Francisco, California: Jossey-Bass Pub., 1993.

Vees-Gulani, Susanne. "Between Reevaluation and Repetition: Illa Hahn's *Unscharfe Bilder* and the Lasting Influence of Family Conflicts about the Nazi Past in Current Literature of the 1968 Generation." *Generational Shifts in Contemporary German Culture*, edited by Susanne Vees- and Laurel Cohen-Pfister, 56–76. Rochester, New York: Camden House, 2010.

Vees-Gulani, Susanne and Laurel Cohen-Pfister. "Introduction." *Generational Shifts in Contemporary German Culture*, edited by Susanne Vees-Gulani and Laurel Cohen-Pfister, 1–23. Rochester, New York: Camden House, 2010.

Chapter 6

An Impossible Homecoming
Ruth Klüger's Austria
Sarah Painitz

Ruth Klüger came to literary fame late in life. She was sixty-one when her autobiography *weiter leben: Eine Jugend* (*continue living: A Youth*) was published to great acclaim in 1992. After being rejected by the highly regarded German publisher Suhrkamp, the book came out with Wallenstein, a small, new publishing house in Göttingen. Its success surprised everyone, including Klüger. In her second autobiography *unterwegs verloren* (*lost on the way*), she describes sitting in front of her television, dumbstruck, as she heard her "modest" book showered with praise on *Das Literarische Quartett*, a popular German TV show.[1] Following its enthusiastic recommendation on that program and consistently positive reviews in the German and Austrian presses in 1993, *weiter leben* sold out.[2] Klüger had written a bestseller.

weiter leben, which chronicles Klüger's experiences during her youth, is widely regarded as going beyond a straight-forward Holocaust memoir. It has been called a landmark among representations because it seeks a new language and a new discourse for the events of the Holocaust.[3] Since it was first published, *weiter leben* has won numerous awards and has become the subject of more than forty scholarly articles, book chapters, and monographs. Today it is routinely taught in university German programs on both sides of the Atlantic. Nine years after writing the original German text, Klüger translated it into English and in the process, she revised it for an American audience. *Still Alive: A Holocaust Girlhood Remembered* appeared in 2001 with the Feminist Press at the City University of New York. In 2008, Klüger published *unterwegs verloren*, which recounts the years following those described in *weiter leben*.

Born in 1931, Klüger experienced anti-Semitism and the systematic exclusion of Jews from public life in Vienna during her childhood. Her father, a pediatrician and gynecologist, and her older half-brother, were murdered in the Holocaust. When she was eleven, Klüger and her mother were deported and incarcerated, first in Theresienstadt, and later in Auschwitz and Groß-Rosen. In 1945, they escaped from a death march, eventually making their way to Straubing, Bavaria, where Klüger was able to graduate from Gymnasium in 1946, and to study philosophy in Regensburg at the age of fifteen in 1947.[4] Later that year, Klüger and her mother emigrated to the United States. Klüger studied library science and English in New York, and German literature at the University of California, Berkeley, earning an MA in 1952 and a PhD in 1967. From 1965 until 1995, she taught German language and literature in Cleveland, Kansas, Virginia, Princeton, and Irvine, forging a reputation as a well-regarded scholar of Baroque poetry, eighteenth and nineteenth-century German literature, and feminism.

This chapter will focus on Klüger's complex relationship to Austria, her childhood home and, as she puts it, "Ort vergangener Bedrohung schlechthin" (place of past threats par excellence).[5] In the course of my analysis, I will consider how Klüger understands her position as author and her connection to the reader, as well as how her notion of "timescapes" allows her to conceptualize the relationship between place and memory. Although I will draw on *weiter leben* and *Still Alive*, the focus of my discussion will be *unterwegs verloren*, which has to date received far less scholarly attention. This second autobiographical text sheds new light on how Klüger attempts to negotiate her relationship with the Viennas of the past and the present, a negotiation that both goes back in time to consider Austria's anti-Semitic legacy, and stretches across space to encompass Germany, the United States, and Senegal.

RUTH KLÜGER AND HER AUDIENCE

In her essays, Klüger has repeatedly commented on the important role of the reader's personal and socio-cultural background in understanding the meaning of a text. "Die Gegenstände der Literaturwissenschaft sind, anders als die der Naturwissenschaften, abhängig von unseren Lebensumständen" (The subjects of literary studies are, unlike those of the natural sciences, dependent on our life circumstances),[6] she notes in "Fakten und Fiktionen." Thus, she begins the preface to *Katastrophen*, a collection of critical essays, with an image of books as ropes that connect the author, who speaks a language drawn from her experiences, with the reader, also shaped by personal experiences. Both author and reader pull on the rope, "zwischen uns ist die Spannung" (between us is the tension).[7] How we read, and how we understand what we read, is influenced by our individual circumstances and experiences. It is shaped by our historical context, too. This is most apparent when present-day readers read older texts differently from the way in which they were understood at the time of their production. But how we read is also influenced by where we are, and it is how she deals with issues of cultural context that has left the most significant mark on Klüger's texts. According to her, it is obvious "dass wir Bücher aus einer anderen Kultur ganz anders lesen als die Einheimischen" (that we read books from another culture completely differently than those from our own).[8] Great, love this. Do you think we have to say anything about reader-response theory here?

While Klüger insists on the specificity and uniqueness of each individual's experience, she importantly argues that we do not live like "isolated monads."[9] Indeed, she believes that comparisons—"the bridges from one unique life to another"[10]—are crucial in creating connections between people. As I have argued elsewhere,[11] what is important to Klüger is not the erasure of differences through comparison but rather our ability to relate *despite* differences. She wants her readers to understand the importance of creating connections and finding similarities. Such connections are the basis for empathy and understanding between people of vastly different backgrounds. Thus, Klüger's texts must be understood as a call for dialogue between author and reader. Indeed, throughout *weiter leben,* Klüger addresses her reader directly, often provocatively. Although her abrasive tone and skeptical attitude take some aback, by addressing her readers directly, Klüger hopes to bring about a dialogue between Jews and German and Austrian non-Jews. When she calls on her reader to become "streitsüchtig," (quarrelsome) and seek "Auseinandersetzung" (debate),[12] she acknowledges that this dialogue may be contentious and difficult. Yet it is clearly preferable to the alternative: "verschanzt euch nicht, sagt nicht von vornherein, das gehe euch nichts an" (don't barricade yourselves, don't say from the outset that it's none of your business).[13] In her autobiographies, Klüger tosses us the rope and asks that we pull it. The resulting dialogue between author and reader is not going to be easy; yet the tension of the rope is a good thing. It indicates a sincere effort, a struggle, an attempt to think about and come to terms with difficult matters.

Understanding Klüger's insistence on positionality is crucial for the questions of who she is, where she is, and when—they mark her life and her autobiographical texts as perhaps no others do. Marcel Reich-Ranicki's description of Klüger as "an Austrian Jew, an American professor, a German writer"[14] is emblematic of the fact that she does not have an easily definable identity, nationality, or position. Yet identity and place play a crucial role in her texts. This is immediately apparent when opening *weiter leben,* whose table of contents essentially consists of place names: Vienna, Theresienstadt, Auschwitz-Birkenau, Christianstadt (Groß-Rosen), Germany, Bavaria, New York, Göttingen. The place names narrate the stations of Klüger's suffering, and eventual liberation, but they also tell us something about her identity as Austrian, Jew, and immigrant. The connection between identity and place is clear, too, in *unterwegs verloren*: its very title means "lost on the way." While place again figures prominently in the chapter headings (they include exile, the old world, the new world, the academic village, German scholar abroad), what is even more striking is that the title underlines a state of being lost while moving. Indeed, this second autobiographical text illustrates Klüger's sense of homelessness and unbelonging and how these absences contribute to her identity. I will return to these points in detail in the third part of my chapter.

A place does not exist in a vacuum; it means different things at different times. Klüger is acutely aware of this, and she is critical about the concentration camp as memorial site. Auschwitz as memorial cannot possibly convey what Auschwitz was like as a concentration camp: "Es ist unsinnig, die Lager räumlich so darstellen zu wollen, wie sie damals waren" (It is nonsense to want to represent the physical reality of the camps as they were back then).[15] She contemplates the possibility of timescapes: "Ortschaft, Landschaft, landscape, seascape—das Wort Zeitschaft sollte es geben, um zu vermitteln, was ein Ort in der Zeit ist, zu einer gewissen Zeit, weder vorher noch nachher" (Place, landscape, seascape—there should be a word like timescape, to convey what a place is in time, at a specific point of time, neither before nor after).[16] "Timescape" describes a place at a concrete historical moment; as a term, it inextricably ties together place and time. For Klüger, this concept is crucial to her ability to convey her experiences to her reader, because those experiences derive from a specific place at a specific moment of time. Conveying such experiences requires Klüger to bridge a spatial and temporal gulf, and empathizing with her requires her reader to do the same.[17]

As I have already noted, cultural and temporal context are not just important in understanding the position from which the author speaks but are equally important in regard to the reader. If Klüger is right—that we read books from other cultures differently than those from our own—this has implications for translation, and any discussion of *weiter leben* must also take into account its English-language version *Still Alive*.[18] *Still Alive* moves significantly beyond what we conventionally think of as a literary translation; Klüger revises, rewrites, and changes her original text to create a new, or, as she calls it, a parallel, text. Many of the changes Klüger implements in the English-language version of her text stem from her desire to address an American audience that is far removed—temporally, geographically, and culturally—from the crimes of the Holocaust. *Still Alive* must thus be understood as a kind of cultural translation,[19] which allows Klüger to adapt her English text to her American readers' context in order to render her story relatable and relevant. One of the most apparent changes is her substitution of references to Austrian writers like Schnitzer, Werfel, and Zweig, and even well-known German authors like Lessing, Goethe, and Schiller, with American ones, such as Mark Twain, Toni Morrison, Maya Angelou, Emily Dickinson, and others. For example, to express her feelings of ambivalence upon immigrating to New York, she quotes from Adrienne Rich's "Prospective Immigrants Please Note."[20] This underlines that Klüger's experiences in New York are a recognizable story for her American audience, for whom the idea of the city as the quintessential immigrant melting pot is a familiar part of their culture.

Klüger also changes chapter titles. Instead of cataloging the names of the camps in which she and her mother were incarcerated, the English version lists the words "ghetto," "death camp," and "forced labor camp." Klüger assumes that her American audience is less familiar with the camps' names, and such descriptive terminology will accurately impart the stages of persecution to which she was subjected. Indeed, the result of removing such culturally and geographically specific references is minimal. *Still Alive* remains a book firmly rooted in the place and time it describes. This holds true despite a third change in which Klüger compares her experience of discrimination and repression as a Jew in Austria with that of slaves and minorities in the United States. For example, in describing the feeling of entering "enemy territory" as soon as she left her house in Vienna after the Anschluss, she writes about "facing a sea of hostile white faces. No white can understand, [blacks] say. I do, I say. But no, you have white skin, they counter. But I wore a *Judenstern* to alert other pedestrians that I wasn't really white."[21] By comparing her experiences of persecution as a Jew to that of African-Americans in the United States, she attempts to build bridges with her American readers. Knowing that such comparisons are imperfect, Klüger does not equate or erase differences. When she dismisses comparing her transport to Auschwitz with being in a stuck elevator, she admits, "again I am stumbling through the labyrinth of conflicting comparisons and asking the question how we can understand anything if we can't relate to it."[22] Not all comparisons are apt. But only through comparing can we relate the experiences of our individual lives to those of others, ultimately gaining greater understanding of people with backgrounds different from our own.

THE AUSTRIAN CONTEXT

"Kein Land der Welt hat sich selbst öffentlich so wenig problematisisert und grundsätzlich reflektiert wie die Zweite österreichische Republik" (No country in the world has publicly problematized itself and reflected on itself as little as the Second Austrian Republic),[23] writes the Austrian author Robert Menasse in his essay *Das Land ohne Eigenschaften*. In Germany during the 1960s, three events in particular contributed to a heightened awareness of the war crimes perpetrated by ordinary Germans: the Eichmann trial in

Israel, the Auschwitz trials in Frankfurt, and the debate surrounding the statute of limitations for capital offenses. The discussions surrounding these events led the younger generation of Germans to confront their parents, criticize their (in)actions, and demand accountability. In Austria, on the other hand, this process of working through the past did not take place until much later. The "Opferthese," a pattern of argumentation that presents Austria as Nazi Germany's first victim, for decades fostered the collective denial and repression of Austria's complicity in Nazi atrocities, glossing over the broad support of the country's annexation among the public, who famously welcomed Hitler at the Vienna Heldenplatz in 1938 by the tens of thousands. Echoing the Moscow Declaration of 1943, the Declaration of Independence in 1945 exonerated Austria's actions during World War II and inscribed its status as German's first victim into the founding documents of the new nation. Members of the Wehrmacht and even the SS could be seen as victims of German aggression rather than perpetrators of atrocities and war crimes. The National Socialist Law of 1947 placed the responsibility for denazification in the hands of Austria's provisional government, and because the political parties were vying for the votes of re-enfranchised former members of the Nazi Party, there was never a rigorous purge of former Nazis from public life: "approximately 90 percent of former party members were deemed 'less incriminated' [. . .] and granted amnesty."[24] Therefore, the condemnation of Nazism occurred "at only the most superficial level."[25] The country's self-conception as victim was propped up by a wide range of cultural institutions and products. Popular "Heimatfilme" portrayed an idyllic world of mountains, lakes, and villages with plots centering on love and family; concerts, plays, and operas drew on Austria's rich cultural tradition while astutely avoiding any political or controversial topics. The few dissenting voices, such as authors who wrote critically of Austria and its past, were vilified as "Nestbeschmutzer" ("nest-soilers") in the conservative media.

Only the Waldheim Affair of 1986 and the commemorative year 1988 led to a more nuanced public debate about Austria's complicity during the Third Reich. In 1986, Kurt Waldheim was elected president just after the disclosure of his Nazi past. Revelations in the press pointed toward his possible complicity in the commission of war crimes and accused him of dishonesty in how he portrayed his past. The World Jewish Congress and the international press increasingly brought attention to the affair and, when Waldheim was nevertheless elected, criticism shifted from the person of Waldheim to the nation. The scandal not only seriously tarnished Austria's international reputation but also forced the country to engage with its Nazi past, in the process laying bare "deep divisions within the Austrian populace."[26] And although broad swaths of the population defended Austria in the face of international scrutiny, a small but vocal circle of critics eventually brought about the public dialogue the country had avoided for so long.

Chancellor Franz Vranitzky had the difficult task of addressing these rifts and fostering a national dialogue about the country's past, one result being the "Bedenkjahr" (year of reflection) in 1988. In his speech to the National Assembly in 1991, Vranitzky for the first time acknowledged Austrian complicity for the war crimes of the Nazi era. Nevertheless, as Menasse astutely argues, responsibility continued to be relegated to the individual level:

> Es habe eine Mitschuld gegeben—aber nur von seiten einzelner Österreicher, jedoch nicht von seiten Österreichs. Mit anderen Worten, es bleibt dabei: Österreich war ein Opfer. Weil keiner damals die Republik wollte, und weil es sie dann auch gar nicht mehr gab. Nur die Staatsbürger waren Täter. Nicht einmal die Staatsbürger, da es ja den Staat nicht mehr gab, sondern die einzelnen, die da lebten, in dieser Gegend, in diesem Raum, wo erst später, als der Nazi-Spuk vorbei war, wieder ein Staat gegründet wurde, der daher als Staat als unschuldig zu gelten hat.

> (There had been complicity—but only on the part of single Austrians, not on the part of Austria. In other words, the fact remains: Austria was a victim. Because nobody back then wanted the Republic, and because later it didn't even exist anymore. Only the citizens were perpetrators. Not even the citizens, because the state didn't exist anymore, just the individuals, who lived there, in that area, in that region, where only later, when the Nazi-spook was over, a state was founded again, a state which therefore must be considered innocent.)[27]

Identifying in this type of argumentation a principle of "Entweder-und-Oder" (Either-and-Or), a "unerträglich sich spreizende Verrenkung" (unbearably contorted maneuver),[28] Menasse reveals how the Austrian discourse about its responsibility during the Third Reich is based on contradictory impulses. Complicity is tied to national identity, and that national identity can be explained away. Austria as a country cannot be held responsible, because "Austria" did not really exist at the time when the atrocities were committed. The contradictions cancel each other out, thus absolving the country of any and all responsibility.

Within this context of national denial and excuses, Klüger's self-image as Austrian would certainly be difficult. As a matter of fact, it may seem counterintuitive to call her an Austrian writer at all, considering she only lived in the country as a child, and provocatively dedicates her first autobiography to "den Göttinger Freunden" (my friends in Göttingen) as "ein deutsches Buch" (a German book). Yet there are multiple reasons why Klüger might be considered Austrian. For one thing, her narrative language is distinctly Austrian.

In describing her relationship with Austrian literature, Klüger states: "[D]ie Literatur dieses Landes, von Adalbert Stifter bis Thomas Bernhard, redet mich intimer an als andere Bücher, nämlich im bequemen Tonfall einer vertraut hinterfotzigen Kindersprache" (The literature of this country, from Adalbert Stifter to Thomas Bernhard, speaks more intimately to me than other books, that is to say in the comfortable voice, familiarly sassy, of a child),[29] and it is clear from other statements she makes that her connection to Austria runs largely through its language and literature.[30] Hans Höller also argues that *weiter leben* is marked by the analytical logic and *Sprachkritik* that stem from a distinctly Austrian intellectual history. The text not only includes many references to and quotations from Austrian writers but also echoes the writing of Adalbert Stifter, Arthur Schnitzler, Ilse Aichinger, Ingeborg Bachmann, Thomas Bernhard, and Elfriede Jelinek.[31] Like Achinger, Bachmann, and Bernhard, Klüger writes from a place of rage. Her anger, it seems, not only stems from her childhood experiences in a Vienna that is "[b]is ins Mark hinein judenkinderfeindlich" (to the core hostile toward Jewish children)[32] but also is directed at an Austria that relied on maintaining continuity and tradition after 1945.

Of course, one might question what it means to be "Austrian" at all. Considering Austria's long and complex history, this question is not easily answered. The multi-ethnic state that was the Austro-Hungarian Empire—consisting of a dozen different nationalities and languages—still looms large in the imagination of Austrian identity. And in just the first half of the twentieth century, Austrians experienced five different forms of government. Thus, a writer like Kafka (Jewish, German-speaking, born in Prague, at that time part of the Austro-Hungarian Empire) is largely considered Austrian. The same goes for the many writers—from Stefan Zweig to Rose Ausländer—who were forced into exile during the Third Reich, settled in another country, and often spent years or decades away from Austria, some of them to never return. Klüger's identity, comprised of multiple influences, then, is characteristic of an Austrian writer.

Yet perhaps most important, Klüger's relationship to her birthplace and childhood home should be probed because it figures prominently in her autobiographical texts. In *weiter leben*, where she describes the growing marginalization, social ostracism, and persecution to which she was subjected during the first eleven years of her life, she says very little about her perceptions of Austria after the war. She calls Vienna "Urschleim" (primordial slime)[33] when she recounts a few weeks there immediately following the war. She no longer has any friends or relatives in the city, which she describes as "weder fremd noch vertraut" (neither foreign nor familiar).[34] Yet since she wrote *weiter leben*, her relationship with Vienna has changed, as Klüger herself acknowledges: "Es gibt jetzt für mich zweierlei Wien. Seit 1992 mein Buch 'weiter leben' über meine Kindheitserinnerungen erschienen ist, habe ich eine neue Beziehung zu dieser Stadt" (For me, there are two Viennas now. Since my book 'weiter leben' about my childhood memories was published in 1992, I have had a new relationship to this city).[35] This new relationship, and its complexities, forms a significant part of *unterwegs verloren*, Klüger's second autobiographical text.

PLACE IN *UNTERWEGS VERLOREN*

In two consecutive chapters entitled "Göttinger Neurosen" and "Wiener Neurosen," Klüger probes her present-day relationship with these two cities. And although the titles may appear to imply some kind of affinity between the chapters, their content and tone diverge. Klüger begins the chapter on Göttingen with the assertion that she has a second home there, only to immediately retract by saying "[i]ch bin hier fast zu Hause" (I am almost at home here).[36] Indeed, the remainder of the chapter retells three incidences that illustrate in varying ways how Klüger feels mistreated, unwelcomed, or taken advantage of in Göttingen. The chapter on Vienna, in contrast, is both more reflective and disjointed than the one on Göttingen. The main reason for these differences is that, for Klüger, Vienna is a timescape, whereas Göttingen exists largely only in the present. This is also clear from comments Klüger has made in interviews. "Göttingen war die Gegenwart, nicht Erinnerung" (Göttingen was the present, not memory),[37] she notes in *Spiegel* in 2008. And in further explaining the two Viennas Klüger perceives, she describes that her new relationship to the city "hat allerdings mein Verhältnis zu dem Wien, an das ich mich erinnere, nicht verändert. Das Wien der Gespenster ist noch immer da, aber das neue ist darüber gestülpt" (has, however, not changed my relationship to the Vienna I remember. The Vienna of the ghosts is still here, but the new one overlays it).[38]

Thus, the old Vienna, the new Vienna, and the process of remembering figure prominently in "Wiener Neurosen." Because of frequent narrative digressions and temporal changes that take us to different moments in Klüger's life as well as in Vienna's history, the chapter feels disjointed and disorienting. This effect is, perhaps, intentional. Klüger, too, experiences Vienna as discomforting. Throughout these pages, the old Vienna of Klüger's memories figures as "Feindesland" (enemy territory),[39] "Ort der schnürenden Verengung" (place of binding constriction),[40] and "Gefängnis" (prison).[41] These images illustrate the social ostracism and marginalization Klüger experienced during her childhood, when she was increasingly excluded from visiting public places and confined to one small, dark room in a crowded collection apartment. Yet she describes experiencing exclusion in the new Vienna, too, especially during the semester she spent as a visiting lecturer at the University of Vienna in 2003.[42] Other images invoked for the present-day Vienna, such as a knot, at which she tugs until bleeding under the fingernails,[43] and a wound, which does not heal,[44] suggest her antagonism toward the city.

Yet for Klüger, Vienna also holds positive connotations. She becomes an Austrian citizen again and likes that the new passport "belongs" to her.[45] She describes feeling "schon irgendwie verankert in Wien" (kind of anchored in Vienna),[46] mainly through female friends. And she recounts feeling honored when invited to give a lecture at city hall.[47] Yet the writer's most important connection to Vienna is through language. In explaining why she chose to write her first autobiography in German, after having lived and worked in the United States for decades, she writes: "Die deutsche Sprache, latent im Gehirn, aber nicht immer robust, hatte mich gewählt, nicht umgekehrt" (The German language, latent in the brain, but still robust, chose me, not the other way around).[48] In intensively recollecting her childhood, she had to return to the language of that childhood, specifically "das wienerische Hochdeutsch" (Viennese standard German).[49] Thus, place and time are tied together in the specific cadences and expressions that Klüger knows so well from the Vienna of her past. The pain associated with that Vienna presides and continues to inflect her perceptions. It cannot be pushed away or ignored. She knows, of course that there is a present and a past Vienna, "aber die beiden lassen sich vom Gedächtnis her nicht so auseinanderhalten, wie man gern möchte. Das Gedächtnis ist hartnäckig und will nicht verdrängt werden" (but in one's memory, the two don't let themselves be kept apart like one wants to. Memory is tenacious and doesn't want to be repressed).[50] It is clear here and in other parts of Klüger's writing that the process of remembering is not entirely within the individual's control. She frequently discusses the subjectivity and unreliability of memory; even so, here, memories intrude and get in the way, bubbling up from the subconscious. She likens buried memories to impressions that are still on the hard-drive of a computer, even though they had never been displayed on its screen. These impressions are triggered by innocuous things, like a design on a door or stairway.[51]

Memories of the old Vienna thus continually affect her perception of the new Vienna. Although she recognizes the many ways in which Vienna has changed, its places remain deadly to her; she perceives the present-day city as "voller Schlaglöcher [. . .] als könne sie auf der Mariahilferstraße stolpern und im Prater im Gebüsch versacken, in einem Schönbrunner Brunnen ertrinken und am Graben verschluckt werden" (full of potholes [. . .] as if she might stumble on Mariahilfer Street and get stuck in the shrubbery in the Prater, drown in a Schönbrunn fountain and be swallowed up on the Graben).[52] Here, the everyday places of the city—shopping streets, parks, and landmarks—become menacing and dangerous. The fear of falling, being entangled, even ingested by inanimate objects is reminiscent of a striking passage in *weiter leben*, in which she describes falling onto the ramp upon her arrival in Auschwitz as "der Boden, auf dem du stehst, will, daß du verschwindest" (the ground on which you are standing wants you to disappear). She continues:

> Auf diese Rampe fall ich immer noch. Aus einer Narkose erwachend, fall ich, erleichtert und entsetzt zugleich, aus der aufgerissenen Tür des bislang versiegelten Wagens auf diese seither berühmt gewordene Rampe, damals noch unberühmt, Sackgasse im Amoklauf einer besessenen Kultur. Unvergessener Augenblick, verhärtet und verknöchert in ein Lebensgefühl.
>
> (I still fall onto this ramp. Waking up from anesthesia I fall, relived and horrified at the same time, from the suddenly opened door of a sealed wagon onto this now famous ramp, then not yet famous, dead end to the rampage of a civilization gone mad. Unforgotten moment, hardened and ossified into a feeling of life).[53]

In *weiter leben*, this sense of falling—utter loss of control—extends into the present, the time during which Klüger began to write her first autobiographical text, forty-four years later. The moment of falling onto the ramp, emblematic for the trauma of Auschwitz, continually returns, marking her life. The same traumatic moment reappears in Vienna, where the city's sites emanate danger and death.

Yet it is not being swallowed up by the ground but going underwater—drowning—that preoccupies Klüger in Vienna. Like *weiter leben*, *unterwegs verloren* includes poems written by Klüger; one of these, "Bauernmarkt eins," addresses Saint Nepomuk, who is believed to protect one from floods and drowning. She asks a statue of Nepomuk in the courtyard of the house in which she is staying to pray for her "daß ich nicht ins Gewässer falle, [. . .] damit ich nicht ertrinken tu am Bauernmarkt eins" (that I don't fall into the waters, [. . .] so that I don't drown at Bauernmarkt number one).[54] Klüger writes her poem for St. Nepomuk during an extended visit in Vienna in 1997; she gives a few lectures and writes essays, but she wants to stay longer so that she can cure "die alten Phobien" (the old phobias).[55] This proves difficult because she is repeatedly reminded not only of her own childhood experiences but also of the persecution of the Jews throughout the history of the city. She recounts, "jedes Mal wenn ich auf den Judenplatz ging, dachte ich ans Ertrinken" (every time I crossed Judenplatz I thought about drowning).[56] Thus, the fear of drowning is tied to specific places in the city; it is a manifestation of her experiences of marginalization and ostracism, of her otherness as a Jew.

Her thoughts of drowning every time she crosses Judenplatz, which was the center of the Jewish Ghetto during the Middle Ages, are tied up with the Pogroms of 1420 and 1421, the largest and bloodiest in medieval Austria. Jews throughout the country were rounded up and imprisoned. Those of little means were expelled, others were dispossessed and tortured. The few Jews remaining in the Ghetto in Vienna locked themselves into the synagogue and committed mass suicide to escape forced baptism in the fall of 1420. The following spring, the last surviving Jews were rounded up outside of Vienna and burned alive. On the so-called Jordan-House, today the oldest building on Judenplatz, a relief depicting Jesus's baptism in the River Jordan with a Latin inscription can still be seen. The anti-Semitic inscription, probably erected in 1497, refers to the cleansing power of the River Jordan and celebrates the murder of the Jews as a "purging from sickness and evil" through fire.[57]

For Klüger, the burnings of the Jews during the medieval Pogroms are comparable to the murder of the Jews in the crematoria of Auschwitz. Rachel Whiteread's memorial for the Austrian Jewish victims of the Holocaust, which today stands on Judenplatz, also underlines this association. Similarly, about her cousin Heinz's death from an accidental fire, Klüger notes: "Welche Juden denken da nicht an die Krematorien der Vernichtungslager, auch wenn sie das als unangebracht gleich wieder verwerfen?" (Which Jews don't think of the crematoria of the death camps, even if they immediately dismiss it as inappropriate?).[58] Accordingly, whenever she crosses Judenplatz, the oppressive knowledge of Vienna's anti-Semitic history make her feel like she is drowning.[59] In calling on St. Nepomuk to save her, she addresses the martyr priest who himself was executed by drowning in the Vltava River in Prague during the conflicts between church and state at the end of the fourteenth century. She asks his wooden statue to pray for her, and to protect her from a river that is invisible and waters that she does not see.[60] These invisible waters are not just the painful memories of a traumatic childhood but also the continuous reminders of the state's persecution of the Jews—reminders that are still present and visible throughout the city today.

Klüger thus addresses this Catholic saint, who represents the religion of the vast majority of the Austrian populace, not only as a Jewish woman but also as a representative of a religious minority that has suffered greatly at the hand of Catholic Austrians. Indeed, Duke Albrecht's decree of 1421 condemning the Viennese Jews to death claimed that they had desecrated the host; such accusations were typical pretexts for anti-Semitic aggressions. Yet in her appeal to St. Nepomuk, Klüger seeks to establish a dialogue. As protector from drowning, he is also known as the "bridge saint." His statues are frequently found on or near bridges; the most famous of these is on the Charles Bridge in Prague, where, after being tortured and badly burned, presumably by King Wenceslaus IV of Bohemia himself, he was thrown into the river.[61]

Death by drowning was the customary form of execution for the clergy at the time. In "Bauernmarkt eins," Klüger imagines how the statue of St. Nepomuk stands "auf brüchiger Brücke" (on a brittle bridge)[62]—a bridge that, like the river beneath it, is invisible. The wooden statue "füllt die Lücke / und begrenzt die Gefahr" (fills the gap / and limits the danger).[63] Here, the statue becomes part of the bridge, thereby permitting safe passage over the invisible waters. Klüger has evoked such imaginary bridges before. In her conceptualization of comparisons as the bridges connecting individual in *weiter leben*, she contemplates that, if there are no bridges, we might have to invent them: "es könnte ja sein, daß sie, obwohl erfunden, trotzdem tragfähig sind" (it could be that, despite being invented, they can bear weight).[64] These passages about imaginary bridges make clear that, while comparisons between individual experiences are necessary for understanding and empathy, what really matters—where the work really happens—is not in the comparisons in and of themselves but in the process of building connections. This building can only occur through contemplation, discussion, and debate with others, others who have had vastly different life experiences from our own. The process cannot be easy. It is fraught and painful, but it is only by working through these difficulties that "bridges of understanding" can be formed.

Thus, it is no coincidence that Klüger seeks dialogue with a Catholic saint. The invisible waters against which she hopes he can protect her are everywhere in the city; wherever she goes, "berühre ich eine wunde Stelle" (I touch a raw spot).[65] "Wiens Wunde, die ich bin, und meine Wunde, die Wien ist, sind unheilbar" (Vienna's wound, which is me, and my wound, which is Vienna, are incurable),[66] she acknowledges. It is clear here that there can never be any "Versöhnung" (reconciliation),[67] any resolution or closure from the traumas of the past. Indeed, since the point of Klüger's imaginary bridges is to bring about understanding through communication and debate, it is the process, not the end-result, that matters. Working through the past does not mean that the wounds themselves go away; rather, it means learning to live with them: "eitern und den ganzen Körper infizieren müssen und sollen solche Wunden nicht, das kann durch Nachdenken und Reden verhindert werden; das wäre doch schon was, und zwar gar nicht wenig" (such wounds mustn't and shouldn't fester and infect the whole body, that can be averted through thinking and talking; that would be something, and not just a little bit).[68] Klüger recognizes that she will never "get over" the pain with which returning to her childhood home presents her, but she can—through contemplation and discussion—hold the pain at bay.

Such hope for working through past traumas notwithstanding, *unterwegs verloren* ends on a somber note. In the epilogue, Klüger acknowledges that her childhood experiences remain ever-present, and that this realization only becomes more apparent as she ages. The past is always already in the present.

So also on Île de Gorée, which Klüger visits during a cruise. For her, this Senegalese island, where slaves were collected before being shipped to the Americas, figures as yet another timescape. She describes how, during her visit to the island, her body suddenly seems to rebel: she gets painful cramps in her feet, a rotten taste rising into her throat.[69] She is struck by a moment of recognition: "Ich kenn das ja, war einmal mitten drin" (I know this, was once in the middle of it).[70] She realizes that she is the only person among the tourists and locals who has personally experienced slave labor. The sudden awareness of the past reaching into the present is underlined by the fact that for this two-page passage, Klüger switches from the grammatical past tense to the present, giving the scene a sense of imminence. Just as she is suddenly transported to her own childhood experiences, so the reader, too, imagines herself to be on Île de Gorée alongside her. Here, Klüger compares her own experiences as "a slave girl"[71] to those of Africans sold into slavery—similar to the way in which she had compared aspects of the Holocaust to the medieval pogroms, the bombing of Hiroshima,[72] American slavery, and the discrimination of African-Americans in the United States. Her comparisons function as bridges to help her reader understand and empathize with her experiences.

But this moment is further complicated by the conflicting notions of identity they evoke for Klüger. Île de Gorée is the point where, in Klüger's imagination, two ships intersect. One is the "Rotterdam," a cruise ship of the Holland American Line, on which Klüger and her friend Maria share a cabin. Such luxury, she reluctantly admits, means that she now belongs to the rich people of the world. The other ship is the "Dunera," a British vessel that deported over 2,500 enemy aliens from Liverpool to Sydney in 1940. The voyage has become infamous for the horrendous physical conditions, abuse, and maltreatment the detainees – one of whom was Klüger's cousin—had to endure. Thus, the painful memories of being a slave girl that Klüger's visit on Île de Gorée evoke are complicated by the fact that she is making this very visit as a tourist living in luxury. "Wer bin ich denn, die oder jene?" (Who am I, she or the other one?), she asks.[73] The "Dunera," a ship from the past, epitomizes the worst kind of depravity, of which Klüger was also a victim. The "Rotterdam," in the present, represents the position of privilege that allows those who are well-off to tour sites of the slave trade from a comfortable distance. Klüger, now part of this class, looks back on her own past self. We see here that the notion of timescapes is relevant to understanding not only a place throughout time but also to an individual throughout her life. A timescape encompasses multiple identities and experiences. Oscillating between her past and her present selves, Klüger struggles to reconcile her disparate identities.

The imaginary crossings of the "Rotterdam" and the "Dunera" are important in yet another way, for they both suggest continuous movement. "Dieses Schiff ist ein Niemandsland" (This ship is a no man's land),[74] Klüger writes about the "Rotterdam." The two ships represent Klüger's past exile, which was forced upon her (as it was on those who were on the "Dunera") and her present homelessness, which she has chosen for herself. A constant "Pendeln zwischen Amerika und Europa" (oscillation between America and Europe),[75] always being on the move, not really belonging in one single place, has indeed defined her entire life. She is not really at home anywhere: "Ich kann nicht sagen, dass ich mich als Amerikanerin oder als Europäerin fühle, man ist irgendwie dazwischen" (I cannot say that I feel like an American or a European, one is somehow in between).[76] Neither Austrian, nor German, nor American, Klüger's identity is marked by a continuous sense of in-between-ness. Indeed, it is this very identity that has sensitized her to the importance of cultural context and the necessity of comparisons so that we might bridge differences arising from that context.

Thus, the answer to Klüger's struggle in reconciling her disparate selves lies in accepting her position of being in-between, the result of a life marked by exile, homelessness, and constant journeying.[77] In an interview in 2012, Klüger gave the following explanation for the title of her second autobiographical text, which is from the lines "einmal ging ich unterwegs verloren, / einmal kam ich an, wo ich nicht war" (once I became lost on the way, / once I arrived where I was not) of a poem by Herta Müller:

> Was mir daran so gut gefällt, ist eben, dass sie nicht sagt, "wo ich nicht gewesen war"—denn das heißt ja einfach "jetzt bin ich da"—sondern "ich bin da und ich bin nicht da." Diese Frage nach dem Standpunkt und Zeitpunkt der Umwelt, in der man sich befindet, und die Unsicherheit über diese Umwelt scheint mir *grammatisch* da gegeben zu sein in diesem "einmal kam ich an, wo ich nicht war." Wie kann man ankommen und nicht da sein, das ist die Frage, das Paradox in dieser Formulierung.
>
> (What I like so much is exactly that she doesn't say, "where I had not been"—because that simply means "now I am here"—but rather "I am here and I am not here." This question about the position in space and point in time of the environment in which one is situated and the uncertainty about this environment, appears to me to be given *grammatically* in this "once I arrived where I was not." How can one arrive and not be here, that is the question, the paradox, of this formulation).[78]

This paradox of simultaneous presence and absence is what suffuses Klüger's autobiographical writing. It informs the position—both in time and in space—from which she writes and from which she addresses her reader. It points toward the role of memory and Klüger's notion of timescapes to capture that memory and make it relatable to others. And it epitomizes her identity as an oscillating, continuous movement between different places and times.

After publishing *unterwegs verloren*, Klüger was repeatedly asked why she had written a second autobiographical text. In the sense that *weiter leben* tells the story of her youth, beginning with Klüger's earliest memories of discrimination and ending with her leaving her mother's home in New York, it appears complete. Yet in her responses, Klüger talks about how she did not feel "done" after writing her first autobiography, how she still had things to say.[79] In one answer, she notes: "Es gab ein Vorher, das mit der extremen Diskriminierung als jüdisches Kind in Wien zusammenhängt, und es gab ein Nachher, mit dem man sich noch herumschlagen musste" (There was a before, that is linked to the extreme discrimination as a Jewish child in Vienna, and there was an after, with which one still has to struggle).[80] What is left unsaid is that the event separating Klüger's life into a "before" and an "after" is the Holocaust. Indeed, *unterwegs verloren* is a poignant illustration of the long-term effects of living through the Holocaust and the ways in which it continues to determine her life. Yet even in the face of the ever-present past, there is change. One such change is Klüger's new relationship with the city of her birth—which, amid all its complexity and ambivalence, is a step toward rapprochement.

NOTES

1. Klüger, *weiter leben*, 156.
2. Braese and Gehle note that by November 1993, over 130 reviews of the book had been published, and all major German-language newspapers had run substantial reviews ("Von 'deutschen Freunden,'" 76), and Schaumann writes: "Never before had a Holocaust testimony been so successful in Germany" ("From *weiter leben*," 324).
3. Lorenz, "Memory and Criticism," 207; Heidelberger-Leonard, "Eine weibliche Autobiographie," 188.
4. Klüger had had virtually no formal schooling. She took a "Notabitur," exams required to graduate from Gymnasium and attend the university, after one year of private tutoring. By her own admission, she was not as well prepared as students who had attended Gymnasium, but passed anyway. See *weiter leben*, 205–08.
5. Klüger, "Wien als Fluchtpunkt," 99. All translations noted in the text are my own. For passages from *weiter leben* that are also in *Still Alive*, I sometimes use Klüger's phrasing, but stay closer than she does to the original text.
6. Klüger, "Fakten und Fiktionen," 84.
7. Klüger, *Katastrophen*, 7.
8. Schmidtkunz, *Im Gespräch*, 47.
9. Klüger, *Still Alive*, 64.
10. Klüger, *Still Alive*, 64
11. See Painitz, "Ruth Klüger's Autobiographical Project," 380–96. On Klüger's insistence of comparing despite differences, see also Heidelberger-Leonard, "Eine weibliche Autobiographie," 196.

12. Klüger, *weiter leben*, 142.
13. Klüger, *weiter leben*, 142.
14. Alfers, "Ruth Klüger."
15. Klüger, *weiter leben*, 78.
16. Klüger, *weiter leben*, 78.
17. On Klüger's concept of timescapes and how they relate to memory and identity in *weiter leben*, see Wickerson, "Seeing the Sites."
18. See Painitz, "Ruth Klüger's Autobiographical Project," for a discussion of *Still Alive* as a self-translation that continues the autobiographical writing process of *weiter leben*. See also Machtans, *Zwischen Wissenschaft und autobiographischem Projekt*, 215–20, Schaumann, "From *weiter leben* (1992)," and McGlothlin, "Autobiographical Re-vision," for comparisons between *weiter leben* and *Still Alive*.
19. Like Schaumann, I use the term "cultural translation" to refer to the important fact that Klüger goes beyond a straightforward translation from one language to another by incorporating changes that take into account her American audience's socio-cultural context.
20. Klüger, *Still Alive*, 171.
21. Klüger, *Still Alive*, 22–3.
22. Klüger, *Still Alive*, 93.
23. Menasse, *Das Land ohne Eigenschaften*, 13.
24. Herzog, *Vienna Is Different*, 176.
25. Herzog, *Vienna Is Different*, 177.
26. Herzog, *Vienna Is Different*, 220.
27. Menasse, *Das Land ohne Eigenschaften*, 17.
28. Menasse, *Das Land ohne Eigenschaften*, 17.
29. Klüger, *weiter leben*, 66.
30. For example, when Klüger recalls the memories of Vienna that her renewed study of German evoke in *weiter leben*, 67. See also "Wien als Fluchtpunkt," 100–01.
31. Höller, "Ruth Klüger," 139.
32. Klüger, *weiter leben*, 68.
33. Klüger, *weiter leben*, 66.
34. Klüger, *weiter leben*, 68.
35. Kospach, "Ein Brocken."
36. Klüger, *unterwegs verloren*, 177.
37. Doerry, "Man ist irrsinnig indiskret.."
38. Kospach, "Ein Brocken."
39. Klüger, *unterwegs verloren*, 196.
40. Klüger, *unterwegs verloren*, 197.
41. Klüger, *unterwegs verloren*, 213.
42. Klüger, *unterwegs verloren*, 206–09.
43. Klüger, *unterwegs verloren*, 215.
44. Klüger, *unterwegs verloren*, 199.
45. Klüger, *unterwegs verloren*, 214.
46. Klüger, *unterwegs verloren*, 211.
47. Klüger, *unterwegs verloren*, 212.

48. Klüger, *unterwegs verloren*, 213.
49. Klüger, *unterwegs verloren*, 213.
50. Klüger, *unterwegs verloren*, 195.
51. Klüger, *unterwegs verloren*, 196.
52. Klüger, *unterwegs verloren*, 195.
53. Klüger, *weiter leben*, 113.
54. Klüger, *unterwegs verloren*, 202.
55. Klüger, *unterwegs verloren*, 200.
56. Klüger, *unterwegs verloren*, 203.
57. Austria-Forum. "Jordanhaus."
58. Klüger, *unterwegs verloren*, 49.
59. Klüger, *unterwegs verloren*, 203.
60. Klüger, *unterwegs verloren*, 202.
61. Austria-Forum. "Der Fünfsterne-Heilige."
62. Klüger, *unterwegs verloren*, 202.
63. Klüger, *unterwegs verloren*, 202.
64. Klüger, *weiter leben*, 79.
65. Klüger, *unterwegs verloren*, 200.
66. Klüger, *unterwegs verloren*, 200.
67. Klüger, *unterwegs verloren*, 200.
68. Klüger, *unterwegs verloren*, 200.
69. Klüger, *unterwegs verloren*, 232–33.
70. Klüger, *unterwegs verloren*, 233.
71. Klüger, *unterwegs verloren*, 234.
72. In the context of discussing the bombing of Hiroshima, Klüger argues that "some aspects of the Shoah have been repeated elsewhere (*Still Alive*, 64).
73. Klüger, *unterwegs verloren*, 234.
74. Klüger, *unterwegs verloren*, 226.
75. Pletter, "Der Pazifik."
76. Hofmann-Wellenhof, *Autobiographische Darstellungen*.
77. See also Taberner, *Aging and Old-Age Style*, and Yowa, *Eine Poetik des Widerstandes*, who both discuss the question of (not) belonging in Klüger's *unterwegs verloren*.
78. Hofmann-Wellenhof, *Autobiographische Darstellungen*, emphasis in original.
79. See, for example, Hofmann-Wellenhof, *Autobiographische Darstellungen*, and Kospach, "Ein Brocken."
80. Kospach, "Ein Brocken."

REFERENCES

Alfers, Sandra. "Ruth Klüger." In *Jewish Women: A Comprehensive Historical Encyclopedia*. Jewish Women's Archive, February 27, 2009. https://jwa.org/encyclopedia/article/klueger-ruth.

Austria-Forum. "Der Fünfsterne-Heilige – Johannes Nepomuk." Last modified April 26, 2015. https://austriaforum.org/af/Wissenssammlungen/ABC_zur_Volkskunde_Österreichs/Johannes_Nepomuk,_hl./Der_Fünfsterne-Heilige.

Austria-Forum. "Jordanhaus." Last modified January 11, 2020. https://austria-forum.org/af/Wissenssammlungen/Denkmale/Jordanhaus,_Judenplatz.

Braese, Stephan, and Holger Gehle. "Von 'deutschen Freunden.' Ruth Klügers *weiter leben – Eine Jugend* in der deutschen Rezeption." *Der Deutschunterricht* 47, no. 6 (1995): 76–87.

Doerry, Martin, and Cordula Meyer. "Man ist irrsinnig indiskret." *Spiegel*, August 11, 2008. https://www.spiegel.de/spiegel/print/d-58853033.html.

Heidelberger-Leonard, Irene. "Eine weibliche Autobiographie nach Auschwitz? Zu '*weiter leben. Eine Jugend*' von Ruth Klüger." In *Das erdichtete Ich – eine echte Erfindung. Studien zu autobiographischer Literatur von Schriftstellerinnen*, edited by Heidy Margit Müller, 187–200. Aarau: Verlag Sauerländer, 1998.

Herzog, Hillary Hope. *"Vienna Is Different." Jewish Writers in Austria from the Fin de Siècle to the Present.* New York: Berghahn Books, 2011.

Hofmann-Wellenhof, Dominik. *Autobiographische Darstellungen von Identitätskrisen im Exil. Frederic Mortons und Ruth Klügers Suche nach Brücken in einer neuen Heimat.* Innsbruck: Studien Verlag, 2016. ProQuest Ebook.

Höller, Hans. "Ruth Klüger: *weiter leben. Eine Jugend* (1992)." In *Grundbücher der österreichischen Literatur seit 1945. Zweite Lieferung*, edited by Klaus Kastberger and Kurt Neumann, 133–40. Vienna: Zsolnay, 2013.

Klüger, Ruth. "Fakten und Fiktionen." In *Gelesene Wirklichkeit: Fakten und Fiktionen in der Literatur*, edited by Ruth Klüger, 68–93. Göttingen: Wallstein, 2006.

———. *Katastrophen: Über deutsche Literatur*. Göttingen: Wallstein, 1994.

———. *Still Alive. A Holocaust Girlhood Remembered*. New York: The Feminist Press, 2001.

———. *unterwegs verloren. Erinnerungen*. Vienna: Zsolney, 2008.

———. "Wien als Fluchtpunkt. Dankesrede zur Entgegennahme des Bruno-Kreisky-Preises." In *Gelesene Wirklichkeit: Fakten und Fiktionen in der Literatur*, edited by Ruth Klüger, 94–103. Göttingen: Wallstein, 2006.

———. *weiter leben. Eine Jugend*. Munich: dtv, 1994.

Kospach, Julia. "Ein Brocken, der mir im Magen liegt." *Frankfurter Rundschau*, February 13, 2009. https://www.fr.de/kultur/ein-brocken-magen-liegt-11476963.html.

Lorenz, Dagmar C.G. "Memory and Criticism: Ruth Klüger's *weiter leben*." *Women in German Yearbook* 9 (1993): 207–24.

Machtans, Karolin. *Zwischen Wissenschaft und autobiographischem Projekt: Saul Friedländer und Ruth Klüger*. Tübingen: Max Niemeyer, 2009.

McGlothlin, Erin. "Autobiographical Re-Vision: Ruth Klüger's *weiter leben* and *Still Alive*." *Gegenwartsliteratur* 3 (2004): 46–70.

Menasse, Robert. *Das Land ohne Eigenschaften. Essay zur österreichischen Identität*. Frankfurt a.M.: Suhrkamp, 1995.

Painitz, Sarah. "Trauma, Memory and the Act of Writing in Ruth Klüger's Autobiographical Project." *Forum for Modern Language Studies* 55, no. 4 (2019): 380–96.

Pletter, Marita. "Der Pazifik hat die richtige Farbe." *Die Zeit*, March 3, 1995. https://www.zeit.de/1995/10/Der_Pazifik_hat_die_richtige_Farbe.

Schaumann, Caroline. "From *weiter leben* (1992) to *Still Alive* (2001): Ruth Klüger's Cultural Translation of Her 'German Book' for an American Audience." *The German Quarterly* 77, no. 3 (Summer 2004): 324–39.

Schmidtkunz, Renata. *Im Gespräch. Ruth Klüger*. Vienna: Mandelbaum, 2008.

Taberner, Stuart. *Aging and Old-Age Style in Günter Grass, Ruth Klüger, Christa Wolf, and Martin Walser: The Mannerism of a Late Period*. Rochester: Camden House, 2013.

Yowa, Serge. *Eine Poetik des Widerstandes. Exil, Sprache und Identitätsproblematik bei Fred Wander und Ruth Klüger*. Würzburg: Königshausen und Neumann, 2014.

Wickerson, Erica. "Seeing the Sites: The Topography of Memory and Identity in Ruth Klüger's *weiter leben*." *The Modern Language Review* 108, no. 1 (January 2013): 202–20.

Chapter 7

Fractures and Refractions in Argentina

Prosthetic Memory and Edgardo Cozarinsky's Lejos de dónde

Amy Kaminsky

When in 1943 the great Argentinean writer Jorge Luis Borges published a short story called "The Secret Miracle," followed in 1946 by "Deutsches Requiem," he established himself, as Federico Finchelstein notes, as "one of the first writers to view the Holocaust as part of global history."[1] Although much of Borges's work is deeply rooted in Argentine history and geography, these two Holocaust-themed fictions are not. In them, Borges leaves Argentina itself out of the Holocaust story, unlike subsequent Argentine writers and artists. For, Borges notwithstanding, Argentina's cultural memory of the Holocaust, like any other nation's, is in some way a measure of its relationship to the events of the Shoah and its aftermath. Argentina's own connection is a complex and paradoxical mix of diasporas, refractions, and repetitions. It is indirect, contradictory, and complex, an amalgam of Holocaust memory, survival, impunity, and—if not imitation—something like it: Homage, perhaps, or fragmentary replication.

Two modern Jewish diasporas brought a significant number of Jews to Argentina. The first took place in the decades bracketing the turn of the century when Jewish flight from Europe was about escaping pogroms and poverty. By 1920, the Jewish community in Argentina was robust enough to open a space for a second wave of Jews made up primarily of those fleeing the rise of National Socialism in Europe, as well as some who lived through the Holocaust and survived to see Nazism's eventual defeat. During the same post-war period another scattering, this one of Nazi war criminals desperate to escape trial and punishment, were welcomed, not by distant relatives who had already made a life in Argentina, but by a leader, Juan Domingo Perón, who cultivated his own paternalistic, nationalist cult of personality, and whose fall and subsequent rise decades later would pave the way for a fractured repetition of some of the Holocaust's brutal practices.

Jews seeking to leave Europe during Hitler's ascendency found greater restrictions on immigration to Argentina than earlier generations of immigrants had, a reality echoed not only in most of Latin America but in the United States as well. In the nineteenth century, successive Argentine governments had encouraged European immigration as a way to develop and modernize the new nation. This policy was eventually extended to include eastern European Jews. By World War I, more than 100,000 Jews lived in Argentina.[2] But barriers to Jewish immigration began to spring up in the 1920s. Argentina's strong pro-immigration policy in the nineteenth century and early twentieth century was replaced by a far less liberal law that granted entry only to people "beneficial" to the nation.[3] Nevertheless, at approximately 75,000, the number of Jews entering Argentina between 1920 and 1931 was startlingly similar to the number that entered in the decade between 1903 and 1913. It wasn't until 1933 that new restrictive immigration laws began closing Argentina's borders. The world economic crisis that occasioned these new immigration restrictions coincided, fatally, with Hitler's rise; and in 1938, just as the Nazi machinery of death was being consolidated, Argentina closed its borders to Jews altogether. In 1939, some 4,400 made their way into the country despite the restrictions, but both during and after the war Argentina was no longer the haven for Jews that it once (and always problematically) had been.[4] Still, many Jewish survivors made their way to Argentina. Previous Jewish immigration to that nation had established Latin America's largest Jewish population there. Buenos Aires had a thriving Jewish community, and the countryside was dotted with Jewish agricultural settlements. Not a few Holocaust survivors had relatives in Argentina.

Argentina had been neutral for most of World War II; ultimately, as the conflict was coming to an end, it declared war on the Axis. Nevertheless Perón, a charismatic populist with a military background, found much to like in National Socialism. When he came to power in 1946, he was in a position to make it relatively easy for Nazi war criminals to relocate to Argentina and hide in plain sight. After the fall of the Third Reich, a network of anti-Communist Catholic clergy developed escape routes to help war criminals make their way to clandestine lives outside Western Europe and the Soviet Union after the fall of the Third Reich. These escape routes, now known as "ratlines," ran both through Franco's Spain and Italy, not infrequently ending in Perón's Argentina. Two particularly high-profile war criminals, Adolf Eichmann and Josef Mengele, used the ratlines to make their way there.

In 1961, six years after a coup overthrew Perón, the Israeli Mossad located Eichmann living in a small town in the outskirts of Buenos Aires, seized him, and brought him to trial in Israel for war crimes. Argentina was thus crystalized in the global imaginary as the quintessential post-war Nazi haven. Within Argentina, the Eichmann kidnapping triggered anti-Israeli sentiment that played out locally as anti-Semitism.[5] In his succinct and enlightening discussion of Argentina as a haven for Nazi war criminals and collaborators, Raanan Rein makes the point that Argentina was hardly the only nation to harbor them. Although Rein in the end faults Argentina for allowing "so many criminals" and collaborators to enter the nation, he suggests that the number of former Nazis who made their way to Argentina actually was lower than many assume.[6] By contrasting the actual, perhaps rather small, number of Nazi criminals in Argentina to the idea that Argentina was thought to be a singular haven for them, Rein suggests what I wish to argue: that their presence at all, in however small a number, punctuated by Eichmann's capture and Mengele's escape, profoundly reconfigures the nation in its own, and in the global, imaginary as a uniquely welcoming place for them. When proto-Nazi ideology and practices reemerge in the 1976–1983 dictatorship, they both reinforce this belief and demonstrate just how deeply rooted Nazi ideology has run in Argentina.

The broad outlines of the Nazi–Argentina connection range from the government to the neighborhood and from Buenos Aires to Patagonia. The secret lives of who-knows-how-many living underground in plain sight, together with the spectacular kidnapping of Eichmann and the failure to apprehend Mengele, who fled Argentina, winding up in Brazil, fuel the fascination with Argentina as a place of Nazi refuge. In the Argentine imaginary, the actual numbers are less important than the reverberations that ring back and forth in crescendo.[7] It is unsurprising that the exploration of the nation's willingness to absorb the perpetrators of unthinkable crimes, together with the tension between Argentina as a haven for Jewish survivors and as a hiding place for their tormentors, is an important feature of post-Holocaust literature in Argentina.[8] Written largely, but not exclusively, by Jews, these texts prod the tender places where Nazism festers just below the skin. Edgardo Cozarinsky's 2009 novel, *Lejos de dónde* (Far From Where?), approaches this thematic by imagining the life of a German woman who evades arrest when Auschwitz is liberated and, passing as a Jew, makes her way to Argentina.[9]

Lejos de dónde has two protagonists. The first, whose story occupies the first part of the narrative, is a woman who worked in the bureaucracy of the death camps. Her son, Federico, takes her place a little more than halfway through the novel. As a clerk at Auschwitz, the woman compiled names and ordered records. The almost ritualistic work of filing the documents of incoming prisoners and then transferring those documents to other files when the prisoners were killed is the textual counterpart of the actual violence done to the people whose names and documents she moves from one file drawer to another. She has neither the empathy nor the imagination to be disturbed by her chilling participation in the bureaucracy of death. Early on, Cozarinsky establishes her as a character whose great instinct for survival compensates for her paltry intellect. She has happily internalized the notion of her own racial superiority, even as she senses that she isn't very bright herself.

The woman's understanding of Jews is made up wholly of anti-Semitic tropes; early in her escape, lugging a bag of gold teeth taken from the dead at Auschwitz, she tries to find her mother's former employer and lover, a Viennese jeweler to whom she hopes to sell the grisly booty. Until she gets to the site where his shop had been and asks a neighbor where he might be, it never occurs to her that he was Jewish. Her distress when this knowledge dawns on her is born of her need to reassess both her admiration for her mother (who must have known she was sleeping with a Jew) and her memory of the kind and generous fellow she herself knew, to bring them in line with her unshakeable anti-Semitism.

As the Red Army approaches Auschwitz, the woman runs away, carrying with her not only the sack of gold teeth but also the passport of a recently killed Jewish woman named Taube Fischbein, a document she was supposed to have consigned to the file cabinet of the dead. Bearing no real resemblance to the photograph in the passport, but linked now to Taube Fischbein's identity, she makes her way to Argentina along the ratlines. On her journey, she manages to find a parish priest in Vienna who locates her baptismal certificate, and therefore agrees to help her escape. Here the narrator has the opportunity to make the woman's name known to the reader, but he does not. Instead, the priest suggests another name she might adopt–Therese Feldkirch—with the flimsy justification that it has the same initials as those on her stolen passport. The woman sheds her own identity, and the narrator allows her to continue with none. Cozarinsky deftly portrays her with the same level of sympathy that she affords to the dead woman whose passport she has taken. He gives the original Taube Fischbein a name, but he denies one to his protagonist. She is empty of humanity, which her lack of an identifying name underscores.

The priest who can get the woman out of Europe and to Argentina explains his dilemma: he knows she is Catholic and at risk of being caught and punished as a Nazi collaborator, but the only document she has identifies her as a Jew, and Argentina now refuses to accept Jews into the country. The fiction here is stamped by reality. The woman's itinerary, from Poland to Vienna to Trieste to Genoa and finally to Buenos Aires, is that of the historical ratlines, peopled by historical figures. In Genoa she is given work as a cook and sometime maid in a ratline guest-house run by the Croatian prelate, Monsignor Karlo Petranović. There she hears the whispered the name of Father Dömöter, the Hungarian priest who provided Eichmann with the false passport that got him to Argentina.

The narrative returns to the woman's baptismal records periodically, always eliding the name that appears on it, as if to remind the reader that her birth name is not so much gone as it is utterly unavailable to her. Even her son never learns who she had been. Although he remembers that she "sometimes called herself Therese Feldkirch," it is Taube Fischbein's name that will stick to her.[10] Moreover, Federico believes that his mother is Jewish, burying her, in a final irony, in a Jewish cemetery. Moreover, following the custom of embedding a photograph of the deceased on the tombstone, he uses the only image of her he can find: the photograph on the stolen passport. Wary of being discovered, Federico's mother had always refused to have her picture taken. Along with a name carved into stone, a photograph is a declaration of identity and a reminder of the life the deceased had led. The name and the photograph on this tombstone reinforce the falsified identity, stolen from another woman, by now long dead. Buried in the Jewish cemetery, she has disappeared entirely into a name that was never hers and into a Jewishness she reviled.

Cozarinsky has written more than once about tangled identities that are anything but straightforward: discarded, rearranged, falsified, hidden, and lost. He has even written before of a Gentile woman who leaves her own name behind and takes a Jewish identity to leave behind a constricting Europe in favor of freedom in Argentina. But unlike the title character of his 2002 novella, "The Bride from Odessa," who exuberantly claims her new name, taking on a Jewish identity to migrate to Argentina in the 1920s, the protagonist of *Lejos de dónde* never becomes one with her stolen identity.[11] The Odessa bride becomes the matriarch of a thriving Jewish family, much loved and respected. In contrast, whenever the name Taube Fischbein is written, it is in the context of its *not* being this woman, reinforcing the readers' knowledge that she has lost her own name, never uttered or remembered during the course of the novel. The woman is always a stranger to the name she goes by, and she is always a stranger in Argentina. Yet traveling as a Jew is hardly a guarantee of safety. Apart from the anti-Semitism she is likely to encounter, the theft and possession of Taube Fischbein's passport are themselves crimes, and her Nazi past also puts her in the way of arrest and deportation. All the identities available to her put her in peril. Fearful of being discovered, she lives estranged from her self and from her history, and certainly from the world that she enters. She seems to go through life in Argentina with no identity at all.

The woman's life in Buenos Aires is reduced to two nodes: the German restaurant, where she works, and the boarding house, where she lives.[12] The route between the restaurant and the boarding house is a space of muddled, vaguely distressing, confusion. Walking home one night after work, she is gang-raped and left pregnant, but what for others would be a traumatizing experience does not much register with her. As the narrator says, "no le despertó asco ni placer" (it awakened in her neither disgust nor pleasure).[13] After her attackers leave, she considers that, neither robbed nor injured, not much damage was done her. Intensely estranged from her surroundings and from her own body, she goes home and waits out her pregnancy.

In her daily walk from her restaurant job to her cramped room, the woman passes by the back of the presidential palace, symbolically remaining at the periphery of the nation in which she lives. One holiday, drawn by the commotion of the crowd filling the Plaza de Mayo on the other side of that building, she finds herself facing the front of the Casa Rosada. There she is witness to an historic speech by Eva Perón, the importance of which simply does not register with her. She senses the emotional meaning of the speech and the response it evokes without being able to understand their content, no less their historical significance. At that rally she first notices the odor of charred meat emanating from the makeshift grills that are ubiquitous at gatherings of Buenos Aires's working class. This sign of Argentine fellowship and nourishment brings back to her the smell of burning bodies in the camp's overloaded crematoria in the last days of the war. That sense memory, which even at its strongest does not much trouble the woman, is attenuated as time passes without ever bringing her nearer to participating in the Argentine culture that the street barbecues represent. Eventually, she altogether stops recalling the Nazi ovens when she smells the *parrillas*. The woman's diminishing olfactory memory is a veritable leitmotif of the novel; its recurrence keeps the connection to Auschwitz present in the reader's consciousness even as it hammers home the character's incapacity to live anything like a morally accountable life. Moreover, the narrator's repeated observation of his protagonist's low affect serves to reinforce the reader's lack of sympathy for her. Her dull-wittedness might explain, if not justify, her moral emptiness; but by invoking it, Cozarinsky makes an implicit claim on the reader's intelligence, which, by extension calls forth a moral response of which the character is apparently incapable.

Cozarinsky's claim on his readers takes the form of what I have called "prosthetic memory," a form of secondary memory of traumatic events in which narrative is called into play in an appeal to others to take on a memory that they never fully developed for themselves.[14] Prosthetic memory is a pedagogical device designed to keep historical memory alive in the face of attempts at erasure and denial, but it aims at more than giving readers information. It is characterized by a multifaceted response achieved by both imparting knowledge and evoking emotional, intellectual, and political reactions to that knowledge, primarily via aesthetic representation. Visual art, film, literature, theater, and music have all been called into service as instruments of prosthetic memory.

Prosthetic memory is a form of secondary memory, and in that way it is similar to the phenomenon that Marianne Hirsch has named "postmemory."[15]

However, in its deliberate nature, it differs importantly from postmemory. If postmemory, as Hirsch has characterized it, is transmitted to and carried in the body of the children of survivors, prosthetic memory is deliberately crafted and brought to subjects who avoided or escaped knowledge of violence done in their names. When postmemory is represented in texts, that representation and its reception constitute the mechanism of prosthetic memory. The primary addressee of prosthetic memory typically shares a history, language, and culture with the author. As Naomi Scheman has pointed out to me, "the author is drawing on what they can take their readers to know—the work of writing is an intervention into a particular time and place, evoking responses that require breaking through numbness and willed ignorance but requiring that, under the resistance, the knowledge is there. That doesn't/shouldn't mean that the writing is inaccessible to the rest of us."[16] What is more, the responsibility the author implicitly asks the reader to assume need not be limited to a local audience. Although most North American readers are unlikely to understand all of Cozarinsky's culturally specific references, they are not exempt from accountability. The United States trained Argentine military personnel through the 1970s, and the US government supported the 1976 military coup and subsequent state violence.

In Argentina, the fashioning of prosthetic memory occurs primarily in films and literature that thematize the state violence perpetrated by the 1976–83 military dictatorship, in which 30,000 people considered subversive were disappeared.[17] In *Lejos de dónde,* the primary historical correlative for that period is the Holocaust. In most texts of prosthetic memory, the narrator forges a sympathetic bond between reader and protagonist, so that when, for example, the character suffers at the hand of the repressive state, the reader experiences vicarious pain. In *Lejos de dónde,* Cozarinsky takes a neo-Brechtian approach and denies the reader easy identification with the protagonists, who may be pitiable on some accounts, but whose vapidity and amorality evoke anything but empathy in the reader. Cozarinsky instead carves out a different path to prosthetic memory. Relying on his readers' partial knowledge of events and historic figures, he engages their collaboration in the production of the text. He flatters them by giving them credit for possessing knowledge that his characters do not have. Once he places his protagonist among a massive working-class crowd in the Plaza de Mayo on an October day, for example, Cozarinsky's readers do not need him to name Eva Perón. They will immediately recognize her and her speech from the balcony of the presidential palace. Presenting Evita through the eyes of a character who does not know who she is immediately establishes his readers' superiority to that character, making them complicit instead with the ironic stance of the author.

Cozarinsky also omits the names of Mengele and Eichmann. Like Evita, they are so well known that their names are unnecessary for the reader to identify them. When the habitués of the German restaurant where the protagonist worked recount, in hushed tones, the story of Eichmann's capture, his name need not be mentioned; here the characters as well as the reader understand the reference. The silence around Eichmann and Mengele thus has an additional function in the novel. Not only the narrator, but also the German exiles, avoid speaking their names because they know that to say it aloud would put all of them in danger. Among them, only the protagonist does not ever quite understand that Mengele is reviled and that the community of Nazi exiles in Argentina is therefore committed to not revealing his whereabouts. Unlike them, she seems really not to know his name. For her, Mengele is "el médico idealista" (the idealistic doctor) whose experiments would have the happy effects of making everyone's eyes blue.[18] Her secret desire was to be worthy of being his assistant:

> Quién sabe si, en vez de ordenar en un fichero los documentos de los prisioneros que llegaban al campo, para luego mudarlos a un fichero paralelo cuando ya habían sido liquidados, no hubiese podido trabajar como asistente de ese médico, merecer su confianza, participar en el programa de eugenesia (había oído la palabra en el campo y la había guardado, humilde retazo de un saber del que se sentía excluida), en la elaboración de una humanidad superior, suscitar así el respeto de los oficiales . . .[19]

> (Who knows if, instead of filing the documents of the prisoners who arrived at the camp in one drawer, only to move them to another file drawer when they had been liquidated, she had been able to work in the eugenics program (she had heard the word in the camp and she had held onto it, a humble shard of a knowledge from which she felt excluded), in the creation of a superior humanity, to inspire in that way the respect of the officers . . .)

In recording the woman's aspiration to be worthy of the company of Mengele and the Nazi officers, the narrator opens a space for the reader both to see the protagonist's point of view and to judge her for it.

Because she has admired him from afar in Auschwitz, the woman recognizes Mengele through his disguise. When she approaches him and calls him Herr Doktor, it is to signal deference and respect; he, however, recoils in fear. The woman seems truly to have no idea that he is fleeing from that identity. She gushes over him; the effect is to further alienate the reader and to reiterate her ignorance. Mengele denies the woman her last bit of nostalgia and reveals just how dangerous she might be to the others who frequent the restaurant. A few days later, the woman is hit by a car. Her death is banal; narratively it comes out of the blue. Cozarinsky gets rid of her without batting an eye.

Cozarinsky does, however invoke the names of historical figures whose names are necessary to speak if they are to be recognized. As we have seen, as the woman makes her way across Europe, Cozarinsky names two of the Catholic priests who facilitated the war criminals' escape. Within the woman's hearing, but always speaking in lowered voices, the restaurant's regulars discuss figures like Kurt Tank, the creator of the Fokker war plane, and the assassination attempt against "un tal Pavelić" (someone named Pavelić) whose name sounds vaguely familiar to her, as well as to organizations like Vianord, set up as a travel agency, which provided documents and passage to fleeing Nazis.[20] The novel thus serves as a brief history lesson with those names anchoring the novel to reality. The restaurant regulars also read and discuss *Der Weg,* a pro-Nazi, German language newspaper founded in Argentina in 1947. Cozarinsky thereby weaves into the narrative the link between those who can continue to spread Nazi propaganda because they are outside Germany and those in Germany who still want that message, with the implication that Argentina holds some responsibility for perpetuating Nazi ideology:

> Escucha a los hombres contar que la difusión de *Der Weg* está prohibida en Alemania por decisión de los nuevos amos, alemanes que colaboraron con los vencedores. En Austria, sin embargo, hay un correligionario que recibe de Buenos Aires paquetes de ejemplares y los hace llegar a quienes corresponde.[21]

> (She listens to the men say that the distribution of *Der Weg* is prohibited in Germany by the decision of the new masters, Germans who collaborated with the victors. In Austria, nevertheless, there is a sympathizer who receives packages from Buenos Aires and gets them to the right people.)

When Frau Dorsch's boarders, identified only by nationality, move away (the Hungarian couple to the city's outskirts, the Rumanian woman to Paraguay), they serve as markers of the Nazi scattering. One boarder, however, is given a fuller, if schematic and somewhat bizarre, story. Identified not by nationality, but simply as "the podiatrist," he meets Harald Kreutzberg, an internationally renowned dancer he had always idolized and who subsequently takes him back to Europe as his secretary and, presumably, his lover. To invoke an image by Marianne Moore, the imaginary toads in the garden are the woman and her son Federico; the poison garden of Argentina's post-War German subculture is real.[22]

Cozarinsky also uses references to specific food and drink to mark a Nazi past. The Bavarian restaurant owner serves his ordinary customers a counterfeit version of a popular German aquavit, saving his stash of authentic Malteser Kreuz for his regulars. The first time the reader comes across this quintessentially German liquor, it is at Auschwitz:

> El cabo, ya alcoholozado, [. . .] abrió otra botella de Malteser Kreuz. Ella se mojó los labios mientras él tragaba el contenido del vaso.[23]

> (The corporal, already drunk [. . .] opened another bottle of Malteser Kreuz. She moistened her lips while he drank a whole glass.)

This apparently throwaway detail occurs in a scene in which the woman steals the key to the storeroom where bags of shorn hair and the gold teeth that she later tries to sell are kept. But the aquavit is also important: it is what makes it possible for the woman to manipulate the soldier into a drunken seduction during which he passes out. She engineers this failed human connection for purely transactional purposes.

In Argentina, the sharing of authentic Malteser Kreuz is a mark of connection and fellowship. But when the Mengele *faux pas* seals her isolation, the silence of the Bavarian as he offers her a final glass of the aquavit propels the woman to her death:

> En los días siguientes querrá volver al restaurant con la esperanza de ver al desconocido, aunque sabe que ya no se atreverá a hablarle; pero se avergüenza del impulso por el que se dejó llevar y posterga todas las noches la visita. Cuando finalmente se atreve, nadie ocupa la mesa poco iluminada del rincón. Es una noche cálida de septiembre, el aire tibio ya anuncia el verano. El bávaro la saluda parcamente y le ofrece sin una palabra el vaso habitual de Malteser Kreuz. Ella lo bebe de un trago y se despide.
>
> Al cruzar la calle Maipú en la esquina donde la plaza San Martín termina al borde de Leandro Alem, un automóvil pasa a toda velocidad y la atropella sin detenerse.[24]

> (In the following days she will want to go back to the restaurant with the hope of seeing the stranger, although she knows she will not dare speak to him again. But she is ashamed of the impulse that drove her to speak in the first place and every night she puts off her visit. When she finally works up the courage, no one is sitting at the dark corner table. It is a hot September night; the warm air is a harbinger of the coming summer. The Bavarian greets her tersely and without a word offers her the habitual glass of Malteser Kreuz. She drinks it in a single swallow and says goodnight.

As she crosses Calle Maipú, at the corner where the Plaza de San Martín ends at the edge of Leandro Alem, a car speeds by and runs into her without stopping.)

The German aquavit ties the fictional woman even more firmly to history, trailing affect and judgment. Cozarinsky packs this short novel full of such historical details in a deeply pedagogical act, building in his readers a visceral secondary prosthetic memory with a composite of facts and affect.

As a project of prosthetic memory, *Lejos de dónde* is a Jewish novel without Jews. Instead, Jews haunt the novel, and they especially haunt the main character. Actual Jews appear only once at the level of the récit, when the woman is sent across town to a delicatessen to buy provisions for the restaurant and discovers that the purveyors are Jewish. These Jews know they are selling to former Nazis, one remarking, "La envía nuestro nuevo amigo, el viejo enemigo de la calle Maipú, ¿no?"[25] (Our new friend, our old enemy from Calle Maipú, sent you, no?) The woman is clearly uncomfortable: Incapaz de pronunciar una palabra, ella esbozó una mueca que no llegó a sonrisa.[26] (Unable to say a word, she twisted her face into something that was not quite a smile.)

The Jewish delicatessen owner is eager to have a new wholesale customer, telling her that her employer will be happy with both the quality and the price of the pickles and herring—food that German Jews and non-Jews consider their own. The owner sends her off with a disconcerting, perhaps ironic, *mazel tov* "que sonó burlón a sus oídos cristianos" (85) (that sounded mocking to her Christian ears). As she makes her way out of the store and through the neighborhood, the woman can only perceive the scene through the screen of anti-Semitic stereotype and her own dull unease:

> Ella salió a una calle que, en ese mismo momento, sintió que se le había transformado en territorio peligroso. Las piezas de tela de colores vivos desplegadas a la entrada de las tiendas le repugnaban como si ese comercio escondiera en sus fondos uno de esos prostíbulos de niñas secuestradas que, le habían explicado en Viena, eran el tráfico frecuente de la raza inferior. El chico que lamía perezosamente un cucurucho de helado le echaba una mirada torva. Dos mujeres que intercambiaban chismes en voz baja se callaron cuando ella pasó a su lado. En la vereda de enfrente se había detenido un anciano de barba blanca, sombrero negro de ala ancha y levita también negra. No despegaba los ojos de ella.
>
> ¿Sería posible que entre ellos hubiese sobrevivientes? ¿Sería posible que alguno la reconociera?[27]

(She went out into a street that she felt had turned into dangerous territory for her at that very moment. The brightly colored pieces of cloth hanging in the entryways of the stores repelled her as if behind them were hidden one of those brothels full of kidnapped girls in which, they had told her in Vienna, the inferior race frequently trafficked. The little boy who lazily licked an ice cream cone gave her a cross-eyed look. Two women who were exchanging gossip fell silent as she passed. In the doorway across the street an old man with a white beard, wide-brimmed black hat, and black coat had stopped. He didn't take his eyes off her.

Could it be possible that there might have been survivors among them? Could one of them have recognized her?)

Although *Lejos de dónde* is virtually devoid of Jewish characters, Cozarinsky includes among the historical figures he invokes one who was, in fact, Jewish: Yevgeni Khaldei, a photojournalist who documented aftermath of the war for TASS. Khaldei's presence in the novel serves quite a different purpose from that of the Nazis and their sympathizers whose lives somehow touch the woman's. Although, like them, Khaldei occupies both the real world of the reader and, tangentially, the fictional world of the novel's characters, he serves as a point of reference rather than as either a character in the novel or a vector of prosthetic memory. Something like a mirror for self-reflection for the author, he is linked only in the most tentative way to the novel's story line. The woman never actually crosses paths with the Soviet Jewish photographer, but they occasionally reverberate ever so faintly with each other's story. Early in the novel, during her flight along the ratlines, Cozarinsky places the woman on a park bench in Vienna that is likely the one photographed a few months later by Khaldei:

> Pocos meses más tarde, en el mismo banco en que esa mujer abatida, asustada, buscó descanso en una pausa de su huida, o en otro idéntico del Volkspark, iba a haber cadáveres. Ya no en medio de la nieve, sino en la verdísima primavera que coincidió con el final de la guerra.
>
> Los va a fotografiar, en los primeros días de ocupación soviética en Viena, el joven Yevgueni Khaldei, que acompaña el Ejército Rojo como corresponsal de la agencia de noticias Tass. En su imagen aparecen tres cadáveres, dos de ellos sentados, el tercero acostado, sobre bancos contiguos. La vestimenta de esas personas es decorosa: abrigos de paño, piernas cubiertas por medias oscuras, knickerbockers en un caso, zapatos sencillos.[28]

(Just a few months later, on the same bench on which this beaten-down, frightened woman looked for rest in a pause from her flight, or on another identical one in the Volkspark, there would be corpses. This time not with snow all around, but in the bright green spring that coincided with the end of the war.

They will be photographed, in the first days of Soviet occupation in Vienna, by the young Yevgeny Khaldei, who accompanies the Red Army as a correspondent for TASS. In his image we see three dead bodies, two of them seated, the third lying down, on adjoining benches. The clothing of these people is decorous: cloth coats, legs covered with dark stockings, knickerbockers in one case, simple shoes.)

Cozarinsky's dispassionate, detailed description matches Khaldei's in both content and form. If you search for the photo on the internet, you will find it the same in every detail as Cozarinsky's description. It is his introduction to a figure to whom he will return many times in the novel, most often with reference to the photograph that obsesses the narrator: Khaldei's famous image of the raising of the Soviet flag on the ruins of the Reichstag. In contrast to the apparently unretouched photograph of the three corpses on the park bench, the victory photograph was both reenacted and altered. The narrator's fascination with this image consists largely in its being a staged version of a real event that both does and does not pass itself off as being "authentic." His recurrent meditation on the photograph functions as an examination of the ethics and practice of prosthetic memory. Both Khaldei's photographs and the locations are significant, allowing the narrator to comment on the larger themes they represent.[29]

A novel that is about as devastating an event as the Holocaust carries with it a responsibility to keep, or make, its readers aware of that history. The prosthetic memory that I believe Cozarinsky is intent on shaping for his readers carries with it an obligation to them as well as to the past. The work must be internally coherent; it must be, in its way, authentic. Prosthetic memory, however, is always manipulative; it offers the reader facts, but it presents them in ways meant to elicit an emotional response that fuels a call to action, or at least to awareness. The story told in a fictional account cannot claim to be "authentic," if by that word we refer to absolute faithfulness to reality. The novel is by definition artificial. Insofar as the project of prosthetic memory is to provide readers knowledge of something they did not previously know, which they can incorporate into their own consciousness, producing an experience to which they respond as if the memory were their own, the novel form as a maker of prosthetic memory is rife with ethical implications.

To what extent it is ethical to use artifice to evoke a visceral response to real-life atrocity? Cozarinsky raises this question within the novel by displacing it onto his consideration of Khaledi's staged photograph. The narrator revisits the photograph multiple times, as if nursing a wound, pressing deeper with each return. To transmit the moment most convincingly, Khaldei had to recreate the scene, which in fact had taken place days earlier. The only Soviet flags he could find were too small, and even a quick trip to Moscow failed to produce an adequate one, so the photographer, with the help of his uncle, a tailor, literally fabricated a flag with appliqued hammer and sickle out of tablecloths. The narrator ends by recalling the darkroom addition of smoke to the scene. Because the photograph was made three days after the event, the sky was clear; the fake smoke, he notes, adds a sense of authenticity. Like this photograph, the novel, by definition a fiction, nevertheless lashes itself to historical fact, and in so doing elicits from the reader a sense of urgency that comes from its manufactured authenticity. By engaging in the pedagogical gesture of embedding historical figures like Khaldei himself into the narrative, Cozarinsky creates a sense of authenticity. This is the fundamental process of prosthetic memory. Put another way, prosthetic memory, whose goal is to create in the reader a visceral response to the narrative, to internalize it and make it one's own, traffics in artificial authenticity.

Cozarinsky recognizes the danger of constructing memory for his reader; the ramifications of prosthetic memory cannot be contained in or by the narrative. His avatar, Khaldei, makes an image that promotes a nation-state whose actions are themselves problematic. If the Red Army victory over the Nazis is to be applauded and memorialized, the Soviets' anti-Semitism also must be made known:

> Pero en ese 1948 en que ella explora la ciudad donde busca hacerse una vida nueva, protegida por una identidad ficticia que no necesita, Khaldei va a ver sacudida la suya por acontecimientos imprevistos. La creación del Estado de Israel suscita pedidos de emigracion de miles de judíos de la Unión Soviética y este movimiento dispara en el Kremlin una ola de antisemitismo. Stalin, que en 1939 había firmado con el Tercer Reich el pacto de no agresión que permitió repartirse Polonia entre ambas potencias, y dos años más tarde, ante la invasión alemana, declaró la "Gran Guerra Patriótica" y creyó un "Comité Judío Antifascista" donde enroló a Ilya Ehrenburg, a Serguéi Eisenstein y a otros notables, no vacila en hacer liquidar con un accidente fraguado a Solomon Mikhoels, director del teatro judío de Moscú.[30]

> (But in that year of 1948, while she explores the city in which she is trying to create a new life for herself, protected by a fictitious identity she does not need, Khaldei is going to see his own (life) shaken by unforeseen occurrences. The creation of the State of Israel gives rise to emigration requests from thousands of Jews in the Soviet Union, and this movement triggers a wave of antisemitism in the Kremlin. Stalin, who in 1939 signed the non-aggression pact with the Third Reich that allowed the partition of Poland between the two powers, and two years later, faced with the German invasion, declared "the Great Patriotic War" and created a "Jewish Anti-Fascist Committee" into which he enrolled Ilya Ehrenberg, Sergei Eisenstein, and other notables, does not hesitate to order the liquidation of Solomon Mikhoels, the director of the Moscow State Yiddish Theater, in a faked accident.)

This passage reinforces the tenuous link between the woman and Khaldei, which began with her resting on the park bench where he would later photograph the dead Germans. They are part of the same broad history, and by joining them in this passage, Cozarinsky implies that there is a real connection between this all-but-anonymous woman, who embraced Nazi ideology and worked in Auschwitz until the Soviet Army set her on her flight to Argentina, and the fact of Jewish conscription into the Soviet project, followed by Stalin's betrayal of some of the same Jews who had supported him.

Lejos de dónde brings the Nazi legacy forward some thirty years, when the woman's son, Federico, joins and then betrays the resistance to the military dictatorship that emerged after Perón's death and the ouster of Isabel Perón, who had been his vice president as well as his wife.[31] In this, the novel joins a cluster of texts that explore the fallout of Nazi ideology and practice, including Sara Rosenberg's *Un hilo rojo* and Manuela Fingueret's *Daughter of Silence*.[32] These texts take up a second peculiarly Argentine theme in Holocaust-related literature and art, namely the parallels between the state violence that was perpetrated during the 1976–1983 dictatorship and the Holocaust. The rhetorical echo that rings between the trope of Argentina as a haven for Nazi war criminals and the language of the Holocaust, both used by the dictatorship and employed to talk critically about it, has its counterpart in visual representations as well. As part of a large multimedia project on Nazism and the dictatorship, Marcelo Brodsky juxtaposes a large-format photograph of a German signpost giving direction and distance to Nazi concentration camps with a physical copy of that signpost that replaces the names of the Nazi camps with those of the junta's torture centers. This work, marking direction and distance to the clandestine prisons where people the dictatorship deemed "subversive" were held, tortured, and killed, is installed the outdoor walkway of a popular Buenos Aires cultural center where can be seen by vast numbers of people. Brodsky calls the piece "Nexo 7: Los Campos" (Nexus 7: The Camps).[33]

Argentina's particular mix of Jewish immigration, Nazi sympathizers, and state violence is the witches' brew out of which emerges this recombination: the dictatorship is bound up, rhetorically and materially, with the Holocaust. The fact that a disproportionate number of Jews were disappeared during the years of state violence serves to further cement the link between the Holocaust and the Argentine dictatorship. The testimony of Jewish survivors attests to the specifically anti-Semitic nature of their treatment in detention, as their jailers and torturers threatened them with, and subjected them to, Nazi practices.[34] Amalia Ran notes that

> The discourse of the Holocaust [. . .] functions like a prism for bringing into focus the past of Argentina [. . .] and its present consequences by means of

inscribing certain images, tropes, and moral and political evaluation within national history.³⁵

Florinda Goldberg agrees:

> The perception of a certain resemblance between the persecution of Jews throughout history, especially during the Holocaust, and the action of state and para-state terrorism during the dictatorship of 1976–1983, has become part of the Argentine collective imaginary. The Nazi as the incarnation of evil already possessed a certain tradition in Argentine literature [. . .] To the documented presence of Nazi symbols and rhetoric among the perpetrators of repression, corresponded, almost automatically, the homologizing of the victims of both. Argentine discourse about/against the dictatorship adopted terms like "concentration camp," "ghetto," "genocide," "final solution," and even "Holocaust" together with toponyms turned into archetypes of a specific kind of horror.³⁶

Importantly, Goldberg sorts out the levels on which Nazi Germany and Argentina under dictatorship resonate. First, there is the demonization of an internal "other," who is represented as a danger to the body politic that must be extirpated, first by confining those others and finally by eliminating them. The second is the experience of diaspora among the survivors, and the third is the indifference of the larger society to what was done in their name.³⁷

As Goldberg indicates, even though all Argentina lived through the historical period during which the brutality was carried out and some of the practices, like arrests on public transportation and paramilitary incursions into homes to take its victims away, were carried out in full public view, the broader society turned a blind eye to the state violence carried out in its name. Prosthetic memory makes its demands on this sort of willed ignorance. Artists, filmmakers, and writers who depict the government-sponsored disappearances and torture engage in the production of prosthetic memory to challenge and overcome it. This overt attempt to create memory of what was deliberately ignored is a call to responsibility of the larger society. Although by no means all the prosthetic memory texts of the dictatorship explicitly link Argentina from 1976 to 1983 to Nazi Germany, some most certainly do.

Fingueret, Rosenberg, Brodsky, and others engage a readership that includes many who avoided full awareness of the crimes that were committed in their name. Their self-imposed task is to create that awareness. Fingueret's novel, *Daughter of Silence*, does so by tying the Holocaust to the dictatorship through the mechanisms of memory and silence. The author dedicates *Daughter of Silence* "to our generation, sons and daughters of the Shoah and survivors of the Argentine military dictatorship," drawing a bright connecting line between the two instances of deadly state violence.[38] The novel's protagonist, Rita, is one of Argentina's disappeared: kidnapped, imprisoned, and tortured in the Naval Mechanics School, a building close to downtown Buenos Aires. Her mother, Tinkeleh, a survivor of Terezin, had kept her Holocaust experiences to herself, as had so many others. Rita struggles to keep herself sane under conditions of torture by piecing together her mother's story. Rita's struggle to create a usable narrative out of the fragments of memory her mother afforded her echoes Borges's conceit in "The Secret Miracle."[39] In that story, the single moment between the discharge of the gun and the bullet that kills a Jewish writer becomes a year in which he can complete his work. In *Daughter of Silence*, the creation of the text itself keeps Rita from falling apart psychologically; when she abruptly falls silent, the novel ends.

Whereas Fingueret, Brodsky, and others draw a clear line connecting the Holocaust to Argentina's right-wing military dictatorship, Cozarinsky blurs that line by suggesting that it was not only the right that internalized Argentina's Nazi legacy. Anti-Semitism permeates Argentine society at all levels. As a child, Federico's classmates tease him for being Jewish, relying on Holocaust tropes, and when he is a young man his activist comrades reveal their own unexplored anti-Semitic attitudes. Cozarinsky engages the complexity of Argentine anti-Semitism in the context of Federico's short-lived participation in anti-dictatorship militancy in the late 1970s. By early 1977, Evita is long dead, and Perón, whose commitment to the working class made him appealing to a later generation of young leftists who cheered his triumphant return to Argentina in 1973, has by now died as well. Argentina's connection to unrepentant Nazis remains unresolved; the right-wing dictatorship that took power in 1976 (and was anticipated by brutal state violence under the Peronist government it deposed) takes up much of its rhetoric and not a few of its practices; but the leftist resistance, some of whose leaders, Cozarinsky suggests, grew up not entirely unsympathetic to National Socialism, is not entirely free of contagion.

Cozarinsky teases out the anti-Semitism of the leftist resistance and even dares to link it to a Nazi past. He takes the term "nationalist socialism," a term invoked by the Peronist youth, which even Wikipedia warns us not to confuse with "national socialism," and dares to suggest how easily they can be confused with each other:

> Pero ¿acaso su esfuerzo por creer, por integrarse, por asimilarse, no era el mismo de esos compañeros, persuadidos por tenaces acrobacias ideológicas de que el líder senil, largo tiempo adulado hasta que finalmente los rechazara, anciano menos inaccesible que Mao, más benigno que Pol Pot, era un legítimo mesías del socialismo? En el socialismo nacional, a cuya realización orientaban

su militancia, no aceptaban reconocer la mera permutación de los últimos términos del nacional socialismo.[40]

(But, perhaps, his effort to believe, to become a part of it, to assimilate, was not the same as that of those comrades, persuaded by tenacious ideological acrobatics, that their senile leader, whom they worshiped so long, until he rejected them, an old man less accessible than Mao, more benign than Pol Pot, was a true messiah of socialism? They refused to see the slight permutation between the words "nationalist socialism," which they were trying to build with their activism, and "national socialism.")

With references to Mao and Pol Pot, as well as to its demand for absolute loyalty, Cozarinsky points to the propensity for totalitarianism in the revolutionary left. Moreover, although the anti-Semitism of the left may be more subtle, it is ingrained; its perpetrators deny its existence in terms that lay it bare:

Federico no supo si como prueba de amistad o argumento proselitista, [un compañero] le había dicho, apoyando una mano fraterna en su hombro:
 –¿Sabés cuántos moishes están con nosotros? Para la orga sos un argentino más. –Luego, dejando que la sonrisa le invadiese el rostro–: Las finanzas de la orga, son los tuyos quienes las manejan . . .[41]

(Federico didn't know if it was as proof of friendship or as a proselytizing argument, that (one comrade) had said to him, resting a fraternal hand on his shoulder:
 "Do you know how many Moishes are with us? For the orga (short for "organization"), you're just another Argentine." Then, letting a smile invade his face, "The finances of the orga, it's your people who manage them . . .")

Unlike the writers and artists who see a unique connection between Nazism and the dictatorship, Cozarinsky refuses to let go the left off the hook. At the same time, Federico is no hero; after he learns that they consider him expendable, he blows up his comrades with a package bomb he was to have placed at police headquarters. He then makes his escape—both from the police, who would have considered the explosion a lucky accident, and from the organization, who, the narrator asserts, would have known he had betrayed them deliberately.

Like his mother, Federico has obtained a false passport: the narrator points out that his trajectory of escape mirrors hers. She is untethered, and her son similarly floats off, bereft of family and national ties, with no ethical grounding. Feeling betrayed by his comrades in the resistance, he in turn betrays them, leaves the country, and spends the rest of his life engaged in shady transnational dealings. Federico winds up trafficking in jewels and artwork whose provenance is unclear, perhaps once belonging to victims of the camps, and the booty, perhaps, of other political expropriations. He travels on false passports, crosses borders with money hidden under his clothing, is as alone as his mother was. In the end, he crosses paths with his half-sister, but since they are both so deracinated, neither of them knowing their mother's story, there is no way that they can know that they are siblings. Their history has been shredded. She tells him that she was a byproduct of the war, the child of an Austrian woman who for some reason was in Poland, that she was left with a family that did not, or would not, remember her mother's name. Here again the reader is given the pleasure of knowledge that is greater than the character's, but the mother's name is lost to both. The suggestion that the Polish family might have known but deliberately withheld it underscores the narrative choice of keeping that name silent. With this final stroke, the narrator obliterates the woman's identity absolutely.

Toward the end of the novel, Cozarinsky comes back to the uses of fiction, this time within the storyline itself. Federico, whose reading had been limited to mind-emptying detective stories, comes to learn that novels can be a source of knowledge:

Lo imaginario no sólo había llegado a iluminarle los años confusos que había dejado atrás; le permitía entender un presente que ya no podía ver en negro y blanco, que se le presentaba en innumerables, engañosos matices de gris, pero siempre gobernado por mentiras no encubiertas. Y en ese presente Federico había aprendido a abrirse paso sin ilusiones sobre el personaje que ahora representaba.[42]

(What was imaginary had not only come to illuminate the confusing years he had left behind; it allowed him to understand a present that he could no longer see as black and white, which presented itself in innumerable, deceptive shades of gray, but always governed by unhidden lies. And in that present Federico had learned to create a path for himself with no illusions about the role he now played.)

Ironically, Federico has come to embody the figure of the wandering Jew, a figure out of Christian tradition, deeply bound up with Europe's long history of anti-Semitism, that one of his clients, a shady but learned Jewish diamond merchant in Antwerp, explains to him in detail. The merchant tries and fails to interest Federico in a story by Borges, recognizable to the reader as "The

Immortal," but he does persuade him to read an Italian novel in which the wandering Jew is romanticized and redeemed:

> Leía todas las noches, una hora o dos antes de dormir. Y el sueño consiguiente se poblaba con imágenes y episodios que parafraseaban libremente esas lecturas. Las novelas policiales, consumidas rápidamente y desechadas en su juventud, habían cedido su lugar a una literatura sólo guiada por el deseo de internarse en dominios ajenos de su vida, donde sin embargo hallaba la explicación de ésta.[43]

> (He read every night, an hour or two before sleeping. And his ensuing dreams were populated with images and episodes that freely paraphrased those readings. Detective novels, rapidly consumed and discarded in his youth, had given way to reading guided only by the desire to enter into worlds far from his own, where nevertheless he found an understanding of his life.)

This paean to something akin to prosthetic memory is, however, diluted by its near juxtaposition to a final return to Khaldei's Reichstag photograph. Federico watches a documentary about Khaldei in which the already compromised image provokes the memory of the soldiers who were there that day, each contradicting the others, "hasta la insignificancia total" (to the point of total meaninglessness).[44] The only detail that retains meaning undercuts the very heroism the photograph is meant to show: the Chief Command ordered the original photograph retouched to remove from the arms of one soldier "varios relojes pulsera, signo elocuente del saqueo al que se entregaron los liberadores" (several wristwatches, an eloquent mark of the liberators' enthusiastic looting).[45]

Every redemptive representation also struggles to keep its own secrets. Our best hope, Cozarinsky suggests, is to wrest from fiction perhaps not truth but something approaching understanding, always aware that even as time burnishes, memory distorts, and that the makers of representations have more than one agenda. The best we can get is approximation, but it is essential that we do.

NOTES

1. Federico Finchelstein, "An Argentine Experience? Borges, Judaism, and the Holocaust" in *The New Jewish Argentina,* ed. Adriana Brodsky and Raanan Rein (Boston: Brill, 2013), 148. Finchelstein in fact includes earlier anti-Fascist essays by Borges as part of his anti-Nazi oevre. Also, Jorge Luis Borges, "Deutsches Requiem" in *El Aleph* (Buenos Aires: Alianza/Emecé 1971, 83–92, and "El Milagro

Secreto" [The Secret Miracle] in *Ficciones,* (Buenos Aires: Emecé, 1956), 149–157. For a lucid discussion of Borges's importance as a post-Holocaust writer, see also Edna Aizenberg, "Postmodern or Post-Auschwitz: Borges and the Limits of Representation," *Variaciones Borges* 3 (1997), 141–152.

2. Haim Avni, *Argentina and the Jews A History of Jewish Immigration,* trans. Gila Brand (Tuscaloosa: University of Alabama Press), 1991, 91.

3. Ibid., 102.

4. Ibid., chapters 4–5.

5. Raanan Rein, *Argentine Jews or Jewish Argentines? Essays on Ethnicity, Identity, and Diaspora* (Boston: Brill, 2010), 173.

6. Ibid., 88.

7. Saúl Sosnowski, "Counting Nazis in Argentina." *Jewish Quarterly* 46.1: 45–48 (May 2013), makes this point persuasively.

8. See, for example, José Pablo Feinmann, *Heidegger's Shadow,* trans. Joshua Price and María Constanza Guzmán (Lubbock: Texas Tech University Press, 2016). Originally published as *La sombra de Heidegger* (Buenos Aires: Seix Barral, 2005), and Patricia Suárez's cycle of plays, *La Germania* (Buenos Aires: Losada, 2006).

9. Edgardo Cozarinsky, *Lejos de dónde.* Buenos Aires: Tusquets, 2009. I have quoted liberally from the text to give English-language readers a sense of the novel because as of this writing *Lejos de dónde* has been translated only into French (Cozarinsky, *Loin d'où,* trans. Jean-Marie Saint-Lu. [*Éditions Grasset & Fasquelle,* 2011]). All translations from the novel are my own.

10. Ibid., 134.

11. Edgardo Cozarinsky, "The Bride from Odessa" in *The Bride from Odessa,* trans. Nick Caistor (New York: Farrar, Strauss and Giroux, 2004). In addition to the title story, several others in the collection deal with identity and displacement.

12. The landlady's surname, Dorsch, is, not incidentially, that of the chief engineer who worked with, and was the rival of, Albert Speer.

13. Cozarinsky, *Lejos de dónde,* 77.

14. See Amy Kaminsky, "Memory, Postmemory, Prosthetic Memory: Reflections on the Holocaust and the Dirty War in Argentine Narrative." *Hispanic Issues on Line* (Spring 2014), 104–117.

15. Marianne Hirsch, "The Generation of Postmemory," *Poetics Today* 29:1 (Spring 2008), 103–128. Postmemory accounts tend to be the work of second-generation writers, filmmakers, and artists. Visual artist Mirta Kupferminc, for example, has taken the Holocaust as one of her central themes. Images of a stylized, darkened Lodz ghetto, of the number tattooed on her mother's arm, of wanderers –some carrying their past with them and others uncannily unburdened-- recur in her work. She invokes the displacement and scattering of survivors with maps of her parents' trajectories, and with landscapes that are sometimes dreamlike and sometimes nightmarish into which she places figures on the move. Literary works in this vein include Sergio Chejfec's 1999 novel, *Lenta biografía* [Slow Biography] (Buenos Aires: Puntosur, 1990). In Chejfec's novel a group of survivors who meet regularly are caught in a narrative cycle of repetition, unable either to make sense of the past or to move into the present. See also Pablo Solarz's 2017 film, *The Last Suit* [*El último traje*], (Argentina/

Spain 2017), the story of an elderly survivor who makes his way back to Poland to fulfill a promise.

16. Naomi Scheman, personal correspondence, March 2020.

17. While the exact number of disappeared can never be known, 30,000 is the number agreed upon by human rights groups.

18. Cozarinsky, *Lejos de dónde*, 76.

19. Ibid., 76–77.

20. Ibid., 89. Founder of the fascist Ustase party and head of the Croatian government under the Nazis, Ante Pavelić was protected by the Vatican after the War and eventually settled in Argentina. In 1957 he was shot by a would-be assassin, but survived, escaping evenually to Spain, where he later died. According to Misha Glenny, *The Balkans: Nationalism, War, and the Great Powers, 1804–1999* (New York: Viking Penguin, 2000), he was responsible for the death of hundreds of thousands of Serbs, Roma, and Jews.

21. Ibid., 90–91.

22. Marianne Moore, "Poetry." *Others for 1919: An Anthology of the New Verse*, ed., Alfred Kreymborg (New York: N.L. Brown, 1920).

23. Cozarinsky, *Lejos de dónde*, 15.

24. Ibid., 112.

25. Ibid., 85.

26. Ibid.

27. Ibid., 85–86.

28. Ibid., 29–30.

29. The narrator also remarks repeatedly on Khaldei's photographs of the Nuremburg Trials.

30. Ibid., 62–63.

31. Perón married Isabel in 1961 (Eva, as much reviled as beloved, died of cancer in 1952.)

32. Manuela, Fingueret, *Daughter of Silence,* trans. Darrell B. Lockhart (Lubbock: Texas Tech University Press, 2012). The novel originally appeared as *Hija del silencio* (Buenos Aires: Planeta, 1999). Sara Rosenberg, *Un hilo rojo* (Madrid: Espasa Menor, 2000).

33. Marcelo Brodsky, "Nexo 7: Los campos." Digital photograph and installation at the Recoleta Cultural Center, Buenos Aires, 2001.

34. See Daniel Goldman and Hernán Dobry, *Ser judío en los años setenta: Testimonios del horror y la resistencia durante la última dictadura* (Buenos Aires: Siglo Veintiuno, 2014).

35. Amelia Ran, "Nuestra Shoá: Dictaduras, Holocausto y represión en tres novelas judeorioplatenses," *Letras Hispanas* 6: 1 (2009), 26 (my translation).

36. Florinda F, Goldberg, "Judíos del Sur: el modelo judío en la narrativa de la catástrofe argentina," *Estudios Interdisciplinarios de América Latina y el Caribe* 12: 2 (2000–2001), 140 (my translation).

37. Ibid., 141.

38. Manuela, *Daughter of Silence*, n.p. (orginally published as *Hija del silencio*. Buenos Aires: Planeta, 1999.)

39. Jorge Luis Borges, "El Milagro Secreto" [The Secret Miracle] *Ficciones.* Buenos Aires: Emecé, 1956, 149–157.
40. Cozarinsky, *Lejos de dónde*, 123.
41. Ibid., 123.
42. Ibid., 145.
43. Ibid., 148.
44. Ibid., 150.
45. Ibid., 151.

BIBLIOGRAPHY

Aizenberg, Edna. *On the Edge of the Holocaust: The Shoah in Latin American Literature and Culture.* Brandeis University Press, 2015.
———. "Postmodern or Post-Auschwitz: Borges and the Limits of Representation." *Variaciones Borges* 3 (1997): 141–152.
Avni, Haim. *Argentina and the Jews A History of Jewish Immigration.* Translated by Gila Brand. Tuscaloosa: University of Alabama Press, 1991.
Borges, Jorge Luis. "Deutsches Requiem." In *El Aleph*, 165–174. Buenos Aires: Alianza/Emecé, 1971.
———. "El inmortal." In *El Aleph,* 7–28. Buenos Aires: Alianza/Emecé, 1956.
———. "El milagro secreto." In *Ficciones,* 149–157. Buenos Aires: Alianza/Emecé, 1956.
Chejfec, Sergio. *Lenta biografía.* Buenos Aires: Puntosur, 1990.
Cozarinsky, Edgardo. *Lejos de dónde.* Buenos Aires: Tusquets, 2009.
———. *Loin d'où.* Translated by Jean-Marie Saint-Lu. Paris: *Éditions Grasset & Fasquelle*, 2011.
———. *The Bride from Odessa.* Translated by Nick Caistor. New York: Farrar, Strauss and Giroux, 2004.
Feinmann, José Pablo. *Heidegger's Shadow.* Translated by Joshua Price and María Constanza Guzmán. Lubbock: Texas Tech University Press, 2016.
———. *La sombra de Heidegger* Buenos Aires: Seix Barral, 2005.
Finchelstein, Federico. "An Argentine Experience? Borges, Judaism, and the Holocaust." In *The New Jewish Argentina,* edited by Adriana Brodsky and Raanan Rein, 147–178. Boston: Brill, 2013.
Fingueret, Manuela. *Daughter of Silence.* Translated by Darrell B. Lockhart. Lubbock: Texas Tech University Press, 2012.
———. *Hija del silencio.* Buenos Aires: Planeta, 1999.
Glenny, Misha. *The Balkans: Nationalism, War, and the Great Powers, 1804–1999.* New York: Viking Penguin, 2000.
Goldberg, Florinda F. "Judíos del Sur: el modelo judío en la narrativa de la catástrofe argentina" *Estudios Interdisciplinarios de América Latina y el Caribe* 12, no. 2 (2000–2001), accessed March 25, 2020. http://eial.tau.ac.il/index.php/eial/article/view/983.

Goldman, Daniel and Hernán Dobry, eds. *Ser judío en los años setenta: Testimonios del horror y la resistencia durante la última dictadura.* Buenos Aires: Siglo Veintiuno, 2014.

Hirsch Marianne. "The Generation of Postmemory." *Poetics Today* 29, no. 1 (Spring 2008): 103–128.

Kaminsky, Amy. "Memory, Postmemory, Prosthetic Memory: Reflections on the Holocaust and the Dirty War in Argentine Narrative." *Hispanic Issues On Line* (Spring 2014): 104–117.

Moore, Marianne. "Poetry." In *Others for 1919: An Anthology of the New Verse*, ed., Alfred Kreymborg. New York: N.L. Brown, 1920.

Ran, Amelia. "Nuestra Shoá: Dictaduras, Holocausto y represión en tres novelas judeorioplatenses," *Letras Hispanas* 6, no. 1 (2009): 17–28.

Rein, Raanan. *Argentine Jews or Jewish Argentines? Essays on Ethnicity, Identity, and Diaspora.* Boston: Brill, 2010.

Rosenberg, Sara. *Un hilo rojo.* Madrid: Espasa Menor, 2000.

Sosnowski, Saúl. "Counting Nazis in Argentina." *Jewish Quarterly* 46, no. 1 (May 2013): 45–48.

Suárez, Patricia. *La Germania.* Buenos Aires: Losada, 2006.

Chapter 8

Anglicization and the Holocaust in Judith Kerr and Eva Tucker's Fictions

Joshua Lander

The disconnection between Anglo-Jewry and the Holocaust is a recurring motif in British Jewish fiction. Such detachment has resulted in a relative paucity of British Jewish novels concerning the Holocaust. As Sue Vice explains, "[t]his is partly because much British Jewish Holocaust fiction adheres to the reality of Britain's relation to the events of the Holocaust, 'on the edges of history.'"[1] However, there has been a notable upswing in British Jewish writings, as Alex Stähler and Sue Vice observe, "this shift is characterized by a new confidence that, in terms of postcolonial theory, has been called a form of writing back."[2] Novelists such as Alison Macleod, David Baddiel, and Howard Jacobson write explicitly on Britain's response to the Holocaust. Their fictions challenge mythologies of Britain's wartime self-image by drawing attention to British anti-Semitism that testifies as a Jewish form of writing back. Similarly, Judith Kerr and Eva Tucker's autobiographical fictions respond to Britain's liberalist ideology that sought to elide Jewish differences. Both novelists' protagonists seek to "become English" and as such, struggle against Britain's anti-Semitism and the country's complex response to the liberation of Bergen-Belsen that initially, and intentionally, overlooked the disproportionate number of Jewish victims.

No death camps or pogroms ever occurred in Britain, nor was the country occupied by Nazi Germany.[3] Nevertheless, Tony Kushner argues, the "Holocaust was not just part of the history Nazi-controlled Europe—it impinged, even on the level of everyday life, on the individual and collective histories of Allied nations."[4] This is especially true for those Jewish refugees who fled to Britain to escape the Nazis. Their experiences, although distanced from the "concentration camp universe," remain bound to the multifarious histories of the Holocaust. Furthermore, as Ruth Gilbert observes, "British Jews who may not have been overtly affected by the Holocaust were nevertheless reminded that the position of Jews might always be precarious."[5] Here, I will examine how the Holocaust emerges in Judith Kerr and Eva Tucker's fiction, specifically focusing on the contested mother–daughter relations as a means of further unpacking the precarious identities of Jewish refugees dwelling in Britain during World War II and thereafter. While the geographic distance of the Holocaust has created a separation between Anglo-Jews and European Jewry, the fictions of Kerr and Tucker examine the traumatic experiences of Jewish refugees that managed to escape Nazi persecution. These narratives unpack the evolving ways in which the Holocaust shaped Kerr and Tucker's protagonists' quest to assimilate into British society. According to Phyllis Lassner, "[t]he liminal space occupied by these Jewish refugees—neither open nor closed yet both—invited neither reinvention nor hybridity. Their identities would remain hyphenated."[6] In both Kerr and Tucker's fiction, the hyphenated identities of German-Jewish refugees are bound up with the Holocaust, which symbolizes their otherness and undermines their protagonists' attempts to become English.

BE ENGLISH!

Judith Kerr left Germany with her parents and brother in 1933, after her father, Alfred Kerr, a prominent writer, discovered the Nazis were plotting to arrest him. The family fled, temporarily residing in Switzerland and France, before arriving in Britain in 1936. The *Out of Hitler Time* trilogy is Kerr's semi-autobiographical narrative of life as a German-Jewish refugee. The first installment, *When Hitler Stole Pink Rabbit* (1971), tells the story from the third-person perspective of Anna, enabling her to give a child's account of anti-Semitism and displacement. The second, *Bombs on Aunt Dainty* (1975), is a more mature work that explores the social and political realities of life as a German-Jewish refugee in Britain during World War II. The third and final installment, *A Small Person Far Away* (1978), focuses on Anna and Max returning to Germany after their mother's failed suicide attempt. Set during the Hungarian uprising and collapse of the USSR, the novel examines Anna and her mother's troubled relationship as they struggle to come to terms with the aftermath of the Holocaust.

Eva Tucker's two novels are also autobiographical. Tucker and her mother Margot evacuated to Britain after receiving sponsorship from the Quakers in 1936. Tucker's two novels, *Berlin Mosaic* (2005) and *Becoming English* (2009), focus on her and her mother's flight from Germany and their assimilation in England. Madelyn Travis argues that in Kerr's novel Anna "demonstrate[s] not a negotiation of identity but a desire to exchange one identity for another,"[7] and this is especially true of *Becoming English*. Both Kerr and Tucker's texts, then, are connected by their protagonists' shared desire to "become British." Such efforts, of course, affirm their foreignness: only the foreigner is required to adapt their bodies, language, and behavior to exist within this refuge. As Homi K. Bhabha has argued, "to be Anglicized is *emphatically* not to be English."[8] Yet the unattainability of Englishness further imbues the identity marker with a mythologic weight that does little to abate Laura or Anna's desire to become English. Englishness represents a totalized form of being that starkly contrasts the fractured identities both Anna and Laura are labeled with as "refugees."

The very structure of Kerr's trilogy suggests that England is a site of completion for Anna. *When Hitler Stole Pink Rabbit* ends with Kerr's protagonist and her family landing in Great Britain after fleeing from Nazi Germany and living as refugees in Switzerland and France. Upon arriving in England, Anna is greeted by an English porter who asks her nationality. After learning she is German, the porter asks, "Ittla?" much to the puzzlement of Anna and her brother, Max. He persists, "plac[ing] one finger under his nose like a moustache and rais[ing] the hand in the Nazi salute. 'Ittla?'" Realizing his meaning, the two children, alarmed, ask if there are Nazis here and profusely shake their heads in protest. Satisfied that the youngsters are not Nazi sympathizers, the porter "spat forcefully on the platform. 'Ittla,' he said. That was what he thought of him."[9] The phlegm, expectorated with violence, has a doubled meaning here. On the surface, the porter's revulsion at Hitler represents a welcome sign of security in England for Kerr's young Jewish protagonist. However, his action also signals England's guardedness against Germany. As German Jewish refugees, Anna and her family are in a precarious space where their nationality, rather than their religion/ "race," assumes a significant position. As such, Anna and her family occupy a doubled identity: they are determined to be enemies by approximation of their Germanness, and yet as Jews they of course are racially codified as aliens within Germany, despite their secularity. Their very bodies possess an uncanniness[10] in Britain that dislocates binaries between England and Germany, and this precarity is marked by the porter's spit; they are both welcome and unwelcome, safe and unsafe, German but Jewish, an enemy that is also the enemy of their enemy. Nevertheless, the novel ends optimistically, as the family "piled into [a] taxi. Cousin Otto gave the address of the hotel. Anna pressed her face against the window, and the taxi started."[11] The ignition of the vehicle signifies yet another journey of acculturation and assimilation, but with a distinct and meaningful difference: here, in England, Anna and her family are moving into, rather than out of, a country; their journey, literally signified by the end of the novel, appears to be complete.

This sense of finality, however, is troubled by the sequels to Kerr's novel, *Bombs on Aunt Dainty* (originally titled, *The Other Way Round*) and *A Small Person Far Away*. In both Kerr and Tucker's novels, their protagonists are connected by their quest for "wholeness," which each locates in the fetishized identity of Englishness. After arriving in England, Laura comes to understand that she, like Kerr's Anna, "realizes she has just thought at *home* meaning Berlin, meaning her granny and grandpa, her father. But that is not at *home* any longer. Where is that now?"[12] Laura has moved away from her grandparents and father, and therefore the conceptual stability of home is thrown into question. Likewise, Kerr's Anna articulates a similar disconnect, but sees such fracturing as an exciting adventure and claims to love being a refugee.[13] As Anna reflects in *A Small Person Far Away*, "[m]y parents got us out before any of it happened. In fact, my brother and I rather enjoyed it."[14] The journeys through Switzerland and France are exciting for the children, both of whom are shielded from the terrifying realities underpinning their emigration.

For Tucker's Laura, becoming a refugee offers her the opportunity to reconceptualize her identity, one that is removed from the conflict of being a German-Jew:

> At her Jewish school in Berlin the others would say incredulously: *your father's a goy?* She never got to know *his* parents, who live in Thüringen. In case her being half Jewish might have been embarrassing for them. Here in England she can grow whole.[15]

In her Jewish school in Germany, Laura is demarcated by her father's "goyishness," while her father's family ostracizes her and her mother for their "embarrassing" Jewishness. Tucker writes from the child's perspective, meaning that the dehumanization of Jews in Nazi Germany is stripped of its politically racialized framework. Rather, Laura understands the implications of Nazi ideology through the familiar and familial: Being a Jew in Germany means being disconnected from her father's family; it is a fractured identity that creates consternation, division, and alienation. Germanness is likewise defined by strife and tension; indeed, neither identities, which in Nazi Germany are delineated through racial qualifications, are desirable. England, on the other hand, is concisely mythologized as a site in which cultivation is possible, where her differences (religious, "racial," and national) can be elided.

Kerr's Max and Anna continuously echo the same desire to ingratiate themselves into the dominant culture and cease to be "different." During their time in France, Kerr underscores the consternation of being a Jewish German refugee and the performative strategies the children adopt to overcome this sense of alienation:

"Well—it doesn't bother you?" said Max. "I mean—being so different from everyone else?"

"No," said Anna. Then she looked at Max. He was wearing a pair of outgrown shorts and had turned them up to make them even shorter. There was a scarf dashingly tucked into the collar of his jacket and his hair was brushed in an unfamiliar way.

"You look exactly like a French boy," said Anna.

Max brightened for a moment. Then he said, "But I can't speak like one."[16]

The clothing Max dons make him look as though he is French, yet Anna's identification as such simultaneously affirms his otherness, as she notes his uncanniness, encapsulating his proximity that retains an inherent sense of detachment. Furthermore, the joy he feels from this disguise is undermined by his recognition that his inability to speak fluent French registers him as other, non-native foreigner.[17] Thus, difference signifies an alien non-belonging that cannot be hidden by wearing French attire. Max and Anna imbue language with an immutable connection to the nation that may be more important than appearance.

Nevertheless, the corporeal is a site where racial identity is performed first. At the beginning of *Bombs on Aunt Dainty*, Anna laments her dark hair: "Why couldn't she at least have been blonde? Everyone knew that blonde hair was better. All the film stars were blonde, from Shirley Temple to Marlene Dietrich."[18] For Anna, blondeness becomes desirable because it represents the normative look, both in Germany and in England. As Gillian Lathey points out, "[b]londe hair was fashionable in post-war Britain of course, yet Anna's desire carries echoes of Third Reich propaganda."[19] By choosing to name Temple and Dietrich, Kerr creates a pointed connection between Anglo and Germanic cultures. Both, Kerr implies, fetishize Aryan white bodies as desirable, implicitly placing Jewishness into a negated and "ugly" form that is thus positioned as undesirable.

Despite Anna's unhappiness at her appearance, however, *Bombs on Aunt Dainty* begins at a point in which Max and Anna feel acculturated. Set several years after the end of *When Hitler Stole Pink Rabbit*, Kerr's novel starts after Anna and Max have gone through the tumultuous process of adapting to English culture. Thus, Kerr omits the transitional stage Anna and Max undergo in "becoming English." On a train journey to Cambridge, Anna talks with a woman who asks where she is from. When she replies that she is German, the woman is incredulous:

The woman stopped in her tracks.

"Berlin?" she cried. "But you're English!"

"No," said Anna, feeling like Mama at the Refugee Relief Organisation. "My father is an anti-Nazi German writer. We left Germany in 1933." [. . .]

> "I should never have thought it," said the tweedy woman. "You haven't got a trace of an accent. I could have sworn that you were just a nice, ordinary English gel."[20]

The woman attempts to negate Anna's Germanness and preserve the monolithic singularity of Englishness. Her remark that Anna has no "trace" of an accent underscores how Englishness is conceptualized through speech, yet Anna's ability to sound English undermines the fundamental ways in which this nationality is conceived as unique. The woman's understanding of enunciation as an indicator of nationality reflects the hegemonic binary of wartime Britain that demarcated Germans as the enemy of the British. When faced with Anna, a German Jewish refugee, the woman's conceptualization of national distinctions dissolves when presented with a German who sounds and thus becomes English. The homogeneity of Englishness is troubled by the German-Jew capable of mimicking the "nice, ordinary English gel [meaning girl]" the woman imagined her to be.

German Jews were seen as a threat to British culture, and refugees were therefore expected to adapt their behavior to appear "less" German. Kushner highlights the key role British Jewish refugee organizations had in ensuring this unwritten condition was kept up:

> The refugees who were under the control of such organizations soon learnt the message. An article in the *Kitchener Camp Review*, on "One Refugee's Advice to the Other," concluded: "behave like the English people. Do not dress conspicuously, do not speak loudly, be polite, smile and be thankful. Once more, BE ENGLISH!"[21]

Jewish refugees were expected to show gratitude, love, and an uncritical appreciation of their host nation-state, and most important, to obfuscate all difference that would make them identifiably "un-English." Jewish refugee organizations, keen to assist in this acculturative process, published a pamphlet entitled, *While You are in England: Helpful Information and Guidance for Every Refugee*.[22] The fact such productions were made by Jews illuminates how British anti-Semitism shaped Jewish performances of their own identities. As Todd Endelman explains, "Britain's genteel intolerance exacted a toll, but not by blocking Jewish mobility, but by preventing Jews who were mobile from embracing their Jewishness unreservedly."[23] In other words, Jews were able to acquire capital, but the cost of upward mobility was a muting of their Jewishness. As such, Lassner, writes, Jewish refugees were expected to "remake themselves in a British image by revising their European Jewish identities and styles of being."[24]

The term "refugee" was stigmatic, and both Tucker's Laura and Kerr's Max detest it. Laura, for example, wonders: "'When will I stop being a refugee?' She does not feel like one. She feels like her grandpa's 'little rascal,' like her granny's 'darling goldfinch,' like her father's 'big girl' who is allowed to ask him any questions she likes."[25] The pontification is marked by a return to those family members now absent, with whom her identity was not centered around dislocation. Indeed, in identifying her father's willingness to let her ask whatever she likes, Laura connects her family with a freedom that she does not localize to a particular place (she isolates home as being in Meadow House, the temporary residence she is installed in Somerset). The multiple appellations afforded to her by her absent-family members starkly contrast to the singular and reductive phrase she is labeled with as a refugee.

The notion of "feeling" is particularly pertinent. Emotion plays an immensely significant role in the construction of national identity. Sara Ahmed argues that "becoming British is indeed a labour of love for the migrant, whose reward is the 'promise' of being loved in return."[26] Such a process is evident in Tucker and Kerr's novels. Six pages after pondering when she will cease to be considered a refugee, Tucker marks a shift in the narrative, as she writes: "Laura begins to feel it is her country."[27] The sense of ownership is evoked through emotion, an intangible connection to England that is purely abstract. As such, when Laura hears Churchill's eponymous speech, she expresses a desire to belong to the mythical "we": *We shall not flag . . . we shall never surrender. . . .* Laura so much wants to be included in that *we.*"[28] Laura's longing for inclusion is not predicated on the underlying understanding that Nazi Germany's defeat of Britain would result in her annihilation. There is nothing here indicating this affinity is borne from anxiety surrounding her precariousness as a Jew; rather, she is motivated entirely by her desire to be included, and identified, as British. In effect, she longs for Britain to reciprocate her love.

A similar pattern emerges in Kerr's fiction. Max shows an unwavering loyalty to Britain despite being arrested and deported to an internment camp on the Isle of Man. In a letter to his parents, Max writes, "I still feel like I belong in this country, even though they don't seem to agree with me at the moment."[29] This unflinching devotion, however, is not unanimously shared by his family. Max and Anna's mother rails against Britain's treatment of its refugees, noting the English's sympathy for German Jews is precariously conditional: "They can be sympathetic when the people are stuck in Germany, but see what happens they get to England? They put them in internment camps."[30] To which Anna's father replies, "We are guests in this country—one should not criticize one's host."[31] Anna's father parrots the ideology put forth by Anglo-Jewish Refugee organizations that set out to police and elide Jewish-German differences within Britain's public spaces.

Kerr mentions British ambivalence toward Jewish refugees but quickly shifts away from the topic, as Anna's father draws on his status to have

Max released. The social capital their father possesses means that they are more privileged than Tucker's Laura, for example, and infinitely more so than Karen Gershon's protagonist Inge of *The Bread of Exile* (1985). While Anna's father struggles financially—he is a German author who can't speak or write in English —he possesses enough clout as a notorious anti-Nazi activist to garner leverage and political support. Subsequently, Anna father's praises the English as "extraordinary," noting how "the Home Secretary can find time to right an injustice to an unknown boy who wasn't even born here."[32] This statement reflects the degree of privilege and power Anna's parents wield, and problematically overlooks the more difficult and unpleasant ambivalences of the British toward Jewish refugees. As Endelman highlights, the internment camps emerged as a result of anti-refugee hysteria centered around anti-Semitic notions of Jews being "unassimilable."[33] Yet Kerr's portrayal underplays Britain's racial politics, instead depicting the British as an "extraordinary" peoples, even though it was the British themselves who arrested and interned Max. Kerr's apolitical account of Britain's internment camps provides a simplistic perspective of German-Jewish refugee life that upholds the myth of Britain as a savior. Max, for example, continues to express his commitment to Britain, even after his arrest: "I know it sounds arrogant to say so, but I know I belong in this country."[34] Such belonging, however, is always complicated by Britain's ambivalence toward its Jewish refugees, an ambivalence that continues to creep into Kerr and Tucker's fiction.

IST MAMI DA?

While Laura, Anna, and Max can assume new identities as Englishmen/women, their parents' age, profession, commitment to Germany, and English anti-Semitism prevent them from being as socially malleable as their children. As Max tells Anna, "'[y]ou and I will be alright, but they'll never belong. Not here.' He made a face. 'Not anywhere, I suppose.'"[35] The parents of Anna and Laura remain *too German* to pass as English. In Tucker's fiction, the unassimilable mother is a profound source of consternation for Laura, who is ashamed of her mother's perceived excessive Germanic mannerisms. The disconnect between the two is marked by Laura's unwillingness to call Ruth "mother."

Incapable of ingratiating herself into British culture, Laura's mother becomes an unwelcome reminder of the German past, yet unlike Anna's Mama, Laura's mother Ruth is far more resistant to English culture. As Laura laments, "[h]aving Ruth about was making it much harder to try and become English."[36] Tucker accentuates Ruth's English speech with inflections that represent her Germanness, symbolizing her inability and/or unwillingness to become English. Her German-inflected accent undermines Laura's anglicized performance, creating a conflict between the mother and daughter. Unsympathetic and dismissive of her mother, Laura sees Ruth only as an impediment to acculturation. The narrative, centered around Laura, still enables readers to glean Ruth's character beyond what Laura perceives. For example, after finishing a shift at the factory, Ruth returns:

> looking pale and tired and spends a long time in the bathroom cleaning up. Her nails are broken, the pink nail polish chipped. [...] "How can I give people a massage viz hands like zese!" She holds them up. "All zat training at home vasted!"
> At home: Berlin.[37]

Ruth suffers from such laborious work: her cracked nails indicate the intensity of her job. The saddest aspect of her lamentation is the reference to Berlin. The last succinct sentence bluntly underpins a key division between Laura and Ruth, the latter of whom cannot conceive of England as "home." For her, England remains a site of estrangement, while Germany—the country in which she was born—remains home to her, even if the country is inaccessible, and lethal.

Ruth's desire to return to Berlin means that she is skeptical of England and resistant toward Englishness. For example, Ruth criticizes English Jews when she receives *A Helpful Guide for Every Refugee*, as she says, "Ze English Jews tell us how ve have to behave. Zey sink ve give zem a bad name!"[38] Her German-accented pronunciations invert and distort the English language and mark her out as foreign. While Laura is afforded an education, and thus an opportunity to immerse herself in the institutions and societies of Britain, Ruth's opportunities are far more limited. Indeed, even in Germany, Ruth's prospects were limited by her family, as Tucker writes in *Berlin Mosaic*: "The best she could do as far as they [her parents] were concerned was to find herself a husband they liked."[39] Ruth's accidental pregnancy with Laura consigns her to a marriage with Hugo in which she is made to give up her job as a school gym teacher. For Ruth, Laura's birth catapulted her into a life of conformity: "She did not say that Laura too had ruined her life. But she had—Laura even more than Hugo."[40]

While Laura ingratiates herself further into English culture, Ruth works across the country in labor-intensive jobs for little money. Their disparate experiences of England create a barrier between the two that reflects the strained conditions Ruth lives in:

> She has no idea what went on in Ruth's day at the factory; Ruth has no idea what Spenser and Shaw are about. [...] Sometimes she fantasizes about having

an English mother without forming any distinct image of what such a mother might look like. An English mother would probably have been brought up in the country, part of a large family. It would be fun to have English aunts and uncles and cousins. An English mother might be widowed, certainly not divorced. She does not fantasize about having an English father: she loves her real father.[41]

The disconnection between the two leads Laura to fantasize about an indistinct "English" mother sculptured as a fantastical opposite to Ruth, whose divorce from Laura's father, Hugo, represents yet another example of Ruth's improperness. The fact that Laura does not need to reinvent Hugo reflects how the absent father is adoringly mythologized, while the materially present mother, a living embodiment of undesirable Germanness, is reconceptualized in a pseudo-matricidal fantasy. The mythic English mother Laura imagines in Ruth's stead, raised of all places in the country—the quintessentially English pastoral setting—represents Laura's desire to erase her German-Jewish identity. Her mother represents a transfixed German pastness that Laura seeks to progress beyond, reducing Ruth to an abject figure of foreignness that occludes her humanity, suffering, and complexity.

The tension between Anna, Max, and her mother comes to the fore in the trilogy's final installment, *A Small Person Far Away*. Before that, Anna's primary concern is her father's inability to acculturate. He is defined as a "writer without a language,"[42] effectively leaving him unable to work, estranged from the German language and culture he knows. Shortly after the end of World War II, Anna's father dies in the United Kingdom, and his coffin is draped with the Union Jack. "It seemed strange," writes Kerr, "for Papa had never managed to speak English properly and had been a British subject only for the last year of his life."[43] Despite having lived the majority of his life in Germany, he is given a British burial, an incongruous ending for such a Germanic figure. Anna's mother goes back to Germany, and the novel dramatizes Anna and Max's return to Berlin, the city of their childhood, after learning of their mother's failed suicide attempt. The title of the book to be refers to Anna, who feels dwarfed by the emotional tumult of returning to the places of her childhood. Lathey makes a good case for such a reading, noting how "Judith Kerr's 'small person far away' is here not merely distant, but lost forever."[44] Lathey understands the title to refer to Anna's childhood, but it can also describe Anna's mother, whose presence is marked by her distance from the immediate world around her. Her fragile mental state and dislocation from her family render her a "small person far away."

In this third installment, Kerr focuses on Anna's mother and the prominent role she played in their acculturation in Britain. As Lathey points out, "it was [Anna's] mother who had dealt with the practical necessities of life and provided the meagre family income."[45] *A Small Person Far Away* examines the traumatic effects displacement has had on Anna's mother and her struggle to ascertain meaningful attention from the family she committed her life to. As Kerr writes, "Her cries of 'I wish I was dead!' and 'Why should I go on?' had been so frequent that both Anna and Papa had soon learned to ignore them."[46] This dismissiveness toward Anna's Mama recurs in the novel, as both children express impatience with their mother's fragile mental health. Anna and her mother's friend, Hildy, discuss her condition, which illuminates the way in which her suffering is perceived in relation to those German-Jews who survived the concentration camps:

> "It's just—she had a bad time for so many years." "Listen!" Hildy peered at her across the tea-cups. "My Erwin worked at Nuremberg. I know what happened to Jews who stayed behind. *They* had a bad time."[47]

Anna's mother's displacement and deculturation is framed in relation to concentration camp survivors. Obviously, her mother's experience is nowhere near as traumatic or as violent as those who survived the camps, and Hildy's allusion therefore nullifies and dismisses her mother's sorrow. Thus, the trauma Anna's mother endured is not given any space to be meaningfully considered, by either her friends or family.

Anna's frustration with her mother is further complicated by the gender politics underpinning the two's relationship. When the siblings visit their mother in hospital, she apologizes to Max for interrupting his holiday in Greece. When Anna asks why her mother hasn't apologized to her, she replies: "I mean, you weren't doing anything special, and I knew you hadn't been away in the summer."[48] Their mother's bias toward Max, her son the engineer, reflects the ways their mother distinguishes between her children. Anna, her daughter the artist, is expected to gratefully attend her mother's side. Both children express a contemptuous attitude toward their mother's mental collapse. They view her suicide attempt as a nuisance and a stain on their social standing. Anna, for example, observes that if "Mama dies, she thought suddenly with a kind of impatience, I'll be the child of two suicides."[49]

Anna's irritation with her mother seems to stem from having to return to Germany, the country of their childhood and the space in which they were displaced from. Such a return, I contest, threatens to upset their efforts to be like everyone else, that is, to be English.

Anna's return to Germany means she must confront the German language, which heightens her sense of disconnection from her English self. Unsurprisingly, given the setting of the novel, the German language assumes a significant space in *A Small Person Far Away*. Vice highlights how the "texts' *énonciation* (their utterance in the present by a first-person narrator) is in English, although the *énoncé* (what is represented) is German. Englishness thus supersedes Germanness, even when words are directly quoted, as specimens to be instantly translated."[50] While Englishness does, as Vice observes, possess a dominant ideological position within the novel that reflects Anna's (and indeed, Kerr's) preference for England and Englishness over Germany and Germanness, the interplay of languages threatens to disrupt Anna's self-conceived identity as English. During a call with her husband Richard, Anna wonders if she is speaking to him with a German accent, reflecting that their conversation "reconnected to some essential part of herself—something that might, otherwise, have come dangerously loose."[51] The irony, of course, is that Anna's notion of English as being essential to her identity. The essential "part of herself" that is threatened by her return to Germany is the mask of Englishness she has worn and embraced as her own over the years, yet in Germany, the performativity of her identity is made apparent. When Anna is greeted by a fellow hotel guest the next morning, she "emphasized her English accent and spoke more haltingly than necessary. She had no wish to be thought even remotely German."[52] Anna's excessive, drag-like caricaturing of Englishness serves to mask her Germanness, highlighting the porousness of nationality, and the central role language plays in identity formation. As Anne Emmanuelle Berger observes, "[t]here is no nation-state [. . .] which does not form a language policy."[53] Ironically, Anna now adopts the very strategies that were used to preclude her family enjoining English society, assuming an exuberantly staged speech to present herself as a singular, non-hyphenated English woman.

The discomfort with the German language reinforces the traumatic dispossession both Laura and Anna suffered as a consequence of Nazism. Germanness becomes emblematic of loss for both characters. In *Becoming English*, Laura remembers "one of the last things her grandpa said to her: *Don't forget your mother tongue.*"[54] Tucker's choice to write the grandfather's German-spoken statement in English reflects the disconnection between Laura and her German childhood. Similarly, Anna's memory of her childhood in Germany is tainted by a profound sense of loss, best understood in relation to her detachment from the German language. Upon learning that she is pregnant, Anna realizes that her children will not speak German:

"I suppose it won't speak any German."
"You could teach it if you liked."
"No," she said. "No, I don't think so. Anyway, it wouldn't be the same."[55]

It did not even bear thinking about
"The past life of emigrés is, as we know, annulled. Earlier it was the warrant of arrest, today it is intellectual experience, that is declared non-transferable

and unnaturalizable."[56] Theodor Adorno's gleaning of émigré experiences in the modern age raises an important question: How did Jewish German refugees living in Britain—a space in which German-Jewish difference was to be elided—speak, write, or even contemplate the ensuing persecution of their fellow Jews? How could they, to borrow the fragment's title, turn their thoughts toward the Holocaust, if their pasts—traumatic or otherwise—were silenced? The marginality of the Holocaust in Tucker and Kerr's fiction is not merely borne from the geographic distance separating Britain from the rest of Europe; rather, the country's ideological impetus toward silencing German-Jewish differences prevented them from thinking about Jews being slaughtered across Europe.

When Laura learns her grandparents have died at Theresienstadt, she is consoled by the women caring for her, much to her chagrin: "Laura feels all three of them looking at her with pity. She cannot bear that; she does not want to be pitiable."[57] The sympathy the news evokes is perceived by Laura as threatening because such pity reifies her difference as a Jewish refugee. The attention around Laura illuminates her foreignness, her past that marks her as un-English.

In Kerr's novels, Nazi Germany's persecution of Jews is less directly connected to Anna and her family. Upon meeting recently arrived refugees, Anna is told by one woman, "'You don't know what it's like,' she said. Anna closed her mind automatically. She never thought about what it was like in Germany."[58] There are two readings of this passage I want to draw on. The first is from Louise Sylvester, who contends that the silence surrounding the issue of the Holocaust in Kerr's novel indicates the British Jewish community's response.[59] Travis takes issue with Sylvester's argument, stressing that Kerr's family were not members of the Anglo-Jewish community but belonged to the German-Jewish refugee municipals.[60] Travis makes a well-reasoned counter-argument that "Anna avoids the subject not because she wishes to deny her German-Jewishness, but because she finds the consequences too awful to contemplate."[61] I would agree that Anna is unable to consider such violence because of how traumatic and unfathomable the Nazi Germany's persecution of the Jewish people, yet Sylvester's point remains valid. After all, Anglo-Jewish communities worked closely with refugees to ensure they understood the cultural requirements of life in Britain. Thus, Anna's unwillingness to reflect on the ensuing events in Nazi Germany should not be decontextualized. Her dismissal of the Holocaust assumes a doubled meaning: it represents her inability to conceive of the inconceivable, but also symbolizes her commitment to ensuring that her "host" nation's requirements are fulfilled. The plight of European Jewry is indelibly bound up with her identity as a German Jew, an identity that she is required to make invisible.

Yet, the Holocaust ruptures Anna and Laura's attempt to anglicize and serves as an unsettling reminder of their precariousness as Jewish refugees. *Bombs on Aunt Dainty*, for example, features a scene in which Anna and her mother visit the titular Aunt Dainty. During this reunion, Anna meets Aunt Dainty's husband Otto, whom we learn was interned at a concentration camp. Kerr's description of Otto is worth quoting in full:

> The figure at the door was old and quite bald and there was a curious lopsided look above the head which had a scar running down one side. It was dressed in a kind of shift and as Anna looked at it, it had moved one hand in a vague gesture of silence or farewell. Like a ghost, thought Anna, but the eyes that stared back at her were human.[62]

The language used here to describe Otto is bereft of any humanity: the words the narrator uses, written from the perspective of Anna, are "figure" and "it," suggesting that the survivor is perceived as surpassing or exceeding humanness itself. Anna cannot locate the human in the body she is seeing and it is she, as witness, who makes the distinction; that is, her inability to recognize Otto as human, she places him in threshold between human and inhuman.[63] Her failure, however, does not serve as an affirmation of Nazi Germany's dehumanization of Jews, of course; rather, Anna's inability to locate Otto's humanness through the corporeal reflects the unfathomably wretched violence Nazi Germany has inflicted on the Jewish peoples. Yet this psychological distancing is also born from a desire to separate herself from the Jewish people. Dehumanizing Otto serves an ideological purpose that ensures she is detached from the Jewish people, meaning she is able to continue performing as "English."

However, the encounter with Otto invasively brings the Holocaust into focus for Anna. She imagines her father in such a situation: "She wondered what it would feel like to be Otto. Supposing it had been Papa in the concentration camp.... It did not bear even thinking about."[64] The Holocaust is made manifest through Aunt Dainty and Otto, the latter of whom brings Anna to imagine her father in a concentration camp, which Anna cannot stand to fathom. Here, I find Travis convincing in her argument that Anna resists contemplating the realities of her situation.[65] Otto's presence in the novel brings Nazi Germany into focus, reminding Anna of her and her family's Jewishness, the very identity that brought them here to England in the first place and that they are trying to suppress.

In both Kerr and Tucker's novels, the protagonists must negotiate multiple identities, which includes confronting the ensuing mass murder of European Jewry. In *Bombs on Aunt Dainty*, Anna attempts to separate herself from the Holocaust. Anna learns on the news that the Grunewald, a woodland near her home where she and Max had played, has been destroyed, and feels "something stir [. . .] inside of her."[66] She recalls in detail where she and Max went sledging, noting how "[t]heir sledges had made tracks in the snow and it had smelled of cold air and pine needles,"[67] and remembers in the summer when "they had played in the patchy light under the trees, [and how] their feet had sunk deep into the sand at the edge of the lake—and hadn't there once been a picnic? She couldn't remember."[68] The sensory connection to the land returns us to a past in which Anna is physically connected to the German ground, and yet such intimacy is severed in her hesitant uncertainty as to whether or not they had once had a picnic. The lack of clarity represents the separation she feels toward her German past that has been violently seized from her. As such, Anna can only now conceive of the Grunewald as a separate space in which she does not belong.

> The Grunewald that was burned was not the one she had played in. It was a place where Jewish children were not allowed, where Nazis clicked heels and saluted and probably hid behind trees, ready to club people down. They had guns and fierce dogs and swastikas and if anyone got in their way, they beat them up and set the dogs on them and sent them to concentration camps where they'd be starved and tortured and killed . . .
> But that's nothing to do with me now, thought Anna. I belong here, in England.
> When Max said to her later, "Did you hear about the fire in the Grunewald?" she nodded and said, deadpan, "It's just as well we left."[69]

This is the most extensive meditation of Nazi Germany in Kerr's entire trilogy. The spaces in which Anna had previously connected to home are now emptied of all warmth. The overwhelming violence of Nazism, imagined by the Anna, from a distance, destroys any connection she once felt toward the Grunewald woodlands. Now, such a space represents the ideological consequences of Nazism and is filled with the sounds of marching black boots, the Hitlerian salute, the clubs, guns, dogs, and swastikas, all of which culminates in the concentration camp. The tactile connection Anna once felt to the lands, the sunken feet in the sand, the smell of pine needles, is now drowned out by the imagined Nazis enacting their genocidal campaign against the Jews. The ellipsis acts as the signifier between her past and present self, a gap that represents the violent decimation of her German childhood, as well as the separateness of her being in England, away from such brutality.

As the Allies began to overwhelm Nazi Germany, news emerged in Britain of the concentration camps, and this outbreak of information is detailed in both novelists' works. In *Bombs on Aunt Dainty*, Anna is "astonished at the reaction. Why was everyone so surprised? She had known about concentration camps since she was nine years old. At least now the English will understand what it was like, she thought."[70] Conversely, Tucker's Laura expresses shock at seeing the bodies on the newsreels: "In April, Belsen concentration camp is liberated; what newsreels and paper reveals sends shockwaves through the nation. *These almost-corpses are people I might have known*? Laura thinks."[71] Both writers illuminate Britain's shock at the emerging images of the concentration camp, however, Anna's optimistic suggestion that the English will now have an understanding of "what it was like" reflects the protagonist's problematic and overly simplistic hopefulness regarding Britain's tolerance of its Jewish refugees. The vagueness of the word "it," a rather meager choice for the diverse constellatory experiences European Jewry suffered, ultimately falsifies the actuality of Britain's response to the liberation of Belsen concentration camp. As Kushner explains, "the perception of German atrocities was confined to the concentration camps and would, even then, rarely refer to Jewish sufferings."[72] The particularity of Jewishness was ignored in Britain's initial coverage of the concentration camps, and this erasure was hardly accidental. Indeed, as Kushner notes, "[t]he liberal imagination demands that the concept of progress be restored as quickly as possible."[73] Essential to that progression was the universalization of the concentration camps that worked to further empty Jewish particularity as a means of assimilating Britain's Jewish refugees into English society.[74] Jewish difference, in other words, had to remain invisible, which meant that Britain avoided confronting the ideological kernel underpinning Nazi Germany's concentration camps: anti-Semitism.

In *Bombs on Aunt Dainty*, Britain's complex response to the Belsen footage is emptied of its nuance. Anna's hopefulness serves as a reification of the liberal will toward a progression, or regression, that erases Jewish difference. Britain's unwillingness to confront the Jewish specificity of the Holocaust greatly affected how Jewish refugees were, or rather weren't, able to publicly acknowledge Germany's destruction of Jewish people and their culture. Tucker explores the inarticulability of the Holocaust through Laura after she learns of her father's death in Dresden. "Like her granny and grandpa," Tucker writes, "her father is safe inside her, but she cannot explain that to her mother."[75] Laura's inability to tell her mother what her family's deaths mean suggests the powerlessness of those Jewish refugees in Britain, whose distance from Nazi Germany's persecution has meant that they are, to borrow Lassner's term, displaced witnesses. Their displacement has granted them freedom and security, yet they remain indelibly connected to the events of the Holocaust, even from afar.

Both Kerr and Tucker's protagonists feel marked by the Holocaust and their fractured identities as refugees, while their English husbands are defined by their "clean" histories that are undisrupted, linear, and monolithically situated within England. Anna ponders whether, "[c]ould she really belong with anyone so unburdened?"[76] Still, her attachment to him affirms her own place in England: "For the first time since she'd left him, she felt all of one piece. There were no more doubts. This was where she belonged. She was home."[77] Laura's lover Francis provides a similar role. After she reveals her family's plight during World War II, Francis is shocked, both by the suffering she has endured, and that she is not English: "'My god, that's monstrous! One has only heard, read about it, hardly believed . . .' he squeezes her hand hard. 'I'd never, never have known you weren't born and bred British; you haven't the least trace of an accent!' Laura likes Francis better and better."[78] Francis's inability to detect her accent—a marker of her otherness—makes Laura confident that she has become English.

Both protagonists' assimilative fantasies, however, are always conditional, performative, and unstable, reflecting the porous conceptuality of Britishness itself. Both novelists' illuminate how Jewish female refugees struggled to stake their place in Britain's society that was structurally designed to delimit their identities as Jews. Within both Kerr and Tucker's novels, each author illuminates how the Holocaust pervaded Jewish refugee experiences of Britain and the spectral remnants of their German-Jewish pasts, affirming Tucker's powerful proclamation that "the past is always present."[79]

NOTES

1. Sue Vice, "British Jewish Holocaust Fiction," in *The Edinburgh Companion to Modern Jewish Fiction*, ed. David Brauner and Axel Staehler (Edinburgh: Edinburgh University Press, 2015), 267–78, p. 277.

2. Axel Stähler and Sue Vice, "Introduction: Writing Jews and Jewishness in Contemporary Britain," *European Judaism: A Journal for the New Europe* 47, no. 2 (2014): 3–11, p. 3.

3. Caroline Sharples and Olaf Jensen, "Introduction," in *Britain and the Holocaust: Remembering and Representing War and Genocide* (Edinburgh: Palgrave Macmillan, 2013), 1–13, p. 2.

4. Tony Kushner, *The Holocaust and the Liberal Imagination: A Social and Cultural History* (Oxford, UK ; Cambridge, MA: John Wiley & Sons, 1994), p. 18.

5. Ruth Gilbert, *Writing Jewish: Contemporary British-Jewish Literature* (Houndmills, Basingstoke, Hampshire; New York: Palgrave, 2013), p. 39.

6. Phyllis Lassner, *Anglo-Jewish Women Writing the Holocaust: Displaced Witnesses*, (Basingstoke England ; New York: AIAA, 2008), p. 12.

7. Madelyn J. Travis, *Jews and Jewishness in British Children's Literature*, Children's Literature and Culture (New York: Routledge, 2013), p. 54.

8. Homi K. Bhabha, *The Location of Culture* (London: Routledge, 1994), p. 125.

9. Judith Kerr, *When Hitler Stole Pink Rabbit* (London: HarperCollins Children's Books, 2017), p. 279.

10. My use of the term is Freudian in that 'the uncanny is that class of the frightening which leads back to what is known of old and long familiar.' As I will show throughout this article, Anna and Laura are uncanny figures to the English people they encounter, as their English accents are familiar and recognizable, yet their accents conceal their foreignness, their un-Englishness. See Sigmund Freud, "The 'Uncanny,'" *New Literary History; Baltimore, Etc.* 7, no. 3 (Spring 1976): 619–645, p. 620.

11. Judith Kerr, *When Hitler Stole Pink Rabbit*, p. 282.

12. Eva Tucker, *Becoming English* (London: Starhaven, 2009), p. 3.

13. Kerr, *When Hitler Stole Pink Rabbit*, p. 265.

14. Judith Kerr, *A Small Person Far Away* (London: HarperCollins Children's Books, 2017), p. 21.

15. Tucker, *Becoming English*, p. 4.

16. Kerr, *When Hitler Stole Pink Rabbit*, p. 186–7.

17. Marc Canani's essay on *When Hitler Stole Pink Rabbit* is excellent in its Derridean analysis of the novel that unpacks the ways in which identity and displacement interplay through languages. See Marco Canani's, "Displacement, Trauma, and Identity in Judith Kerr's 'When Hitler Stole Pink Rabbit,'" *Cultural Perspectives - Journal for Literary and British Cultural Studies in Romania*, no. 19 (2014): 32–44.

18. Judith Kerr, *Bombs on Aunt Dainty* (London: Collins, 2017), p. 2.

19. Gillian Lathey, *The Impossible Legacy: Identity and Purpose in Autobiographical Children's Literature Set in the Third Reich and the Second World War* (New York: P. Lang, 1999), p. 74.

20. Kerr, *Bombs on Aunt Dainty*, p. 39.

21. Kushner, *The Holocaust and the Liberal Imagination: A Social and Cultural History*, p. 57.

22. Anne Karpf, *The War After: Living with the Holocaust* (London: Minerva, 1996), p. 178. See also, Lassner, *Anglo-Jewish Women Writing the Holocaust*, p. 10.

23. Todd Endelman, *The Jews of Britain, 1656 to 2000* (Los Angeles: University of California Press, 2002), p. 247.

24. Lassner, *Anglo-Jewish Women Writing the Holocaust: Displaced Witnesses*, p. 9.

25. Tucker, *Becoming English*, p. 5.

26. Sara Ahmed, *The Cultural Politics of Emotion*, Second edition (Edinburgh: Edinburgh University Press, 2014), p. 134.

27. Tucker, *Becoming English*, p. 11.

28. Ibid., p. 29.

29. Kerr, *Bombs on Aunt Dainty*, p. 105.

30. Ibid., p. 112.

31. Ibid.

32. Ibid., p. 114.

33. Endelman, *The Jews of Britain, 1656 to 2000*, pp. 224–5.

34. Kerr, *Bombs on Aunt Dainty*, p. 121.

35. Kerr, *Bombs on Aunt Dainty*, p. 384.

36. Tucker, *Becoming English*, p. 4.
37. Ibid., p. 67.
38. Ibid., p. 9.
39. Eva Tucker, *Berlin Mosaic* (London: Starhaven, 2005), p. 71.
40. Ibid., p. 90.
41. Tucker, *Becoming English*, p. 68.
42. Ibid., p. 27.
43. *A Small Person Far Away*, pp. 22–3.
44. Lathey, *The Impossible Legacy*, p. 23.
45. Ibid., p. 102.
46. Kerr, *A Small Person Far Away*, p. 39.
47. Ibid., p. 105.
48. Ibid., p. 167.
49. Ibid., p. 40.
50. Sue Vice, "'Almost an Englishwoman': Jewish Women Refugee Writers in Britain," in *Jewish Women Writers in Britain*, ed. Nadia Valman (Detroit: Wayne State University Press, 2014), 97–115, p. 101.
51. Kerr, *A Small Person Far Away*, p. 40.
52. Ibid., p. 72.
53. Anne Emmanuelle Berger, "Politics of the Mother Tongue," *Parallax* 18, no. 3 (August 1, 2012): 9–26, p. 10.
54. Tucker, *Becoming English*, p. 14.
55. Kerr, *A Small Person Far Away*, p. 259.
56. Theodor W. Adorno, *Minima Moralia: Reflections on a Damaged Life*, trans. E. F. N. Jephcott, Radical Thinkers (New York: Verso, 2005), pp. 46–7.
57. Tucker, *Becoming English*, p. 38.
58. Kerr, *Bombs on Aunt Dainty*, p. 25.
59. Louise Sylvester, "A Knock at the Door: Reading Judith Kerr's Picture Books in the Context of Her Holocaust Fiction," *The Lion and the Unicorn* 26, no. 1 (January 1, 2002): 16–30, https://doi.org/10.1353/uni.2002.0011, p. 18.
60. Travis, *Jews and Jewishness in British Children's Literature*, p. 55.
61. Ibid., p. 54.
62. Kerr, *Bombs on Aunt Dainty*, p. 217.
63. Kerr's description echoes Primo Levi's account of the *Muselmann* (the 'Muslim'), whom Giorgio Agamben describes as 'not only or not so much a limit between life and death; rather, he marks the threshold between the human and the inhuman.' See
64. Kerr, *Bombs on Aunt Dainty*, p. 221.
65. Travis, *Jews and Jewishness in British Children's Literature*, p. 54.
66. Kerr, *Bombs on Aunt Dainty*, p. 373.
67. Ibid.
68. Ibid.
69. Ibid., pp. 373–4.
70. Ibid., p. 378.
71. Tucker, *Becoming English*, p. 73.

72. Kushner, *The Holocaust and the Liberal Imagination: A Social and Cultural History*, p. 128.
73. Ibid., p. 213.
74. Elsewhere, Kushner argues that '[f]rom the end of the war until at least the 1980s British society as a whole was, for the most part, at best indifferent and at worst antipathetic to recognizing that Jews had, in fact, been subject to specific treatment by the Nazis.' See Tony Kushner, "Too Little, Too Late? Reflections on Britain's Holocaust Memorial Day," in *After Eichmann: Collective Memory and the Holocaust Since 1961*, ed. David Cesarani (New York: Routledge, 2005), 116–30, p. 116.
75. Tucker, *Becoming English*, p. 77.
76. Kerr, *A Small Person Far Away*, p. 254.
77. Ibid., p. 255.
78. Tucker, *Becoming English*, p. 84.
79. Tucker, *Berlin Mosaic*, p. 151.

REFERENCES

Adorno, Theodor W. 2005. *Minima Moralia: Reflections on a Damaged Life*. Translated by E. F. N. Jephcott. Radical Thinkers. New York: Verso.

Agamben, Giorgio. 2002. *Remnants of Auschwitz: The Witness and the Archive*. Translated by Daniel Heller-Roazen. Revised edition. New York: Zone Books.

Ahmed, Sara. 2014. *The Cultural Politics of Emotion*. Second edition. Edinburgh: Edinburgh University Press.

Berger, Anne Emmanuelle. 2012. "Politics of the Mother Tongue." *Parallax* 18 (3): 9–26. https://doi.org/10.1080/13534645.2012.688631.

Bhabha, Homi K. *The Location of Culture*. London: Routledge, 1994.

Brauner, David, and Axel Stähler, eds. 2015. *The Edinburgh Companion to Modern Jewish Fiction*. Edinburgh: Edinburgh University Press.

Canani, Marco. 2014. "Displacement, Trauma, and Identity in Judith Kerr's 'When Hitler Stole Pink Rabbit.'" *Cultural Perspectives - Journal for Literary and British Cultural Studies in Romania*, 19: 32–44.

Cesarani, David. 1990. *The Making of Modern Anglo-Jewry*. Oxford England, UK ; Cambridge, MA: Wiley-Blackwell.

———, ed. 2013. *After Eichmann : Collective Memory and Holocaust Since 1961*. Hoboken: Routledge. http://search.ebscohost.com/login.aspx?direct=true&db=nlebk&AN=699065&site=ehost-live.

Endelman, Todd. 2002. *The Jews of Britain, 1656 to 2000*. Subsequent edition. Berkeley ; Los Angeles: University of California Press.

Freud, Sigmund. "The 'Uncanny.'" *New Literary History; Baltimore, Etc.* 7, no. 3 (Spring 1976): 619–645.

Gilbert, Ruth. 2013. *Writing Jewish: Contemporary British-Jewish Literature*. 2013 edition. Houndmills, Basingstoke, Hampshire ; New York: Palgrave.

Jacobson, Howard. 2007. *Kalooki Nights*. London: Vintage Books.

Karpf, Anne. 1996. *The War after: Living with the Holocaust*. London: Minerva.

Kerr, Judith. 2017a. *A Small Person Far Away*. London: HarperCollins Children's Books.
———. 2017b. *Bombs on Aunt Dainty*. London: Collins.
———. 2017c. *When Hitler Stole Pink Rabbit*. London: HarperCollins Children's Books.
Kushner, Tony. 1994. *Holocaust and the Liberal Imagination: A Social and Cultural History*. First edition. Oxford, UK ; Cambridge, MA: John Wiley & Sons.
———. 2005. "Too Little, Too Late? Reflections on Britain's Holocaust Memorial Day." In *After Eichmann: Collective Memory and the Holocaust Since 1961*, edited by David Cesarani, 116–30. New York: Routledge.
Lassner, Phyllis. 2008. *Anglo-Jewish Women Writing the Holocaust: Displaced Witnesses*. 2008 edition. Basingstoke England ; New York: AIAA.
———. 2015. "Jewish Exile in Englishness: Eva Tucker and Natasha Solomons." In *The Edinburgh Companion to Modern Jewish Fiction*, edited by David Brauner, 199–210. Edinburgh: Edinburgh University Press.
Lathey, Gillian. 1999. *The Impossible Legacy: Identity and Purpose in Autobiographical Children's Literature Set in the Third Reich and the Second World War*. New York: P. Lang.
Pearce, Andy. 2014. *Holocaust Consciousness in Contemporary Britain*. New York: Routledge.
Sharples, Caroline, and Olaf Jensen, eds. 2013. *Britain and the Holocaust: Remembering and Representing War and Genocide*. Edinburgh: Palgrave Macmillan.
Stähler, Alex, and Sue Vice. 2013. "Writing Jews in Contemporary Britain." *Jewish Quarterly* 60 (3–4): 117–18. https://doi.org/10.1080/0449010X.2013.855458.
Stähler, Axel, and Sue Vice. 2014. "Introduction: Writing Jews and Jewishness in Contemporary Britain." *European Judaism: A Journal for the New Europe* 47 (2): 3–11.
Sylvester, Louise. 2002. "A Knock at the Door: Reading Judith Kerr's Picture Books in the Context of Her Holocaust Fiction." *The Lion and the Unicorn* 26 (1): 16–30. https://doi.org/10.1353/uni.2002.0011.
Tollerton, David. 2020. *Holocaust Memory and Britain's Religious-Secular Landscape: Politics, Sacrality, and Diversity*. First edition. New York: Routledge.
Travis, Madelyn J. *Jews and Jewishness in British Children's Literature*. Children's Literature and Culture, 94. New York: Routledge, 2013.
Tucker, Eva. 2005. *Berlin Mosaic*. London ; La Jolla, CA: Starhaven.
———. 2009. *Becoming English*. London: Starhaven.
Valman, Nadia, ed. 2014. "Introduction: Feeling at Home: Jewish Women Writers in Britain, 1830–2010." In *Jewish Women Writers in Britain*, 1–9. Detroit, United States: Wayne State University Press.
Vice, Sue. 2013. "'Becoming English': Assimilation and Its Discontents in Contemporary British-Jewish Literature." *Jewish Culture and History* 14 (2–3): 100–111. https://doi.org/10.1080/1462169X.2013.805900.
———. 2014. "'Almost an Englishwoman': Jewish Women Refugee Writers in Britain." In *Jewish Women Writers in Britain*, edited by Nadia Valman, 97–115. Detroit, United States: Wayne State University Press.

———. 2015. "British Jewish Holocaust Fiction." In *The Edinburgh Companion to Modern Jewish Fiction*, edited by David Brauner and Axel Staehler, 267–78. Edinburgh: Edinburgh University Press.

———. 2016. "British Representations of the Camps." *Holocaust Studies* 22 (2–3): 303–17. https://doi.org/10.1080/17504902.2016.1148881.

Chapter 9

Collective Disengagement
Canada's National Holocaust Monument
Lizy Mostowski

In Prime Minister Justin Trudeau's inauguration speech, he described the National Holocaust Monument as having "walls that simultaneously cut visitors off from their surroundings while directing their gaze to the sky and the freedom and the hope that it represents," he continued, "and the view from the terrace where you can see the Peace Tower, a beacon of hope for many."[1] Trudeau reads the National Holocaust Monument (NHM) through his agenda of collective memory: the NHM is interpreted for the Canadian public as a sign of peace and hope, a sign of the prosperity of Canadian Jews, and symbolizes the acceptance of Jews into Canadian society. He does not fail to mention the SS St. Louis, highlighting a positive trajectory from closed borders to open arms, attempting to write Canada into Canadian collective memory as a promised land for European Jewry. When he refers to the SS St. Louis, Trudeau gestures toward engaging with Canada's Holocaust history; yet the representation of the Holocaust provided by the NHM disengages the event from Canadian temporal memory.

On my first visit to the NHM in December of 2017, the hope and freedom which Trudeau claimed the view of the Peace Tower symbolized wasn't accessible. Inside the NHM, only the new condominium buildings of LeBreton Flats peered over and into the Monument. Even outside of the Monument, the Peace Tower was hidden by a smoke stack. Senator Frum, in her petition to keep the NHM open year-round, noted that she had visited Auschwitz in the winter and that the experience allowed her to see the cold and horrible experience that the victims of the Holocaust faced.[2] "The potential for that impact in our monument here in Ottawa is the same. It's a very moving emotional experience to be inside that monument and its starkness, but to do that while it's also extremely cold out, it potentially could be part of the experience,"[3] Frum told *The Star*. Indeed, my visit on a negative-twenty-degrees-Celsius day did not leave me feeling optimistic. The triangle-shaped reflection room of the Monument,

Figure 9.1 National Holocaust Monument Development Council. The National Holocaust Monument. Accessed: December 2017. *Source:* Screenshot from holocaustmonument.ca showing the homepage of the site.

where the eternal flame is located was covered in snow and cordoned off. The eternal flame of the NHM was out, both literally and metaphorically.[4] The eternal flame of the National Holocaust Monument was out on Channukah, the Jewish festival of lights, while the Centennial Flame on Parliament Hill burns year-round. Being inside the cordoned-off reflection room was overwhelming: its high walls do not direct one's gaze toward the sky. Instead, one is separated from the rest of the Monument and the surrounding landscape.

The seats in the space were set up to allow visitors to gaze into the eternal flame as they reflected on the architecture, imagery, and narrative of the Monument that they encountered before entering. The small entrances on either side of the space force visitors to feel closed-in from the world. Perhaps these small entrances on either side account for the lack of winter-maintenance, conveniently accounting for the extinguished eternal flame. The NHM stands as a metaphor for the memory of the Holocaust in Canada: frozen, forgotten, non-reflective. How could this frozen, snow-covered monument symbolize hope and freedom from its bunker-like foundation? Can inclusion and tolerance be articulated through a space that is forgotten by its guardian? How can the conversation around the NHM become more than Senator Frum single-handedly pointing out the ways in which it was mishandled? How can the memory of the Holocaust in Canada become multidirectional through a monument which produces disjointed memory?

On Thursday, September 28th, 2017, Prime Minister Justin Trudeau unveiled Canada's National Holocaust Monument to the public. Until then,

Canada was the only Allied Nation without a Holocaust memorial in its capital. In London, England, the Hyde Park Holocaust Memorial was erected in 1983 by the Board of Deputies of British Jews, endorsed by Greville Janner, a Labor Party MP. The United States Holocaust Memorial Museum in Washington, D.C., was dedicated in 1993. Before the National Holocaust Monument, Canada had only one monument commemorating the Holocaust in Edmonton, Alberta as well as three educational institutions dedicated to preserving the memory of the Holocaust: (1) The Montreal Holocaust Memorial Centre in Montreal, Quebec, (2) The Sarah and Chaim Neuberger Holocaust Education Centre in Toronto, Ontario, and (3) The Vancouver Holocaust Education Centre in Vancouver, British Columbia.

The Nation's Capital, Ottawa, Ontario, boasts a large number of monuments and memorials which acknowledge various wars and forms of human suffering: The Response, National War Memorial (1939) dedicated to all Canadians who have served in times of war—it was rededicated to include World War II and the Korean War—this memorial is located centrally between the Chateau Laurier, the Parliament, and the National Arts Centre in downtown Ottawa; the Never Again War, Monument to Peace and Remembrance (1992) located across the river in Gatineau which is meant to broadly illustrate "the harmony and balance toward which individuals and nations should strive"[5]; the Tomb of the Unknown Soldier which lies in front of the National War Memorial containing the remains of an unknown Canadian soldier buried near Vimy Ridge, the site of a famous Canadian World War I victory; and the Canadian Tribute to Human Rights (1990), a declaration of Canada's belief in universal human rights located across from Ottawa's City Hall and Courthouse.

Ottawa's National Holocaust Monument fails for many reasons. While the memorial landscape of Canada's Capital did not include the Holocaust until recently, only the structural absence has been corrected. Scholars have aptly written about the National Holocaust Monument as a legitimization of settler-colonialism[6] and as a failed project in terms of its potential for creating a space for multidirectional[7] memory.[8] The National Holocaust Monument in Ottawa, Canada, reveals the problem of the Holocaust in Canadian collective memory, as the Monument allows disengagement and distancing from the Holocaust and the reality of human rights in Canada. The NHM reveals a collective understanding of the Holocaust as a unique event that cannot be compared with other traumas, this concept is used to legitimize settler-colonialism and inhibit multidirectional memory which would allow the Holocaust, communism, and colonialism to come into dialogue with one another. Furthermore, as I will argue, the NHM allows a vague, disinterested, and stereotypical understanding of the Holocaust to prevail in Canada. In this chapter, I will examine the language of the two versions of the controversial

NHM introductory plaque: the photography exhibited inside of the monument and the NHM in relation to Berlin's Memorial to the Murdered Jews of Europe and architect Daniel Libeskind's other Holocaust-related projects. The NHM represents a collective disengagement from memory of the Holocaust, pushing the event to the periphery of Canadian collective memory.

In 2017, Canada celebrated a hundred-and-fifty years since the Canadian Confederation of 1867, when the British colonies of Canada joined Nova Scotia and New Brunswick to create the Dominion of Canada which included four provinces: Ontario, Quebec, Nova Scotia, and New Brunswick. The national commemorative series of events, "Canada 150," gave all Canadians a free National Parks pass for the year, added Nunavut to the Centennial Flame located in front of Parliament, displayed illuminated tipis in front of the Canadian Museum of History, and listed particularly elaborate events for Canada Day on July 1st. Roots, the Canadian retailer, launched a line of patriotic red-and-white clothing commemorating what would be called Canada's 150th Birthday. This series of events and celebrations allowed Canada to once again reframe its national narrative, as was attempted in the controversial lineup of events in the opening ceremonies of the Vancouver 2010 Olympics.[9] The intention of these events was overt: to reframe the ways in which Canada is seen internationally, displaying itself as a nation that is accepting, multicultural, valiant, and honorable.

In his article "Identity and Trauma: Two Forms of the Will to Memory," Gil Eyal defines collective memory as "a crisis of memory" or "a historically specific *will to memory*, a constellation of discourses and practices within which memory is entrusted with a certain goal and function, and is invested, routinely, as an institutional matter, with certain hopes and fears as to what it can do."[10] While the National Holocaust Monument was unveiled in this historic year, the unveiling, unlike the addition of Nunavut to the Centennial Flame, was not listed as one of these celebratory events. The attention drawn toward celebrating Canadian identity and the focus on the redefinition of Canadian collective memory in 2017 point to the unveiling of the NHM as another motion toward refocusing Canadian collective memory, however much the unveiling of the NHM was kept in the periphery. Illustrating the ambivalent position of the Holocaust within that memory, even as the rise of right-wing governments and anti-Semitism around the world demonstrates the need for Canada to build such a memorial. The NHM illustrates the will to memory of a specific group of Canadians, while the disinterest of the media and the lack of discourse around the NHM illustrate failure in writing the Holocaust into Canadian collective memory.

Yet Nadine Blumer notes in her article "Memorials are built of public discussion as much as stone," the development of the NHM did not provoke dialogue in Canada:

Criticisms of the Memorial to the Victims of Communism have centered on its location near the Supreme Court of Canada, its sombre and massive design, and allegations of the government's pandering to Canada's almost eight million constituents who originate in former communist countries. In contrast, almost nothing has been said about the National Holocaust Memorial, a project of similar scope, size, government funding and geographic prominence, whose construction in the National Capital Region is also set to coincide with the federal election later this year.[11]

Canada's Memorial to the Victims of Communism has been hotly debated in the media—the progress of design selection and other factors had been publicized—yet, the same developments in the creation of the NHM attracted scant attention. While the number of Holocaust survivors in Canada is only a small fraction of the number of Canada's victims of Communism—it is estimated that about 40,000 Holocaust survivors settled in Canada after the Holocaust, in contrast, waves of thousands of refugees fled communist regimes in Eastern and Central Europe, China, and Cambodia from as early as 1920 to the 1980s[12]—the number of descendants and those who were affected by the legacy of the Holocaust in Canada is both large and unknown. Regardless, the development of the NHM had gone relatively unnoticed and undiscussed. Blumer writes: "The debate *is* the memorial. Memory scholar James Young wrote this in the 1990s as a newly reunified German state argued over the parameters of the country's first central Holocaust memorial."[13] In his *The Stages of Memory*, Young elaborates:

> In Berlin, when asked by the Bundestag in 1997 to explain why I thought Germany's 1995 international design competition for a national 'memorial for the murdered Jews of Europe' has failed, I answered that even if they had failed to produce a monument, the debate itself had produced a profound search for such memory and that it had actually begun to constitute the memorial they had so desired.[14]

Thus, in Young's terms, the lack of debate, in some way, erases memory. The Canadian National Holocaust Monument is a hollow symbol that signals a national distancing from the Holocaust, the lack of media commentary and interest point to the collective feeling that the NHM lacks relevance for the Canadian mainstream. In its creation, the NHM becomes the fulfillment of a criteria to reinforce Canada's desired national image. As Blumer highlights, "communism and the Holocaust are shorthand for 'evil' that happened 'over there', Canada, by contrast, is framed as an idealized site of freedom, refuge and diversity."[15] Maurice Halbwachs writes in his *On Collective Memory*: "the mind reconstructs its memories under the pressure of society."[16] Halbwachs highlights the problem of reconstructing a truly collective memory for Canadians around the Holocaust without the pressure of a public discourse.

REWRITING THE PLAQUE'S INSCRIPTION

Only after the National Holocaust Monument was unveiled did it strike outrage and provoke some discussion. Trudeau's controversial statement on the plaque of the NHM, in which he forgot to mention the Jews and all other minority groups targeted by the Nazis, attracted attention. The original plaque read as follows:

> The National Holocaust Monument commemorates the millions of men, women and children murdered during the Holocaust and honours the survivors who persevered and were able to make their way to Canada after one of the darkest chapters in history. The monument recognizes the contribution these survivors have made to Canada and serves as a reminder that we must be vigilant in standing guard against hate, intolerance and discrimination.[17]

Below this inscription, the following was written: "Inaugurated by the Right Honourable Justin Trudeau, PC, MP, Prime Minister of Canada, on September 27, 2017."[18] Senator Linda Frum, a Jewish Conservative member of the Senate of Canada, took a photo of the original plaque and tweeted, "In Justin Trudeau's Canada the New Holocaust Monument plaque doesn't mention Jews, Anti-Semitism or the 6 Million."[19] Frum points to Trudeau's lack of acknowledgment of the six million victims of the Holocaust and the architecture of the evil Nazi regime itself on his original plaque. Further outrage in the Canadian media prompted the plaque to be taken down and rewritten. As of December 17, 2017, almost three months after the unveiling and the controversy that overshadowed Trudeau's intended effect on Canadian collective memory, the plaque had still not been replaced. An empty space with holes where the original plaque was bolted ominously looked back at visitors.[20] Some argued that the shape of the memorial (a Star of David from the bird's-eye-view perspective) compensated for the omission. Others argued that the photographs stenciled on the walls inside of the NHM depicting Jewish suffering under the Nazi regime did the work; however, Senator Frum rightly pointed to the importance of the acknowledgment of these facts on the official plaque.[21]

Today the rewritten plaque reads:

> The National Holocaust Monument commemorates the six million Jewish men, women and children murdered during the Holocaust and the millions of other

victims of Nazi Germany and its collaborators. It also stands as a tribute to the courage and resilience of the survivors who were able to make their way to Canada following one of the darkest chapters in human history. The monument recognizes the immense contributions these survivors have made to Canada and serves as a reminder that we must be vigilant in standing guard against antisemitism, hatred and intolerance.[22]

Trudeau's original plaque had not mentioned the Nazis or any of their victims: Jews, Roma, Slavs, homosexuals, and other targeted groups. The original plaque grouped those targeted by the Nazis with those who fought against them, highlighting the resilience of the survivors in the second clause of the first sentence and in the second sentence. The rewritten inscription on the updated plaque creates a distinction between Jews and the other groups targeted by Nazi policies. Discrimination in general is translated to anti-Semitism in specific. The new plaque valorizes Jewish suffering and persecution over the suffering of other groups rather than naming and recognizing each group alongside the Jews. The updated inscription reinforces Rebecca Dolgoy and Jerzy Elżanowski's argument about the NHM being resistant to the potential of multidirectional memory. Of course, Jews were the main group targeted by the Nazis, yet in Canada, the Jews are written into the memorial landscape as the *only* group targeted by the Nazis. Both plaques are problematic, though the updated plaque is a motion in the right direction as it begins to name the victims of the Holocaust. The updated plaque, along with other elements of the NHM which I will discuss, can be read as unfinished as public discussion and debate must force the Prime Minister to include all groups persecuted by the Nazis. A Holocaust memorial that manages to exclude the public, many groups of victims of the Holocaust, and parallel discourses on the topic produces *disjointed* memory, which is only *tolerated* by the public, becomes a memorial for *Jews* and not necessarily all *Canadians*.

The National Holocaust Monument is located in the periphery of Ottawa's downtown in LeBreton Flats—unlike other previously mentioned memorials and monuments in Ottawa which are more centrally located—and across the street from Ottawa's Canadian War Museum[23] which focuses on Canadian military history. In May of 2013, the competition for the design of the NHM was opened, the initial Call for Qualifications "invited teams of professional artists, architects, landscape architects and other design professionals to submit their credentials and examples of prior work at the first stage of a two-phase national design competition."[24] Designs for the NHM were to be presented to the jury in Winter of 2014, and the Monument was initially set to be completed in the Fall of 2015. The team that was selected to build the NHM in the end was made up of Daniel Libeskind, architect of the Jewish Museum Berlin, Edward Burtynsky, a Canadian landscape photographer of

Ukrainian heritage, Claude Cormier, a landscape artist, Gail Lord, a museum planner, and University of Toronto Professor Doris Bergen, a Holocaust scholar. Dov Goldstein of Lord Cultural Resources, a firm of which Gail Lord is co-President, credits the initial motion for a need for the National Holocaust Monument about a decade ago to a student named Laura Grossman.[25] "[I]n 2009, the idea of a national Holocaust monument was introduced as a private member's bill in Parliament by Conservative MP Tim Uppal. It received Royal Assent in 2011, and fundraising began."[26] Lord Cultural Resources assembled the team that won the competition in 2014.

PHOTOGRAPHY AND SNOWY SYMBOLISM

As I walked through the entrance of the snow-covered National Holocaust Monument on December 17th, 2017—the only entrance opened to the public, the others were ice-covered and cordoned off—I noticed a Channukea, planted by Chabad of Centrepointe, which stood to the left of the Monument, in stark contrast to the extinguished eternal flame in the heart of the Monument.

After the initial controversy around Trudeau's plaque, controversy ensued in November of 2017 when Senator Frum was informed that the National Capital Commission did not have any snow-clearing plans for the Monument,

Figure 9.2 Mostowski, Lizy. "Entrance of National Holocaust Monument." Ottawa, Canadada. December 2017. *Source:* Photo by Lizy Mostowski.

which meant that it would be closed over the winter, about one-third of the calendar year in Ottawa. Heritage Minister Melanie Joly quickly righted the wrong, announcing on Twitter that snow would be cleared from the monument.[27] Joly commented: "The death camps operated all year round. Why shouldn't Canada's commemoration?"[28] A device to melt snow off the monument was included in the original design plans; however, it was scaled back due to budget restrictions. While one can enter the NHM from the main entrance, the stairway leading to the terrace where Trudeau stated the Peace Tower could be seen, was closed, as was the elevator and the other eastward-facing entrances to the NHM. The symbolism built into the NHM was snowed over; the frozen NHM stood as a metaphor for the place of the Holocaust in Canadian collective memory.

Upon entering the Monument, I first saw the sign declaring "National Holocaust Monument," and around the corner, the empty wall where Trudeau's plaque was once bolted across from the plaque detailing the private donors who contributed half of the funds for building the NHM, the half that the public, or the Canadian government did not contribute. A "Canada 150" flag as well as flags of the Nation's provinces decorated the skyline above this corner of the Monument. As I entered the core of the NHM's exhibition space, I was met with Burtynsky's photograph of the iconic barbed-wire gates of Auschwitz.

Aside from the Holocaust narrative that is presented inside the Monument, the viewer focuses on Edward Burtynsky's photographs which have been transformed into gray stencils and painted onto the inner walls of the Monument. Many of these walls are angled inward, creating for the visitor a sense of entrapment. One must view the photographs on these inward-angled walls from a closer range than those on walls without an angle. Yet, as one approaches the stenciled photographs more closely, the images they portray become indecipherable. The majority of the photographs, some on large walls as high as a two- or three-story home, must be viewed from a distance. The photographs are contemporary—all taken in 2014 by Burtynsky, presumably after their team won the competition to create the NHM—and picture stereotypical depictions of the Holocaust: the barbed wire gate of a death camp, the abandoned railroad tracks leading to Treblinka, the broken tombstones of Warsaw's Okopowa Street Cemetery, a makeshift prayer room in Theresienstadt, another railway track in Berlin, and the site of a death march near Mathausen which today is a roundabout for automobile traffic. Many of the photographs lack punctum—defined by Roland Barthes as that which "pricks"[29] the viewer of the photograph and that which the viewer "add[s] to the photograph and *what is nonetheless already there*"[30]—the style in which the photographs are stenciled onto the walls of the Monument does not allow for such a connection; they do not pierce their viewer. The predictable and stereotypical nature of the photographs enforce a well-known and predictable

Figure 9.3 Mostowski, Lizy. "Reflection Room of National Holocaust Monument." Ottawa, Canada. December 2017. Pictured cordoned-off & snow-covered. *Source:* Photo by Lizy Mostowski.

Holocaust narrative—that which has already been perpetuated by popular culture, that which highlights suffering, that which highlights the death camp experience. Furthermore, these photographs, in their general lack of punctum, do not allow visitors to the Monument to connect with or to sympathize with or to understand the Holocaust experience in a textured and nuanced way. Though the photograph of the Theresienstadt prayer room allows the viewer

Figure 9.4 Mostowski, Andy. "Trudeau's Missing Plaque." Ottawa, Canada. December 2017. *Source:* Photo by Andy Mostowski.

to imagine themselves within the space, once more, the lack of specific narrative does not allow the photograph to "prick" the viewer, to allow the viewer to understand the prayer room's history and significance. The features of the prayer room—the Stars of David painted on the ceiling and the Hebrew script across the top arches of the walls—resemble many Eastern European synagogues. This photograph, like the rest, lacks detail, specificity, punctum. The descriptions of the photographs further distance the viewer from the experience they are meant to sympathize with. The description of the Theresienstadt prayer room reads: "In the face of misery, torture, sickness and death and in the desperate, crowded conditions of this 'camp-ghetto,' Jewish prisoners managed to create and adorn a place of prayer. Such acts of devotion, defiance and spirit are the legacy of the Holocaust."[31] The description does not name the creators of the prayer room, the sacrifices likely endured for its creation, nor does the description help the viewer to identify the punctum of the photograph.

Burtynsky's landscapes contain only studium, as Barthes defines it:

> the studium is inevitably to encounter the photographer's intentions, to enter into harmony with them, to approve or disapprove of them, but always to understand them, to argue them within [one]self, for culture (from which the studium derives) is a contract arrived at between creators and consumers. The studium

Figure 9.5 Mostowski, Andy. "Edward Burtynsky's 'Hiding Place' (left) & 'Prayer Room.' (right.)" Ottawa, Canada. Decemer 2017. *Source:* Photo by Andy Mostowski.

is a king of education (knowledge and civility, 'politeness') which allows [the viewer] to discover the Operator, to experience the intentions which establish and animate his practices, but to experience them 'in reverse', according to [one's] will as a Spectator. It is rather as if [one] had to read the Photographer's myths in the Photograph, fraternizing with them but not quite believing in them.[32]

Burtynsky's photographs featured within the NHM allow the reader to see his intentions—to portray the Holocaust as the average Canadian understands it, via the horrors of death camps, death marches, cattle cars—and allows one to see the myths of the Holocaust which the photographer holds—the Holocaust as impersonal, far away, Holocaust as fragmented memories in contemporary Europe. According to Barthes, the functions of the studium include: to inform, to represent, to surprise, to cause, to signify, to provoke desire.[33] Burtynsky's photographs certainly inform and represent, though seldom do they surprise. Furthermore, the photographs fail to display a narrative, allowing these images to signify only to those with a personal connection to these specific landscapes. Visitors of the NHM become disjointed: those who are unfamiliar with the landscapes presented in Burtynsky's photographs are alienated and those who are intimate with them are decontextualized by the contemporary temporal spaces that they inhabit.

Burtynsky's photograph entitled "Hiding Place" captures the ground of Warsaw's Okopowa Street Cemetery covered in leaves and broken—illegible—*matzevot* with a space in the ground beneath them which invites the viewer to imagine themselves hiding in the space beneath the shards of *matzevot*, beneath the Cemetery. The caption of the photograph once again removes punctum for the viewer:

> The Jewish cemetery in Warsaw was outside the walls of the ghetto. This trench beneath the tombstones became a hiding place for the Jewish prisoners—cemetery workers and their families—during raids and deportations. This photograph is a reminder that much of the Holocaust took place, literally and figuratively, underground.[34]

This caption describes the photograph and explains its intended meaning to the visitor of the Monument—the Resistance fighters, the Warsaw Uprising, the many who were hiding in attics and forests are not mentioned. The lack of specificity of the name given to the Cemetery above the description—"Warsaw Jewish Cemetery" is what they name the Okopowa Street Jewish Cemetery—distances the viewer from the place and context of the Cemetery and simultaneously sanitizes and domesticates the scene for the viewer. Moving closer to this photograph in particular, brings one further away from it—the photograph becomes even more vague, one cannot see any trace of thimbles, jewelry, or the things that may have been left behind by these victims from this photographer's contemporary perspective. One cannot read the name on the tombstone, the punctum is torn from the viewer effectively pushing the viewer away from the underground of the Holocaust, disengaging them from learning more about it—the photograph together with its description articulate that Holocaust happened underground in places like this, but we do not know and cannot see what happened here.

The captions of Burtynsky's photographs discourage dialogue within and among visitors to the NHM.[35] Instead, the photographs are decontextualized—falsified if you will—in the NHM by their vague, sanitized captions. In 2018, an exhibition entitled "Anthropocene" at the National Art Gallery of Canada featured Burtynsky's photographs of landscapes from around the world—from the United States to Russia to Nigeria—depicting the impact of human activities on our planet. The photographs were captioned by their provenance, followed by the history and context of the landscape depicted in the photograph. Such context inspires within visitors a curiosity to learn more about the highways, mines, and plants depicted in the photographs if they so choose, allowing discourse to form around the subjects of the photographs. Another example of captions which provoke dialogue and curiosity can be found within the Core Exhibition of POLIN Museum of the History of the

Polish Jews in Warsaw, Poland, which cites scholarship in place of writing its own narrative, allowing visitors to digest the information on their own, to develop their own ideas around the content. In the NHM, however, the captions of Burtynsky's photos summarize various aspects of the Holocaust in broad strokes, they are polite and overly explained, preventing viewers from feeling either curiosity or punctum, imprinting history onto contemporary landscapes without addressing the temporal gap. Stenciled in shades of gray onto a gray concrete background, these photos and their captions leave the visitor unmoved.

ARCHITECTURE AND EDUCATION

Montreal, Canada, was home to the largest number of Holocaust survivors in Canada and had the third largest population of Holocaust survivors in the world after Israel and New York City. The Montreal Holocaust Memorial Centre, attached to the Jewish Public Library, was created for and by the city's many survivors and their descendants. The Centre, along with the United States Holocaust Memorial Museum, served as sources for the narrative panel presented in the National Holocaust Monument. Before Jewish refugees were welcomed to Canada in the 1940s, Canada famously turned away 908 German Jews who were aboard the SS St Louis. Canada's Prime Minister MacKenzie King famously said, "None is too many," when the SS St Louis sought to dock on Canada's shores in 1939. In Halifax, where the ship was turned away, this incident has its own memorial on the harbor.

Trudeau mentioned the event in his dedication of the NHM, and the narrative presented within the NHM itself does discuss Canada's closed borders, the SS St Louis, and that Canada only admitted 5,000 Jews during World War II. While Montreal has a Holocaust museum which acts primarily as an educational centre, the Monument in Ottawa, unlike Berlin's Memorial to the Murdered Jews of Europe, does not have an information centre beneath it. The Information Centre which is located below the German Memorial "audaciously illustrates both that commemoration is 'rooted' in historical information and that the historical presentation is necessarily 'shaped' formally by the commemorative space above it."[36] Ottawa's National Holocaust Monument has a rootlessness to it, depicted best through Edward Burtynsky's stenciled, cold, vague, stereotypical, and punctum-less photographs which inhibit rather than reconstruct memory. Trudeau's vague inscription, even the updated one, misdirects memory. The narrative on the wall feels forced yet insufficient in articulating what is at stake in such a monument.[37] Yet, the Monument itself does not reflect Canada's dark history during the Holocaust in its architecture, photography, nor in Trudeau's interpretation of the effect of these combined elements. Trudeau's unhurried rewriting of the official plaque of the Monument, like the lack of public discussion around the building and design of the Monument, points to the distance that Canadian collective memory has created between itself as a nation and the history of the Holocaust.

Daniel Libeskind, born in Łódź, Poland to Polish-Jewish Holocaust survivors in 1946, has designed many Holocaust-related buildings and monuments, including the Jewish Museum Berlin in Berlin, Germany (2001), the Danish Jewish Museum in Copenhagen, Denmark (2003), the Contemporary Jewish Museum in Sanfrancisco, California (2008), the Dutch Holocaust Memorial of Names in Amersterdam, Netherlands (2013), the Ohio Statehouse Holocaust Memorial in Columbus, Ohio (2014), and most recently, *Through the Lens of Faith* outdoor installation at the Auschwitz-Birkenau State Museum in Oświęcim, Poland (2019). The Jewish Museum Berlin, was conceived, designed, built, and inaugurated before the city's Memorial to the Murdered Jews of Europe; therefore it was the first to represent "the repercussions of the Holocaust"[38] in postwar Germany. The overall tone, texture, style, and design of the Jewish Museum Berlin is very similar to the NHM: concrete and sharp angular lines, intentional and symbolic pathways. Yet, a substantial difference lies between the two.

The architect's website explains the intentions behind his designs and the symbolism of his architecture. When a visitor enters the Jewish Museum Berlin, they descend underground and must choose between three paths: "The first leads to a dead end—the Holocaust Tower. The second leads out of the building and into the Garden of Exile and Emigration, remembering those who were forced to leave Berlin. The third and longest, traces a path leading to the Stair of Continuity, then up to the exhibition spaces of the museum, emphasizing the continuum of history."[39] The design of the Jewish Museum Berlin reflects the city's history, the three possible paths that the city's Jews could find themselves on: to a concentration camp, to exile, or struggling to cross the void and into the contemporary which they encounter after the Stair of Continuity. The void of the Museum is explained as "a space that embodies absence[,] a straight line whose impenetrability becomes the central focus around which exhibitions are organized. In order to move from one side of the museum to the other, visitors must cross one of the 60 bridges that open onto this void."[40] These bridges, it is clear, symbolize the many ways through which survivors could find themselves on the other side of the void. The design of the NHM is similarly symbolic, the Star of David is claimed to be a "visual symbol of the Holocaust"[41] which "millions of Jews were forced to wear"[42] during the Holocaust, while the tighter, smaller triangular spaces such as the reflection room of the NHM, and the other tight corners of the Star of David are interpreted as being "representative of the badges the Nazis and their collaborators used to label homosexuals, Roma-Sinti, Jehovah's Witnesses and political and religious prisoners for murder."[43] Clearly, the official plaques posted by Trudeau on the Monument do not reflect as much diversity as the architect intended to represent. Studio Libeskind does not echo Trudeau's interpretation of the staircase to the terrace where the Peace Tower can be seen as "a beacon of hope for many."[44] Instead, an interpretation which better reflects the reality is given by Studio Libeskind: "Surrounding the monument, a rough landscape of various coniferous trees will emerge from the rocky pebbled ground. This landscape will evolve over time representative of how Canadian survivors and their children have contributed to Canada."[45] As we see in the Jewish Museum Berlin and the NHM, Libeskind's designs themselves serve as commentaries on collective national memories of the Holocaust: Germany's must intentionally ascend and find its way through a void, through a deep fracture, while Canada's finds itself on uncertain ground where it passively grows and begins to blend in with the landscape.

The design of the NHM should be considered next to other Holocaust memorials designed by Libeskind of a similar scale. For example, the Ohio Statehouse Holocaust Memorial in Columbus, Ohio, which carries similar design motifs found in the Jewish Museum Berlin and the NHM: the Ohio Statehouse Holocaust Memorial features heavy concrete, angled walls, and a Star of David split through the center is the focal point of the Memorial in two eighteen-foot bronze panels. The Memorial, however, features a key element that is lacking in the NHM: the panels are "Embossed with a story told by a survivor of Auschwitz."[46] The NHM includes no survivor testimony, a fundamental element of our understanding of the history of the Holocaust. Testimony, in all of its complexities and nuances, forms the basis of dialogue around a traumatic historical event, such as the Holocaust. The surrounding flora will persevere in the austere environment the Monument was allotted and one day will overtake the Monument, just as the collective memory of the Holocaust in Canada has been obscured.

The design of the NHM reflects the collective disengagement of Canadians in reckoning with national Holocaust inheritance. As a metaphor for the place of the Holocaust in Canadian collective memory, the extinguished and snow-covered eternal flame, the omission of any group targeted by Nazi policies other than the Jews, the stenciled photographs of stereotypical Holocaust landscapes with vague captions, and the lack of space for education, all combine to distance the Holocaust from Canadian collective memory. In contrast to the common usage of broken Jewish tombstones to construct Holocaust memorials in contemporary Poland,[47] the Canadian memorial landscape reveals its lack of aura—defined by Walter Benjamin as the authenticity of an original object, an essence that is irreproducible in mediums like photography[48]—through stencils of contemporary photographs of overly familiar Holocaust landscapes onto imposing concrete walls. While the Polish landscape—the site of much of the horrors of the Holocaust—can construct, with the aura of the fragments of *matzevot*, a powerful memory of the Shoah. Burtynsky's photograph from the Okopowa Street Cemetery shows the Canadian take—indecipherable, blurred, and unfocused. Regardless of the efforts of individuals like Senator Frum, in Trudeau's Canada, the Holocaust has become irrelevant, pushed to the periphery of collective memory, just as the Monument itself sits on the periphery of the Nation's Capital.

NOTES

1. The Canadian Press. "Holocaust monument plaque that didn't mention Jews to be replaced." *CBC News*. Published: October 6th, 2017. Accessed: December, 2017. Online. http://www.cbc.ca/news/politics/holocaust-plaque-memorial-plaque-1.4343829

2. Levitz, Stephanie. "Newly opened National Holocaust Monument to close in winter to avoid damage." The Star. Published: October 26, 2017. Accessed: December, 2017. Online. https://www.thestar.com/news/canada/2017/10/26/newly-opened-national-holocaust-monument-to-close-in-winter-to-avoid-damage.html

3. Ibid.

4. Leah Sandals notes in her article that the Monument "is fractured and exploded into six separate triangle forms—a choice that not only evokes the destruction wrought by the Holocaust, but also suggests the triangular shapes that other oppressed groups were marked by." [Sandals, Leah. "6 Questions About Canada's New National Holocaust Monument." *Canadian Art*. Published October 4, 2017. Accessed November 2017. Online. http://canadianart.ca/features/national-holocaust-monument-canada/]

5. Government of Canada. "Monuments—Experience Canada's capital." Last Updated: October 2, 2017. Accessed: December 2017. Online. https://www.canada.ca/en/canadian-heritage/services/art-monuments/monuments.html

6. Chalmers, Jason. "Settled Memories on Stolen Land: Settler Mythology at Canada's National Holocaust Monument." American Indian Quarterly, vol. 43, no. 4, 2019, p. 379. EBSCOhost, doi:10.5250/amerindiquar.43.4.0379.

7. Multidirectional memory creates dialogue between different memories, cultures, and traumas. "[M]ultidirectional memory," writes Michael Rothberg, "is irreducibly transversal; it cuts across genres, national contexts, periods, and cultural traditions." (Rothberg, Michael. *Multidirectional Memory: Remembering the Holocaust in the Age of Decolonization*. Stanford: Stanford University Press, 2009. Print. Pg. 18).

8. Dolgoy, R. C. (. 1.)., and J. (. 2.). Elżanowski. "Working through the Limits of Multidirectional Memory: Ottawa's Memorial to the Victims of Communism and

National Holocaust Monument." Citizenship Studies, vol. 22, no. 4, pp. 433–451. EBSCOhost, doi:10.1080/13621025.2018.1462507. Accessed 9 June 2020.

9. Articles on the opening ceremonies of the Vancouver 2010 Olympics are readily available from various journalism publications such as *The Globe and Mail* and *The Wall Street Journal*. See also Linda Solomon Wood's critique in the *Vancouver Observer*: "Perhaps above all else, the ceremony attempted to make a statement about the place of First Nations people in Canada. It celebrated four First Nations bands that chose to participate in the event and the First Nations culture in general, putting it up front and central in the production as if to suggest a level of visibility in the mainstream culture that is what Canada hopes for, rather than what Canada is." (Linda Solomon Wood. "What We Saw at the Opening Ceremonies of the Vancouver 2010 Olympic Games." *Vancouver Observer.* Published February 13th, 2010. Accessed: July 2020. Online. https://www.vancouverobserver.com/blogs/overheardolympics/20 10/02/13/what-we-saw-opening-ceremonies-vancouver-2010-olympic-games)

10. Eyal, Gil. "Identity and Trauma: Two Forms of the Will to Memory." *History & Memory*, no. 1, 2004, p. 5. EBSCOhost, doi:10.2979/HIS.2004.16.1.5. pgs. 6–7.

11. Blumer, Nadine. "Memorials are built of public discussion as much as stone." *Ottawa Citizen*. Published: May 8, 2015. Accessed: December 2017. Online. http://ottawacitizen.com/news/politics/nadine-blumer-memorials-are-built-of-public-discussion-as-much-as-stone

12. "Canada: A History of Refuge." Government of Canada. Date modified: 2020–01–16. Accessed: June 2020. Online. https://www.canada.ca/en/immigration-refugees-citizenship/services/refugees/canada-role/timeline.html

13. Ibid.

14. Young, James E. *The Stages of Memory: Reflections on Memorial Art, Loss, and the Spaces Between*. Amherst: University of Massachusetts Press, 2016. Project MUSE., https://muse.jhu.edu/ Pg. 7

15. Blumer, Nadine. "Memorials are built of public discussion as much as stone." *Ottawa Citizen*.

16. Halbwachs, Maurice. *On Collective Memory*. Transl. Lewis A. Coser. Chicago: The
   University of Chicago. 1992. Pg. 51.

17. Photo of original plaque. @LindaFrum. "In Justin Trudeau's Canada the new Holocaust Monument plaque doesn't mention Jews, Anti-Semitism or the 6 Million." *Twitter*, October 3, 2017, 7:06AM, https://twitter.com/LindaFrum/status/915216401979383814

18. Ibid.

19. @LindaFrum. "In Justin Trudeau's Canada the new Holocaust Monument plaque doesn't mention Jews, Anti-Semitism or the 6 Million." *Twitter*, October 3, 2017, 7:06AM, https://twitter.com/LindaFrum/status/915216401979383814

20. See Figure 5.

21. Wyld, Adrian. "National Holocaust Monument plaque pulled after panel omits mention of Jews." The Toronto Star. Published: October 5, 2017. Accessed: December, 2017. Online. https://www.thestar.com/news/canada/2017/10/05/plaque-pulled-after-national-holocaust-monument-in-ottawa-omits-mention-of-jews.html

22. National Holocaust Monument.

23. The Museum's website reads: "The Museum's collections are among the finest military holdings in the world, including rare vehicles, artillery, uniforms, medals, personal memoirs and more than 14,000 works in the Beaverbrook Collection of War Art" (warmuseum.ca). The Museum's focus is in valorizing war and Canadian involvement in war rather than its prevention. The Museum boasts a large gallery of real fighter jets and other military vehicles from various wars.

24. Daniels. "Daniel Lieberman part of a team selected to submit a design proposal for the National Holocaust Monument." University of Toronto John H. Daniels Faculty of Architecture, Landscape, and Design. Published: November 4th, 2013. Accessed: December, 2017. Online. https://www.daniels.utoronto.ca/news/2013/11/04/david-lieberman-part-team-selected-submit-design-proposal-national-holocaust

25. Sandals, Leah. "6 Questions About Canada's New National Holocaust Monument." *Canadian Art*. Published October 4, 2017. Accessed November 2017. Online. http://canadianart.ca/features/national-holocaust-monument-canada/

26. Ibid.

27. The Canadian Press. "Holocaust monument plaque."

28. Levitz, Stephanie. "Newly opened National Holocaust Monument to close in winter to avoid damage." The Star. Published: October 26, 2017. Accessed: December, 2017. Online. https://www.thestar.com/news/canada/2017/10/26/newly-opened-national-holocaust-monument-to-close-in-winter-to-avoid-damage.html

29. Barthes, Roland. *Camera Lucida: Reflections on Photography*. Transl. Richard Howard. New York: Hill and Wang: A Division of Farrar, Straus, and Giroux, 1980. Print. Pg. 27

30. Ibid. pg. 55.

31. National Holocaust Monument.

32. Ibid. pg. 27–8.

33. Ibid. pg. 28.

34. National Holocaust Monument.

35. "[A]ll photographs," writes Susan Sontag in her *Regarding the Pain of Others*, "wait to be explained or falsified by their captions." New York: Picador, 2004. Pg.10.

36. James Young elaborates: "Here we have a 'place of memory' literally undergirded by a 'place of history,' which is in turn inversely shaped by commemoration, and we are asked to navigate the spaces in between memory and history for our knowledge of events." Young, James E. *Texture of Memory: Holocaust Memorials and Meaning*. New Haven: Yale University Press, 1993. Print. pg. 11.

37. Ibid. James Young in his *The Texture of Memory* writes: "a monument turns pliant memory to stone" (13). What memory, exactly, was turned into stone in the making of the NHM?

38. "Jewish Museum Berlin." Studio Libeskind. Accessed: June 2020. Online. https://libeskind.com/work/jewish-museum-berlin/

39. Ibid.

40. Ibid.

41. "National Holocaust Monument." Studio Libeskind. Accessed: June 2020. Online. https://libeskind.com/work/national-holocaust-monument/

42. Ibid.
43. Ibid.
44. The Canadian Press. "Holocaust monument plaque."
45. "National Holocaust Monument." Studio Libeskind. Accessed: June 2020. Online. https://libeskind.com/work/national-holocaust-monument/
46. "Ohio Statehouse Holocaust Memorial." Studio Libeskind. Accessed: June 2020. Online. https://libeskind.com/work/ohio-statehouse-holocaust-memorial/
47. James Young writes of Poland's memorial landscape: "In an architectural impulse akin to the poet's broken epitaph, fragments of shattered Jewish tombstones have become the predominant iconographic figure by which public memory of the Shoah is constructed in Poland today" (185). Young, James E. *Texture of Memory: Holocaust Memorials and Meaning*. New Haven: Yale University Press, 1993.
48. Benjamin, Walter. "The Work of Art in the Age of Mechanical Reproduction." *Illuminations: Essays and Reflections*. Ed. Hannah Arendt. Transl. Harry Zohn. New York: Schocken Books, 1968. Print. pgs. 217–242.

REFERENCES

"About the Museum." Canadian War Museum. Accessed: January 2021. Online. https://warmuseum.ca/about

Barthes, Roland. *Camera Lucida: Reflections on Photography*. Transl. Richard Howard. New York: Hill and Wang: A Division of Farrar, Straus, and Giroux, 1980. Print.

Benjamin, Walter. "The Work of Art in the Age of Mechanical Reproduction." *Illuminations: Essays and Reflections*. Ed. Hannah Arendt. Transl. Harry Zohn. New York: Schocken Books, 1968. Print. pgs. 217–242.

Blumer, Nadine. "Memorials Are Built of Public Discussion as Much as Stone." *Ottawa Citizen*. Published: May 8, 2015. Accessed: December 2017. Online. http://ottawacitizen.com/news/politics/nadine-blumer-memorials-are-built-of-public-discussion-as-much-as-stone

"Canada: A History of Refuge." Government of Canada. Date modified: 2020–01–16. Accessed: June 2020. Online. https://www.canada.ca/en/immigration-refugees-citizenship/services/refugees/canada-role/timeline.html

Chalmers, Jason. "Settled Memories on Stolen Land: Settler Mythology at Canada's National Holocaust Monument." American Indian Quarterly, vol. 43, no. 4, 2019, p. 379. EBSCOhost, doi:10.5250/amerindiquar.43.4.0379.

Daniels. "Daniel Lieberman part of a team selected to submit a design proposal for the National Holocaust Monument." University of Toronto John H. Daniels Faculty of Architecture, Landscape, and Design. Published: November 4th, 2013. Accessed: December, 2017. Online. https://www.daniels.utoronto.ca/news/2013/11/04/david-lieberman-part-team-selected-submit-design-proposal-national-holocaust

Dolgoy, Rebecca Clare, and Jerzy Elzanowski. "Working through the Limits of Multidirectional Memory: Ottawa's Memorial to the Victims of Communism and National Holocaust Monument." *CITIZENSHIP STUDIES* 22, no. 4 (January 1, 2018): 433–51. doi:10.1080/13621025.2018.1462507.

Eyal, Gil. "Identity and Trauma: Two Forms of the Will to Memory." *History & Memory*, no. 1, 2004, p. 5. EBSCOhost, doi:10.2979/HIS.2004.16.1.5. pgs 6–7.

Government of Canada. "Monuments—Experience Canada's capital." Last Updated: October 2, 2017. Accessed: December 2017. Online. https://www.canada.ca/en/canadian-heritage/services/art-monuments/monuments.html

Halbwachs, Maurice. *On Collective Memory.* Transl. Lewis A. Coser. Chicago: The University of Chicago. 1992. Pg. 51.

"Jewish Museum Berlin." Studio Libeskind. Accessed: June 2020. Online. https://libeskind.com/work/jewish-museum-berlin/

Levitz, Stephanie. "Newly opened National Holocaust Monument to close in winter to avoid damage." The Star. Published: October 26, 2017. Accessed: December, 2017. Online. https://www.thestar.com/news/canada/2017/10/26/newly-opened-national-holocaust-monument-to-close-in-winter-to-avoid-damage.html

@LindaFrum. "In Justin Trudeau's Canada the new Holocaust Monument plaque doesn't mention Jews, Anti-Semitism or the 6 Million." *Twitter*, October 3, 2017, 7:06AM, https://twitter.com/LindaFrum/status/915216401979383814

"National Holocaust Monument." Studio Libeskind. Accessed: June 2020. Online. https://libeskind.com/work/national-holocaust-monument/

"Ohio Statehouse Holocaust Memorial." Studio Libeskind. Accessed: June 2020. Online. https://libeskind.com/work/ohio-statehouse-holocaust-memorial/

Rothberg, Michael. *Multidirectional Memory: Remembering the Holocaust in the Age of Decolonization.* Stanford: Stanford University Press, 2009. Print. Pg. 18.

Sandals, Leah. "6 Questions About Canada's New National Holocaust Monument." *Canadian Art.* Published October 4, 2017. Accessed November 2017. Online. http://canadianart.ca/features/national-holocaust-monument-canada/

Sontag, Susan. *Regarding the Pain of Others.* New York: Picador, 2004. Print.

Solomon Wood, Linda. "What We Saw at the Opening Ceremonies of the Vancouver 2010 Olympic Games." *Vancouver Observer.* Published February 13th, 2010. Accessed: July 2020. Online. https://www.vancouverobserver.com/blogs/overheardolympics/2010/02/13/what-we-saw-opening-ceremonies-vancouver-2010-olympic-games

The Canadian Press. "Holocaust monument plaque that didn't mention Jews to be replaced." *CBC News.* Published: October 6th, 2017. Accessed: December, 2017. Online. http://www.cbc.ca/news/politics/holocaust-plaque-memorial-plaque-1.4343829

Wyld, Adrian. "National Holocaust Monument plaque pulled after panel omits mention of Jews." The Toronto Star. Published: October 5, 2017. Accessed: December, 2017. Online. https://www.thestar.com/news/canada/2017/10/05/plaque-pulled-after-national-holocaust-monument-in-ottawa-omits-mention-of-jews.html

Young, James E. *Texture of Memory: Holocaust Memorials and Meaning.* New Haven: Yale University Press, 1993.

———. *The Stages of Memory: Reflections on Memorial Art, Loss, and the Spaces Between.* Amherst: University of Massachusetts Press, 2016. Project MUSE., https://muse.jhu.edu/ Online. pg. 7.

Chapter 10

Forgetting and Remembering
The Holocaust in Contemporary Australian Fiction
Ira Nadel

Australian Holocaust Fiction is the literature of evasion. Almost from its inception it has supported a Holocaust metanarrative derived from testimony but altered by literary practice in its narrativizing of events. Acting as a buffer between the past and present, the fiction effectively distances and makes acceptable, through its tropes of loss and renewal (essentially relying on the archetype of romance), the engagement with a dark, often unspeakable, past. But in doing so, it transforms that tragic past into an evasive engagement with previous guilt and wrongs. Replacing literature as a chronicle is the creation of texts as we want them to be rather than reflections of what might have happened, avoiding conflict with an actual Holocaust past. A literature of evasion emerges with the outcome, as the critic and historian Anna Clare Hunter describes, "an 'easy' cultural frame of reference that screens the true horror of the event and facilitates an inappropriate sense of cultural redemption." The result has been acceptable, popular Holocaust fiction which transforms guilt into innocence, pain into restitution.[1]

To illustrate this contested effort to simultaneously evade and confront the Holocaust will be an analysis of three recent Australian texts: Liam Pieper's *The Toymaker* (2015), Bram Presser's *The Book of Dirt* (2017), and Heather Morris's *The Tattooist of Auschwitz* (2018). Introducing the topic will be Patrick White's *Riders in the Chariot* (1961), his "Jewish novel" as he deemed it. What the texts collectively reveal is the doubled theme of engagement and distance, of a need to both recreate and avoid a past that in its experience was unbearable, yet in its re-creation disappears either because of the impulse to evade the tragedy and replace the camp settings with scenes of contemporary Australia, or simply to forget it. Erasure of the tragic past replaces an encounter with its horror and loss. Should a character seek to recreate it, they fail, as seen in Bram Presser's *The Book of Dirt* (2017), or paradoxically manage to reframe it (actually re-write it), as in Liam Pieper's *The Toymaker* (2015).

The challenge and responsibility of Australian Holocaust writing was to maintain a valid cultural memory of a bitter past at the same time it sought to avoid it. For refugee writers, it was trying to make a new home without nullifying their personal history, while functioning within a government policy of refugees recruited only as "suitable immigrants" which meant Jews who would assimilate and presumably forget their recent past.[2] In White's novel, the identity of the Jewish survivor Himmelfarb is of no importance to a mob prepared to crucify him; an older woman angrily cries out, "Go home to Germany."[3] Here is the purity of avoidance through an act of erasure, a refusal to acknowledge a Holocaust past that is, nevertheless, ever-present. Yet, the entire twelve-page episode becomes a vivid, disturbing moment in the text unleashing unrestrained xenophobia and anti-Semitism, a smoldering long-term attitude in Australia.[4]

But what makes recent Australian Holocaust novels Australian? The answer is not their geographical settings or local references (both of which are generally limited), but their attempt to diminish the Holocaust in a country that had neglected or eliminated the reality of its own genocide against its aboriginal population. Evasion dominates Australia's telling of its history. But the Holocaust could not be entirely forgotten, and one way to reverse the neglect was to use recognizable tropes as posited by popular culture. Television, movies, or books like Leon Uris's *Exodus* (1958) and *Mila 18* (1961) reaffirmed the success of such an approach.[5] The strategy relied on a simplistic division between the good and the bad: violence and the willful destruction of defenseless Jews versus the survival of heroic individuals often defined by daring, romantic action.

In the popular Holocaust metanarratives, audiences quickly and easily identified with the suffering of victim-focused narratives which required no awareness of the origins of Nazism or Fascism, or interest in the psychology of the perpetrators. The Holocaust was packaged with a one-sided representation of the events shaped by a series of quick-ready markers: striped uniforms, train tracks, the Auschwitz entrance gate, torture, smoking chimneys, and the Star of David.[6]

What explains the appeal and popularity of recent Australian Holocaust fiction is the inscription of an accepted cultural narrative of the Holocaust in an effort to overcome a broader, national sense of forgetfulness. The Holocaust metanarrative, even when the author bases his or her story on actual events, becomes the vehicle for another, often idealistic, account of redemption or renewal. And with their roots in the Jewish family rather than

Jewish cultural history, they privilege personal history over re-imagined political facts.

To evade the past was understandable: among the many the postwar Jewish immigrants to Australia, the Holocaust was never mentioned. Silence rather than speech was their currency. Or if they did speak, it was often in Yiddish and what they said was generally unrecorded and rarely translated. It was not until the Eichmann trial in 1961 that survivors began to feel secure and reveal their stories. Television and the movies soon began to portray the Holocaust experience worldwide. With the establishment of the Jewish Holocaust Centre in Melbourne (1984) and the Sydney Jewish Museum (1992), survivors felt they could at last speak on the record. That same year, 1992, saw the establishment of the Australian Centre for Jewish Civilization at Monash University in Melbourne with its the Holocaust Autobiographies Catalogue, a database of over 180 memoirs published in Australia.

Distance and time also plays a role. For Australian Holocaust survivors and writers, geography interfered with and isolated the re-creation of the past at the same time it protected it. But if physically absent, the Holocaust remained as a psychological presence. A survivor's route of travel was no guarantee of safety. Escape often meant escape from Danzig or Warsaw or Vienna to Shanghai and then Melbourne or Sydney as in Peter Kohn's *Rachel's Chance* (1987). In that text, a Viennese Jewish family departs for Shanghai in 1938 before moving to Israel and then to Australia. But no one in the family can forget their origins or painful past.

In the evolution of Australian Holocaust writing, distance joins time. The appearance of Holocaust fiction in Australia has been late. Early efforts from 1945 onward were scattered and inconsistent. There was also an initial resistance to telling stories about the horrors and the suffering, and further resistance to making it up. But for the survivors and the witnesses, it was critical that some form of fact shape the narrative, although determining the "facts" was not easy. Helen Demidenko's *The Hand That Signed the Paper* (1994) was originally presented as non-fiction but later marketed as fiction. Heather Morris's *The Tattooist of Auschwitz*, based on the actual story of Lale Sokolov and his wife Gita, tattooed by Lale in July 1942, was similarly unsure of its genre. The author's initial goal was to write a screenplay; when that failed, it became a novel—yet, some bookshops still assigned it to the non-fiction section.

The source of these stories, family histories re-fictionalized, has become not only the overriding trope Australian Holocaust literature but also a site of contestation: What is real and what is made up? What is self-serving and what is invented? The current dispute over Morris' new novel, *Cilka's Journey* (2019), something of an extension of *The Tattooist*, is an example, about which the Auschwitz Memorial Research Centre published an extensive report pointing to errors and information inconsistent with the facts in her first novel, *The Tatooist*. Concerning the more recent novel, the Research Centre is just as critical—although Morris claims that she wanted to use the life of Cilka only as inspiration for her latest work. Cilka had supposedly been carrying on a love affair with a high-ranking SS member in the camp, allegedly based on a true story of her becoming a sex slave to the commandant. Cilka's stepson has called the book lurid and hurtful.[7]

Only through such re-imaginings, however, can the "facts" be faced. Literary narrative becomes the means to approach the physical and psychological engagement with the sites of death and their memories. For Australian writers, it is the removal of these narratives from their European foundations that makes their telling possible; such displacement, however, is largely evasive. Paradoxically, "objective" stories as recounted to, or discovered by, Australian authors will be re-imagined by them. Before such exercises, the treatment of the Holocaust in Australian fiction was rarely invented.[8]

Further contributing to this effort of renewal and forgetting is psychological distancing. The Holocaust happened decades ago and thousands of miles away, and those survivors who arrived in Australia—like those who came to the United States and other locations—either did not want, or were not asked, to discuss it. Evasion became the means of their inner peace and outward security. But those who remained in Europe had visual reminders; those who went to the United States had survivor communities. Holocaust survivors who found postwar refuge in Australia sought a tranquil haven, far from visual, psychological or political reminders: the isolation of the country became their reason for emigrating. Disremembering became their epistemological stance encouraged by their physical separation from Europe—yet still interrupted, as always, by visions of the past. The collection *We are Here* interviews with Australian Holocaust survivors edited by Fiona Harai, who records the experience of survivor "Phillip Maisel who walked for several months in a zig-zag pattern after his release and arrival in Australia because he had marched for so long in a straight line. He could now exercise his freedom crossing from one side of the street to another. The movement is a metaphor of the constant shifting between forgetting and remembering experienced by Holocaust survivors in Australia."[9]

History frequently fragments itself into conscious or unconscious forgetting and a compelling feature of Australian Holocaust writing in the postwar period was a certain cultural amnesia regarding the Holocaust *per se*, linked, perhaps, to a broader amnesia regarding the massacre of Australian aboriginals in the nineteenth and early twentieth centuries.[10] Neglecting the aboriginal past of Australia in certain ways prepared the way for the absence of the Holocaust in the Australian consciousness and writing.[11] In its extreme, the historical void even allowed for Australian writers to incorporate a Nazi point of view if not directly, then through collaborators. Helen Demidenko's (actual name Helen Darville) prize-winning *The Hand that Signed the Paper* (1994), about two Ukrainian brothers who join the SS, is one example. Political and personal motivations center the novel which, according to one critic, could not have been published and nor win any prizes in Europe, though it won several in Australia, because of its favorable depiction of accomplices to the Third Reich.[12]

The work demonstrates the appropriation of the Holocaust by non-Jews and the dilemma of Australian Holocaust fiction in adjusting fact to fiction: originally presented as non-fiction based on recorded interviews, Darville later claimed that her text was a work of fiction.[13] Its success, however, suggests a welcomed cultural forgetting (no doubt aided by the reluctance of survivors to speak out) in relation to Australia and the Holocaust. Those Jewish and non-Jewish writers that were determined to remember and establish a place for the Holocaust in the Australian psyche relied by default on the methods of popularization, exemplified by Heather Morris's work.

Australian writers of the second and third generations faced another challenge: uncertainty about the agency of the imagination in addressing such a devastating subject. This directed them to history but seen from a corruptible distance. The documentary fictions of *The Toymaker, The Book of Dirt,* and *Tattooist* find action in memory rather than fact, conscious of Bram Presser's troubling question in *The Book of Dirt*: "how can we claim that there *is* an objective narrative, floating above individual experience"?[14] One response is to incorporate what the late Croatian novelist Daša Drndić identified in reference to her powerful Holocaust novel *Trieste* (2007; Eng. 2015), that "the document (even in fiction) is more powerful than the 'invention' which often rings as false as a construction."[15] *The Book of Dirt*, in particular, incorporates documents, photographs, time sheets, and symbols to reinforce fiction with fact, or seeming fact, causing the narrator at one point to write "back in Australia, I floated on a paper lake, trapped in a gorge of boxes . . . a vast hall of souls."[16]

Postmemory also became an important element of Australian Holocaust fiction; indeed, such writing collectively became a site of postmemory which "implies temporal, but also spatial distance from the site of trauma," as Zuzana Buráková has explained.[17] This prompts, or makes permissible, evasion, the situation of the contemporary Australian Holocaust writer who fictionalizes about a tragedy more than seventy years ago separated by time and space. Contemporary writers have no direct knowledge of the Holocaust past nor any immediate experience with the Shoah. Their link is only secondary, often through parents or grandparents or memoirs or documents. The family is the space of transmission as Australian Holocaust Fiction assumes, in the words of Marianne Hirsch, "the guardianship of a traumatic personal and generational past."[18] But this raises questions about ownership and substitution: do second and third Jewish generations have any legitimate claim to the experiences of the first? Presser repeatedly confronts the problematics of this question in *The Book of Dirt*.

The Book of Dirt takes chances, repeatedly juxtaposing fiction and non-fiction in the author's quest to know more and legitimize his right to write about what he doesn't know, while conscious of the conundrum that "to doubt is improper."[19] "The thing with survival," he states, is that "it cannot be challenged. It cannot be subjected to interrogation . . . every survivor is a hero."[20] Hence, the necessary textual fluctuations between naturalism and fabulism, between a direct narrative and an imaginative re-writing incorporating songs and dreams, demons and spirits, rumors and scriptures. Textual evasion compliments thematic evasion, while expressing the inability to capture directly the Holocaust experience.

The non-fictional element in Presser's novel is his own account of his quest to learn the experiences of his grandparents, Holocaust survivors who almost never spoke about their past in the war. He relays his quest in the first two-thirds of the book more or less chronologically, setting it alongside the fictionalized lives of Presser's family leading up to, and during, the occupation of Prague by the Wermacht. The focus is Jakub, Presser's grandfather and his great grandmother Františka (the mother of his grandmother, Daša met by Jakub at Theresienstadt); what begins as a broad family and cultural history narrows to focus on individual characters. At Theresienstadt, Jakub Rand sorts through Jewish books for a so-called Museum of the Extinct Race. Hidden in a tattered prayer book, with its pages hollowed out, is a small pile of dirt. The story explains this dirt, as fiction amplifies memory through materiality.

The Book of Dirt tracks the intergenerational action between fiction and non-fiction leading up to the goal of Presser's writing: to fashion an image, an understanding of his grandparents' time in the Theresienstadt ghetto and concentration camp. But only when he visits the site of the former camp at the end of his quest does Presser realize that it is too late to learn any more about them and that their story is now his to weave together from what little he has. With this, Presser is able to begin the final third of the book, a sustained fictional rendering of Jakub and Daša's time as prisoners at Theresienstadt.

The Book of Dirt, similar to Drndić's *Trieste*, incorporates photographs both historical and contemporary, real and imaginary. People and documents appear as caption-less images. To the reader, they convey factual impressions also available to Presser's grandparents but also mystery. But the facts, and certainly the images, do not tell all, despite Presser's efforts to track down his grandparents' story by visiting Prague, Theresienstadt and Israel and reading the correspondence and journals of his relatives, several of the letters republished in the novel. Yet the fragments and elisions allow the novelist to fictionalize the story, a form of memorialization where truth trumps fact. What does unite these documentary fictions, however, is the focus on names. As Daša Drndić succinctly states, "BEHIND EVERY NAME THERE IS A STORY," lamenting in her final novel *EEG* that "history remembers the names of criminals, while the names of victims are forgotten."[21]

But *The Book of Dirt* is not as experimentally extreme in terms of documentary fiction as Drndić's *Trieste* (pub. as *Sonnenschien*, 2007; Eng. tr. as *Trieste*, 2012) where a forty-three page chapter consists only of the names of 9,000 Italian Jews killed during the war and printed in four alphabetical columns on each page. The existence of the names recalls Derrida's painful point in *The Work of Mourning* that death without a name, as at Auschwitz, forbids mourning. The first step in mourning must be to speak the name of the dead.[22]

A similar task of turning fact into fiction shapes *The Tattooist of Auschwitz*, the story of an actual couple that met and survived Auschwitz, the protagonist a *Tätowierer* (tattooist) who almost instantly falls in love with a young woman when he tattoos her arm with her number. Written by the journalist Heather Morris, the novel is a text that jars because of the transparency of its characterizations, flat and factually close to the actual figures but too far from them emotionally. The novel is an event, not an experience that reveals the shortcomings of such historically manipulated fiction.

Morris (a New Zealander living in Australia) interviewed at length the late Lale Sokolov, the Slovakian Jew at the center of the story, but cannot gain the fictional or narrative distance from the details to fashion a novel.[23] Yet the very weaknesses of the romance became the source of its popularity. The limpid prose, clichéd writing and external, rather than internal, reaction of the characters to events makes it an undemanding text whose sensational story erases an actual past but explains its wide appeal. Here, the literature of evasion takes on a different hue. It evades not history but an authenticity of feeling. This becomes writing to a formula, the text suffering because the author substitutes romance for experience. The "emotionless" voice Lale hears from the prisoner Nadya in the novel is representative of what's missing: "Whether she's relaying stories of happy times with her family or talking about the tragedy of being here, there is no change in her tone."[24] Everything is strangely the same.

Liam Pieper's *The Toymaker* similarly relies on sensationalism to develop an incomplete trope of an Auschwitz inmate, previously a medical student, who survives by making roughly constructed toys for the children of the camp. Alternating between the terrible experiments on children and adults—Mengele appears more than once in the novel—and the temporary happiness generated by the dolls and toys the Russian prisoner Arkady Kurlakov creates, the text shuttles between contemporary Melbourne where the survivor Arkady (now a grandfather) has a successful toy company distributing throughout Asia and the horrors of Auschwitz. The grandson Adam, an alcoholic and philanderer, especially with teenage girls, now runs and virtually ruins the toy business, ironically saved by his wife who keeps promising to leave her husband but, attached to the grandfather, cannot.

The plot, however, is improbable: Adam's exploitation of young girls, his reform, the actual story of Arkady (his identity assumed by an SS doctor, Dieter, who murdered him in the camp), the implausible hiding of funds in Europe, the sudden outburst of Arkady slashing his 7yr. old grandson with a cane, the continued attachment of his daughter-in-law to her husband after confirmation of his sexual abuse of young women, the offset of the grandfather's trying to save children through his toys (motivated by guilt)—all of these themes collide as the story proceeds with one dominant theme: "people are known by the secrets they keep."[25] But secrets are, perhaps, the most dangerous form of evasion.

Although *The Toymaker* reveals little about the craft or even theory of toys (although details on manufacturing appear), Pieper does disclose one process of creating toys, those generated by the sound of individual words such as "puggle," the name of a small Australian mammal, the echidnas, a small spiny anteater whose name suggests a creature from Greek mythology, half woman, half snake: the animal was to have qualities of both mammals and reptiles (and not the crossbreed of a beagle and a pug). The process is simple: first the word and then the toy to fit the sound, not the meaning, of the term.[26]

But thematic confusions mar the text with the Auschwitz horrors included almost as a distraction as the novel bounces between the past and the present, the kindly grandfather (the suspiciously redeemed SS doctor) ironically passing on history and tradition to this Jewish daughter-in-law. A blackmail attempt disappears, even after the grandson, Adam, finagles $50,000 from a company account as he moves production from China to Indonesia, while the discovery of a compromising photo of him with the fourteen-year-old Carla seems to have little consequence for the wife. The son also repeats his grandfather's story of how he survived and how he helped others survive, especially the parents in the camp, by making toys for their children.[27] The irony of the tale he tells is that replacing its moral urgency is its use as a marketing and promotional tool for the company.

Nevertheless, despite the evasion of identity and truth, there are several observations that extend the treatment of the Shoah in contemporary Australian fiction. The most obvious is the familiar tale of escaping the past by settling in the future of a distant land. And keeping that past secret. But the alternate story of Dieter, the S.S. doctor, atoning for his actions at the camp and murder of Arkady (and then assuming his Jewish identity), seems unlikely and melodramatic; indeed, it is even unclear if the actual Arkady was Jewish.[28] This is also an ironic treatment of the perpetrator as potential victim, assuming a victim's identity.

Stylistically, the book veers from cliché to platitude, while the characters lack emotional resonance, this very simplicity aiding the evasive nature of the novel. Occasionally, a few sentences possess aphoristic value: Russia is "an empire that had carved itself out of snow and sadness." Walking through the Jewish cemetery of Krakow and seeing the sinking graves, tipped by tree roots, "the dead are tossed and tumbled by time, just like the living. No one stays the person they were buried, not for long;" "I'm a Russian after all—without some kind of angst we feel lonely." And then, the hopeful "if we cannot let go of fear and hatred, we will always be in the camps."[29]

But can Australia actually function as a site of refuge for the Australian Holocaust novel? Tentatively "yes," achieved through the act of fictionalizing a fact-based past which it ironically avoids, as the Australian novelist and critic Mireille Juchac explains in her 2016 essay, "The Most Holy Object in the House." In this essay, Juchac attempts to connect with her grandmother, a German Jew and wartime refugee in Australia. After her death, Juchac writes that 'I've inherited an imperative to represent this past, to prevent this history from crystallising into myth." But eliminating fiction or emotion is impossible: "If our recollections don't align with the facts, the feelings accompanying them can still testify to what's astonishing."[30] Paradoxically, surviving the past is possible only by evading it, erasing what was unthinkable while also acknowledging that it must not be forgotten. The contradiction is at the center of Australian Holocaust writing posing the challenges Presser, Morris, and Pieper address in conflicting ways.

The issue may be one of inheritance as Walter Benjamin outlined. When "'the stability and self-identity of the inheritance is taken for granted,'" he argued, there is blindness to how the inheritance (in our case, the Holocaust) resists appropriation. A more accurate purchase on the past would be to understand the "'irreducible enigma'" that it is and attempt to interpret it again.[31] But such an act of reinterpretation resists closure and completion as Presser understands. Morris, by contrast, takes things "for granted" and never questions her inheritance—hence, the weakness of her novel. Its pseudo-certainty of what the Holocaust experience was like neglects its complex actuality which Charlotte Delbo, French Resistance fighter and Auschwitz survivor, made clear. In her memoir *Days and Memory*, she writes that

> In Auschwitz reality was so overwhelming, the suffering, the fatigue, the cold so extreme that we had no energy left for . . . pretending. . . . Reality was right there, killing.[32]

The situation of accepting and denying the past might be summed up by another Australian work: Arnold Zable's *Cafe Scheherazade* (2001). The son of Polish-Jewish refugees, Zable's work is both fiction and non-fiction but more than Presser's novel, *Cafe Scheherazade* anchors the experience of World War II refugees *in* Australia. The book begins and ends in Melbourne and Zable uses a journalist-narrator, who visits the eponymous establishment in the suburb of St Kilda where refugees from Odessa gather. This becomes a device to record their unease expressed by the protagonist Zalman from Warsaw when he explains that

> Our centre of gravity had shifted. This is what I sensed as I stood aboard the boat on the day of our departure . . . our centre of gravity had shifted: away from Poland, Russia, Europe, away from our childhood homes . . . [and] I feel rootless. . . . Though I have lived in Melbourne for over fifty years, I have no sense of belonging.

But, he adds, "in losing everything, I have come to value everything."[33]

Zable, himself, had traveled from Warsaw and Vilna to Kobe, Shanghai and finally Australia. Once settled, he published the important memoir *Jewels and Ashes* (1992), an account by a second-generation writer who returns to Poland to understand the tragic legacy of his parents. Anticipating such discomfort was the German refugee Walter Adamson who, when he arrived at Port Melbourne in 1939, felt that he had not arrived "but had been expelled from the world. . . . What happened between '33 and '45 destroyed my ability to belong," he adds. Disenfranchised, he explained that he felt "as if I stand between at least two worlds if not more."[34] Such liminality, culturally and physically imposed, naturally meant historical and spatial evasion.

Evading the past simultaneously creates a desire to be closer to it but this makes its representation doubly difficult. Incorporating even incomplete documents, memoirs, and photographs from the past maintains its materiality, while the literary forms used to represent the Holocaust initiate methods that distance its immediacy. History and fiction differ, the former pursuing details of the past, the latter often seeking ways to remake them. Inaccurate memories, confused images, and indecipherable documents then become not forms of record but signs of absence as Presser illustrates throughout *The Book of Dirt*. For Australian Holocaust writers, the past exists in half-forgotten memories and in fragments that enforce the materiality of the past into its own form of erasure.³⁵

The question faced by Jewish writers everywhere is how can fiction reconstitute the experiences of the Holocaust? In an interview, Presser explicitly faced the issue:

> The weight I felt was not so much about documenting the unrecorded stories, but to consider the place and responsibility of the novelist in a post-survivor world. What is left to be told?³⁶

Answering that last sentence is the duty of the novelist who must foreground himself in the quest for story because the past and its participants have evaded him. But ironically, by overtaking the narrative and making it his own, narrative evasion survives because of the disruptions to materials and memory necessary to fashion story.

The narrator's statement at the beginning of *The Book of Dirt* best outlines the responsibilities and position of Australian Jewish writers on the Holocaust from an historical and epistemological point of view: "They [the survivors] chose not to speak and now they are gone. . . . What's left to fill the silence is no longer theirs. This is my story, woven from the threads of rumor and legend, post-memory." But it is a story defined by absence, elusion: an emptiness that creates a vacuum as Presser writes, "We cannot find the pieces of the puzzle that make up those few years of their life."³⁷ History is the source but the literary imagination is the means to re-inscribe it.

NOTES

1. Anna Clare Hunter, "'To Tell The Story:' Cultural Trauma and Holocaust Metanarrative," *Holocaust Studies*, 25, nos. 1–2 (2019): 12–27. Special issue: "Trauma & Memory: the Holocaust in Contemporary Culture." Hunter adds that the metanarrative of the Holocaust "militates against the integration of the Holocaust into cultural memory." https://www-tandfonline-com.ezproxy.library.ubc.ca/doi/full/10.1080/17504902.2018.1472872?src=recsys.

Also useful is Christine Berberich, "Introduction: The Holocaust in contemporary culture," *Holocaust Studies* Vol. 25, nos. 1–2 (2019): 1–11. https://www-tandfonline-com.ezproxy.library.ubc.ca/doi/full/10.1080/17504902.2018.1472871.

2. Klaus Neumann, "'Thinking the forbidden concept:' refugees as immigrants and exiles," *Antipodes* Vol. 19, no. 1 (2005): 11.

Australia preferred Jews who would integrate. Historically, Australia welcomed a limited number of Holocaust survivors, government policy restricting Jews to only 3,000 in the immediate postwar years, compared to 9,000 in the prewar period. There was also resistance from the public to Jewish immigrants because they were perceived as less assimilable. A 1936 document from the Australian Department of the Interior stated that Jews dangerously "'preserve their identity as Jews.'" The Anglo-Australian "monoculture" felt comfortable only with non-Jewish Europeans, including a sizeable number of former Nazis who resettled between 1945 and 1950; such anti-Jewish discourse continued for years. (Quoted in Kirril Shields, "Reshaping the Holocaust: Australian fiction, an Australian past, and the reconfiguration of 'traditional' Holocaust narratives, *"Holocaust Studies*, 22, no. 1 (2016): 67, 68. Also see Paul R. Bartrop, *Australia and the Holocaust 1933–1945* [Melbourne: Australian Scholarly Publishing 1994]).

Nevertheless, the country became second only to Israel as a haven for Holocaust survivors on a per capita basis. From 1946 to 1961, 27,000 Jewish survivors migrated to Australia, more than doubling the size of the pre-war community. See Fiona Harari, "Introduction,*"* We are Here, Talking with Australia's oldest Holocaust survivors* (Melbourne: Scribe, 2018), 2.

3. Patrick White, *Riders in the Chariot* (New York: Viking Press, 1961), 439.

4. White included two other Jews in the novel, Harry and Shirl Rosetree who enthusiastically welcomed Australia's assimilationist ethos, burying their Jewish identity underneath a new materialism. The mock crucifixion in Chapter 13, however, dominates the treatment of Judaism in the novel.

5. Both Uris novels, *Exodus,* the story of the founding of Israel, and *Mila 18,* the story of the uprising in the Warsaw ghetto were bestsellers and made into successful movies, yet their utility as a source of history is debatable.

6. These very signs were used in a tasteless Russian ice-skating extravaganza on a Russian reality-celebrity television show in late November 2016. See http://edition.cnn.com/2016/11/27/europe/russian-ice-skating-holocaust-trnd/index.html.

7. Alison Flood, "Sequel to The Tattooist of Auschwitz branded 'lurid and titillating' by survivor's stepson," *Guardian*, 3 October 2019. https://www.theguardian.com/books/2019/oct/03/cilkas-journey-heather-morris-sequel-tattooist-of-auschwitz-branded-titillating.

8. Early texts included Walter Kaufmann's *Voices in the Story* (1953) and Dymphna Cusak *Heat Wave in Berlin* (1962). Jean Devanny published an allegorical novella, *Roll Back the Night* in 1945. The year of the Eichmann trial, White published *Riders in the Chariot* (1961); nineteen years later, Thomas Keneally published *Schindler's Ark* (1982), although Australia does not figure in the novel.

For a general survey, see Serge Liberman, "Australian Jewish Fiction: A Bibliographical Survey," *Edinburgh Companion to Modern Jewish Fiction* (Edinburgh: Edinburgh UP, 2015). 332–345.

9. Anne Susskind, "We Are Here review: The triumph of the last witnesses," *Sydney Morning Herald*, 21 March 2018. https://www.smh.com.au/culture/books/the-triumph-of-the-last-witnesses-20180321-h0xrbn.html.

10. Aboriginals were not included in the Australian census until 1967.

11. The issues of Aboriginal identity, in response to invasion, dispersal, and disease, originating in colonization, have increasingly gained importance, although it was only in 1967 that Australia voted to finally include Aboriginal and Torres Strait Islanders in its census. In 1992, in what is known as the Redfern Speech, then prime minister Paul Keating admitted the government's role in the dispossession,

violence and oppression that colonialization imposed on Australian Aboriginals. But some argue little has changed, while history becomes, according to one elder Aboriginal, only "what people choose to remember." See Paul Daley," It's 50 years since Indigenous Australians first 'counted.' Why has so little changed?" *Guardian* 18 May 2017. https://www.theguardian.com/inequality/2017/may/18/50-years-since-indigenous-australians-first-counted-why-has-so-little-changed-1967-referendum.

However, by 2002 the *Protocols for Producing Indigenous Australian Writing* appeared (2nd ed. 2007), published by the Australian Council for the Arts. It begins with "Principles and protocols" followed by "Implementation." But until these late 20th century and early 21st century developments, Aboriginal life and culture had been at best over looked, and at worst, forgotten. See Emmanuel S. Nelson, "Literature against History: An Approach to Australian Aboriginal Writing," *World Literature Today* 64, no. 1 (1990): 30–34. For a contemporary review of the situation, see Clair Andersen, "Exploring Aboriginal identity in Australia and Building Resilience," Intechopen Books, 2019; https://www.intechopen.com/books/indigenous-aboriginal-fugitive-and-ethnic-groups-around-the-globe/exploring-aboriginal-identity-in-australia-and-building-resilience.

12. The novel focuses on Ukrainian anti-Semitism and the suffering of Jews in the Holocaust tracing a family's cooperation with the Nazis with greater sympathy for their militaristic sons than their Jewish victims. The novel won the prestigious Miles Franklin literary award (as did *Riders in the Chariot*), but to the surprise of many, the author was unmasked as Helen Darville, daughter of British immigrants, pretending to be Ukrainian. See Robert Manne, *The Culture of Forgetting: Helen Demidenko and the Holocaust* (Text, 1996).

The controversy over the novel's SS focus anticipated reaction to the Australian born Rachel Seiffert's *The Dark Room* (2001) concentrating on the German people's reaction to Nazism, as well as Jonathan Littell's novel, *The Kindly Ones* (2006) narrated by a former SS officer and mass murderer. It won the *Prix Goncourt*.

13. Two books addressed the issue of authenticity in the novel: Robert Manne's *The Culture of Forgetting: Helen Demidenko and the Holocaust* and Andrew Riemer, *The Demidenko Debate*. Both appeared in 1996.

14. Bram Presser, *The Book of Dirt* (Melbourne: Text Publishing, 2017) 69.

15. Drndić in Katharina Bielenberg, "The Editor's Chair: On Daša Drndić," *Granta* 16 November 2018. https://granta.com/katharina-bielenberg-editors-chair/.

16. Presser, *The Book of Dirt* 74.

17. Zuzana Buráková, "Whose trauma is it? A trauma–theoretical reading of *The Book Thief* by Marcus Zusak," *Holocaust Studies* 25.1-2 (2019). https://www-tandfonline-com.ezproxy.library.ubc.ca/doi/full/10.1080/17504902.2018.1472874.

18. Marianne Hirsch, "The Generation of Postmemory," *Poetics Today* 29:1(2008) 104 rpt. in *The Generation of Postmemory, Writing and Visual Culture After the Holocaust* (New York: Columbia UP, 2012).

19. The actual Jan Randa (1911-1996) emigrated to Melbourne where he married his wife Daša, first met in Theresienstadt.

20. Presser, *The Book of Dirt* 11.

21. Drndić, *Trieste* 141; Drndić, *EEG* in Alison Flood, "Daša Drndić . . . dies aged 71," *Guardian*, 6 June 2018. https://www.theguardian.com/books/2018/jun/06/dasa-drndic-unflinching-croatian-novelist-dies-aged-71. Also see Bielenberg, "The Editor's Chair: on Daša Drndić."

22. For the list, see *Trieste*, tr. Ellen Elias-Bursać (Mariner Books, 2015) 143–86. In the Croatian edition of the novel, the lists of names were printed on perforated pages. At a Jewish Book Week in London, Drndić passed around a copy and invited the audience to tear out the pages containing the names they recognized. In *Belladonna* (2017) there is a list of the 2,061 Jewish children deported from the Netherlands. On death and naming, see Derrida, *The Work of Mourning*, ed. Pascale-Anne Brault and Michael Naas (Univ. of Chicago Press, 2001) 237.

23. A parallel is Antonio Iturbe's young adult novel, *The Librarian of Auschwitz,* tr. L. Z. Thwaites (2012; Eng. Godwin/Henry Holt, 2017). It focuses on the so-called children's library in Block 31 based on the true story of Dita Kraus. Iturbe interviewed the real Dita Krause who was 80 and at the time lived in Israel. She was 14 in the camp when she protected a ragged assortment of twelve or so books and secretly circulated them to teachers to share with the 500 children in Block 31. The titles included *A Short History of the World* by H.G. Wells, a Russian grammar, a book of analytical geometry and *The Count of Monte Cristo* in French. Her autobiography, *A Delayed Life,* appeared in 2020.

24. Heather Morris, *The Tattooist of Auschwitz, A Novel* (New York: Harper 2018), 107.

25. Liam Pieper, *The Toymaker* (Melbourne: Penguin/ Random House Australia, 2016), 190–91.

26. Pieper, *Toymaker*, 187–9.

27. Pieper, *Toymaker* 28–9.

28. Pieper, *Toymaker* 242–5.

29. Pieper, *Toymaker* 101, 114, 164, 165.

30. Mireille Juchac, "The Most Holy Object in the House," *Tablet 27 July 2016.* https://www.tabletmag.com/jewish-life-and-religion/208749/the-most-holy-object-in-the-house.

31. Walter Benjamin in Gerhard Richter, *Inheriting Walter Benjamin* (London: Bloomsbury, 2016) 10.

32. Charlotte Delbo, *Days and Memory*, tr. Rosette Lamont (Marlboro, VT: Marlboro Press, 1990), 1–2.

33. Arnold Zable, *Café Scheherazade* (Melbourne: Text Publishing, 2001), 101.

34. Walter Adamson, *Matilda Stops Waltzing* (Scarsdale: Papyrus, 1996) 108, 114. Adamson in Josef Vondra, *German Speaking Settlers in Australia* (Melbourne: Cavalier Press, 1981) 199.

Adamson's father died in a concentration camp. Adamson was best-known for his 1974 satiric novel *Die Anstalt* (*The Institution*). In 1984 he published *Australia of All Places.*

35. This may parallel Heidegger's notion of *sous rature*, translated as "under erasure" and used by Derrida as the elimination but yet presence of a word or a concept in a text. Meaning derives from difference, not reference, to already existing concepts.

Evasion does not eliminate the Holocaust in contemporary Australian Holocaust writing but deflects its realism. It is simultaneously present and absent, creating a contested space. As Derrida notes, "the continued legibility of a term placed under erasure is crucial." This has implications for the historical and literary treatment of the Holocaust in Australian writing and its reliance on evasion. See Raphael Rubinstein, Missing: / Must include: *Erasure," sous rature, An exhibition* 28 November 2018-27 January 2019. https://www.under-erasure.com/.

36. Presser in Jerath Head, "What Fills the Silence: *The Book of Dirt* by Bram Presser," *Sydney Review of Books*, 1 May 2018. https://sydneyreviewofbooks.com/the-book-of-dirt-by-bram-presser/.

37. Presser, *The Book of Dirt* 80, 188.

REFERENCES

Adamson, Walter. *Matilda Stops Waltzing*. Scarsdale: Papyrus, 1996.
Bielenberg, Katharina. "The Editor's Chair: On Daša Drndić," *Granta* 16 November 2018. https://granta.com/katharina-bielenberg-editors-chair/.
Delbo, Charlotte. *Days and Memory*, tr. Rosette Lamont. Marlboro: Marlboro Press, 1990.
Drndić, Daša. *Trieste, a Novel*. Tr. Ellen Elias-Bursać. Boston: Mariner Books, 2015.
Flood, Alison. "Daša Drndić . . . dies aged 71," *Guardian*, 6 June 2018. https://www.theguardian.com/books/2018/jun/06/dasa-drndic-unflinching-croatian-novelist-dies-aged-71.
Harari, Fiona. "Introduction," *We are Here, Talking with Australia's oldest Holocaust survivors*. Melbourne: Scribe, 2018. 1–7.
Head, Jerath. "What Fills the Silence: *The Book of Dirt* by Bram Presser," *Sydney Review of Books*, 1 May 2018. https://sydneyreviewofbooks.com/the-book-of-dirt-by-bram-presser/.
Hirsch, Marianne. *The Generation of Postmemory: Writing and Visual Culture After the Holocaust*. New York: Columbia UP, 2012.
Hunter, Anna Clare. "'To tell the Story:' Cultural Trauma and Holocaust Metanarrative," *Holocaust Studies*, 25, nos. 1–2 (2019): 12–27.
Juchac, Mireille. "The Most Holy Object in the House," *Tablet, 27 July 2016*. https://www.tabletmag.com/jewish-life-and-religion/208749/the-most-holy-object-in-the-house.
Morris, Heather. *The Tattooist of Auschwitz, A Novel*. New York: Harper, 2018.
Neumann, Klaus. "'Thinking the Forbidden Concept:' Refugees as Immigrants and Exiles," *Antipodes*, 19, no. 1 (2005) 6–11.
Pieper, Liam. *The Toymaker*. Melbourne: Penguin/Random House Australia, 2016.
Presser, Bram. *The Book of Dirt*. Melbourne: Text Publishing, 2017.
Richter, Gerhard. *Inheriting Walter Benjamin*. London: Bloomsbury, 2016.
White, Patrick. *Riders in the Chariot*. New York: Viking Press, 1961.
Zable, Arnold. *Café Scheherazade*. Melbourne: Text Publishing, 2001.

Chapter 11

"We Are the New Children"
Shoah and Israeli Childhood in *Nava Semel's* And the Rat Laughed

Ranen Omer-Sherman

In her tragically short lifetime, the aesthetically bold and morally audacious works of Nava Semel (1954–2017) made a significant transformation in the Israeli reading public's appreciation of the Holocaust's complexity as a profoundly consequential factor in both domestic and national life. This was accomplished through her perspicacious portrayals of the struggle of children and young people growing up in families in which the trauma of "over there" was suppressed, if never quite fully *unexpressed* in ways that often left them uneasily at odds with their own Israeli identities, as if they inherited the vague shame of a "difference" or "otherness" they cannot fully comprehend but which sets them adrift from the normative, heavily masculinized "Israeliness" that ostensibly fortifies their peers (if only because the latter have been spared that direct proximity). In Hanna Yaoz' incisive discussion, she describes the weight that fell on the children of survivors

> The transgenerational transfer of the survivors' syndrome turned children of survivors into 'memorial candles' who immortalized by their very existence the memory of family members who had perished. The way in which this phenomenon was expressed in parental overprotection and anxieties with food, illness, security, family relations, and career has been noted by psychologists . . . [and] provided raw material for second-generation writers . . . projected on the world model they built in their imagination.[1]

Among their salient concerns, Yaoz writes, are "the conspiracy of silence, guilt feelings, traumatic anxieties and fears, the burden of immortalizing memory, and the legacy of suffering" (161). In indelible ways, Semel's work measures these distances and gaps, between the suffering and pain of intimate familial memory (what the author once dubbed their "private Shoah") and ceremonial, nationalistic forms of Holocaust memory, the apartness felt by the children of survivors struggling with a legacy that prevents their seamless sense of inclusion. In Semel's moral imagination, Israel is not so much the proverbial Phoenix rising from the ashes of the Holocaust as a reminder that nation-states are at best reminders of how poorly its legacy is understood or applied even by those who claim to own it. As she recounts it, in these so-called "silent families" there was often muted evidence of the unspeakable torment survivor parents had endured and struggled to suppress, often expressed through intimate familial cues such as their body language. And these disturbing hints and signs were readily discernable by their children even if their full meaning remained elusive.

Such visceral examples of "non-verbal transmissions" are alluded to by Semel in a few salient instances in her penetrating series of conversations with Israeli-Irish sociologist Ronit Lentin. Here she recalls her early memory of:

> my mother listening to the radio at six, at twilight, when Ben Gurion announced in the Knesset that Eichmann had been caught. And my mother standing by the radio and physically shaking. I remember myself pulling at her dress and asking who this man was and she said only the name, Eichmann, I don't remember anybody explaining to me who he was. Because the man who owned the grocery store, at the end of our street, Brandeis street, was called Astman and . . . they used to send me to buy half a loaf of bread, which I used to bite at on the way home. I was afraid for a very long time to go to the grocery store and buy bread, because I thought that the man who owned the grocery store was a criminal. By the way, this man and his wife were Shoah survivors. (Lentin, 33)[2]

Elsewhere, she evocatively describes such instances of the traumatic past trickling into her childhood cognition as "seeping information" (Lentin, 34). Semel's mother, Margalit (Mimi) Artzi (nee Liquornik), born in Bukovina, was a survivor of several concentration camps, including Auschwitz. Though Semel was born in a *ma'abara* (transit camp), she always insisted that she experienced no special deprivation in childhood.[3]

If still regrettably less familiar to readers outside Israel than David Grossman (not himself the child of survivors), whose *See Under: Love* (Ayen Erech: Ahava) was published to wide acclaim and also addressed second-generation themes, Semel's oeuvre includes the very first collection of "second generation" fiction collection ever published in Israel, *Kova Zekhukhit* (*A Hat of Glass* [1985]) which appeared the year before Grossman's extraordinary novel (and was unjustly eclipsed in the wake of its fame).[4] This ground-breaking collection, which today is generally lauded by Hebrew critics crediting Semel for launching a vigorous literary and cultural conversation that continues in Israel to this day, proved initially unpopular among mainstream Israelis who were simply unaccustomed (or even hostile) to encountering the Shoah as a complex intergenerational legacy.[5] Fortunately she persevered, and in addition to numerous works for adults, Semel's Holocaust-oriented fiction includes two novels for younger readers, *Gershona Shona* (*Becoming Gershona* [1988/1990]) and *Maurice Havivel Melamed Lauf* (*Flying Lessons* [1991/1995]) portraying the interactions of young Israelis living among Shoah survivors struggling to create new lives in the early years of the state, a time when their very existence sometimes seemed an affront to the heroic and almost exclusively masculinist ideal of the "New Hebrew."

For Semel, "writing about the scar of the Holocaust is my rebellion against the rigid model of the neo-Israeli, supposedly untainted by the past."[6] More specifically, her voice constitutes an explicitly feminist rebuttal to Zionist culture, for as Lani Ravin argues persuasively, a significant aspect of Semel's achievement resides in "writing about the Holocaust for an Israeli audience, Semel is firmly putting female experience front and center. It is rare for women's experiences to be widely considered the norm or an archetype for Jewish or Israeli themes" (60). Ravin's point cannot be overemphasized, except to add that depictions of female childhoods are an even rarer subject in Israeli Holocaust literature. Yet as notable as this contribution is, at a certain point, Semel's imaginative focus moved beyond absorption with the gendered limitations of Israeli identity toward a near-universalist orientation.

As Yaoz observes, an unusual feature distinguishing the writing of the second-generation in Israel is the turn "from the real to the fantastic" (161), a quality that certainly includes Semel's extraordinary 2001 novel *Tzchok Shel Achbarosh* (*And the Rat Laughed*), featuring one of the youngest protagonists in the global canon of Shoah literature, a nameless five-year-old girl whose Jewish parents entrust her to the care of an anti-Semitic farming family living in a remote village who agree to take her in strictly for financial gain. For nearly a year, she is kept in a dark potato cellar with only the titular rat for company—where she is raped repeatedly by the farmers' teenage son, Stefan. Encompassing 150 years (1944–2099), the novel's five disparate sections and genres (story, legend, poetry, scientific report, diary), range from the time of that abuse to the Tel Aviv of 1999, to the investigations of an anthropologist in the year 2099, and back again to the past told from the perspective of Father Stanislaw, a priest who struggled to rescue and restore the child. Except for the latter, each features intellectually curious and bold female protagonists of different generations, each driven by their moral passion to unseal the past. The exquisite fragmentation of their interwoven stories performs a powerful interrogation of the imperative to remember while paying heed to the unpredictable and sometimes even dangerous effects of the story on those who willingly or otherwise become its conduits. Indeed, in an important sense, the entire novel is a prolonged meditation on just how complicated this moral calculus is. Over the years, many of my students have reported that when it comes to the ethics of identification, this is one of the most stirring works they encountered. Accordingly, here it bears stressing that this often neglected work warrants far more inclusion in classroom syllabi than it receives for *And the Rat Laughed* is a multilayered work that can be taught at almost every level (and by way of comparison, unlike Grossman's epic *See Under: Love*, which in its entirety can be unwieldy even for university courses, it comes in at a slim 232 pages). But more than for its convenient brevity or even its imaginative audacity, Semel's work warrants greater attention for its critical focus on sexual violence in the Holocaust, a topic rarely addressed in Holocaust fiction even though descriptions of vicious sexual abuse directed toward both females and males of all ages are pervasive in the testimonies collected at the Fortunoff Video Archives for Holocaust Testimonies, US Holocaust Memorial Museum, University of Southern California Shoah Foundation, Yad Vashem, and others.[7]

After the fraught introduction ("The Story") to the grandmother struggling to bring her past to light, the second section ("The Legend") consists of the granddaughter's naïve retelling in her school report; the third section ("The Poems") set a decade later takes the form of a lyrical sequence, putatively written by the grandmother and released by a mysterious website. In Part Four ("The Dream"), an anthropologist labors over piecing together the origins of a strange myth, or "encrypted historical memory," while Part Five ("The Diary") cycles back to the horrific genesis of the story in the form of the diary kept by Father Stanislaw, who has taken in the speechless child (the looming enigma that perpetually nags at the reader is how this child, catatonic after enduring such cruelty, survives to become the affectionate if somewhat prickly mother and grandmother we meet in the first story and it is here that we receive an answer, albeit one that is a source of yet more heartbreak). In his compassionate struggle to restore the humanity of the-little-girl-who-once-was, Stanislaw is undone himself, anguished and driven into silence by the moral turpitude of his congregants.

To fully appreciate the ambition behind Semel's tour de force, it is important to considering the environment that inspired her initial foray into Holocaust fiction. Most crucially, one must bear in mind that even if the Israeli society of Semel's childhood years putatively commemorated the Shoah as Yom Hazikaron laShoah ve-laG'vurah (Holocaust and Heroism Remembrance Day), she insisted that it was "more the 'Heroism and Shoah day' than the other way round" (Lentin, 34) and that the heavily ritualized and decorous ceremonies at her school only increased the distance between her limited understanding and her mother's painful history: "I never, never imagined that I should have gone home [from school], on that very day, and asked my mother directly, because she had been there. I mean there was a complete dissociation. I think that in this respect I am representative of a whole generation for whom there was a dissociation relating to the ritualism, which undoubtedly was also based on heroic rituals in these years of shaping the Israeli psyche" (Lentin, 34).[8] Not so unlike many young people, she had simply been incurious about her mother's personal history.

Only years later did it dawn on her that whenever alluding to her younger years, her mother would freely refer to anything up to her 18th year or beyond the age of 23, while leaving a blank gap of five years. And yet: "I never gave it a thought until I became an adult myself and understood that a part was missing in this chain" (Lentin, 35).[9] As one Israeli reviewer of *And the Rat Laughed* incisively observed, for those living in Israel, Holocaust stories "sink in deep and become part of a collective trauma, below and in addition to the more immediate stresses of life in Israel. On another level, the exaggerated horrors (even if factually true) become trite, over-used and political gimmickry. Kids tell Holocaust jokes and roll their eyes during solemn assemblies."[10] In ways that arguably mirrored the embryonic society in which she was raised (immured within its mythic tropes of heroism and repudiation of the European past), Semel's gradual awakening that led her to appreciate her mother's complex layers as a survivor and most importantly her own responsibility to bear witness to it, as a daughter and as an artist. Hence, in significant ways, Semel's own journey, in response to her mother's traumatic history, was analogous to that of many of her readers:

[T]he Israeli climate was, if not hostile, certainly alien and not aware of how to digest these people who arrived with traumas, and with a lot of guilt on the part of the Yishuv (pre-state Jewish settlement) in Eretz Israel. Because, it transpires that some of the facts (about the Shoah) did reach (the Yishuv) and no one wanted to believe them. Plus the fact that the survivors themselves . . . because they felt there was no one listening, they closed up and this suited their psychic state of surviving as a result of a life urge and fast rehabilitation. So they chose to deal with the practical aspects of life. I always think that what saved them from such a large collective trauma, which, by the way, they did not even clarify to themselves, was the fact that very fast they were sucked into the giant vacuum cleaner of building Israel, into the momentum of doing, of practice, of livelihood, of bread, of moving from tents in a transit camp to an apartment in some apartment block and so on. And then they had to send the child to school and have him bring home good grades. Therefore their children saw them as the ultimate, absolute model of parenthood . . . the disbelief was even greater, because you could not have suspected that behind the parent who is chasing you with a banana and a jumper the whole day and the whole night, could hide such enormous dramas. It was almost impossible to link that parental model with a human model. My dialogue with my mother began when I decided she was a human being, not only my mother. And I was going to examine the biography of that human being. (Lentin, 40)

The cataclysm of her mother's opening up led to Semel's new awareness that her mother was a far more complex being than she had previously imagined; that painful cognition led to the thematically linked stories of *A Hat of Glass* (published in 1985 when she was just twenty-five years old), reflecting a new-found sense of identity and identification.[11] Years later she would recall that sometime during that heady new period of open questioning and disclosures in their relationship, she had been startled by the visible display of relief on her mother's face, simply because "someone was asking at last" (Lentin, 43). As Semel's interlocutor in this revelatory exchange argues, Semel gradually became confident in her new role as her mother's chronicler and began to insist on identifying "openly as a daughter of survivors and exit the isolation resulting from having grown up in a 'silent family'" (Lentin, 38). Hence, in assembling the missing gaps in the fabric of her mother's story, she was also constructing her own.[12] Not surprisingly given that burdened history, *And the Rat Laughed* sharply interrogates the limits of language, repression, and representation.

Accordingly, in portraying the halting attempts of an aged survivor struggling to impart her story for the first time, Semel first renders the near-impossibility of that task: "The old woman has no illusions. Her story is made of stumps. The chances that it will be mended at this late stage are very slim" (*And the Rat Laughed*, 22). Accordingly, the first section begins with what would best be characterized as a series of wavering, vacillations, hesitations, and deferral on the part of its narrator, a quality that bears comparison both with the lived experience of many survivors as well as some of their notable fictional surrogates. This phenomenon occurs most strikingly in the works of Polish-born survivor Ida Fink, beginning with the title story of the latter's *A Scrap of Time* (1987) where the narrator announces that she intends to "talk about a certain time" dug out of "the ruins of memory" (*Scrap of Time*, 3) while refraining from actually doing so for some pages, as if signaling the writer's own incapacity to bring the enormity of what she must describe (the murder of a little boy) under full emotional or aesthetic control. Similarly, Semel's first narrator vacillates over how, or whether, to transmit her childhood trauma to her Israeli granddaughter who knows only the familiar, cosmopolitan life of Tel Aviv: "How to tell this story?"; "But maybe there's no need to tell it"; "How should the story be told?" "It's as if she has no choice but to assume the role of the storyteller" (*And the Rat Laughed*, 3). Until at last this:

[J]ust as she has repressed the story, so too does she now repress the very question of how to tell it. Because if she were to give it a voice, the story would burst through without her being able to contain it, and its severed limbs would scatter in all directions, unfamiliar even to her. . . . Even when she pent it up inside her, the story would stab its way through, jabbing its spikes into her . . . foisting itself on her and dragging her deep into the entrails of the story. (4)

Even after this visceral acknowledgement of the impossibility of the story's further concealment, a series of false starts ensue until it becomes clear to the woman that there will never be a fully satisfactory form or structure to express what she endured, let alone any possibility of healing after so many years. For a time, this litany of self-doubt ("What good will it do? Why now"?) buffers her from the pain revisiting "the story" can still inflict (5). Yet, even more than that pain, what she most fears is that in the very telling, once out in the world, "the story will become incoherent" or "in an effort to disguise its own ugliness will turn into something completely different" (5). And this latter anxiety would seem the essence of Semel's own moral quandary as a second-generation artist, the urgent necessity of witnessing and the utter impossibility of it, since it is the way of human beings to sanitize, sentimentalize, and conceal what is abhorrent or inconceivable.[13] Indeed, it is the inevitable realization of the protagonist's fears that proves the creative stimulus behind the almost unrecognizable new meanings and distortions her story acquires later, in an unimaginably distant future society with its own pre-conceived notions of the primitive past. But as the novel begins, in the here and now of sunny Tel Aviv, it seems that the granddaughter, who breezily insists on obtaining the bare facts required for her family genealogical assignment for school, will not be left unsatisfied (no matter how poorly she is prepared to absorb the horror of what her grandmother actually endured) as a child.

In the end, the process proves oddly synchronous, for even as the grandmother slowly yields to the girl's pressure, a mysterious "urgency" builds up within her: "Maybe it's old age. She cannot afford to let the story disappear as if it never happened" (5). Yet her will to tell it ebbs and flows; she is nearly paralyzed at crucial moments by anxiety over her toxic narrative's potential to prematurely age or otherwise inflict terrible psychic damage on her granddaughter: "The old woman would try her best to keep the venom from splattering onto the recipient of her story" (13). *And the Rat Laughed* is brimming with the kinds of quiet ironies that might pass unnoticed upon the first reading or whose prophetic resonance emerges only much later such as when she wishes for a more "ideal addressee" than her granddaughter: "Had she been allowed to choose, she would have preferred someone indifferent, unemotional, far-removed from her" (13). In the narrative's ingeniously twisted and unexpected paths that wistful hope reaches its perverse fulfillment in the hands of unimagined recipients, particularly in the section titled "The Dream" where anthropologists in 2099 (a time where any form of traumatic memory is automatically excised) use their technologies to try to trace the origins of the troubling myth of "Girl and Rat," one of the cryptic fragments of the barbaric past inherited by their time.

In her nuanced rendering of the old woman's subjectivity, Semel gives short shrift to any consoling notion a reader might have (and to my mind this lesson bears crucial pedagogical resonance in the classroom for students coming to terms with the subjectivity of survivors) when it comes to potentially cathartic or redeeming effects for the survivor in liberating the trauma they've kept hidden: "The storyteller is supposed to gain something from the very act of telling the story. Release, after all, according to conventional wisdom, is supposed to bring relief. The old woman certainly has a hefty motive then. And yet, no gain seems to present itself in the case of her story. The natural act of returning to the past and rummaging through memories brings solace only to those with very different stories to tell" (16–17). There is never even a hint of redemptive unburdening in Semel's portrayal of the survivor's plight, nor any hope of escaping their status as "an eternal outcast from the world," their "walled off existence" (34), just the overwhelming, almost biological imperative to create some form of bridge to the next generation, however precarious.[14]

Gradually, the grandmother's hesitation gives way to wrenching flashbacks to her earliest memories of abandonment by the parents she would never see again, her first harrowing memories of being handed over to strangers and forced to survive, literally underground as a hidden child:

> They stood with their backs to her. Her mother did not turn around. Didn't say a word. Not even good-bye. Didn't touch her either. The old woman is almost choking. The story is lodged between her throat and her mouth.
>
> The stranger, the one whom she would come to call the "farmer's wife," dragged her down the ladder and said, This is where you stay.
>
> They lowered her into a pit under the ground. The little-girl-who-once-was thought that only the worst creatures in the world lived under the ground. Moles and snakes and worms. And the worst of all were the rats. She was worse than any of them though, if she had to be hidden away from all the people up above. . . . The little-girl-who-once-was thought: Maybe I'm really dead. Because only dead people get pushed so deep down. (17, 18)

No matter how many attempts, never again will she be able to conjure up even a fleeting trace of her mother's face: "God is a mother who turns her back" (24) and "All that remained was her mother's back. A locked-body door" (34). Moreover, the author insinuates that in approaching the end of her life, this subterranean time is more real to the protagonist than her present. Even though she is now forty years older than her mother had been when she turned her back, the sense of abandonment, rage, and yearning are "as razor-sharp as ever" (30). Not unlike Cynthia Ozick's Rosa in the second part of *The Shawl*, clinging fetishistically to the moment of her traumatic loss, and for whom the Miami sunlight is "smothering," an "executioner," Semel's protagonist recoils from the sunny present of Tel Aviv: "Early afternoon . . . is always a difficult time of day. The light is invasive. Only rarely does the old woman let herself take it in. Most of the time, she draws the curtains and shuts the blinds, to let in the darkness, her old ally"; "Tel Aviv deifies the light. In this city, light is the be-all and end-all" and "When her time comes, the old woman will be lowered into the earth, into the familiar darkness. She's not afraid. . . . She emerged from the darkness, and has remained in the darkness" (18, 32, 45).[15] The weight of the suffering that each woman has borne over the decades makes it impossible to be capable of experiencing the benevolence of the sun as anything but a cruelly seductive chimera. That capacity was clearly left behind with "the little-girl-who-once-was [. . .] Anything beyond the darkness, anything that had come before and anything that might come after, became an illusion" (33, 34). As the horrifying details begin to seep out of her in the reluctant act of transmission, recounting the agonizing rapes she endured at the hands of the farmers' son, Stefan, the grandmother notices that her granddaughter is so unprepared for the enormity of the tale that she is unable to lift her pen. Later we learn that the girl is rapidly formulating a more benign version of her grandmother's past, one for which the old woman is insufficiently grateful, or otherwise unable to recall the kindnesses bestowed on her by the altruistic family that sheltered her.

Semel's language concerning the grandchild's innocence, her capacity for comprehending unendurable horror, to record its crucial details dispassionately in a notebook, strikingly recall the plight of Grossman's Momik in *See Under: Love*: "Her granddaughter is indeed young, but she's already at an age where people are capable of working out the codes and deciphering the truth. And although she's decided to get the story, no matter what, the pages of her notebook are blank" (*And the Rat Laughed*, 31). And yet, this child, however ill-equipped, is nevertheless critical to the preservation of memory precisely because communication about the past between the grandmother and her daughter, the girl's mother, has already proved an even worse failure, a dysfunctional relationship representative of many in the second generation who grew up feeling themselves in the shadow of an immensity that threatened to overshadow or stunt their own identities:

> The daughter . . . always suspected that her mother was obsessively repeating the story to herself. She claimed that whenever a person becomes immersed in a story, he doesn't bother to listen to anything around him. Perhaps she was trying to cry that she had a story too, one that was no less important than her mother's. No one had explained to her that her mother was immersed not in the story, but in the question of how to tell it or refrain from telling it. (35)

As noted above, a pervasive theme in Semel's earlier work is the inability of the second generation of Israelis to come to terms with a legacy of vulnerability and suffering that felt so at odds with their own sense of identity. In one salient example, Dafna, the young female protagonist of "A Private Holocaust," raised on kibbutz by survivor parents, flees the smothering weight of the past for a new life in London. She utterly disavows the Shoah's claim on her (and by extension her entire generation's) Sabra identity:

> Leave me out of all this. Why do you keep dealing with the Holocaust? We lock the ceremonies away for one day in the year. It has been, it is finished, we are another generation, and we are the new children. Don't lumber us with your fur of fears. We are new. Shem, Ham and Yefet. Throwing covers over their father's nakedness. All these things happened in a place far away. That period stuck only to the pages of the books. It does not touch me. I seek to find myself, I am after a new girl.[16]

Semel's logic in what unfolds is brutal. Only in the aftermath of suffering the terror of a violent abduction and rape, does something shift within Dafna and she at last begins to truly empathize with her mother's pain and gradually accept and integrate the once incommensurate halves of her being. By way of contrast, *And the Rat Laughed* proffers a rare moment of wry humor and grace as the grandmother contemplates a strand of intergenerational resemblance, leaving open at least a faint prospect of new understandings. When her daughter arrives to retrieve her granddaughter, the old woman watches her daughter's utter dismay as she grasps how they have spent their time. The mother, to whom the story was never told and belatedly accepts that she has long resented that withholding, is angered that her daughter's innocence will be sullied instead. And in this moment, the reader is exposed to the faint presence of acerbic humor as a subterranean coping mechanism within the old woman, one whose existence has sustained her over time.

> Mother, don't you go messing up my daughter's head.
> For the first time on a blinding afternoon, the old woman actually cracked a smile. The realization that the one she had given birth to had become such an expert at survival was gratifying. (36)

Though the story's power is excruciating, smothering, she has one perverse, obstinate resource for denying it total victory over her, even if it is edged with self-mockery: "Humor is the only way of undermining the story, making believe that we're standing over its ruins. Even now, the storyteller makes fun of herself: an old woman spending a blinding afternoon in Tel Aviv, in a room with its shutters closed tight. Paralyzed with fear of what she and her story are inflicting on her granddaughter" (42).[17] Yet her deepest anxiety is the fate of the story once released, the violence that might be done to it by future generations, whether in some way her childhood rapist might somehow come to be misconstrued as a redeemer:

> The old woman is worried about how the stories are liable to evolve. In a world where stages are glossed over, with no apparent sequence, one must take into account the possibility of changes and reframings. Whatever the next storyteller adds worries her even more than what he may leave out. The Stefan must never turn into the main character, God forbid. (43)

Semel stresses that the entire chain of transmission begins on shaky grounds. Having unburdened herself, the survivor forces herself to acknowledge her own complicity in the story's uncertain fate: "She and others like her will never be the perfect storytellers. All they can offer is the shell" and "The story has subplots and untold portions, but since the afternoon has lost the final vestiges of daylight and darkness is falling over Tel Aviv, the old woman leaves the untold portions suspended in the twilight. This was the hour when she would, if she could, have chosen to die" (47, 49). Relentlessly grim, each section of Semel's novel nevertheless leaves off with the barest hint of solitary grace, a sorrowful benediction.

Hence just before parting, the old woman, recalling the horror of her parents' abandonment, commands herself: "Hug your granddaughter. . . . Face to face, hug her. Don't turn your back" (50). But of course the story moves on from there and all too soon it's revealed that not only is the old woman's worry about future embellishments fully justified but her own granddaughter, whose sunny good nature leads her to assume only the very best of the Polish farming family, renders a grotesquely distorted interpretation, reinventing them as "righteous gentiles" in her imagination. Since her grandmother omitted the full dimensions of the evil done to her, the schoolgirl's report presents an account consistent with her own essential goodness (a synchronous polarization between what the teller must convey and the listener's capacity to absorb its horror occurs in the final section recounting Father Stanislaw's spiritual struggle in his encounter with unspeakable evil).

At one point, not long before this harrowing introduction to the ordeal of the-little-girl-who-was breaks off entirely, we learn in passing that the grandmother has belatedly acquired what seems at first to be a casual interest in computers and the internet. The heart of the entire novel, "The Poems," are discovered online ten years later by a young internet surfer who is overwhelmed by their horror but filled with an inexplicable sense of purpose that she must circulate them immediately, as widely as possible. If in some sense lyrical (think Paul Celan), they are the rawest distillation of the pain and horror the-little-girl-who-once-was endured. A young Israeli woman, shaken to the core by the power and sense of urgency of the poems after stumbling across the arcane site, writes to the Polish hacker she hopes will penetrate the mystery of their meaning, "I have no idea who wrote them or why, and maybe it doesn't matter. . . . The writer decomposes the world into the most basic concepts, but presents them the other way around. You'll sense it—the innards pouring out" (95). In Emily Ronay Johnston's perceptive analysis of the narrative's sequence of forty-four poems (which undoubtedly applies to the novel as a whole)[18]:

> What's particularly unique about Semel's fictionalized Holocaust historiography is its sustained meditation on the relationship between trauma and language, and more specifically, on the relationship between what happened and *telling* what happened. . . . Poetry makes room for us to, quite literally, read between the lines. Trauma's un-tellability and its must-tellability converge, creating a new totality of experience. ("A Few Thoughts")

In spare and relentlessly horrifying lines, the speaker of the poems delineates the limits of her underground existence but can only gesture to the extent of the suffering child (referred to only in the third person as "little girl" or "hole-child") whose only companion is a rat who come and goes:

For example, "Steps":
Three steps
Forward
Three steps
To the left
Three steps
Back
Three steps
To the right

That's how you cross yourself
That's how you're blessed
Maybe if I do it
The pain will be less (116)

From this unbearably claustrophobic space of pain, unendurable loneliness, and violation, the narrative suddenly leaps ahead to the futuristic distances of Section IV, "The Dream," where the clash between the polarities of memory and forgetting moves most imaginatively to the fore. In 2099, excitement surrounds the discovery of "the ruins of Madonna of the Rat Church in a geographical place once called 'Poland'" (118). Yet like the best science-fiction, the narrative's gaze never truly departs from the present, especially when it comes to the tensions that divided Semel's own Israel as she wrote and until this day. As Efraim Sicher aptly notes, Semel was among Israel's boldest writers who participated in "a complex deconstruction of the Israeli national consensus and an ongoing Kulturkampf . . . [their] texts are symptomatic of a new questioning of post-Holocaust identity, which challenges the inviolability of official representation of the Holocaust, and they represent the Holocaust victim not as an Other but as someone with whom to identify and whose experience could be internalized, a working-through of a psychological trauma by means of literature."[19] In that important sense, each protagonist of Semel's novel becomes a surrogate for the Israeli reader's own empathic struggle, a beckoning toward a paradigm shift. This even holds true for the feverish satire of "The Dream," set in a time when someone who had suffered as the mythical little girl had easy access to healing technology in "one of the clinics for Memory Excision—a safe and simple operation. . . . Once it is over, the patient resumes normal life, and the memory gap—this black hole they used to refer to as trauma—is completely eradicated" (149, emphasis in original). In this distant future, the legend has grotesquely morphed into virtual games and theme parks (PanEuroDisney replaces Mickey Mouse with Mickey Rat) which may be Semel's satiric dig at the commercialization of Holocaust tourism.[20] This speaker, whose speech is filled with jargon reflecting the futuristic forms of knowledge and history preservation of her time, is an anthropologist whose obsessive investigation of the ultimate source of the Hebrew poems that have miraculously survived since 2011 send her on a surreal global journey.[21]

One of her virtual sojourns takes place in TheIsrael, a curious tiny political entity whose insistence on maintaining sovereignty is atypical for its time. This feverishly present- and future-oriented society is vehemently opposed to preserving any form of ties to tradition or the past. As the anthropologist explains to a colleague, this society is "amazingly vibrant," "addicted to the present, alienated from anything that preceded its establishment as a sovereign state" and changing its

> values and icons at a dizzying pace . . . they always prefer the new to the old, or the not-quite-yet-old. . . . TheIsrael became caught up in the digital revolution with near-theological fervor, maybe because of how it filled the void left when

they obliterated their past, including their Zionist ideology and Jewish religion. (143)

Here, Semel slyly magnifies the novel's deep engagement with the individual's struggle between "memory" and "forgetting" to encompass that of the collective, ironically alluding to classic Zionism's complete repudiation of the Galut and indifference to any historical understanding other than a lachrymose interpretation of the past, in order to form its seamless narrative of Jewish sovereignty in its homeland. Of course anyone familiar with Jewish history will know that Semel's futuristic entities, TheIsrael and Ju-Ideah, not only mirror the societal fissures of her own moment (and the incessant politicization of Holocaust memory by Israel's right-wing parties) but the disastrous post-Solomonic schism that led to the division of the ancient country of Israel into two warring kingdoms, the Kingdom of Israel and the Kingdom of Judea.

The anthropologist finds herself troubled by what she considers the locals' "pathological distortion" of time: "almost every mythological representation of the future is short-term, and includes a cataclysm" which for some readers may evoke their anxieties about a society perpetually preparing for war, unable to imagine alternatives (143). But when she attempts to present her theoretical ideas about their "misperception of time" even her academic peers in TheIsrael respond with chilly hostility (143). Her next virtual sojourn takes her to the adjacent homeland of Ju-Ideah (which apparently resides next to the separate realm of ThePalestine), composed of a closely aligned network of religious communities. Since the latter, in stark contrast to TheIsrael, consider the past "sacrosanct," the anthropologist is sanguine that she will achieve better progress in her investigation. In the anthropologist's musings about the sharp differences she encounters between the discrete societies ("It's really surprising to discover such a striking contrast between two entities with the same historical parents" [143]), Semel deepens her sly allegory, underscoring the inherent absurdities in the Jewish State that outsiders might encounter in our own time. In Ju-Ideah, the anthropologist discovers a society "intent on avoiding anything that's new or different . . . . Even the way they dress in Ju-Ideah is old-fashioned, and my quick investigation revealed that it originated in seventeenth-century Poland—the same geographical space where the Madonna of the Rat Church is located" (143–144). Alas, here too the anthropologist's hopes for tracing the origins of the Girl & Rat legend are thwarted as the libraries of Ju-Ideah contain only "mythological representation [of] male spiritual shepherds known as rabbis" (144). Convinced that she conceals the true reason for her visit, the elders helpfully direct her to various graves of their mythical heroes that will grant her fertility or longevity. However, as was the case in Israel, this visit abruptly ends in bitter acrimony when the anthropologist attempts to engage in a more constructive dialogue and they sever her virtual access to their libraries:

> When I recounted the Girl & Rat legend, the idea of some link between a Polish-born Jewish girl and the Christian faith was categorically rejected, and the Ju-Ideah elders' initial politeness suddenly disappeared. The beaming was interrupted, and my access to the public sources of information was blocked. My apologies were rejected. When I tried to break into the blocked data stores, I discovered that, despite its longstanding separatism, or perhaps precisely because of it, their data security technology is state-of-the-art. It may even be more advanced than ours. I would never have succeeded in breaking into their REMaker—if they even use REMakers there. . . . The exile of memory. . . . What submemoryfolder did they banish the little girl to? (145)

In their own ways, both societies are recognizably descendants of modern-day Israel, and each is a dystopian fulfillment of distinct trends disturbingly visible today (and perhaps not only in the Jewish State).[22] If, according to Kafka's famous dictum, "a book must be the axe for the frozen sea within us," nowhere is such an imperative more applicable than in the realm of Holocaust literature, especially in societies with uneven or problematic histories of empathy or official memorialization such as Nava Semel's Israel.[23]

As Alan Berger argues, in Semel's rendering, "the Holocaust is destined to remain an unmasterable trauma even while future generations bear responsibility for remembering."[24] However faint any note of optimism that *And the Rat Laughed* might linger before its readers is captured by Semel's indefatigable anthropologist, "ferreting through discards of history" in her desperate attempt to make Father Stanislaw's diary of his rescue of the little Jewish girl somehow comprehensible to the remote future where traces of the past are often distorted and misappropriated. In her yearning for some form of sacred covenant with the dead, she doggedly avows that "a historical scar does not guarantee that the horrific events will never happen again, but the very existence of memory—might still leave us some room for hope" (155). Yet more often than not, Semel insists on exposing the hellish logic of such memory, the essentially impenetrable nature of the paradox articulated by the severely depressed Father Stanislaw in the book's wrenching conclusion: "What a monumental concatenation of malignant memories could be avoided if only man could contain the torments of his precursors, imprinted into him like an innate warning system. But had the little girl known in advance what was waiting for her, wouldn't she have refused to be born?" (217). In the wake of his fall from faith and certitude about both humanity and divinity, Stanislaw may serve as a surrogate for Holocaust literature students who at one point or another often experience their own loss of language when facing humanity's untrammeled capacity for evil in this and other narratives. Over time, most readers in such classes (along with the university-trained intellects of their professors) sensing their own internal rupture, grasping that the overflowing horrors they encounter in Holocaust stories which, exceeding the boundaries of most other fiction, will offer them afford few affirmations of the triumph of survival or justice. In the end, the most enduring Holocaust fiction leaves all of us unsettled about such questions, searching within for answers to the burden of memory. As James Young has argued in another context: "the best ... memorial to the fascist era and its victims may be not a single memorial ... but simply the never-to-be-resolved debate over which kind of memory to preserve, how to do it, in whose name, and to what end. That is, what are the consequences of such memory? Instead of a fixed sculptural or architectural icon for Holocaust memory, the debate itself—perpetually unresolved amid ever-changing conditions—might now be enshrined."[25] In that very spirit, *And the Rat Laughed*'s meager "hope" does not begin to provide any form of compensatory solace but nevertheless seems the most apt memorialization of a past that is never really past, raising too many questions to be put to rest.

NOTES

1. See Hanna Yaoz, "Inherited Fear: Second-Generation Poets and Novelists in Israel." In ed. Efraim Sicher, *Breaking Crystal: Writing and Memory after Auschwitz* (Chicago: University of Illinois Press, 1998): 160–181. Quotation appears on pg. 161.

2. In interviews, Semel refers to a childhood of little understanding except the awareness that adult survivors often used a sort of shorthand or "code word," "Auschwitz," and that this word somehow possessed enormous, destructive power. Speaking of her childhood self in the third person, she says that "Because some of that secret pact of silence at home was created by the fact that the child feels that she has great responsibility. She was not to misuse her weapon. She has a grenade and she is holding on to the trigger. If you say the word Auschwitz, something bad would happen to your parent. She would collapse, she would cry, she would scream, she would again have a headache. My mother suffered migraines when I was a child. It was one of my worst memories. Locking herself up in her room, in the dark, drawing the shutters" (Lentin, 42). See "Writing is the Closing of Circles," In *Israel and the Daughters of the Shoah: Re-Occupying the Territories of Silence*. Oxford: Berghahn Books, 2000: 27–68. Reprinted on the author's blog: https://www.ronitlentin.net/2017/12/02/writing-is-the-closing-of-circles-nava-semel/

3. Semel was appointed a member of the Yad Vashem Board of Governors, worked in television and radio as well as journalism and was recipient of many awards for her multidisciplinary creative work, including the American National Jewish Book Award for Children's Literature, the Austrian Best Radio Drama Award,

the Women Writers of the Mediterranean Award, and the Israeli Prime Minister's Award for Literature, among others.

4. Other Israeli writers and poets addressing the second or third-generation experience and Holocaust trauma include Savyon Liebrecht, Amir Gutfreund, Oded Peled, Tanya Hadar Rivka Miriam, Itamar Levi, and Dorit Peleg, to name just a few.

5. As Semel recounts it, there was only one brief and utterly critical response in the wake of *A Hat of Glass*' publication: "*Ha'aretz* published a small box . . . which carried the by-line of someone who...was 23 at the time. He wrote something like, 'Yesterday *A Hat of Glass* by Nava Semel was published. From what it says on the cover, this is a book about children of, about the second generation, sons and daughters of Shoah survivors. I for one have no intention even of reading it. Haven't we had enough with Shoah survivors and their problems, do their children too need to tell us they have problems?'" (Lentin, 54). The response of readers at that time was consistently negative, according to Semel because she had somehow "'spoilt the Israeli stereotype.' How dare I describe, underneath the macho, a trembling Israeli (man), frightened, scared, diaspora-like? I was criticized for having spoilt the beautiful ethos" (Lentin, 59). Fortunately, in later years this book was widely discussed and reprinted at least three times to date.

6. Quoted in Dvir Abramovich, "Nava Semel," Ed. S. Lillian Kremer. *Holocaust Literature: An Encyclopedia of Writers and Their Work*, Vol. II (New York: Routledge, 2003): pgs. 1142–1145. Quotation appears on pg. 1143.

7. Sara R. Horowitz describes the historical resistance among Holocaust scholars to consider the role of gender in the Holocaust: "The focus on gender is relatively recent, still considered controversial by many [who] fear that a focus on women or gender issues would eclipse the horror of genocide, either by domesticating it or by de-emphasizing its centrality to the Holocaust in favor of an emphasis on patriarchy. . . . Many scholars fear that bringing sexuality into the discussion of victims or perpetrators and their respective cultures would be inappropriately titillating or voyeuristic." Horowitz strongly champions the pedagogical value of overcoming such reluctance, proposing that "As students evaluate or criticize gender approaches, they become aware of differences among them and of ongoing debates in feminist and gender theory. Noticing issues of gender enables us not only to consider issues pertaining to women and men during the Holocaust but also to think through broader questions about the nature of Holocaust representation" (112, 113). See Sara R. Horowitz, "Gender and Holocaust Representation," in eds. Marianne Hirsch and Irene Kacandes, *Teaching the Representation of the Holocaust* (New York: The Modern Language Association of America, 2004), 110–122. As Semel herself told the *Forward* in 2011: "Over the years, I've met survivors who told me that they had gone through a horrific experience in hiding, alluding to sexual abuse, but felt like they couldn't talk about it. Although it is fiction, I expected people would approach me with similar stories following publication, and 10 people did. They thanked me for being the voice for their untold hidden story." See Elissa Strauss, "Struggling to Be Heard," *Forward* (March 16, 2011): https://forward.com/articles/136215/struggling-to-be-heard/. Finally, in their illuminating essay, Sonja Hedgepeth and Rochelle Saidel discuss Semel's portrayal of the psyche of an adult

survivor sexually abused in childhood as well as the singular challenges of narrating such trauma for others in "Nava Semel's *And the Rat Laughed*: A Tale of Sexual Violation" in eds. Sonja Hedgepeth and Rochelle Saidel, *Sexual Violence against Jewish Women during the Holocaust* (Hanover and London: Brandeis UP, 2010), 217–233.

8. In response to Lentin's insistent probing about the severe alienation and bewilderment faced by her mother's generation of survivors in their Israeli "rehabilitation", Semel rapidly regurgitated a litany of key words and phrases that are highly illustrative of their struggle in an indifferent environment: "'hostile,' 'alien,' 'no one listening,' 'life urge,' 'fast rehabilitation,' 'sucked into the giant vacuum cleaner of building Israel'" (Lentin, 40).

9. To a striking degree, "Momik," the first section of Grossman's more familiar *See Under: Love*, reads as a precise illustration of Nava Semel's thesis about the topsy-turvy nature of the childhoods of the second generation: "The sense of responsibility you receive as a child, becoming adult before your time …There is something in the basic structure of the family, like who is the source of authority, who is the source of responsibility, who is the source of control. To a certain extent this balance is shaken, and you too assume a source of authority, and a source of responsibility, for your parents' wellbeing" (Lentin, 57).

10. Lani Ravin, "Review of *and the Rat Laughed*." *Femspec*, 9.1 (2008): 57–61. Quotation appears on pg. 57.

11. In her introduction to a later Hebrew edition, Nurit Govrin explicates the book's cryptic title as a trope for the psychic burden of the Israeli children of survivors: "The Glass Hat, its touch is cold. It is transparent and insulated, burdensome . . . vulnerable and may break into pieces at any moment. More than it protects it exposes and bears great danger." "Foreword" in Nava Semel, *Kova Zekhukhit* (Tel Aviv: Sifriat Poalim, 1985), 9–10.

12. Abramovich describes the historical significance and grim impact of this "first Israeli work to give literary voice to the children of the survivors.…Semel replays the difficulty of children living with survivor parents, presenting their anxieties as childhood fragments from a broken home movie. Sooner or later, each tale focuses on the dark underside of the individual to whom a particular pathology has been bequeathed" (1142).

13. With sensitivity but also creative vivacity *And the Rat Laughed* circles back incessantly to the enigmatic imperative and perilous nature of memory. As Father Stanislaw later observes of his struggle to heal the suffering child: "I am tormented for her. Remembering and reminding—this is the only commandment that still has any meaning, and yet I have been doing everything in my power to erase her memory. For her, forgetting is healing, but for the world, forgetting is the very disease itself" (221).

14. As Dvir Abramovich argues, Semel's entire oeuvre is distinguished by its attention to "the recurring comingling of memory, imagination, and fact. . . . At heart, it describes the importance and difficulty of communicating the destructive calamity of the Holocaust to the third generation so as to sustain the fading memory and legacy of the eyewitnesses" ("Nava Semel," 1145).

15. Cynthia Ozick, *The Shawl* (New York: Random House, 1983), 14, 22.

16. I'm grateful to Abramovich's graceful translation of this salient passage from *Kova Zehuvit* (Tel Aviv: Sifriyat Hapoalim, pp.47–48) in "Nava Semel" (1143).

17. Later, in Part Two ("The Legend") we come closer to the critical role nihilist humor plays as a perverse form of philosophic balm, examined from her granddaughter's naïve perspective: "[I]f there's one thing you can't say about my grandmother it's that she doesn't have a sense of humor, although not everyone understands it, especially not my mom. My grandmother, what can I tell you, she laughs at the weirdest things, like people on talk shows arguing about the meaning of life, or the horoscope telling you what's going to happen to you...And once we were watching TV together and we saw this expert talking about a technique for controlling your thoughts and your feelings, and another expert was telling the studio audience how to release anger and talking about energy points—you just have to press on the right places and you get rid of all the garbage inside. And she thought it was hilarious. She gave this strange laugh of hers....A silent laugh as if it isn't coming from her throat, or from her stomach, or wherever people usually laugh, but from somewhere completely different" (56).

18. See Emily Ronay Johnston, "A Few Thoughts on Language, Trauma and *the Rat Laughed*." In *Spoon River Poetry Review*: http://www.srpr.org/blog/a-few-thoughts-on-language-trauma-and-and-the-rat-laughed/

19. Efraim Sicher, "The Burden of Memory: The Writing of the Post-Holocaust Generation," in *Breaking Crystal: Writing and Memory after Auschwitz*: 1–88, Quotation appears on pg. 43.

20. For a wide-ranging discussion of the Holocaust, humor and dark tourism in Israeli culture see Liat Steir-Livny, "The Image of Anne Frank: From Universal Hero to Comic Figure." in eds. David Slucki, Gabriel N. Finder, and Avinoam Patt, *Laughter After: Humor and the Holocaust* (Detroit: Wayne University Press, 2020), 195–214. Semel's novel explores the absurdist outcome of an era in which traumatic memory is completely reduced to commodity, to paraphrase Steir-Livny's argument in another context.

21. It is an age that Father Stanislaw's language ironically anticipates more than he can possibly know when he mournfully imagines that "Some day in the future, memory will be packaged like merchandise, turning into nothing more than a thick cloud, and the story of one little girl will be swallowed up within it" (230). In considering the role of fantastic realism in second-generation writing, Yaoz argues that narrative "moves from literal to hidden and occasionally preternatural meaning, and this forces the reader to redefine reality" ("Inherited Fear," 162).

22. It is worth noting that Semel's use of multiple genres, temporal shifts and imagined Jewish homelands in the futuristic setting of the novel are also employed by her again in the witty and gripping alternative history *Isra Isle* (Yedioth Ahronoth, 2005) that builds on the earlier work's deep engagement with the contingencies of homelands and the uses of Jewish memory, a novel Adam Rovner praises as an "Israeli-feminist *Yiddish Policeman's Union*...a triumph of the imagination." See his fascinating discussion of Semel's postmodern speculation on the global consequences had playwright and journalist Mordecai Manuel Noah (1785–1851) actually succeeded

in creating his planned "city of refuge for the Jews on Grand Island, upriver from Lake Erie and today a suburb of Buffalo, New York" (Rovner 134). Rovner notes that in this later work, "the factual territory we today call Israel, or as it is referred in the novel, Grand-Palestine, remains a far off, desolate land, "the sleepiest place in the world" with few, if any, Jews. Jerusalem is nothing but ruins, a small village whose very name is unrecognizable to the narrator. The prosperous real-world Israel of today thus appears infinitely superior to the backwater of Semel's fictional 'Grand-Palestine.' On the other hand, the 'West Bank' refers not to the contested territory featured on the nightly news but to an exclusive yacht-filled marina on the shores of IsraIsland. A tranquil and self-contained city-state, IsraIsland appears in contrast to the territorial conflicts that wrack present day, real-world Israel. Semel's novel, like allohistories in general, presents possible worlds and . . . that point to reformist, utopian futures, or warn against dystopian nightmares" (136). In "Alternate History: The Case of Nava Semel's *Isralsland* and Michael Chabon's *The Yiddish Policeman's Union*," *Partial Answers: Journal of Literature and the History of Ideas* 9.1 (2011): 131–152.

23. Franz Kafka, Letter to Oskar Pollak *(27 January 1904). In Richard Winston, Clara Winston, Eds. Letters to Friends, Family and Editors* (New York City: Schocken, 1990): 16.

24. Alan L. Berger, "The Holocaust Novel from Israel that America Can't Handle," *Forward*, October 26, 2009: https://forward.com/culture/117704/the-holocaust-novel-from-israel-that-america-can/.

25. James E. Young, "Teaching German Memory and Countermemory: The End of the Holocaust Monument in Germany," in eds. Marianne Hirsch and Irene Kacandes, *Teaching the Representation of the Holocaust* (New York: The Modern Language Association of America, 2004), 274–285. Quotation appears on pg. 284.

REFERENCES

Abramovich Dvir. *Hebrew Classics: A Journey Through Israel's Timeless Fiction and Poetry.* Boston: Academic Studies Press, 2012.

Berger, Alan. "The Holocaust Novel From Israel that America Can't Handle," *Forward*, October 26, 2009: https://forward.com/culture/117704/the-holocaust-novel-from-israel-that-america-can/.

Grossman, David. *See Under: Love,* translation, Betsy Rosenberg. New York: Picador Press, 1989.

Govrin, Nurit. *Nava Semel, Kova Zekhukhit* .Tel Aviv: Sifriat Poalim, 1985: 9–10.

Hedgepeth, Sonia and Saidel, Rochelle Saidel. *Sexual Violence against Jewish Women during the Holocaust.* Hanover and London: Brandeis UP, 2010.

Hirsch, Marianne and Kacandes, Irene. *Teaching the Representation of the Holocaust.* New York: The Modern Language Association, 2004.

Johnston, Emily Ronay. "A Few Thoughts on Language, Trauma and the Rat Laughed." *Spoon River Poetry Review*: http://www.srpr.org/blog/a-few-thoughts-on-language-trauma-and-and-the-rat-laughed/ 19

Kremer, Lillian. *Holocaust Literature: An Encyclopedia of Writers and Their Work*, Vol. II. New York: Routledge, 2003.

Ozick, Cynthia. *The Shawl* New York, Random House, 1983.

Patt, Avinoam and Slucki, David. *Laughter After: Humor and the Holocaust*. Detroit: Wayne University Press, 2020.

Ravin, Lani. "Review of And the Rat Laughed." *Femspec*, 9.1 2008.

Rovner, Adam. "Alternate History: The Case of Nava Semel's *IsraIsland* and Michael Chabon's *The Yiddish Policemen's Union*" *Journal of Literature and the History of Ideas*. Baltimore: JHU Press, Vol. 9: 1. 2011

Sicher, Ed. *Breaking Crystal: Writing and Memory after Auschwitz* (Chicago: University of Illinois Press, 1998), 160–181.

Strauss, Elissa Strauss. "Struggling to Be Heard," *Forward* (March 16, 2011): https://forward.com/articles/136215/struggling-to-be-heard/.

Winston, Richard and Clara, Eds. *Letters to Friends, Family and Editors*. New York City: Schocken, 1990.

Chapter 12

Representing the Holocaust and Jewishness in Contemporary Television

The Cases of The Man in the High Castle, Hunters, *and* Juda

Marat Grinberg

The opening credits to the HBO adaptation of Philip Roth's *The Plot Against America*, which premiered in March 2020, provide a powerful collage of documentary images, whose purpose is to convince the viewer that the alternate history they are about to ponder—Charles Lindberg's short-lived presidency—might not be "real," but could very well have been. The credits begin with Lindbergh's 1927 transatlantic flight and the cheering crowds celebrating it. It is followed by the footage of the economic hardships of the Great Depression, Roosevelt's rise to power and the New Deal programs he initiated. Then there are chilling images of the actual American fascists from a summer camp in upstate New York and a rally in Madison Square Garden. Finally, the footage of Germany and the war rolls out: Chamberlain's "Peace in our time" pact with Hitler, the burning of books, anti-Semitic signs on stores and windows, Hitler speaking to the adoring crowds, and the ravages of air bombardments. The non-diegetic sound accompaniment throughout is the song, "The Road is Open Again," which while purveying the same fascist mood was in fact written for a series of short films produced to popularize Roosevelt's efforts to alleviate the economic depression.

One short grainy image, almost a glimpse of it, stands out in this sequence and, peculiarly, is not discussed in any of the miniseries' reviews: a nude woman—her face invisible—seems to be forcefully marched somewhere. Everything happens in rapid motion and she lingers on screen for no longer than a few seconds. Even for those who are thoroughly familiar with

Holocaust visuals—undoubtedly a very sizable minority of the audience—identifying the shot and how it fits into the overall narrative of the credits may prove to be difficult. Its probable source is a photograph of the massacre of Jews in Western Ukraine, one of the multitudes of ravines on the outskirts of Ukrainian towns, where Germans, with the help of local accomplices, murdered almost their entire Jewish populations in 1941 and later throughout the war. The photograph was taken by someone from the local German administration and shows a throng of nude Jewish women, some clutching their babies, about to be shot by the SS killing squad and members of the Ukrainian auxiliary police. The woman in the opening credits is one of them. In the credits, an illusion of movement is created and the still snapshot appears to come alive.

What is the status of this image, this "document of horror," marked by "inexactness"[1] and fragmentariness? Inserted into the show streaming on a popular TV network and viewed internationally, what moral and ontological weight does this photographic remnant of the catastrophe carry? Is the viewer invited to probe into it or does it inevitably pass unexamined, constituting a failure on part of both the creators and the spectators? The choice of the "Holocaust by bullet" footage is particularly troubling since neither Roth's novel nor the miniseries mention the annihilation of Jews by the Nazis in the occupied Soviet territories or the later death camps, although it might have been less jarring had they integrated the much more familiar camp imagery. There's certainly talk both on screen and page of the persecution of German Jews by Hitler's regime, invoked in the opening credits by the well-known

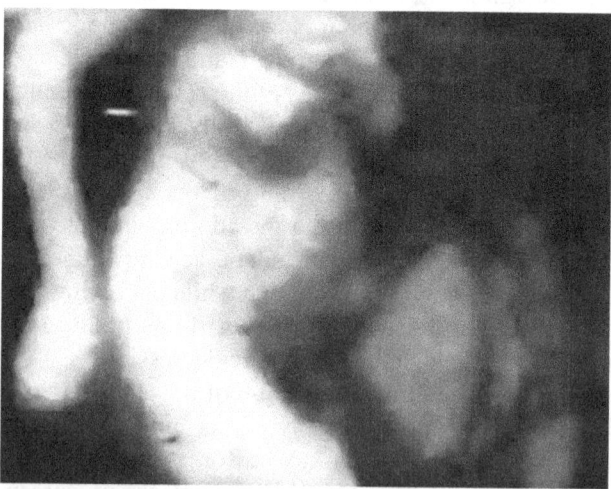

Figure 12.1 A Woman from the Opening Credits. *Source: The Plot Against America.* Opening credits. TV mini-series. 2020.

Figure 12.2 Naked Jewish Women, Some of Whom Are Holding Infants, Wait in a Line before Their Execution by German Sipo and SD, with the Assistance of Ukrainian Auxiliaries. Photograph #17877. *Source:* The United States Holocaust Memorial Museum. Washington DC.

Kristallnacht footage. There is also anti-Jewish violence in Lindberg's America, which parallels the events in Germany, but it seems that Roth, a diligent student of Holocaust history, went out of his way to not mention the atrocities. He did not want to touch their horror in his historical reimagining and thus suggest that this too could happen in America. By omitting the larger Holocaust events from the novel, Roth proposes that the pogrom-type violence fits the historical plausibility for the United States, but not the unprecedented full-scale genocide of the war. The miniseries' creators follow the novel very closely and the inclusion of the ravine photograph falls out of this overall faithfulness.

The glimpse of the unnamed female Jewish body about to be destroyed stands at the "intersection of the phenomenon of cinema and the phenomenon of extermination."[2] French historian of cinema Jean-Michel Frodon provides an exhaustive list of the potential meanings and implications of this intersection: "the cinema as archive; the cinema as material for historical research; the cinema as method for constructing one or several realms of imagination; the cinemas as method of investigation and/or revelation; the Shoah as the subject of film; the Shoah as a backdrop for films whose 'subject' is or appears to be something else; the Shoah as a question mark on an ethic of representation or of narration; the Shoah as a test of the limit to the possibility of representing things, as a threshold to the possibility of the image."³

The Holocaust as a backdrop, a question mark and a test of the limit to the possibility of representing atrocities, which pushes or warps the boundaries of imagination, is most relevant for analyzing how it functions in contemporary cinematic culture in the United States and beyond, a big portion of which is occupied by numerous television series on various streaming platforms, immediately accessible to vast audiences worldwide and dissected in the labyrinths of social media. The driving question in this context is no longer whether a certain depiction is permissible or not, but rather how it is received. Can the Holocaust images, canonized and ingrained in popular iconography and historiography, still shock and remain vital on both a historical and aesthetic level? Can they produce "the imaginative transformation of history"⁴ via what Lawrence Langer called "the atmosphere of monstrous fantasy"⁵ while upholding the historical fact?

This chapter aims to probe these questions through three case studies of two American television series, produced by Amazon, *The Man in the High Castle* (four seasons 2015–2019), *Hunters* (one season 2020), and one Israeli–*Juda* (one season 2017), distributed in the United States by Hulu in 2020. All three tap both into various popular genres (science fiction, horror, graphic novels) and the wider literary and cinematic Holocaust corpus. The American series, in particular, reflect on the current political moment and how the Holocaust intersects with it, especially in terms of black-Jewish relations and the legacy of American racism. There's an obsessive search for the historical veracity in them—what the past looked and smelled like— and the radical, playful overwriting of history by imagination at the same time. All three shows echo each other in their thinking about history: not just how to deal with the past, but how to rewrite it; how to imagine the possibility of Jewish survival in the world where the Jew is perpetually the Other. Unsurprisingly, evil becomes their inevitable main concern and topic of their artistic expression.

THE MAN IN THE HIGH CASTLE

There's a long record of Holocaust representation and coverage in American television, from the early war and post-war newsreels to the 1950s talk shows, which introduced a number of survivor stories to the American public, to the broadcasts of the Eichmann trial from Jerusalem in 1961. The popular TV series from the late 1950s and 1960s, such as *Star Trek* and *The Twilight Zone*, memorably confronted the Holocaust in a number of their episodes while in 1970s, the miniseries, *Holocaust: The Story of the Family Weiss*, became not just "a landmark of Holocaust consciousness in America,"[6] but of American television history in general. There is an element of adaptation and auteurism in the annals of the American "televising of Holocaust," to use Jeffrey Shandler's phrase, which makes it part of the larger cinematic history. The great American auteur Sydney Lumet, who grew up in a Yiddish-speaking household with the father who was an actor in Yiddish theater, directed for television an adaptation of S. Ansky's cult Jewish drama *The Dybbuk* in 1960, which brilliantly suffused the content of the play with symbolic allusions to the Holocaust. Another notable example is Stanley Kramer's groundbreaking *Judgement at Nuremberg*, which premiered first on television in 1959.

Frank Spotnitz, the creator of *The Man in the High Castle*, engages with this television and film legacy and the various tropes it engendered. In choosing Philip K. Dick as the source material, he was turning, on the one hand, to the cult author, whose works have been frequently and legendarily adopted for screen, but, on the other, selecting the text, which, peculiarly, has never been taken on before. The show fills in this lacuna and while it departs dramatically in plotline from the original novel, Spotnitz and the team of showrunners aimed at capturing the spirit and atmosphere of Dick's text, and thus an analysis of it is essential for evaluating the Amazon version.[7]

Published in 1962, *The Man in the High Castle* put Dick on the map as a serious writer and was the only one of his books to have received the prestigious Hugo Award for the best science fiction novel. Describing the post–World War II America, where part of the country is controlled by the Nazis and part by the Japanese, Dick's text has been classified as alternative or counterfactual history,[8] but this is only partially true. As is the case throughout Dick's oeuvre, at the core is not merely an idea that historical events could have turned out differently, as is the case in *The Plot Against America*, for instance, but that it is not at all clear whether the reality we (or his characters) inhabit is indeed *real* or merely a simulacrum, with the true reality(ies) existing on another plane and accessible to only a few. As Frederick Jameson has classically described this conundrum, "Every reader of Dick is familiar with this nightmarish uncertainty, this reality fluctuation, sometimes accounted for by drugs, sometimes by schizophrenia, and sometimes by new SF powers, in which the psychic world as it were goes outside, and reappears in the form of simulacra or of some photographical cunning reproduction of the external."[9]

The trick in *The Man in the High Castle* is that the reality where the Axis have won is false and the one where they are victorious is in fact true. The novel, *The Grasshopper Lies Heavy*, written by Hawthorne Abendsen, "the man in the high castle," depicts the latter in Dick's text. Juliana Crane, the novel's only female protagonist, confronts Abendsen at the end and spells it out for him: "Raising his head, Hawthorne scrutinized her. He had now an almost savage expression. 'It means, does it, that my book is true?' 'Yes,' she said. With anger he said, 'Germany and Japan lost the war?' 'Yes.'"[10] The truth is hard for the creator to accept, as it is for the readers who begin to wonder whether the reality they inhabit and perceive with their minds is in fact *real*. Dick himself was confused and troubled by the ending. As Umberto Rossi puts it, "If Germany and Japan lost World War II, why do the characters of the novel live in a world dominated by those powers? Dick was not satisfied because he did not have a solution to this aporia. No wonder then that it will come back in the rest of Dick's oeuvre"[11]

There's another aspect which deeply concerned and continuously haunted him—the significance and meaning of Jewishness and the annihilation of Jews during the war. Most of the characters in the novel are Jews who painstakingly try to conceal their identity to survive in the world where the Holocaust had never been stopped. While the Japanese, who occupy the West coast, did not kill Jews or build ovens, they're obligated to turn any Jews hiding in their territories to Nazis in the East. Hence the main San Francisco character, Juliana Crane's ex-husband Frank Fink, changes his surname to Frink to camouflage his Jewishness. There's also Mr. Bayne, a German spy, who tries to stop a German nuclear attack against the Japanese. As Baynes explains to an unsuspecting Nazi interlocutor, ridiculing the Nazi racial science, "I do not in any physical way appear Jewish; I have had my nose altered, my large greasy pores made smaller, my skin chemically lightened, the shape of my skull changed. In short, physically I cannot be detected. I can and have often walked in the highest circles of Nazi society. No one will ever discover me. . . . And there are others of us. . . . We did not die. We still exist. We live on unseen."[12] Finally, Abendsen, who resides in the free neutral zone in Colorado, is also Jewish. This "unseen" quality is what allows these characters to penetrate beyond the sham reality and catch a glimpse of the true plane. Fink designs a jewelry piece, meditating on which serves as a conduit to the *real* reality, and Mr. Bayne has knowledge of the parallel realities, an idea Dick was developing in an unfinished sequel to *The Man in the High Castle*.[13] He presents Jewishness as both a biological and an ontological condition, malleable and permanent at the same time.

Dick's Jewish characters are essentially Holocaust survivors, which puts the novel in dialogue with other Holocaust literature of 1960s, such as Edward Lewis Wallant's *The Pawnbroker*, published in 1961, and famously adopted for screen by Sydney Lumet in 1965, and I. B. Singer's stories, translated from Yiddish and appearing throughout the 1960s. Dick engages with these sources and creates believable Jewish portraits—Fink peppers his speech with Yiddishisms while Abendsen and his circle resemble the "family" of New York Jewish intellectuals of the 1950s and beyond. At the same time, Dick was also apprehensive about Jewishness, verging on paranoid. In a piece, "Naziism and the High Castle," written in 1964 in response to a review of the novel, he lashed out against the idea that there was something inherently anti-Semitic about the German character. In deeming the Nazi hatred of the Jew an inexplicable "phobia,"[14] he proclaimed the danger of "Jewish nationalists," that is Zionists and Israel, who committed crimes equal in magnitude to the Nazi evil and would most likely wreak havoc on the whole world, including the Jews themselves.[15]

This thinking is reflected in his manifold oeuvre. In a dystopian novel, *The Simulacra*, published soon after *The Man in the High Castle*, an Israeli agent Goltz masquerades as a leader of the neo-Nazi movement. He concocts a plan to bring Hermann Georring back from the past in order to convince him that in exchange for not perpetrating the Holocaust, Germany would be allowed to win the war and continue the Nazi domination into perpetuity, with the Jews now as its allies. Goltz quickly realizes, however, that "once the Nazis have won World War Two . . . *they will massacre the Jews anyhow*. And not just those in Europe and White Russia but in England and the United States and Latin America as well . . . the objective in the war for the Nazis was the extermination of World Jewry; it was not merely a byproduct."[16] Dick's insight into the Nazi mindset was not insignificant after all.

Dick admired Hannah Arendt and was deeply affected by her *Eichmann in Jerusalem: Report on the Banality of Evil*. He might have derived his disdain of Israel from Arendt's account, which was deeply critical of the Israeli government and suspect of the Zionist project as a whole. Her denunciation of European Jewish leadership and Jewish passivity during the war as responsible for the Holocaust, which made Arendt a pariah in the eyes of the majority of her Jewish readers, must have appealed to Dick as well. His Nazi characters are banal in the Arendtian sense, limited by their meager moral imagination. The Amazon adaptation of *The Man in the High Castle* hearkens back to these qualities in its Nazi and Jewish characters, both following in the footsteps and radically revising Dick's profoundly disturbing and penetrating vision.

In the text of *The Man in the High Castle*, Juliana Crane bemoans the fact that there's no good television in the American Nazi Reich. The reason is that "the Nazis have no sense of humor, so why should they want television? Anyhow, they killed most of the really great comedians. Because most of them were Jewish. In fact, she realized, they killed off most of the entertainment field."[17] Dick imbues the imagined annihilation of Jews in the United States with a palpable historical sense and what it could actually mean for the US life and culture. Television —the American Nazi television—features prominently in the screen adaptation of the novel and takes on a meta-quality. The series itself becomes a response to the Nazi cultural malaise. In changing the text—the novel *The Grasshopper Lies Heavy*—to the newsreels, created and disseminated by "the man in the high castle" to offer a glimpse of the true reality, the show emphasizes the cinematic and the visual as the antidote to Nazism. Newsreels certainly did play an important role in informing the American public both through television and the larger screens of the Holocaust and events of the war.

Throughout its four seasons, the Amazon show replicates the archframework of Dick's text, with the United States divided between the Nazi, Japanese, and neutral zones, but it greatly expands it and fills with new characters and action plotlines, concentrating on the struggle of the homegrown resistance against the Nazis and the Japanese and their attempts to subdue it. The introduction of the new main character, John Smith, a high-ranking American Nazi, who becomes the chief military leader of the Eastern states, echoes Dick's overall preoccupation with Arendt's depiction of the Nazi mindset and her portrayal of the Eichmann trial as a spectacle. Our concern here is the representation of the Holocaust and Jewishness in the series. We shall zero in on a number of crucial scenes which address it both explicitly and obliquely. The show's main Jewish character is Frank Frink (Rupert Evans). Unlike in the novel, where Frink (Fink) conceals his identity in order to survive, but internally is fully in touch with his Jewishness, this Frank has a hard time acknowledging and accepting who he is. His is the case of an identity amnesia and the gradual painful rediscovery of his Jewish roots.

Frank's story intertwines with allusions to the Holocaust. At the beginning of the first season, he is arrested by the Japanese secret police on the assumption that he might know something about his girlfriend's—Juliana Crane's (Alexa Davalos)—resistance activities. To force Frank to speak, his sister (Christine Chatelain) and her two children (Callum Seagram Airlie, Carmen Mikkelsen) are arrested as well. They are placed in a comfortable large room, where the kids watch *Pigs in a Polka* on television, a cartoon from 1943. Neither they nor viewers suspect that the room will turn out to be a gas chamber where they are killed.

First, the scene showcases the advancement of the killing machinery, with the American entertainment industry implicated in it. The choice of the cartoon is ironic and points to Hollywood's anti-Jewish prejudice. *Pigs in a Polka*, produced by the Warner Brothers, was a parody of Walt Disney's *Three Little Pigs* (1933), which contains a number of anti-Semitic images and allusions. Frank's sister and the kids become like the three little pigs, trapped inside the room to be exterminated by the bad wolves in all too familiar guises.

Second, the scene invokes the Nazi obfuscation of their murderous actions—gas chambers as showers—but there's little resemblance between the horror of gassing in Birkenau, Treblinka, and Sobibor, and this imagined

Figure 12.3 The Trapped Door of the Gas Chamber. *Source: The Man in the High Castle. Season 1. 2015.*

masked execution. Importantly, in the novel, the Japanese do not exterminate the Jews and abhor the Nazi practices. Dick also does not depict the mechanics of atrocities. There's a troubling history to the mention of gassing on American television. During the airing of *The Judgment at Nuremberg* on CBS in 1959, the American Gas Association pressured the network into "blanking out four or five references to Nazi 'gas chambers.'"[18] CBS caved in and "although the program was televised live . . . delayed its transmission for a few seconds, long enough for an engineer to bleep out the word gas each time it was mentioned."[19] According to Jeffrey Shandler, "this incident has been frequently cited as a quintessential example of the degree to which sponsors interfered in programming during the early years of television."[20] The scene may have this disturbing prehistory coded into it, but the larger point it makes is evasive: the images, sleek and unambiguous, invoke central familiar points from the debates about the legitimacy and ethics of representing the Holocaust on screen and in popular media, but it's puzzling where they lead the viewers, apart from expecting an emotive response from them.

A similar inscrutability is on display in another scene from the first season, when Juliana Crane comes upon a mass open grave, filled with dead bodies, among whom, she believes, is her sister. There's a pastoral *mis-an-scene* here, whose mood is enhanced by a somber non-diegetic score. Making her way through a forest with the tree tops glimmering in the sunlight, Juliana is carrying a single white flower to place on her sister's grave. Her morose, but inspired facial expression quickly changes as she approaches the horrific sight. Because of the stench of dead bodies, she can hardly breathe and puts a handkerchief against her face. There's white pollen flying all around—another pastoral symbol signifying spring—but the hopefulness associated with it is quickly reversed. Juliana comes to the edge of the pit and as the camera pans back she, and the audience along with her, see dead bodies piled next to and on top of each other. The scene shifts into an aerial shot, which creates an impression that the pit is moving in a circle, its shocking content now appearing miniscule and insignificant. The movement implies that we have entered one of the circles of hell, but it is also rotating from the vantage point of Juliana, who walks around and through it until she locates her sister's body (as she'll later learn, her sister is actually alive in a parallel universe). Juliana covers her face with a scarf and stands over the decomposing corpse, perhaps silently intoning a prayer. Finally, the aerial perspective returns, now suggesting the sacred—the divine mourning over the murdered.

This visually well-orchestrated sequence is skillfully alluding to the iconic Nazi camp imagery—piles of dead bodies—and perhaps also the Holocaust by bullet imagery (recall the opening credits of *The Plot Against America*). *The Man in the High Castle* both sanitizes— the bodies here are not naked,

Figure 12.4 Aerial Shot of the Mass Grave. *Source: The Man in the Castle.* Season 1. 2015.

Figure 12.5 Juliana Crane at the Mass Grave. *Source: The Man in the High Castle.* Season 1. 2015.

but clothed—and aestheticizes it. Perhaps it also dejudaizes the Holocaust through its substitution effect—the victims here are not Jews, but members of the resistance against the occupying Japanese. Appearing in 2015, the show is responding, however, not so much to the actual documentary footage, but the earlier reconstructions of it, such as gas chamber sequences in the TV series *War and Remembrance* (1988), which have been called "spectacular and objectionable."[21] Thus, it participates in the politics and poetics of Holocaust mimicry, but does not seem to carry on an aesthetic program of its own. The image of radical violence that is produced is purely a *picture* which neither shocks nor tests "the limit to the possibility of representing things," to recall Frodon's formulation.[22] It is important to recall that Dick avoids any description of atrocities, choosing to rely on readers' visual memory in filling all the gaps to generate an "ethical recall"[23] of the event. At a much further remove from the events of the war than the novel, the show provides a complete graphic afterimage of the Holocaust-like terrain, but its actual commentary on the nature of capturing a historical atrocity is opaque at best.

The content and intent of the series' depiction of Jewishness and Judaism are much more discernible, admirable, and yet problematic. At the center is Frank's transformation into a pious Jew, which starts in the first season. After learning of the death of his sister, nephew, and niece, Frank screams to the Japanese inspector Kido (Joel de la Fuente), "If you need any more Jews to kill, you know where to find me."[24] He comes in contact with Mark

Sampson (Michael Gaston), a fellow Jew, who recites Kaddish in secret—the mourners' prayer—for Frank's murdered relatives, with Frank deeply moved by it without understanding a single word. Unlike in Dick's novel, where Jewishness is marked by ethnicity, language (Yiddish), and meaningful cultural tropes, here it is purely a religious denomination, which speaks to the perception of Jewishness in contemporary America, rather than that of the 1960s, or at least certain segments of American society where Yiddishkeit was a widespread presence rather than a distant memory or even completely forgotten. It is both hard to imagine Dick's Fink reciting the Kaddish and not knowing what the Kaddish is. During their first encounter, Sampson whispers an enigmatic phrase to Frank, "To life," which, Frank says, he might have heard from his grandfather. To today's American viewer, "to life" signals Jewishness because it is associated with the musical *Fiddler on the Roof*, where Tevye famously sings, "To life, to life, l'chaim," yet it is not by any means a special Jewish motto or a Jewish code word, apart from it being a Hebrew/Yiddish form of "cheers" over drinks. How can such a conscientious Jew as Sampson not know that?

Frank's embrace of Judaism reaches its apogee in the third season. A badly injured seasoned resistance fighter, he finds a refuge in the community of Jews, masked as a catholic convent, in the neutral zone. Their experience resembles that of *marranos* or *conversos*—Jews in medieval Spain, who converted to Catholicism, but continued to practice Judaism in secret under the threat of being discovered by the Inquisition. The community is called "Sabra," which invokes the Zionist ethos and Israeli experience—native-born Israeli Jews are referred to as sabras after a desert fruit prickly on the outside and sweet on the inside—although there's no indication that there is a Jewish state in *The Man in the High Castle* universe. The series is to be commended for its positive portrayal of Jewishness, but in its desire for palatability by the audience, it effaces much of historical authenticity and simplifies the complexities of the Jewish condition in the twentieth century. To that end, the community is like an American Jewish summer camp: it is religious, yet invokes the secular Israeli symbolism and valor;[25] the actual Jewish resistance groups during the war were associated with either left- or right-wing secular Zionist groups or the broader leftist organizations.

In the Sabra camp, under the guidance of Mark Sampson, Frank is preparing for his bar-mitzvah, though there's no requirement that a *baal-teshuvah*—an adult Jewish returnee to Judaism—would need to have one. There's a symbolism to Frank engaging in and embracing the ritual, but the overall purpose is to invoke a Judaism that conforms to the expectations and knowledge of the majority of American viewers. In the third season's 6th episode, "History Ends," the shots of Frank's bar-mitzvah are juxtaposed with the speech Himmler (Kenneth Tigar), the new German Fuehrer, is giving to the roaring crowd in Manhattan in honor of *jahr null* —year zero—which erases history and initiates the new Nazi age. The Nazi apocalypticism is the very opposite of Judaism's attachment to historical continuity and the eternal chain of tradition, which Frank's bar-mitzvah represents. Discovered by Inspector Kito, Frank dies the death of a Jewish martyr at the Japanese man's hands, with the words of *Shema* on his lips. Thus, ultimately, the show privileges the image of the Jew as a perennial victim; yet the idea of finding redemption in death is much more rooted in Christianity than in Judaism.

The Sabra resisters make a very brief appearance in the next final season of the series, which premiered in 2019, where the great bulk of the action is given to BCR—Black Communist Resistance—who fight the Japanese oppression in the Pacific states. Much more in tune with black American culture and politics than Sabra with Jewish, BCR functions also as a site of multidirectional Holocaust memory, to recall Michael Rothberg's term. According to Rothberg, in the works of art and literature, there's "cross-referencing" which occurs between post-Holocaust and post-colonial memory in the West, leading to "the rhetorical and cultural intimacy of seemingly opposed traditions of remembrance."[26] The critic uses Sigmund Freud's idea of "screen memory" to argue that not only can the Holocaust function as a screen for other catastrophes but the other traumatic referents can "screen" the Holocaust.

Thus, "the displacement that takes place in screen memory . . . functions as much to open lines of communication with the past as to close them off."[27]

Figure 12.6 Jahr Null Celebration in New York. *Source: The Man in the High Castle.* Season 3. 2018.

Figure 12.7 Frank's Bar-Mitzvah. *Source: The Man in the High Castle.* Season 3. 2018.

In the case of Amazon's *The Man in the High Castle*, BCR "screens" the Holocaust and vice versa, opening up such lines of communication. Many of its members were in the camps and subjects of medical experiments. There's a tradition of this type of screening in American cinema, if we are to recall *The Pawnbroker* (1964), as well as in African American intellectual history (W. E. B. Dubois's essay on the Warsaw ghetto),[28] and Dick's oeuvre (*Ubik*).[29] Dick also alludes to the murder of blacks in the American Reich and the attempted genocide of Africa's populations in *The Man in the High Castle*. The black and Jewish destinies are further fused toward the series' conclusion with the revelation of the operation "Fire Cross," whose goal is to exterminate, through gassing, the remaining American blacks and Jews.

Yet in confronting the Holocaust and racist legacies, the latter forcefully and painfully resonating in today's America, through the character of John Smith, "a fictional American example of the decent man who derives his strength and character from his duty as an SS officer," the series is most successful.[30] Reminiscent at first of Arendt's notion of the banality of evil, Smith grows in complexity throughout the seasons precisely because he's able to overcome the limitations of his moral imagination through visiting the parallel universe—*die Nebenwelt* (Dick's term)—of the actual America of 1960s, which forces him to confront the horror of the choices he had made. He participated in murdering Jews and betrayed one of his closest friends who was also Jewish. Through Smith, brilliantly played by Rufus Sewell, the series gets at the heart of how the Holocaust would have been possible in America. In the final episode, Smith takes his own life, confessing to Juliana Crane, who was about to kill him, that "to be able to look through that door

Figure 12.8 John Smith at the End. *Source: The Man in the High Castle.* Season 4. 2019.

and glimpse all the people you could have been. And to know that out of all of them this is the one you became."[31] With his demise, the operation "Fire Cross" is thwarted and the multiple parallel worlds meet. But whether Jewish or black lives would be safe because of this union of realities remains highly uncertain and unresolved.

HUNTERS

In Philip K. Dick's *Ubik*, there's an idea that "our world declines, turns back onto itself, bringing to the surface past phases of reality. By the end of the week, we may wake up and find ancient clanging streetcars moving down Fifth Avenue."[32] This notion of recreating the reality of the past epoch to see how our present refracts in it and vice versa, while exposing the instability of this past and reimagining it, links *The Man in the High Castle* with another recent Amazon series, *Hunters*. Both are preoccupied with multidirectional memory in representing the Holocaust and Jewishness and engage in the debate regarding the ethics of Holocaust representation. *Hunters* is also concerned with the Nazi mindset and how to resist it, but its main question is one of the righteousness of vengeance and the moral choices Jews are forced to make in the shadow of the Holocaust.

Steeped in the era of 1970s and the mythology surrounding it, *Hunters* hearkens back to such movies as *The Odessa File* (1974) and *Marathon Man* (1976), but also the much earlier Orson Welles's *The Stranger* (1946). The premise is that the former Nazis reside in America, preparing to turn the United States into the Fourth Reich; a colorful group of Nazi hunters, comprised of Jewish and non-Jewish cultural types, pursues them and kills. The series invokes the long history of "Jewish retribution and vengeance toward the Germans during and after WWII"[33] and incorporates a number of other historical elements, such as operation "Paper Clip," which allowed prominent German war scientists to come to the United States in order to assist with the space program and further Cold War projects. As A. E. Smith put it, "The whole idea of a cabal of unreconstructed Nazis secretly plotting a violent coup in 1970s America seems—and is—ridiculous. But, in explaining the origins of this fictional conspiracy, *Hunters* forces us to consider another historical truth that is largely forgotten. After the war, America scooped up Wernher von Braun and 1,600 other Nazi scientists and engineers, expunging their wartime records and parachuting them into positions of influence in the American scientific establishment, particularly NASA."[34]

The bulk of the series' plotlines derives from "comic books and B-grade movies (kung fu, grindhouse, blaxploitation)."[35] It builds upon the comic book trope of the longevity of Nazism in America, from the mid-1950s and on,[36] and the renewed interest in the topic in 1970s. Notably, Howard Blum's bestselling *Wanted: The Search for Nazis in America* was published in 1977, shockingly accusing the INS agents, who happened to be Jews, of acting as a new *Judenrat* in squashing the attempts to uncover the former Nazis in the American midst. Similarly to *The Man in the High Castle*, the series interweaves the black/Jewish narratives—the Nazi plan is to poison the "colored" population of New York—and directly links its imagined Nazis to the neo-Nazi threat of today. Travis (Greg Austin), a murderous American recruited by the Nazi organization, kills his Jewish lawyer in prison, yelling out the slogan of the 2017 Unite the Right rally in Charlottesville, "Jews will not replace us."[37] To the detriment of her own career, a black female FBI agent, Millie Morris (Jerrika Hinton), drives the anti-Nazi investigation, assisting the hunters and teams up with the female Jewish congresswoman Elizabeth Handelman (Zoe Winters) to uncover the Nazi plot. Notably, the series' co-producer is Jordan Peele, a prominent black filmmaker, famous for probing race through the horror genre.

At the center of the series is the relationship between Jonah Heidelbaum (Logan Lerman), whose Holocaust survivor grandmother Ruth, played by the legendary Jeannie Berlin, is thought to have been killed by a Nazi, and Meyer Offerman, played by Al Pacino. Meyer recruits Jonah into the hunters' brigade and reveals that he's Jonah's grandfather who fell in love with Ruth in the camps. The first season's conclusion is startling: Meyer turns out to be a notorious Mengele-like Nazi surgeon, nicknamed the Butcher, who tormented Ruth and the actual Meyer and was indeed in love with Ruth.

After the liberation of the camp, the Butcher killed Meyer, underwent plastic surgery and proceeded to impersonate him, becoming in the process not just a Jew, but an avenger for the crimes committed against the Jews. Having discovered the truth, Jonah kills the fake Meyer. He proclaims the "hunt" for the Nazis the Jewish "birthright," to which the Butcher has no claim, and the historical Jewish responsibility to guard themselves. Thus, *Hunters* ultimately presents Jewishness as a biological factor, as something that cannot be learned or unlearned. There are religious and cultural elements to it, but they are manifestations of something much more essentialist and inborn, making the Jew the perpetual other.

There's another startling final revelation: Adolf Hitler is alive, living in Argentina with Eva Braun (Lina Olin), who heads the Nazi operations in America, surrounded by Aryan-looking boys who may or may not be his children. With this *Hunters* wanders into the alternative history territory, which forks in two directions: the aesthetics of Holocaust representation and the show's indebtedness to another 1970s cult film, *The Boys from Brazil* (1978), based on Ira Levin's eponymous novel.

Flashbacks are an important part of confronting the Holocaust on screen, made famous by *The Pawnbroker*, and they play a major role in *Hunters*. They're comprised of memories of the camp horrors by Ruth, Meyer/the Nazi surgeon, and the other hunters. Similarly to *The Man in the High Castle*, the series is engaging not only, or not even much with the camp footage, as the history of representing the camp universe on screen. It obeys many of its codes, from barbed wire, striped uniforms, crematorium chimneys, inmates' orchestras, and sadistic Nazis, but breaks the rules in other meaningful ways. One sequence, in particular, had sparked a considerable controversy. In the first episode, Meyer tells Jonah about an incident that he and Ruth witnessed in the camp. A Nazi guard Heinz Richter created a game of human chess, with the Jewish inmates as chess figures forced to kill one another as the game progressed. The main participant was Markus Roth, the "Bobby Fisher of Germany," whom Richter, an aspiring chess player always losing to Jews, resented and admired.

The scene is impressive in its orchestration. As Jonah and Meyer engage in their own chess game, where the pieces bizarrely look like emaciated male human figures, the shot fades into a flashback, narrated by Meyer, of the fortress-like construction of a human chess board, populated by the camp prisoners—the males in striped uniforms and the females nude. Throngs of dead bodies—the killed off figures—surround the chess field. Evocatively— and perhaps consciously so—of the mass grave pit in *The Man in the High Castle* scene, there's an aerial view of the macabre spectacle, with Ruth (Ann Hagg) and Meyer (Zack Schor) (the actual Meyer) witnessing in horror the massacre from the nearby tall grass.

Multiple gazes—from above, Ruth/Meyer, and the game participants killing off each other—create a multiplicity of perspectives, chaotic and affecting, almost verging on cathartic. The murderous game lasts for seven days, making it a ghastly reversal of the biblical creation. The non-diegetic soundtrack of a mournful Yiddish song imbues the scene with a particularly Jewish somber sentiment. Unsuspectingly for the audience and Jonah, everything in the flashback is complicated by the fact that its progenitor is not merely unreliable but a vicious impostor. Did this actually take place or did he make it up to trap Jonah into his game? Since his own chess pieces resemble camp prisoners, we see that something here is askew. The idea of revenge, central to the hunters' code, is invoked here as well, for Roth attempts to kill Richter by slashing his throat. "What I'd give to have killed those mother fuckers," Jonah tells Meyer, as the old man offers him this philosophy of history: "The past is all there's . . . repeating over and over again with new players and new times, hoping for a different outcome."[38] This eternal return which accounts, however, for a possibility of change evokes the Jewish notion of time as moving forward and yet consisting of reenactments of certain central episodes, such as the exodus from Egypt or the destruction of the Temple, in every generation.

The major negative response to the scene came from the Auschwitz memorial museum which tweeted, "Auschwitz was full of horrible pain & suffering documented in the accounts of survivors. Inventing a fake game of human chess for @huntersonprime is not only dangerous foolishness & caricature. It also welcomes future deniers. We honor the victims by preserving factual accuracy."[39] Thus, the scene has reactivated the classical debate about the limits and ethics of imagination when confronting a catastrophic historical

Figure 12.9 Meyer and Jonah Playing Chess. *Source: Hunters.* Season 1. 2020.

Figure 12.10 Aerial Shot of the Human Chess Game in the Camp. *Source: Hunters.* Season 1. 2020.

event. The retort of David Weil, the show's creator, who is Jewish and a grandson of Holocaust survivors, reveals that he foresaw such a reaction and was submitting with *Hunters* an earnest and artistically serious commentary on Holocaust representation; Frodon's "the Shoah as a test of the limit to the possibility of representing things, as a threshold to the possibility of the image" is at play here. This differs *Hunters* from *The Man in the High Castle* which, as I've argued, invokes these debates, but offers no fresh interpretation of them. Weil's statement is an illuminating and eloquent credo about *how* to represent Auschwitz on screen:

> While *Hunters* is a dramatic narrative series, with largely fictional characters, it is inspired by true events. But it is not documentary. And it was never purported to be. In creating this series it was most important for me to consider what I believe to be the ultimate question and challenge of telling a story about the Holocaust: how do I do so without borrowing from a real person's specific life or experience?
>
> It was for this reason that I made the decision that all of the concentration camp prisoners (and survivors) in the series would be given tattoos above the number 202,499. 202,499 is the highest recorded number given to a prisoner at Auschwitz. I didn't want one of our characters to have the number of a real victim or a real survivor, as I did not want to misrepresent a real person or borrow from a specific moment in an actual person's life . . .
>
> In speaking to the "chess match" scene specifically . . . this is a fictionalized event. . . . And why did I feel the need to create a fictional event when there were so many real horrors that existed? After all, it is true that Nazis perpetrated

widespread and extreme acts of sadism and torture—and even incidents of cruel "games"—against their victims. I simply did not want to depict those specific, real acts of trauma.

If the larger philosophical question is can we ever tell stories about the Holocaust that are not documentary, I believe we can and should. . . . This show takes the point of view that symbolic representations provide individuals access to an emotional and symbolic reality that allows us to better understand the experiences of the Shoah and provide it with meaning that can address our urgent present.[40]

Weil speaks forcefully and convincingly not only to the legitimacy and power of imagination, but its ethical advantage. Essentially, the nude and dead bodies in *Hunters* are not *real*; the voyeuristic and to an extent pornographic gaze of the audience does not trespass on the zone of the actual victims at their most vulnerable and exposed, as would be the case with photographs and documentary footage. Here reimagining the past supersedes reproducing it in an almost Aristotelian manner, with poetry and tragedy achieving a higher truth than history. The resulting truth is playfully multifarious and suspect. The whole flashback could be Meyer's/the Butcher's imagining to rehearse his sadistic fantasies or, on the contrary, assuage his guilt. Perhaps he's trying to ensnare Jonah to be eventually discovered for who he is and pay for his crimes or indeed wants to impart to him the truth about history and what it means to be a Jew. The superhero plotlines (Batman, Superman) are important to the series, but so is *Star Wars*.

IS THE BUTCHER A DARTH VADER TO JONAH A LUKE SKYWALKER?

The choice of chess is significant too. Often associated with Jews in European and American imagination, from Stefan Zweig to Stanley Kubrick, the scene acquires a fatalistic quality. The very abilities that make Jews special and allow them to assimilate result in their destruction. There's also a possible paratextual element to the sequence. *The Doomed City* is a novel by the Strugatsky brothers, Soviet Jewish masters of science fiction, translated into English in 2016. It could have certainly been on Weil's radar, especially considering his interest in the genre. Taking place in a parallel universe, not unlike in Philip K. Dick's oeuvre, it describes a Red building where the main character, Andrei Voronin, plays a game of chess with Joseph Stalin nicknamed the Great Strategist, using real humans as pieces and deciding whom to kill. Andrei encounters the tyrant's cruel "wisdom" and tricks which shock and perturb his beliefs: "And Andrei carried on agonizingly trying to understand what sort of game this was that he was playing, what its purpose was, what the rules were, and why all this was happening. . . . It was played not by adversaries but by partners, allies; the game had only one set of goalposts, nobody lost, everybody won . . . apart, of course, from those who would not survive until the victory."[41] Similarly, the relationship between Jonah and Meyer/the Butcher tests who each one is to the depth of their souls and who among the hunters would betray, kill, or survive. The macabre chess game in the camp is a symbolic mirror of the world Jonah finds himself in. This is confirmed by the fact that in the opening credits, all the show's characters are depicted as pieces on a chess board, shot from different angles, including the aerial one.

Like commissar Lyutov in Isaac Babel's *The Red Cavalry*, who is trying to reconcile his Jewish ethics with the violence of the Russian civil war and revolution, Jonah is "imploring fate to grant [him] the simplest of abilities—the ability to kill a human being,"[42] which proves excruciatingly difficult, even if that human being happens to be the very embodiment or evil and your sworn enemy. Jonah is torn between his allegiance to his grandmother Ruth, whose ghost instructs him not to dirty his hands in the Nazis' blood, and Meyer who offers the categorical imperative of revenge, "This is not murder . . . this is mitzvah. The Talmud is wrong. . . . You know what the best revenge is? Revenge!"[43] Ironically, the only time when Jonah kills unapologetically and without any moral compunction is when he slays Meyer/the Butcher. Has he learned Meyer's lessons in revenge then? The central question of the series is what is the proper Jewish response to evil. *The Boys from Brazil* is a central prism for understanding *Hunters*' take on it.[44]

Figure 12.11 Opening Credits. *Source: Hunters.* Season 1. 2020.

Figure 12.12 Opening Credits with the Characters as Chess Pieces. *Source: Hunters.* Season 1. 2020.

Published in 1976 and the film based on it released two years later, *The Boys from Brazil* had not garnered as much as attention as Ira Levin's other cult classics, such as *Rosemary's Baby* and *The Stepford Wives*, though it's arguably the most serious and provocative of his works. The film follows the novel very closely, but the text is much more reflective of the Jewish politics of 1970s. The plot revolves around two antagonists—the historical Dr. Mengele in hiding in Brazil, and the fictionalized Ezra Lieberman, a Holocaust survivor, who has devoted his life to bringing the Nazis to justice. Member of the organization operating across the world with the intent of restoring the Third Reich (not unlike in *Hunters*), Mengele succeeds in cloning multiple boys from Hitler and placing them with adoptive parents in Europe and the United States. To make sure that the boys or at least some of them will grow up to be the next Hitler, Mengele must recreate for them Hitler's childhood and upbringing, which involves killing off their stepfathers. Lieberman uncovers Mengele's plan and the science of human cloning. The two cross paths in the home of one such boy, Bobby Wheelock, in Massachusetts, which results in Mengele dead and Lieberman barely surviving.

The paramount problem is what to do with the boys. Lieberman, who has the list with all their names and where to locate them, refuses to give it up to a young Nazi hunter (John Rubinstein) (in the book, it's the rabbi who heads the Young Jewish Defense organization), who is determined to kill the boys to prevent the next Holocaust. Lieberman destroys the list, pronouncing, "Killing children, any children—it's wrong."[45] The novel's ending is ominous and chilling. It's evident that some of the boys will grow up to be the next Fuhrer. One of them is an aspiring painter who draws crowds of people cheering for their leader: "He bent his sharp nose closer to the paper. . . . His forelock fell. He bit his lip, squinted his pale-blue eyes. . . . He could hear the people cheering, roaring; a beautiful growing love-thunder that built and built, and then pounded, pounded, pounded, pounded. Sort of like in those old Hitler movies."[46]

The film's ending is more ambiguous: Bobby Wheelock (Jeremy Black) admires the photographs he took of the dead Mengele and the bloodied Lieberman; it's almost a certainty that the murderous seed within him will grow and flourish. Thus, the problem of how to confront and prevent evil remains in the state of aporia. Lieberman's position, grounded in traditional Jewish ethics, is admirable, but also possibly a failure on the grand scale. The choice is left up to the reader to decide how to act in real life.[47]

The theme of Jewish national fate and responsibility runs throughout the book. Lieberman, whose character recalls the legendary Nazi hunter Simon Wiesenthal, is said to carry "the whole damned concentration-camp scene pinned to his coat-tails" with "all those Jews wail[ing] at you from the grave every time Lieberman steps in the room"[48] while rabbi Gorin, undoubtedly based on the radical rabbi Meir Kahane, the head of JDL, yells at Lieberman after learning that he disposed of the list, "It wasn't your list. . . . It was everybody's! The Jewish people's!"[49] While Lieberman's moral voice is the strongest and most appealing, Gorin's does not lose its seriousness and justice, reflective of Kahane's status before he became a universally reviled figure.

Hunters is closely attuned to these themes as well as the imagery and tropes of *The Boys from Brazil*. The young boys, surrounding Hitler in the last episode, are a direct spinoff of the cloned little Hitlers. The film's grotesquery

Figure 12.13 Bobby Wheelock at the End. *Source: The Boys from Brazil* (1978).

and playfulness are also carried over into *Hunters*. The Shakespearean Laurence Olivier is cast as Lieberman, with a clear ironic nod to *Marathon Man*, where he played the sadistic Nazi doctor, while the quintessential Hollywood good guy Gregory Peck, a Jew, plays Mengele. Al Pacino's over the top performance as the Butcher in Meyer's Offerman's clothing echoes these acting choices. The Lieberman/Gorin dispute is invoked in *Hunters* in the rivalry between Meyer and Simon Wiesenthal, with Wiesenthal (Judd Hirsch) telling Meyer, "Angels do not get blood on their wings. If we follow your path, . . . we Jews will eradicate ourselves."[50] The true Lieberman character, however, is Ruth, who disdains the idea of vengeful killing and upholds the obligation of remembrance. In the novel, Lieberman confesses,

> In the beginning I only wanted vengeance. . . . Vengeance for the deaths of my parents and sisters, vengeance for my own years in the concentration camps . . . vengeance for *all* the deaths, for *everyone's* years. . . . But the trouble with vengeance . . . is that, one, you can't get it, not really . . . and two, even if you could, would it be of much use? . . . No. So now I want something better than vengeance, and something almost as hard to get. . . . Remembrance. . . . And that's why it's important to capture an Eichmann and a *Stangl* . . . so that they can be made to stand trial—not necessarily to convict them, no, but so that *witnesses can be brought forward*, to remind the world . . . that men no different on the outside from you and me can commit under certain circumstances the most barbarous and inhuman atrocities.[51]

Whether Jonah would kill the potential new Hitlers to stop the next Holocaust remains undecided and thus, *Hunters* does not dare resolve the moral dilemmas offered by *The Boys from Brazil*. Instead it offers the righteousness and legitimacy of Jewish militancy in confronting evil. It's not revenge that becomes a supreme value, but the Jewish obligation, rooted in birthright, to defend themselves. This is what Jonah learns by killing Meyer/the Butcher and reclaiming the "hunt" as a Jewish existential necessity and moral prerogative.

JUDA

I, a demon, bear witness that there are no more demons left. Why demons, when man himself is a demon? Why persuade to evil someone who is already convinced? I am the last of the persuaders. I board in an attic in Tishevitz and draw my sustenance from a Yiddish storybook, a leftover from the days before the great catastrophe. The stories in the book are pablum and duck milk, but the Hebrew letters have a weight of their own. I don't have to tell you that I am a

Jew. What else, a Gentile? I've heard that there are Gentile demons, but I don't know any, nor do I wish to know them. Jacob and Esau don't become in-laws.
(I. B. Singer, "The Last Demon")

Hunters' rich probing of these issues makes it part of the global Jewish television scene where Israeli shows loom large. In *Juda*—the first full-blown Israeli foray into the vampire genre—Juda, a lowly criminal and gambler, played by the series creator Tsion Baruch, is bitten in Romania by Dracula's daughter. The bite transforms him into a vampire. The plot's trick is that the vampires are forbidden from drinking the Jewish blood since the Jew, who becomes a vampire, will vanquish the entire bloodsucking brood. The series follows Juda on his return to Israel where he must deal with his new identity and powers as well as the Romanian vampires who come to the Jewish state to find him and destroy before he obliterates them.

A mysterious rabbi, played by an iconic Israeli Yiddish comic Mike Burstyn, watches over Juda's metamorphosis and educates in what it means to be a Jewish vampire: a messianic figure, who through his beastlike prowess and union with evil, will put an end to it. The show's conclusion reveals that the rabbi is in fact a vampire himself who lay dormant for decades in wait for a replacement. With Juda as such a substitute, the rabbi can now fulfill his mission and destroy the vampires, including the Dracula himself, which is precisely what he does in the last episode's final moments.

History and, particularly, the Holocaust is key in *Juda*. The Israeli present is its main setting, but it does not let go of the pre-state Jewish past. The series' most startling part is an animated sequence in episode two which contains the rabbi's tale to Juda about a Jewish boy named Zadek, who escaped the Nazis in a Romanian forest and was saved by none-other than the Dracula and his son. The Nazis eventually find the boy and murder him. Unable to bear the pain of losing his friend, the young Dracula bites Zadek, turning him into a vampire. The tragedy is that he then has to kill him since he learns that the Jewish vampire will eradicate the parasitic race. Weeping, he plunges the dagger in Zadek's heart and, the audience supposes, finishes him off. What they discover to their shock at the end is that Zadek never died, but learned to harness his powers and thirst for blood, patiently waiting to realize his destiny. Zadek is the rabbi. Having found out the truth, Juda asks him how he could have survived the war, to which the rabbi responds in a typical Jewish fashion with a question, "You still believe that Hitler killed himself?"[52] Thus, the Jewish vampire–a true Jewish superhero—slays the Nazi Amalek and avenges his people.

This counterfactual streak is emblematic of how the series approaches the past and its impact on the present, tying it back to *Hunters* and *The Man in the High Castle*. With its blurring of lines between the good, the bad, and the ugly, and the idea that in order to defeat evil, one, and especially the Jew,

Figure 12.14 Zadek and Dracula's Son. *Source: Juda.* Season 1. 2017.

must give in into their own dark inclinations—ditto for *Hunters*—*Juda* casts a wide pedigree net, where the two sources, in particular, loom large: Roman Polanski's vampire comedy, *The Fearless Vampire Killers* (1967), and the stories of I. B. Singer.

Jewishness is pervasive and meaningful in *The Fearless Vampire Killers*. Polanski situates his tale in a shtetl lying at the feet of the vampire Count von Krolock's castle. There are Jews all around, who seem to have come out of the pages of Sholem Aleichem or the Yiddish vaudeville stage: Yoine Shagal the inn-keeper (Alfie Bass) who becomes a vampire; his dim-witted domineering wife Rebecca (Jessie Robins); and his beautiful daughter Sarah, notably played by Sharon Tate, who also turns into a ravishing vampiress. The young nebbish student Alfred, who accompanies professor Abronsius (Jack MacGowran) on his quest to uncover Krolock's true nature, is suggestively Jewish as well not least because he is played by Polanski himself.

The Holocaust was never far from Polanski's mind—his mother died in Auschwitz while he managed to survive the war in hiding—but it is in this farcical over-the-top comedy that he confronts for the first time the memories of his Polish Jewish past. Polanski described this Jewish subtext in a 1969 interview with the French journal *Positif*, "In the film there's an Eastern European culture which was desolated by the Germans and that's been killed off for good thanks to Polish Stalinism. It's the kind of thing that you can see in the work of figures like Marc Chagall [hence the film's Shagal—MG] and Isaac Babel, and also in certain Polish paintings. This culture, which never reappeared after the war, is part of my childhood memories."⁵³ Polanski's sentiment might have been prompted by the Israeli victory in the Six-Day war—the film was released six months after it—which became a source of pride for many Jews and led to a new anti-Semitic campaign in the Communist Poland.

Via these childhood memories, Polanski tries to imagine what it would have taken to preserve the destroyed Jewish world. He reimagines evil, embodied in the vampires, as an attractive malevolent force which does not, however, threaten the Jews' survival: both Shagal and Sarah succumb to and embrace their new nature. At the end of the film, von Krolock lives on, but so does the shtetl. The evil triumphs: Sarah bites Alfred and they ride into the wider world to spread the vampire scourge. The perseverance of evil persists in Polanski's films, but here, to reiterate, the dark forces do not put an end to the Jew. Polanski proposes his own counter-history, subtler than that of the Amazon shows or *Juda*. For him, it is as if there never was and never will be

Figure 12.15 The Shtetl. *Source: The Fearless Vampire Killers* (1967).

Figure 12.16 Shagal the Jewish Vampire. *Source: The Fearless Vampire Killers* (1967).

a Hitler with his absolute evil, which bitterly and ironically implies that only in a screen fairy tale can the Jew endure.

In addition to Chagall and Babel as the depicters of Yiddishkeit, Polanski could have also mentioned I. B. Singer, who by 1967 had long become not only the leading Yiddish writer but a major American Jewish one thanks to his translations into English; hence Philip K. Dick's indebtedness to him. Singer consistently revels in the demonic and the macabre and suffuses his imagination with the awareness of the Holocaust. Though he never portrays the actual events of the war, concentrating either on the remote Jewish past or the post-war present, the Holocaust is perennially on his mind. Already his first great gothic novel, written in Poland, *Satan in Goray*, was saturated with premonitions of the incoming catastrophe while his Holocaust survivor characters residing in New York resemble the living dead and the vampires.

In 1943, in the midst of the slaughter raging in Europe, Singer, a refugee in New York, began to write short stories where the protagonist was the Jewish devil. Drawing on riches of the Yiddish occult, he offered his own intrinsically and indigenously Jewish version of evil as the alternative to the external and eternal hatred of the Jew. For Singer, the Jewish past could only be memorialized via the demonic route, since evil, as far as he is concerned, is the essential part of what it means to be a human and, especially, what it means to be an artist.

Unlike *Juda*'s vampire superhero, Singer's Yiddish devil cannot murder Hitler or rid the world of Dracula, but he can give voice to the Jewish dead and allow Jews to confront morality on the terms of their own horror tales. *Juda*, *Hunters*, and *The Man in the High Castle* offer provocative even if imperfect addendums to these horror tales—a testament to the vibrancy of contemporary television in its probing of the limits of imagination in confronting historical horror.

NOTES

1. Didi-Huberman, Georges, *Images in Spite of All* (Chicago: The University of Chicago Press, 2008), 33–34.
2. Frodon, Jean-Michel, "Intersecting Paths," in *Cinema & the Shoah*, ed. Jean-Michel Frodon (Albany: SUNY Press, 2010), 4.
3. Ibid., 4.
4. Pickford, Henry, *The Sense of Semblance: Philosophical Analyses of Holocaust Art* (New York: Fordham University Press, 2013), 3.
5. Langer, Lawrence, *The Holocaust and the Literary Imagination* (New Haven: Yale University Press, 1975), 30.

6. Shandler, Jeffrey, *While America Watches: Televising the Holocaust* (New York: Oxford University Press, 1999), 155.

7. See Miller, Liz, "How the Man in the High Castle Expanded on Philip K. Dick's Work for Four Seasons," *SYFY Wire*, November 19, 2019, https://www.syfy.com/syfywire/how-the-man-in-the-high-castle-expanded-on-philip-k-dicks-work-for-four-seasons.

8. See Adams, Jenni, "Relationships to Realism in Post-Holocaust Fiction: Conflicted Realism and the Counterfactual Historical Novel," in *The Bloomsbury Companion to Holocaust Literature*, ed. Jenni Adams (London: Bloomsbury, 2014), 81–101.

9. Jamison, Fredric, *Archaeologies of the Future: The Desire Called Utopia and Other Science Fictions* (London: Verso, 2005), 350.

10. Dick, Philip K., *Four Novels of the 1960s: The Man in the High Castle, The Three Stigmata of Palmer Eldrich, Do Androids Dream of Electric Sheep? Ubik* (New York: The Library of America, 2007), 227.

11. Rossi, Umberto, *The Twisted Worlds of Philip K. Dick: A Reading of Twenty Ontologically Uncertain Novels* (Jefferson, North Carolina: McFarland & Company, 2011), 95.

12. Dick, *Four Novels of the 1960s*, 38–39.

13. See in *The Shifting Realities of Philip K. Dick: Selected Literary and Philosophical Writings*, ed. Lawrence Sutin (New York: Vintage Books, 1995), 119–134.

14. Ibid., 113.

15. Israel is depicted in a much more positive light in Dick's *Martian Time Slip* published in 1964.

16. Dick, Philip K., *The Simulacra* (New York: Ace Books, 1964), 108.

17. Dick, *Four Novels of the 1960s*, 69.

18. Shandler, *While America Watches*, 77.

19. Ibid., 78.

20. Ibid., 78.

21. See in *Cinema & the Shoah*, 246, 349.

22. What shocks and disturbs the public are the images of swastika preponderant in the show. After the series ended, all of its Nazi paraphernalia was destroyed. Amazon also had to pull its advertising campaign, for which seats in New York's subway cars were covered with the show-inspired images of the American flag bearing a swastika. The book dedicated to the series' art removed all swastikas from its illustrations. Notably, the Japanese and Nazi flags were depicted on the cover of the first edition of *The Man in the High Castle*.

23. See in *Film and Genocide*, ed. Kristi M. Wilson and Tomas F. Crowder-Taraborrelli (Madison: The University of Wisconsin Press, 2012), 102.

24. "Sunrise," *The Man in the High Castle*, season 1, episode 2, directed by Daniel Percival, aired October 24, 2015.

25. A similar inconsistency is present in how the series approaches liturgical Hebrew, pronouncing half of it in the Ashkenazi manner, indicative of certain strands of ultra-Orthodox Judaism, and the other half in the contemporary Israeli one.

26. Rothberg, Michael, *Multidirectional Memory: Remembering the Holocaust in the Age of Decolonization* (Stanford: Stanford University Press, 2009), 7.

27. Ibid., 12.

28. See in Rothberg, *Multidirectional Memory*, 111–134.

29. See in Dick, *Four Novels of the 1960s*, 740.

30. Crim, Brian, *Planet Auschwitz: Holocaust Representation in Science Fiction and Horror Film and Television* (New Brunswick: Rutgers University Press, 2020), 170.

31. "Fire from the Gods," *The Man in the High Castle*, season 4, episode 10, directed by Daniel Percival, aired November 15, 2019.

32. Dick, *Four Novels of the 1960s*, 711.

33. Rockaway, Robert, "Jewish Vengeance," *Tablet*, June 1, 2020, https://www.tabletmag.com/sections/arts-letters/articles/jewish-vengeance-wwii.

34. Smith, A. E., "The Best Revenge: a (Qualified) Case for *Hunters*," *Jewish Review of Books*, March 12, 2020, https://jewishreviewofbooks.com/uncategorized/6823/the-best-revenge-a-qualified-case-for-hunters/.

35. Ibid.

36. See Adams, Neal, Medoff, Rafael, Yoe, Craig, *We Spoke Out: Comic Books and the Holocaust* (San Diego: IDW Publishing, 2018).

37. "Eilu v' Eilu," *Hunters*, season 1, episode 10, directed by Michael Uppendahl, aired February 21, 2020.

38. "In the Belly of the Whale," *Hunters*, season 1, episode 1, directed by Alfonso Gomez-Rejon, aired February 21, 2020.

39. See in Moreau, Jordan, "'Hunters' Slammed by Auschwitz Memorial for 'Dangerous' Historical Inaccuracy," *Variety*, February 23, 2020, https://variety.com/2020/tv/news/hunters-chess-scene-auschwitz-historical-innacuracy-1203512474/.

40. Ibid.

41. Strugatsky, Arkady and Boris, *The Doomed City*, tr. Andrew Bromfield (Chicago: Chicago Review Press, 2016), 140.

42. Babel, Isaac, *The Essential Fictions*, tr. Val Vinokur (Evanston: Northwestern University Press, 2018), 287.

43. "In the Belly of the Whale," *Hunters*.

44. Weil himself commented on the importance of *The Boys from Brazil* for him. See in Weiss, Josh, "'Hunters' Creator David Weil Breaks Down The Biggest Moments Of That Jaw-Dropping Season 1 Finale," *Forbes*, February 26, 2020, https://www.forbes.com/sites/joshweiss/2020/02/26/hunters-creator-david-weil-breaks-down-season-1-finale/#2466bced6300.

45. Levin, Ira, *The Boys from Brazil* (London: Bloomsbury, 1998), 242.

46. Ibid., 245.

47. While a long-standing literary and artistic trope, according to memoirs, members of the actual Jewish vengeance brigades had no compunctions about killing the surviving Nazis. See in Rockaway, Robert, "Jewish Vengeance."

48. Levin, *The Boys from Brazil*, 37–38.

49. Ibid., 242.

50. "The Jewish Question," *Hunters*, season 1, episode 8, directed by Michael Uppendahl, aired February 21, 2020.

51. Levin, *The Boys from Brazil*, 53–54.
52. "He Perceives a Matter's Outcome at Its Inception," *Juda*, season 1, episode 8, directed by Tsion Baruch, aired June 15, 2017.
53. *Roman Polanski: Interviews*, ed. Paul Cronin (Jackson: University Press of Mississippi, 2005), 42.

REFERENCES

Adams, Jenni. "Relationships to Realism in Post-Holocaust Fiction: Conflicted Realism and the Counterfactual Historical Novel." In *The Bloomsbury Companion to Holocaust Literature*, 81–101. London: Bloomsbury, 2014.

Adams, Neal, Medoff, Rafael, Yoe, Craig, eds. *We Spoke Out: Comic Books and the Holocaust*. San Diego: IDW Publishing, 2018.

Arendt, Hannah. *Eichmann in Jerusalem: A Report on the Banality of Evil*. New York: Penguin Books, 1994.

Avila, Mike. *The Man in the High Castle: Creating the Alt World*. London: Titan Books, 2019.

Babel, Isaac. *The Essential Fictions*. Translated by Val Vinokur. Evanston: Northwestern University Press, 2018.

Carrere, Emmanuel. *I Am Alive and You Are Dead: A Journey into the Mind of Philip K. Dick*. New York: Metropolitan Books, 2004.

Crim, Brian. *Planet Auschwitz: Holocaust Representation in Science Fiction and Horror Film and Television*. New Brunswick: Rutgers University Press, 2020.

Cronin, Paul, ed. *Roman Polanski: Interviews*. Jackson: University Press of Mississippi, 2005.

Dick, Philip K. *Four Novels of the 1960s: The Man in the High Castle, The Three Stigmata of Palmer Eldrich, Do Androids Dream of Electric Sheep? Ubik*. New York: The Library of America, 2007.

Dick, Philip K. *Martian Time-Slip*. London: Orion Books, 1999.

Dick, Philip K. *The Simulacra*. New York: Ace Books, 1964.

Didi-Huberman, Georges. *Images in Spite of All*. Chicago: The University of Chicago Press, 2008.

Frodon, Jean-Michel, ed. *Cinema & the Shoah*. Albany: SUNY Press, 2010.

Grumberg, Karen. *Hebrew Gothic: History and the Poetics of Persecution*. Bloomington: Indiana University Press, 2019.

Hirsch, Joshua. *Afterimage: Film, Trauma and the Holocaust*. Philadelphia: Temple University Press, 2003.

Jamison, Fredric. *Archaeologies of the Future: The Desire Called Utopia and Other Science Fictions*. London: Verso, 2005.

Langer, Lawrence. *The Holocaust and the Literary Imagination*. New Haven: Yale University Press, 1975.

Levin, Ira. *The Boys from Brazil*. London: Bloomsbury, 1998.

Miller, Liz. "How The Man in the High Castle Expanded on Philip K. Dick's Work for Four Seasons." SYFY Wire, November 19, 2019. https://www.syfy.com/syfy

wire/how-the-man-in-the-high-castle-expanded-on-philip-k-dicks-work-for-four-seasons.

Moreau, Jordan. "'Hunters' Slammed by Auschwitz Memorial for 'Dangerous' Historical Inaccuracy." *Variety*, February 23, 2020. https://variety.com/2020/tv/news/hunters-chess-scene-auschwitz-historical-innacuracy-1203512474/.

Pickford, Henry. *The Sense of Semblance: Philosophical Analyses of Holocaust Art*. New York: Fordham University Press, 2013.

Rockaway, Robert. "Jewish Vengeance." *Tablet*, June 1, 2020. https://www.tabletmag.com/sections/arts-letters/articles/jewish-vengeance-wwii.

Rossi, Umberto. *The Twisted Worlds of Philip K. Dick: A Reading of Twenty Ontologically Uncertain Novels*. Jefferson, North Carolina: McFarland & Company, 2011.

Roth. Philip. *The Plot against America*. Boston: Houghton Mifflin Company, 2004.

Rothberg, Michael. *Multidirectional Memory: Remembering the Holocaust in the Age of Decolonization*. Stanford: Stanford University Press, 2009.

Shandler, Jeffrey. *While America Watches: Televising the Holocaust*. New York: Oxford University Press, 1999.

Singer, I. B. *Collected Stories: "Gimpel the Fool" to "The Letter Writer."* New York: The Library of America, 2004.

Singer, I. B. *The Last Demon*. London: Penguin Classics, 2011.

Smith, A. E. "The Best Revenge: A (Qualified) Case for Hunters." *Jewish Review of Books*, March 12, 2020. https://jewishreviewofbooks.com/uncategorized/6823/the-best-revenge-a-qualified-case-for-hunters/.

Sutin, Lawrence, ed. *The Shifting Realities of Philip K. Dick: Selected Literary and Philosophical Writings*. New York: Vintage Books, 1995.

Strugatsky, Arkady and Boris. Translated by Andrew Bromfield. *The Doomed City*. Chicago: Chicago Review Press, 2016.

Wallant, Lewis. *The Pawnbroker: A Novel*. New York: Fig Tree Books LLC, 2015.

Weiss, Josh. "'Hunters' Creator David Weil Breaks Down The Biggest Moments Of That Jaw-Dropping Season 1 Finale." *Forbes*, February 26, 2020. https://www.forbes.com/sites/joshweiss/2020/02/26/hunters-creator-david-weil-breaks-down-season-1-finale/#2466bced6300.

Wilson, Kristi M., Crowder-Taraborrelli, Tomas F., eds. *Film and Genocide*. Madison: The University of Wisconsin Press, 2012.

Index

NOTE: Page reference in *italics* refer to figures.

aboriginal peoples of Australia: census, 212n10–11; genocide against, 202, 204; *Protocols for Producing Indigenous Australian Writing*, 213n11
Abramovich, Dvir, 234nn12, 14
accountability, 16; German, 90–91, 101–3, 118; and memory, 91; and third-generation Germans, 90, 94, 100
acculturation of German-Jewish refugees, 159, 161–63; inability to, 166; resistance to, 164–66
Adamson, Walter, 214n34
Adorno, Theodore, 83, 168–69
Africa: Italian colonization of, 46
African Americans: interweaving of narratives of Jews and, 117, 126, 242, 252–54
After (Bukiet), 1, 6
Agamben, Giorgio, 175n63
Ahmed, Sara, 163
Aichinger, Ilse, 120
Airlie, Callum Seagram, 246
Altaras, Adriana, 73
alternative history/allohistory, 235n22; of Israel, 229–31; of US, 239–55

Amazon, 267n22. *See also Hunters*; *The Man in the High Castle*
American Jews: view of Poles and Poland, 55–56
American television series: bullet imagery of Holocaust in, 239–41, 248; depiction of vengeance, 253–56, 259, 261, 262; ethics of Holocaust representation on, 242, 247–49, 253, 255–58; gassing and gas chambers on, 247, 249; historical authenticity, 250, 256–57; historical elements in, 254; Jewishness and Judaism in, 246, 249–51; mass grave scene in, 247–49, 255; Swastika preponderance, 267n22
And the Rat Laughed (*Tzchok Shel Achbarosh*) (Semel), 219–20, 222–32, 234nn12–14
animal identities, 59–61, 63, 65
Ansky, S., 243
anti-Semitism: Argentina, 147–49; Australia, 202; Austria, 113–14; Britain, 9, 157, 162, 164; Fascist and Nazi compared, 43–45; German, 80–82, 96, 102, 172; Italy, 33–37, 42–45; of leftist resistance, 149–51;

in *Lejos de dónde*, 135–36; Poland, 55–56, 61–62, 66; Soviet Union, 146–47; Ukrainian, 213n12, 240, *241*; Vienna, 123–25
Apartheid, 12n20
apology: French, 19, 27n20; Vatican, 37
Appiah, Kwame Anthony, 83
architecture: of Jewish Museum Berlin, 193; of NHM, Canada, 185–86, 193–95
Arendt, Hannah, 246, 252; and "Good Italian" myth, 39; impact on Dick, 245
Argentina: anti-Semitism, 147–49; Holocaust memory in, 9–10, 133; Jewish diasporas in, 133–34; military dictatorship, 139, 147–49; post-War German subculture in, 141–43; as refuge, 10, 134–35, 255
Artzi, Margalit, 218; traumatic history of, 220–22
assimilation: Australian ethos of, 202, 211n2, 212n4; of German-Jewish refugees in Britain, 158–64, 172–73
audience. *See* readers/audience
Au Revoir Les Enfants (film: Malle), 18, 27n17
Auschwitz, 14n23, 264; in American TV series, 255–58; in Australian fiction, 203, 207–8; as "code word", 232n2; experiences in, 210; Frankfurt trials, 118; Italian cinematic representation of, 41–42; Klüger's experiences in, 116, 123; Libera's LEGO display of, 1, 10n4; as memorial, 116; olfactory memory of, 138; photograph of, 187; survivor testimony, 194
Auschwitz-Birkenau Memorial and Museum, 256–57
Auschwitz Memorial Research Centre, 204
Ausländer, Rose, 120
Austin, Greg, 254

Australian Centre for Jewish Civilization (Monash University, Melbourne), 203
Australian Holocaust writing, 10, 212n8; distance and time in, 203–4; family histories as source, 203–7; incorporation of Nazi viewpoint, 205, 213n12; and postmemory, 205–6; recent appeal and popularity of, 202–3; second- and third-generation, 205–6
Australian-Jewish refugees: psychological distancing of, 204; silence of, 203; "suitable immigrants", 202, 211n2
Australian-Jewish refugee writers, 202, 210–11
Australia of All Places (Adamson), 214n34
Austria: anti-Semitism, 113–14, 123–25; and identity, 115–16; Klüger's complex relationship with, 114, 120–25; literature of, 119–20; medieval pogroms, 124; national identity, 120; victimhood narrative, 118–19
Austro-Hungarian Empire, 120
authenticity: in American TV series, 242, 250, 254, 256–58; books on, 213n13; in Cozarinsky, 142–43; of family histories, 203–7; in Grjasnowa's novel, 74; and prosthetic memory, 144–46. *See also* alternative history/allohistory
autobiography: Holocaust Autobiographies Catalogue (Australia), 203. *See also individual titles, for e.g., weiter leben: Eine Jugend* (*continue living: A Youth*) (Klüger)

Babel, Isaac, 259, 264, 266
Bachmann, Ingeborg, 120
Baddiel, David, 157
Balkans: Italian occupation of, 46

Index

Baraka, Amiri, 29n32
Bar-On, Dan, 89
Barthes, Roland, 187, 189
Baruch, Tsion, 263
The Battle of the Rails (film: Clément), 17
Becoming English (Tucker), 158, 160, 162–63, 172–73
being in-between, 127
Belladonna (Drndić), 214n22
Belonging: A German Reckons with History and Home (*Heimat*) (Krug), 9, 90, 92–97, 99–100, 104–7
belonging/unbelonging/non-belonging: German-Jewish refugees' sense of, 162–64, 170–71; and homeland, 97–98; and Klüger, 115–16
Benigni, Roberto: awards and reception, 40–41; critique on, 41–42, 45; "the Good Italian" myth, 33–34, 47; and Italian anti-Semitism, 42–44
Benjamin, Walter, 194–95, 209
Bergen, Doris, 186
Bergen-Belsen, 20, 28n23, 157, 172
Berger, Alan, 231
Berlin, Jeannie, 254
Berlin Mosaic (Tucker), 158, 164–66
Bernhard, Thomas, 120
Berr, Hélène, 19, 28n23
Bhaba, Homi K., 159
Bikont, Piotra, 63
Birkenau, 246
Black, Jeremy, 261
Blum, Howard, 254
Blumer, Nadine, 182–83
Bombs on Aunty Dainty (Kerr), 158, 160–63, 170–72
The Book of Dirt (Presser), 201–2, 205–7, 209–11
A Bookshop in Berlin (Frenkel), 19
Borges, Jorge Luis, 133, 151–52
The Boy in the Striped Pajamas (film: Herman), 22
The Boys from Brazil (Levin), 255, 259–62, 268n44

Braun, Eva, 255
The Bread of Exile (Gershon), 164
Brecher, Bob, 104
Britain: anti-Semitism, 9, 157, 162, 164; internment camps, 163, 164; knowledge of concentration camps, 171–72; as a site of completion, 159; as a site of estrangement, 165
British Jew(s), 158; criticism of, 165; disconnect between Holocaust and, 157; response to Holocaust, 169
British-Jewish fiction, 9, 157–58; assimilation and acculturation in, 159–64, 170, 172–73; displacement in, 158, 166–67, 172; interplay of languages in, 167–68; marginality of Holocaust in, 169–71; resistance to acculturation in, 164–66
British Jewish refugee organizations: *While You are in England: Helpful Information and Guidance for Every Refugee*, 162, 165
Brodsky, Marcelo, 148, 149; "Nexo 7: Los Campos", 147
Bukiet, Melvin, 1, 6
Buráková, Zuzana, 205
Burstyn, Mike, 263
Burtynsky, Edward, 185–92, 195

Café Scheherazade (Zable), 210
Cage, Nicholas, 46
Canada: *Anthropocene* exhibition, 191; "Canada 150", 182, 187; and Holocaust, 179–84, 194–95; Holocaust survivors in, 183, 192; memorials in, 181, 185; refugees of Communist regimes in, 183; SS St. Louis incident, 179, 192; Vancouver Olympics, 182, 196n9. *See also* National Holocaust Memorial, Canada (Ottawa)
Canadian Jews, 179
Canadian War Museum (Ottawa), 185, 197n23
Canani, Marc, 174n17

Captain Corelli's Mandolin (film: Madden), 46
Casablanca (film: Curtiz): personal agency in, 16–17
catharsis, 224, 256
CBS (Columbia Broadcasting System), 247
Chagall, Marc, 264, 266
Chatelaine, Christine, 246
Chejfec, Sergio, 153n15
chess match: in Strugatsky brothers' novel, 258–59; symbolic representation in American TV series, 255–58, *259, 260*
children: *Au Revoir les Enfants*, 18, 27n17; from Balkans, 46; in concentration camps, 41–42; Italian and German compared, 43–44; killing of, 260–61
children of survivors: childhood of, 234nn9, 12; coping mechanisms of, 103; fiction on, 233n5; and non–verbal transmissions, 218; and parents' traumatic history, 220–22; and postmemory, 139; and survivors' syndrome, 217–18. See also *And the Rat Laughed* (*Tzchok Shel Achbarosh*) (Semel)
Chirac, Jacques, 19, 27n20
Cilka's Journey (Morris), 203–4
Cohen-Pfister, Laurel, 101, 109n47
collaboration and complicity, 22, 213n12; Austrian, 118–19; French acknowledgement of, 18–19, 27n17; Italian, 36–37; Polish, 15–16, 63; as unintentional, 17–18. See also perpetrators and participators
collective guilt, 91–92, 94–95, 103, 104; acknowledgement of, 98–99
collective memory: Canadian, 179, 181–84, 193–95; notion of, 182
colonialism, 9; Italian, 46; settler-colonialism, 181
comics: Polish reception of, 64

Communism: Black Communist Resistance in TV series, 251–52; Poland, 64, 67
concentration camps: Britain's complex response to, 171–72; Brodsky's multimedia project, 147; screen imagery of, 247–49, 255. See also Auschwitz; survivors
Cormier, Claude, 186
corporeality: and identity, 160–61, 244; and uncanniness, 159, 174n10
cosmopolitan memory, 72, 74, 83
The Courage and the Pity (documentary), 40
Cozarinsky, Edgardo, 9–10; on anti-Semitism of leftist resistance, 149–51; historical figures and details, 138–49; and prosthetic memory, 143–44, 152
Cruz, Penelope, 46
cultural change: France, 19–21, 39–40; Germany, 40
cultural context: and identity, 127; and readers, 116–17
cultural memory: and Australian writings, 202
cultural translation, 116–17, 129n19
Cusak, Dymphna, 212n8

Dark Room (Seiffert), 213n12
Das Lächeln meines unsichtbaren Vaters (*The Smile of My Invisible Father*) (Kapitelman), 74, 76–79, 82, 83
Daughter of Silence (Fingueret), 147–49
Davalos, Alexa, 246
David Golder (Nemirovsky), 23
Days and Memory (Delbo), 209–10
Delbo, Charlotte, 209–10
Demidenko, Helen, 203, 204, 213n12
Denby, David, 42, 45
denial, 6; Austria, 118–19; benign form of, 45; and first-generation Germans, 101–3; France, 26; increase in, 11n10

Denmark, 15
Depardieu, Gérard, 44
Der jüdische Patient (Polak), 73
Der Rabbi und das Böse (Höftmann), 79–80
Derrida, Jacques, 12n20, 207, 214n35
De Rosnay, Tatiana, 9, 19, 24–25
Der Russe ist einer der Birken leibt (Grjasnowa), 73
"Deutsches Requiem" (Borges), 133
Devanny, Jean, 212n8
Dick, Philip K., 243–47, 249, 250, 252, 256, 266. *See also The Man in the High Castle*
Die Anstalt (*The Institution*) (Adamson), 214n34
Die Leinwand (Stein), 73
Die letzte Sünde (Höftmann), 79
Dietrich, Marlene, 161
direct testimony, 11n9, 234n14; of sexual abuse and violence, 220
displacement, 9; German-Jewish refugees, 9, 153n15, 158, 166–67, 172, 174n17
distance: and engagement, 201, 203; psychological distancing, 204; from site of trauma, 172, 205; spatial and temporal, 96–98; temporal, 100, 105; and time in Australian Holocaust writing, 203
documentary fiction, 9, 205–7, 210–11
Doitscha! (Altaras), 73
Dolgoy Rebecca, 185
Dömöter, Edoardo, Father, 136
The Doomed City (Strugatsky brothers), 258–59
double-consciousness: Nemirovsky's, 22–24
Drndić, Daša, 205, 206, 207, 214n22
Dubois, W. E. B., 252
The Dybbuk (Ansky), 243

Editions Denoël, 21
EEG (Drndić), 207

Eichmann, Adolf, 136; in Argentina, 134–35, 140; trial, 80–81, 117–18, 203, 212n8, 242, 246
Eichmann in Jerusalem: Report on the Banality of Evil (Arendt), 39, 245, 246
Elias-Bursać, Ellen, 214n22
Elżanowski, Jerzy, 185
emotional engagement: with characters, 76, 83, 139; and national identity, 163. *See also* punctum
empathy, 76, 83, 115
Endelman, Todd, 162, 164
Englishness: identity of, 158–64, 170, 173; resistance to, 164–66
ethics of Holocaust representation: in popular media, 242, 247–49, 253, 255–58. *See also* moral complexity
Evans, Rupert, 246
evasion (of past): in American TV series, 247; in Australian fiction, 9, 201–2, 204–11, 215n35; and Australian-Jewish refugees, 203
evil, 252; Jewish response to, 259, 261–66
Exodus (Uris), 202, 212n5
Eyal, Gil, 182

family histories/stories: Israeli, 221–22; and postwar generations, 89–90, 100–101; reconstruction of missing pieces in, 95–97; repression of Holocaust in, 102; as site of contention, 203–7
fantastic realism, 219, 229–31, 235n21
Fascism: Italy, 34, 35, 38
"father observation" genre, 74, 78–79
Fearless Vampire Killers (film: Polanski), 264–66
Febbre di Vivere (*Eager to Live*) (film: Gora), 38–39
female childhood, 219. *See also And the Rat Laughed* (*Tzchok Shel Achbarosh*) (Semel)

Fiano, Nedo, 43
Fiddler on the Roof (film: Jewison), 250
films: on French Resistance, 17, 27n9; influencing role of, 46–47; Italian, 38–39; phenomenon of, 241–42. *See also* American television series; Israeli television series; *individual titles, e.g., Schindler's List* (film: Spielberg)
Finchelstein, Federico, 133
Fingueret, Manuela, 147–49
Fink, Ida, 222
Flanzbaum, Hilene, 7–8, 58
flashbacks, 224, 255–58
forgetting: Australian sense of, 202–5, 213n11; as healing, 234n13; and memory, 229–32, 234nn13–14; as psychological distancing, 204
Fortunoff Video Archives for Holocaust Testimonies, 220
France: complicity and collaboration of, 17–19, 27n20; culpability of, 9, 19, 39–40; German-Jewish refugees' alienation in, 161–62; heroic Frenchman, 16–17; Holocaust memory in, 25–26; self-acquitting narrative of, 39
Frank, Anne, 20
Franklin, Ruth, 22
French-Jewish fiction, 9, 19; non-mention of Jews, 16–17, 22–23
French-Jewish women: biographies of, 19
Frenkel, Françoise, 19
Freud, Sigmund, 251
Frodon, Jean-Michel, 241–42, 257
Fromer, Dafna, 89
Frum, Linda, 179–80, 184, 186, 195
Fuchs, Oliver, 89, 100, 101, 103, 104
Funk, Mirna, 71, 79–83

The Garden of the Finzi-Continis (film: de Sica), 39, 41
gas chambers and gassing, 246–47; on American TV, 247, 249

Gayle, Addison, Jr., 29n32
gender politics, 167, 219, 233n7
German Democratic Republic (GDR), 80
German-Jewish fiction writers/writings, 71, 73; absence of Jewish experience in war trauma, 74–76; and Israel as *locus amoenus*, 73–74, 77–78; third-generation, 9. *See also* Krug, Nora
German-Jewish identity, 81, 84n6
German language: and anti-Semitism, 43; disconnect with, 167–68; Klüger's connection with, 122
Germanness, 159, 160; as emblematic of loss, 167–68; negation of, 161–62; retention of, 164–66
Germany: 1960s events, 117–18; anti-Polish sentiments, 59; anti-Semitism, 80, 81, 82, 96, 102, 172; and Argentinian dictatorship compared, 147–49; Austria as first victim of, 118; as cause of Italy's racist turn, 44–46; culpability of, 9, 40; in Dick's novel, 243, 244, 246–47; first ("silent") generation, 91, 98, 100–103, 109n47; generational attitudes and public discourse, 90–92; intergenerational responses to Holocaust, 100; "make-good-again-Jews", 85n13; new right-wing party, 102, 104, 107; occupation of Poland, 53–54; reception of *The Reader*, 2, 5; second-generation, 93, 100, 103, 109n47, 118; self-acquitting narrative, 39. *See also* Nazis/Nazism; third-generation Germans
Gershon, Karen, 164
Gershona Shona (Becoming Gershona) (Semel), 219
Giesen, Bernhard, 91, 102, 103
Gilbert, Ruth, 158
Goering, Hermann, 245
Goldberg, Florinda, 148
Goldhagen, Daniel, 15
Goldstein, Dov, 186

"the Good German" myth, 11n11
"the Good Italian" myth, 9, 33–34, 37–47
Gorelik, Lena, 72–73, 81, 82
Göttingen (Austria), 121
Gott ist nicht schüchtern (*City of Jasmine*) (Grjasnowa), 79, 82, 83; "Jewish book", 74–76
graphic representation, 2–3. *See also A German Reckons with History and Home* (Krug); *Maus* (Spiegelman)
Grass, Günter, 71
Grjasnowa, Olga, 71, 73–76, 79, 82, 83
Gross, Jan, 63–64
Grossman, David, 218, 220, 225, 234n9
Grossman, Laura, 186
guilt: evasive engagement with, 201–2; inherited, 94; and responsibility, 104–5. *See also* collective guilt; survivors' syndrome
Gutfreund, Amir, 233n4

Hadar, Tanya, 233n4
Hagg, Ann, 255
Halbwachs, Maurice, 183–84
The Hand That Signed the Paper (Demidenko), 203, 204
Harai, Fiona, 204
Hardtmann, Gertrud, 102, 103
A Hat of Glass (*Kova Zekhukhit*) (Semel), 218–19, 222, 233n5
HBO, 239
Heat Wave in Berlin (Cusak), 212n8
Hedgepeth, Sonja, 233n7
Heimat. See Belonging: A German Reckons with History and Home (Krug); homeland
Herf, Jeffrey, 91
heroism: of French, 16–17; of Italians, 45; of Poles, 62–63, 66–67
Hinton, Jerrika, 254
Hirsch, Judd, 262
Hirsch, Marianne, 138–39, 206
Hitler, Adolf, 9, 118, 159, 239, 240, 255, 260–61, 265–66

Hochzeit in Jerusalem (*Wedding in Jerusalem*) (Gorelik), 72–73, 81, 82
Hoffman, Eva, 3
Höftmann, Katharina, 79–80
Höller, Hans, 120
The Holocaust: The Story of the Family Weiss (TV miniseries), 242–43
home: for German-Jewish refugees, 160, 162–63, 165, 170–71; sensory connection to, 170–71
homeland (*Heimat*): away from, 96–98; and identity, 93; notion of, 92–93
homelessness: Klüger's, 115–16
Horowitz, Sara R., 233n7
humour, 226–27, 235nn17, 20
Hunter, Anna Clare, 211n1
Hunters (TV series: Amazon), 242, 253–55, 261–64, 266; human chess match scene, 255–58; opening credits, *259*, *260*
Hyde Park Holocaust Memorial (London), 181
hyphenated identity: of German-Jewish refugees in Britain, 158–64, 172–73

identity: animal identities, 59–61, 63, 65; and corporeality, 160–61, 244; and homeland, 97–98; hyphenated, 158–64, 172–73; and language, 167–68; and migration, 78–79; and place, 100–101, 107, 115–16; post-Holocaust, 229; and second-generation Germans, 103; and second-generation Israelis, 225–27; and third-generation Germans, 89–90, 92, 96–98, 100–101, 103–5, 107; and timescapes, 126–27; victim's, 136–37, 208, 209. *See also* national identity
Île de Gorée (Senegal): as a timescape, 126–27
Il Monastero di Santa Chiara (*The Monastery of Santa Chiara*) (film: Sequi), 38
IMDB: ratings for *Life is Beautiful*, 41

"The Immortal" (Borges), 151–52
Inglourious Basterds (film: Tarantino), 22
Israel: alternative history of, 229–31, 235n22; building of, 220–22; Dick's disdain of, 245; as exotic locale, 79; as haven for Holocaust survivors, 212n2; as *locus amoenus*, 73–74, 77–78, 81–83; as *locus terribilis*, 81–83; "New Hebrew", 219; official memorialization in, 220–21, 230–31; as reference point in fiction, 71; in Semel, 229–31
Israeli Holocaust fiction, 218–19, 233n4. See also Israeli television series; Semel, Nava
Israeli-Palestinian conflict, 78, 80
Israeli television series, 242, 263–66. See also American television series
Isra Isle (Semel), 235n22
Italy: anti-Semitic measures, 33–37, 42–45; complicity of, 10; self-acquitting narrative, 33–34, 37–39
Iturbe, Antonio, 214n23

Jacobson, Howard, 157
Jameson, Frederick, 243
Janner, Greville, 181
Japan: in Dick's novel, 243, 244, 246–47, 251, 267n22; Hiroshima, 130n72
Jelinek, Elfriede, 120
Jew(s): in 1938–43 Italy, 34–37, 42–45; dehumanization of, 160, 170; "make-good-again-Jews", 85n13; *marranos/conversos* in Spain, 250; and third-generation Germans, 95; vengeance brigades, 268n47; "wandering Jew", 151–52
Jewels and Ashes (Zable), 210
Jewish Holocaust Centre (Melbourne), 203
Jewish identity/Jewishness, 74; in American TV series, 246, 249–51; as biological factor, 255; concealment of, 160–62, 244; in Dick's novel, 244–45, 249, 250; German-Jewish, 81, 84n6; in Kapitelman, 76–78; and mother-daughter relations, 158, 164–68; in Polanski's comedy, 264; taking on, 136–37, 208, 209
Jewish Museum (New York): LEGO Auschwitz display, 1, 10n4
Jewish Museum Berlin, 193, 194
Johnston, Emily Ronay, 228
Joly, Melanie, 187
Juchac, Mireille, 209
Juda (TV series: Hulu), 242, 263–64; sources, 264–66
Judaism, 74, 76–78, 212n4; depiction in American TV series, 249–51
Judgment at Nuremberg (film: Kramer), 243
Judgment at Nuremberg (*Playhouse 90* TV series episode: CBS), 247

Kafka, Franz, 120, 231
Kahane, Meir, 261
Kapitelman, Dimitrij, 71, 74, 76–79, 82, 83
Kapò (film: Pontecorvo), 39
Katastrophen (Klüger), 114
Kaufmann, Walter, 212n8
Keating, Paul, 212n11
Keneally, Thomas, 212n8
Kerr, Alfred, 158
Kerr, Judith, 9, 175n63; and corporeality, 160–61; hyphenated identity, 158, 172–73; identity of Englishness, 157–62; and interplay of languages, 167–68, 174n17; marginality of Holocaust, 169–72; migration, 158; mother-daughter disconnection, 166–67; portrayal of British racial politics, 164; separation from her past, 171; stigma of "refugee", 162–63; uncanniness, 161–62, 174n10
Khaldei, Yevgeni, 144–45; Reichstag photograph, 145–47, 152
The Kindly Ones (Littell), 213n12

Klein, Ilona, 41
Klüger, Ruth, 9; Auschwitz experiences, 123; being in-between, 126–27; biographical sketch of, 113–14; dialogue with reader, 115; education of, 128n4; experiences of anti-Semitism, 113–14, 117; and Göttingen, 119, 121; and her audience, 114–17; identity as Austrian Jew, 115–16, 119–21; imaginary bridges of, 124–25; reception of, 113, 128n2; and Senegal, 126–27; and Vienna, 120–25, 128
Kohn, Peter, 203
Kramer, Stanley, 243
Krause, Dita, 214n23
Kristallnacht, 240–41
Krug, Nora: *heimat* for, 92–93, 97; on her parents' generation, 103; Holocaust education, 94–95; open engagement with the past, 103–4; parameters of place for, 98–99; public/private dichotomy of, 100–101; relatives' involvement in Nazism, 9, 90, 95–96, 99, 105–7; return narrative, 93–94, 105; sense of shame and guilt, 95–97, 104
Kubrick, Stanley, 258
Kupferminc, Mirta, 153n15
Kushner, Tony, 157, 162, 172

Langer, Lawrence, 242
language: and identity formation, 167–68. *See also* German language
Lassner, Phyllis, 158, 162, 172
The Last Suit [*El ultimo traje*] (film: Solarz), 153n15
Laurien, Ingrid, 101
L'Ebreo Errante (*The Wandering Jew*) (film: Alessandrini), 38
Lejos de dónde (*Far from Where?*) (Cozarinsky), 9–10, 135–52
Le Journal d'Hélène Berr (Berr), 19, 28n23

Lenta biografia [Slow Biography] (Chejfec), 153n15
Le Pen, Jean-Marie, 26
Le Pen, Marine, 26
Levi, Itamar, 233n4
Levi, Primo, 76, 175n63
Levin, Ira, 255; confrontation of evil in, 260–62; influences, 259, 268n44
Levitsky, Holli, 55–56
Levy, Daniel, 72
Libera, Zbigniew, 1, 10n4
Libeskind, Daniel, 182, 185, 193
The Librarian of Auschwitz (Iturbe), 214n23
Liebrecht, Savyon, 233n4
Life is Beautiful (*La Vita è Bella*) (film: Benigni), 33–34, 41–45, 47
Littell, Jonathan, 213n12
locus amoenus: Israel as, 73–74, 77–78, 81–83
locus terribilis: Israel as, 81–83
Lord, Gail, 186
loss, 224–25; and Germanness, 167–68
Lumet, Sydney, 243, 244
Lysak, Tomek, 63

MacLeod, Alison, 157
Maisel, Philip, 204
Malcolm, Janet, 24
Malle, Louis, 18, 27n17
Malteser Kreuz drink, 142–43
The Man in the High Castle (Dick), 243–46, 249, 267n22; *Grasshopper Lies Heavy* (Abendsen), 243–44, 246
The Man in the High Castle (TV series, Amazon), 243–46, 252–54, 257, 263, 266, 267n25; Jewishness and Judaism in, 246, 249–51; mass grave scene in, 247–49, 255; Swastika preponderance in, 267n22
Mann, Thomas, 24
Manne, Robert, 213n13
Mao, Zedong, 149, 150
Marathon Man (film: Schlesinger), 253, 262

Maurice Havivel Melamed Lauf (Flying Lessons) (Semel), 219
Maus (Spiegelman), 8, 9, 54, 58–61, 63–67
memorials: in Canada, 181, 185; in capital cities, 181; compared, 192, 193, 194; and memory, 197n36, 198n47, 232. *See also* National Holocaust Memorial, Canada (Ottawa)
Memorial to the Murdered Jews of Europe (Berlin), 192
Memorial to the Victims of Communism – Canada, a Land of Refuge (Ottawa), 183
memory: and Argentina, 9–10; and forgetting, 229–32, 234nn13–14; and German-Jewish writers, 74, 78–83; and homeland, 93; and migration, 71–72, 78–79; and narrative style, 76; olfactory memory, 138; and place relationship, 98–99, 114. *See also* timescape; in Poland, 198n47; postmemory, 93–94, 138–39, 153n15, 205–6; repression of, 101–2; screen memory, 251–52. *See also* multidirectional memory; prosthetic memory
Menasse, Robert, 117
Mengele, Josef, 134, 135, 140–41, 207, 254, 260, 261, 262
migration, 71–72; ambivalent feelings of, 117; to Argentina, 133–36; of German-Jewish fiction writers, 79–82; and identity, 78–79
Mikkelsen, Carmen, 246
Mila 18 (Uris), 202, 212n5
Miriam, Rivka, 233n4
Miron, Dan, 84n6
Mitterand, Francois, 18–19
Modiano, Patrick, 19
Montreal Holocaust Memorial Centre (Montreal), 181, 192
moral complexity, 3–5, 58. *See also* ethics of Holocaust representation

Morris, Heather, 9, 201, 203–5, 207, 209
"The Most Holy Object in the House" (Juchac), 209
mother-daughter relationship: awareness of parent's traumatic history, 220–22; and identity-formation, 158, 164–68, 225–27
Mueller, Agnes: on *The Reader*, 2
Müller, Herta, 127
multidirectional memory, 72, 195n7; and American TV series, 251–53; of German-Jewish fiction writers, 74, 82–83; and Grjasnowa's novel, 75; and memorials, 181; and NHM, Canada, 185; of Polish non-Jews and Polish Jews, 66–67
Muselmann (Levi), 175n63
Mussolini, Benito, 34, 35, 46

names, 207, 214n22; and mourning, 207
National Holocaust Memorial (NHM), Canada (Ottawa), 9, 179–82; bird's eye view of, *180*; compared to other memorials, 192, 193, 194; design of, 185–87, 193–95; entry to, *186*; lack of public debate on, 182–83; photographs featured within, 184, 187–92, 195; plaque and plaque's inscription, 184–87, 192–94; snowy symbolism of, 186–87, *188*; Trudeau's inauguration speech, 179, 192
national identity: Austrian, 120; and complicity, 119; role of emotions in, 163; Spiegelman's rendering of, 59–61, 65
nationalist socialism, 149–50
National Socialism. *See* Nazi/Nazism
"Nazism and the High Castle" (Dick), 245
Nazis/Nazism: and Argentina connection, 10, 134–35, 147–49, 255; in Austria, 118; Dick's views on, 245; Operation Paper Clip, 254;

popular depiction of, 4, 5; refuge in Australia, 212n2; relations' involvement in, 89–90, 93, 95–96, 98, 99, 101–3, 105–7; viewpoint in Australian fiction, 204–5
Neighbors (Gross), 63–64
Nemirovsky, Denise, 20–21
Nemirovsky, Irene, 8, 19–21, 24, 28n5; judgment and portrayal of French, 23, 29n29; portrayal of Jews, 22, 23; reception of, 9, 19, 20, 24, 25; and Wheatley compared, 22–23
neo-fascism, 102
Nepomuk, St., 124–25
NHM, Canada. *See* National Holocaust Memorial, Canada (Ottawa)
Night (Wiesel), 8, 22
Night and Fog (documentary: Resnais), 17
Niv, Kobi, 41

objective truth, 11n9
The Odessa File (film: Neame), 253
Ohio Statehouse Holocaust Memorial (Columbus), 194
Okopowa Street Cemetery (Warsaw): Burtynsky's photograph, 187, 191, 195
olfactory memory, 138
Olin, Lina, 255
Olivier, Laurence, 262
"One Survivor Remembers" (documentary), 7
Operation Paper Clip, 254
Ophüls, Marcel, 39, 40
Ostrovsky, Tal, 89
Out of Hitler Time trilogy (Kerr), 158. *See also Bombs on Aunty Dainty*; *A Small Person Far Away*; *When Hitler Stole Pink Rabbit*
Ozick, Cynthia, 2, 76, 225

Pacino, Al, 254, 262
The Painted Bird (Kosińki), 8
parallel universe, 248, 252, 258–59

Paris After Dark (film: Moguy), 17
Paris Underground (film: Ratoff), 17
Pavelić, Ante, 154n20
The Pawnbroker (film: Lumet), 244, 255
The Pawnbroker (Wallant), 244, 252
Peck, Gregory, 262
pedagogy: and national context, 57–59, 62–63
Peele, Jordan, 254
Peled, Oded, 233n4
Peleg, Dorit, 233n4
Perón, Eva, 138, 139, 149, 154n31
Perón, Isabel, 147, 154n31
Perón, Juan Domingo, 133–34, 147, 149, 154n31
perpetrators and participators, 9; Argentina as refuge for, 10, 134–35; assumption of victim's identity, 136–37, 208, 209; Australia as refuge for, 212n2; German forebears as, 89–90, 93, 95–96, 98, 99, 101–3, 105–7. *See also* collaboration and complicity
personal memories, 91. *See also* Germany: first ("silent") generation
photographs: incorporation in fiction, 206; of Jewish women waiting to be executed, 240, *241*
photographs (in NHM, Canada), 184; captions of, 191–92; lack of punctum in, 187–89, 191; studium in, 189–90
Pieper, Liam: documentary evidences, 205; engagement and distance in, 207–9; evasion of past in, 201–2, 208–9
Pigs in a Polka (cartoon series: Warner Bros), 246
place: and identity, 100–101, 107, 115–16; and memory, 98–99, 114; romance via, 73, 80–82. *See also* homeland (*Heimat*); timescape
The Plot Against America (Roth), 239, 240, 241
The Plot Against America (TV miniseries, HBO), 239–43, 248

pogroms, 240–41; medieval, 124
Polak, Oliver, 73
Poland: anti-Semitism, 55–56, 61–62, 66; complicity of, 15–16, 62; contemporary, 56–57; depiction of Poles as pigs, 59–61, 63; memorial landscape, 198n47; Okopowa Street Cemetery (Warsaw), 187, 191, 195; "Polack jokes", 55–56; Poles and Polish Jews relations, 53–55, 63–67; secondary education, 62
Polanski, Roman, 264–66
Police Order Number 5 (Italy), 35–37, 44
POLIN Museum of the History of the Polish Jews (Warsaw), 191–92
Polish Jews: under German occupation of Poland, 53–54; history of, 53, 57–58; "misinformation" about, 61–63; and Polish goodwill, 64–67; vilification of, 61–62
Pol Pot, 149, 150
postmemory, 138–39, 153n15; and Australian fiction, 205–6; and return narrative, 93–94
Presser, Bram, 209; documentary evidences, 205, 210; evasion of past in, 201–2; fiction and non-fiction elements in, 206–7; responsibility and position of, 210–11
Priebus, Reince, 16; in Argentina, 139; Argentinian dictatorship compared to Nazi Germany, 147–49; and authenticity, 144–46; notion of, 138; and postmemory compared, 138–39; prosthetic memory, 143–44, 152
psychological distancing, 204
public consciousness (German): shifting generational responses, 90–92
public opinion: France, 19, 39–40; Polish, on *Maus*, 63
punctum: notion of, 187; and photographs featured in NHM, Canada, 187–89, 191

Rachel's Choice (Kohn), 203
racial laws: Italy, 34–35, 42–46
racism: American, 242, 251–52
Ravin, Lani, 219
The Reader (Schlink), 2–5, 58
readers/audience: background and context of, 114–15; cultural and temporal context of, 116–17; empathetic engagement with characters, 76; prosthetic memory, 138–40, 143, 145–46. *See also* punctum
realism, 2–3; in documentaries, 11n9; in films, 45
reality, 141, 210; in Dick's novel, 243–44
The Red Cavalry (Babel), 259
refugees: of Communist regimes in Canada, 183; and stigma, 162–63; Syrian refugee crisis, 74–76; *While You are in England: Helpful Information and Guidance for Every Refugee*, 162, 165
Reich-Ranicki, Marcel, 115
Rein, Raanam, 135
Rensmann, Lars, 91, 100
Resistance: French, 17, 27n9; Italian, 46
Resnais, Alan, 17
responsibility, 15; Argentina's, 141; Austria's acknowledgement, 118–19; France's acknowledgement, 19, 39–40; inherited culpability, 97; national, 9, 16
return narrative, 92, 94, 96, 99, 105–6, 158; and identity-formation, 167–68
Rich, Adrienne, 117
Riders in the Chariot (White), 201, 202, 212n8, 213n12
Riemer, Andrew, 213n13
Rohr, Susanne, 1, 6
Roll Back in the Night (Devanny), 212n8
romance: Australian fiction, 201, 202, 207; via a place, 73, 80–82

Rosenberg, Sara, 147, 148
Rossi, Umberto, 244
Roth, Philip, 23, 239–41
Rothberg, Michael, 12n21, 66, 72, 75, 82, 195n7, 251
Rovner, Adam, 235n22
Russian-Jewish immigrants, 76–77

Safran, William, 105
Saidel, Rochelle, 233n7
Sandals, Leah, 195n4
Sarah and Chaim Neuberger Holocaust Education Centre (Toronto, Ontario), 181
Sarah's Key (de Rosnay), 9, 19, 24–25
Satan in Goray (Singer), 266
Scheman, Naomi, 139
Schindler's Ark (Keneally), 212n8
Schindler's List (film: Spielberg), 22; Amon Göth in, 4; awards, 7; IMDB ratings, 41
Schlink, Bernhard, 71; critique on, 2, 3, 5; and moral complexity, 3–5, 58
Schnitzler, Arthur, 120
Schor, Zack, 255
Schroeder, Doris, 104
science fiction television series, 10, 242. See also American television series; Israeli television series
Scola, Ettore, 44
A Scrap of Time (Fink), 222
screen memory, 251–52
Sebald, W. G., 71
"The Secret Miracle" (Borges), 133
See Under: Love (Ayen Erech: Ahava) (Grossman), 218, 220, 225, 234n9
Seiffert, Rachel, 213n12
Semel, Nava, 10, 217–18, 234n12, 235n22; awards, 232n3; critique on, 229, 233n5; on Holocaust tourism, 229, 235n20; memory and forgetting in, 229–32, 234nn13–14; on non-verbal transmissions, 218; portrayal of survivor's plight, 222–27; relationship with mother, 220–22, 232n2; trauma's un-tellability and must-tellability in, 227–29; on vulnerability and suffering of the second-generation, 225–26; works of, 218–19
Sewell, Rufus, 252
sexual abuse and violence, 220, 234n7
shame, 4; and idea of homeland, 93; and third-generation Germans, 95–97, 104
Shandler, Jeffrey, 243, 247
The Shawl (Ozick), 225
Shoah (documentary: Lanzmann), 11n9
Sicher, Efraim, 229
silence: of Australian Jewish refugees, 203; "silent families", 217–18, 222; "silent" generation, 91, 98, 100–103, 109n47, 222
simulacra, 243–44
The Simulacra (Dick), 245
Singer, I. B., 244, 262–64, 266
A Small Person Far Away (Kerr), 158, 160, 163–64, 166–68
Smith, A. E., 254
Snyder, Timothy, 82
Sobibor, 246
Sokolov, Gita, 203
Sokolov, Lale, 203, 207
Solarz, Pablo, 153n15
Sonnenschein (Drndić), 207. See also *Trieste* (Drndić)
Sontag, Susan, 197n35
The Sorrow and the Pity (documentary: Ophüls), 17–18, 39, 40
South America, 9–10. See also Argentina
Soviet Union: anti-Semitism, 146–47; and Judaism, 77; occupation of Poland, 54; occupation of Vienna, 144–46
Spiegelman, Art: American reception of, 58–59; Jewish and non-Jewish Poles' interactions in, 54, 60, 64–67; Polish

reception and reaction, 9, 59, 61, 63–64; rendering of national identity, 59–61
Spielberg, Steven. *See Schindler's List*
Spotnitz, Frank, 243
SS St. Louis (ship), 179, 192
Stähler, Alex, 157
Stalin, Joseph, 146, 147, 258
Star Trek (TV series), 242
state violence, 147–49
Stein, Benjamin, 73
Stein, Gertrude, 24
Stierlin, Helm, 107
Stifter, Adalbert, 120
Still Alive: A Holocaust Girlhood Remembered (Klüger), 113, 114; a cultural translation, 116–17; *See also weiter leben: Eine Jugend* (Klüger)
The Stranger (film: Welles), 253
Strugatsky brothers, 258–59
Studio Libeskind, 194
studium, 189–90
subjectivity: of survivors, 222–25
Suite Française (Nemirovsky), 8, 9, 25; appendices, 19–20, 22; "Dolce", 20, 22; genre of, 20; as Holocaust literature, 21–22; section three, 20–21; "Storm", 20, 22; third appendix, 28n25
Suleiman, Susan, 22
Survival at Auschwitz (Levi), 8
survivors: alienation of, 221–22, 234n8; Argentina as refuge, 10, 134–35; in Australia, 202, 203, 211n2; in Canada, 183, 192; "code word" usage, 232n2; comparative circumstances, 7–8; displacement and scattering of, 153n15; exoneration/condemnation of, 3–5; humanness of, 170; in Israel, 212n2; and Jewishness, 244–45; listed on NHM, Canada's plaque, 184–85, 194; subjectivity of, 222–25; testimonies of, 194, 220; vilification of, 1, 6, 58. *See also* children of survivors
survivors' syndrome: and children of survivors, 217–18
Sydney Jewish Museum (Sydney), 203
Sylvestor, Louise, 169
Syrian refugee crisis, 74–76
Sznaider, Nathan, 72

Tank, Kurt, 141
The Tattooist of Auschwitz (Morris), 201, 203, 205, 207
television series. *See* American television series; Israeli television series
Temple, Shirley, 161
Theresienstadt, 206, 207, 213n19
Theresienstadt prayer room: Burtynsky's photograph, 187–89, *190*
third-generation Germans, 109n47; and collective guilt, 91–92, 104; Holocaust education, 94–95; and identity formation, 89–90, 92, 96–98, 100–101, 103–5, 107; temporal significance of, 98–100, 105
Three Little Pigs (animated film: Disney), 246
Thwaites, L. Z., 214n23
Tigar, Kenneth, 250–1
time: context of, and readers, 116; and distance, 96–98, 100, 105; and distance in Australian Holocaust writing, 203; "pathological distortion" of, 230; and spatial shift, 98–99
timescape, 114; Île de Gorée as a, 126–27; notion of, 116; Vienna as a, 121–23
Toklas, Alice B., 24
Tonight We Raid Calais (film: Brahm), 17
The Toymaker (Pieper), 201–2, 205, 207–9

trauma, 76; Klüger's, 123–25; studies, 6, 11n9; via a place, 82–83
Travis, Madelyn J., 158–59, 169, 170
Treblinka, 246
Trieste (Drndić), 205, 206, 214n22
Trudeau, Justin, 179, 180, 184, 192–93
Trump, Donald, 16, 26n5
Tucker, Eva, 9, 170; and Germanness, 168; hyphenated identity, 158, 172–73; identity of Englishness, 157, 159, 160, 172; marginality of Holocaust, 169, 172; migration to Britain, 158; mother-daughter disconnection, 164–66; stigma of "refugee", 162–63
The Twilight Zone (TV series), 242
Two Lives: Gertrude and Alice (Malcolm), 24

Ubik (Dick), 252, 253
Ukraine, 213n12, 240, 241
uncanny, 159, 161–62, 174n10
Unfair Competition (*Concorrenza Sleale*) (film: Scola), 44–45
Un hilo rojo (Rosenberg), 147
uniqueness of Holocaust: debate on, 6–7, 12n21
United States (US): in Dick's novel, 243–46; employment of Nazis, 254; gassing on American TV, 247; pervasiveness of Holocaust representation, 7, 10, 22; Polish and Jewish communities in, 55–56; Polish students' identification with American South, 57; in Roth's novel, 239–41; survivor communities, 204; Yiddishkeit in, 250. *See also* American television series
United States Holocaust Memorial Museum (Washington, D.C.), 7, 45–46, 181, 192, 220; photograph #17877, 240, *241*
University of Southern California Shoah Foundation, 220

unterwegs verloren (*lost on the way*) (Klüger), 113–16, 121–28. *See also weiter leben: Eine Jugend* (*continue living: A Youth*) (Klüger)
Uppal, Tim, 186
Uris, Leon, 202, 212n5

vampire genre, 263–66
Vancouver Holocaust Education Centre (Vancouver), 181
Vatican, 37, 154n20
Vees-Gulani, Susanne, 90, 101, 109n47
Vel D'Hiv Roundup Anniversary, 18, 24, 26
vengeance of Jews: on American TV series, 253–56, 259, 261, 262; vengeance brigades, 268n47
vergangenheitsbewältigung, 94, 99–101
Vice, Sue, 157, 167–68
Vichy France (Paxton), 39–40
Vichy Syndrome, 26, 39
victims and victimhood: Austria as, 118–19; names of, 207, 214n22; Poles as, 62–64
Vienna: Klüger's complex relationship with, 114, 120–25; Soviet occupation of, 144–46
violence: and Israel, 80–81; and Nazism, 170–71, 240–41; state, 147–49
Voices in the Story (Kaufmann), 212n8
von Braun, Wernher, 254
Vranitzky, Franz, 119

Waldheim, Kurt, 118
Wallant, Edward Lewis, 244, 252
Wanted: The Search for Nazis in America (Blum), 254
War and Remembrance (TV miniseries: ABC), 249
We Are Here interviews (Harai), 204
Weil, David, 257–58, 268n44
weiter leben: Eine Jugend (*continue living: A Youth*) (Klüger), 113–16,

119–21, 123, 125, 128. *See also Still Alive: A Holocaust Girlhood Remembered* (Klüger); *unterwegs verloren* (Klüger)
Wheatley, Phillis, 29n32; and Nemirovksy compared, 22–23
When Hitler Stole Pink Rabbit (Kerr), 158–59, 161, 174n17
White, Patrick, 201, 202, 212nn4, 8, 213n12
Whiteread, Rachel, 124
wholeness: in identity of Englishness, 160–61
Wiesenthal, Simon, 261, 262
Winfrey, Oprah, 2
Winternähe (Funk), 80–83

Winters, Zoe, 254
women: experiences of, 219. *See also* mother-daughter relationship
Wood, Linda Solomon, 196n9

Yad Vashem, 220
Yaoz, Hanna, 217–19, 235n20
Young, James, 183, 197nn36–37, 198n47, 232

Zable, Arnold, 210
Zionism, 230; depiction in TV series, 250; Dick's apprehensions about, 243, 245; feminist rebuttal of, 219, 229–30
Zweig, Stefan, 120, 258

About the Contributors

Victoria Aarons holds the position of O.R. & Eva Mitchell Distinguished Professor of Literature at Trinity University, where she teaches courses on American Jewish and Holocaust literatures. In addition to over ninety scholarly articles and book chapters, she is author or editor of eleven books, including, most recently, *Holocaust Graphic Narratives: Generation, Trauma, and Memory* (Rutgers UP, 2020). She is on the editorial board of Philip Roth Studies, Studies in American Jewish Literature, and Women in Judaism, and she is series editor for Lexington Studies in Jewish Literature.

Hilene Flanzbaum is the Allegra Stewart Chair of Modern Literature at Butler University, where she co-founded the MFA program and leads expressive writing workshops throughout Indianapolis. She is the editor of, and a contributor to, *The Americanization of the Holocaust* and the managing editor of *Jewish-American Literature: A Norton Anthology*. She has published over two dozen critical essays on Literature of the Holocaust and Jewish American literature, as well as non-fiction and poetry about third-generation survivors, in places as various as *Tikkun*, *O! magazine* and *Ploughshares*.

Marat Grinberg teaches Russian language, literature, and culture at Reed College and is the author of *"I am to be read not from left to right, but in Jewish: from right to left": The Poetics of Boris Slutsky* and co-editor of *Woody on Rye: Jewishness in the Films and Plays of Woody Allen* (2013). His latest book, 2016, is the study of the great banned Soviet film *The Commissar*.

Amy Kaminsky is professor emerita of gender, women, and sexuality studies at the University of Minnesota. She has written widely on Latin American literature and film. Kaminsky's latest book, *The Other/*

Argentina: Jews, Gender, and Sexuality in the Making of a Modern Nation, is forthcoming.

Shira Klein is an associate professor of history at Chapman University. Her book *Italy's Jews from Emancipation to Fascism* was selected double-finalist for the 2018 National Jewish Book Award. Winner of the Barbieri Grant in Modern Italian History and the USC Shoah Foundation Fellowship, her essays have appeared in *Modern Judaism*, *Nashim*, and the *Israel Studies Review*. She is creator of the podcast *Forgetting Fascism*.

Joshua Lander completed his PhD at the University of Glasgow in 2019 which focused on the novels of Philip Roth and has recently obtained a PGDE from Strathclyde University. Lander has been published by *Philip Roth Studies* and the Scottish literary magazine, *Gutter*. His research focuses on antisemitism, Jewish identity, and Holocaust literature.

Holli Levitsky is professor of English/director of Jewish Studies at Loyola Marymount University. She works in the areas of Jewish American literature, Holocaust studies, and Exile studies, and has published extensively in these areas. Most recently, she is the co-editor of *New Directions in Jewish American and Holocaust Literature: Reading and Teaching* (2018), *The Literature of Exile and Displacement: American Identity in a Time of Crisis* (2016), and *Summer Haven: The Catskills, the Holocaust and the Literary Imagination* (2015).

Lizy Mostowski is a PhD student at the University of Illinois at Urbana Champaign in the Program for Comparative & World Literature in conjunction with the Program in Jewish Culture and Society's Holocaust, Genocide, and Memory Studies Initiative with a graduate minor in museum studies. She was recently awarded the Gendell–Shiner Fellowship from the Program in Jewish Culture and Society as well as a Doctoral Fellowship from the Social Sciences and Humanities Research Council of Canada.

Agnes C. Mueller (PhD) is College of Arts & Sciences Distinguished Professor of the Humanities and Professor of German and Comparative Literature at the University of South Carolina. In addition to directing the Program in Global Studies, she is core faculty in Comparative Literature and in Jewish Studies and affiliated with Women's and Gender Studies. Her most recent monograph is *The Inability to Love: Jews, Gender, and America in Recent German Literature* (in German translation 2017), and she is co-editor of *German Jewish Literature After 1990* (2018). Mueller's 2004 anthology *German Pop Culture: How "American" Is It?* is still widely used for teaching and research.

Ira Nadel, professor of English at the University of British Columbia, Vancouver, BC, has published biographies of Leonard Cohen, Tom Stoppard, David Mamet, and Leon Uris, in addition to *Biography: Fiction, Fact & Form, Joyce and the Jews* and *Modernism's Second Act*. He has also edited *The Cambridge Companion to Ezra Pound* and *The Letters of Ezra Pound to Alice Corbin Henderson*. Forthcoming is a critical biography, *Philip Roth, A Counterlife*.

Ranen Omer-Sherman is The Jewish Heritage Fund for Excellence Endowed Chair in Judaic Studies at the University of Louisville. He is the author or editor of five books including *Diaspora and Zionism in Jewish American Literature* (2002), *Israel in Exile: Jewish Writing and the Desert* (2006), *The Jewish Graphic Novel: Critical Approaches* (2008), *Narratives of Dissent: War in Contemporary Israeli Arts and Culture* (2013), and most recently *Imagining Kibbutz: Visions of Utopia in Literature and Film* (2015), as well as numerous essays on Jewish writers from Israel and North America. In addition, he serves as co-editor of *Shofar: An Interdisciplinary Journal of Jewish Studies*. He was a founder of a desert kibbutz and worked for many years as a desert guide in the Sinai and Negev.

Sarah Painitz is assistant professor and German program director at Butler University. Her research focuses on twentieth-century Austrian literature, and she has published essays on Hugo von Hofmannsthal, Veza Canetti, Mela Hartwig, Marta Karlweis, Robert Neumann, Ingeborg Bachmann, and Ruth Klüger. Her current research examines the continuous engagement with trauma through the writing, translating, and rewriting of texts.

www.ingramcontent.com/pod-product-compliance
Lightning Source LLC
Chambersburg PA
CBHW061707300426
44115CB00014B/2591